# 12,000

## DREAMS
### *interpreted*

A New Edition for the 21st Century

# 12,000

# DREAMS
## *interpreted*

## GUSTAVUS HINDMAN MILLER

Revised and updated by
### Linda Shields and Lenore M. Skomal

STERLING
New York

STERLING
New York

An Imprint of Sterling Publishing
1166 Avenue of the Americas
New York, NY 10036

New material © 2011 by Sterling Publishing Co., Inc. Portions of this book
previously appeared in *10,000 Dreams Interpreted: A Dictionary of Dreams*,
published in 2007 by Sterling Publishing Co., Inc., previously published by
Barnes & Noble, Inc., © 1995 by Barnes & Noble, Inc.

ISBN 978-1-4027-8417-0 (Trade Paperback)
ISBN 978-1-4027-9083-6 (ebook)

Library of Congress Cataloging-in-Publication Data

Miller, Gustavus Hindman, 1857-
12,000 dreams interpreted : a new edition for the 21st century / Gustavus Hindman Miller.
-- Rev. and updated / by Linda Shields and Lenore M. Skomal.
    p. cm.
Rev. ed. of: 10,000 dreams interpreted / by Gustavus Hindman Miller. 2007.
ISBN 978-1-4027-8417-0
1. Dream interpretation. 2. Dreams. I. Shields, Linda. II. Skomal, Lenore. III. Miller,
Gustavus Hindman, 1857- 10,000 dreams interpreted. IV. Title.
BF1091.M6 2012
154.6'3--dc23
                    2011023587

Distributed in Canada by Sterling Publishing
c/o Canadian Manda Group, 664 Annette Street
Toronto, Ontario, Canada M6S 2C8
Distributed in the United Kingdom by GMC Distribution Services
Castle Place, 166 High Street, Lewes, East Sussex, England BN7 1XU
Distributed in Australia by Capricorn Link (Australia) Pty. Ltd.
P.O. Box 704, Windsor, NSW 2756, Australia

For information about custom editions, special sales, and premium and corporate purchases,
please contact Sterling Special Sales at 800-805-5489 or specialsales@sterlingpublishing.com.

Manufactured in the United States of America

12  14  16  18  20  19  17  15  13

www.sterlingpublishing.com

# INTRODUCTION

*W*HAT IS A DREAM? IS IT SOMEWHERE WE GO TO ESCAPE LIFE'S UPS and downs? Is it a prophecy of what is to come in the future? Or perhaps a message from the past, a long-deceased loved one reaching out from the misty depths of the spirit world? Or could it be the spirit world trying to warn or tell us something that we need at that moment for clarity? Might it be our subconscious mind, clarifying a problem in our lives or giving us a glimpse of future events to come? Or is it simply that pickle that we ate before bed?

The answer to all these questions is "yes." In our waking lives, our brains subconsciously store information, events, and feelings as we go through our days and years. At the same time, we have a spiritual subconscious that is operating full-bore below the surface of our conscious, material life. The combined power of these dual consciousnesses emerges in our dreams. We may dream of a solution to a problem that has eluded us when awake. Or we might come up with a predictive vision, dreaming of an upcoming birth or death, celebration or sadness. We can even receive numbers to play games of chance. Sometimes there is no such voice behind the vision, and our dreams have no obvious rhythm or reason—which could be our "pickle before bed" dreams.

For most of us, dreams materialize in the form of a story. And, as with any story, there are components that together make up the whole, whether or not they make sense individually. A person, a house, a certain food, a strong feeling or emotion—these are some of the pieces of the whole. And though, while dreaming, we are immersed in this whole, often upon waking we can only recall a single item or fleeting feeling from a dream, our waking lives haunted by the ghosts of our night wanderings.

Sometimes it is not our days but our nights that are haunted by hazy visions of past events. Or certain dreams may recur night after night, telling us the same confusing story.

Though it may seem counterintuitive, such dreams can act as a kind of Band-Aid to keep our minds balanced. Some components of a such a dream are things we'd like to forget but may need to bring up again and again, so that we can use the lesson in our waking lives in order to move on.

Sometimes people we don't know play starring roles in our dreams. Sometimes we see deceased loved ones, or friends, or even celebrities. These people could be really present in our dreams, visiting us or giving us messages. More often than not, though, they are spirit guides—ethereal mentors or angels there to help us, giving us information and guidance that we cannot receive in our waking, skeptical state.

That's where this book comes in. This dictionary has some twelve thousand definitions to help you interpret your dreams. With a little practice, interpreting a dream can be easy and enjoyable. Over time, you will find that you can interpret your dreams on an intuitive level, using this guide as a reference only when needed.

## HOW TO DREAM

Everyone dreams. It is one thing that all human beings have in common. It's just that some of us can't remember our dreams upon waking, and so our waking perceptions tell us (wrongly) that we don't dream. Since dreams are not merely amusing fantasies, but can serve as strong tools to help you work out problems in your life, we suggest that you learn how to immerse yourself in your dreams and remember them.

Prior to falling asleep, try to clear your mind as much as you can. If you have a problem in your life, this is the time to think about it. You are not trying to solve it; just think about it and analyze some of the aspects of your dilemma. What are the elements of the problem, and how is it making you feel? Who is involved, and why? Consider these questions from an objective point of view, removing yourself from the issue, or you may very well find yourself obsessing about your problem instead of falling asleep. View the problem as if from a distance; you are merely observing what is going on. Don't think too hard or too long, and remember to keep the goal of solving it through your sleep foremost in your mind.

As you settle the pieces in place mentally, assure yourself: *I will have clarity through my sleep.* Then allow yourself to fall into sleep. You may have to do this several nights in a row, but eventually your dreaming mind will provide a solution to the problem. If you don't have a specific problem but are looking to see farther into your future, you can do the same exercise; just focus on what it is you want to know before you slumber. Your subconscious is taking in and processing tiny particles of information about the world around you all the time, without your even realizing it, and it can see the hidden connections and subtle indicators that your waking mind cannot. If you calmly and repeatedly direct your mind toward this purpose, your dreams will show you more than your eyes can see of what is to come.

## TYPES OF DREAMS

Professional dream interpreters divide dreams into the following categories:

### NIGHTMARES

The definition of a nightmare is in the mind of the dreamer. If you wake up frightened, then it's a nightmare. While once believed to be the exclusive bailiwick of young children, nightmares are very real—and very terrifying—to many, many people. But most of us focus on the feeling of fear we're left with, rather than the details of the dream that created it. Understanding the components of the nightmare will give valuable insight into the underlying fears that give rise to these dream monsters. Indeed, many people who suffer from chronic nightmares are plagued by very real traumas in their waking lives, whether present-day or remembered. Uncovering and addressing these problems and getting help is the best way to banish nightmares, particularly those that make repeat visits.

### RECURRING DREAMS

Many of us have had the same dream over and over again. A dream may visit you every night for several weeks, or resurface only occasionally over the course of many years. These may be dreams of fears that you need to address in your waking life. These dreams are worth noting and keeping track of. They can have a profound meaning and, if examined closely, usually offer much-needed assistance with a part of your personality that you would benefit from looking at more closely, a fear you've been mastered by, or a trauma that seeks healing. Sometimes recurring dreams will visit for years until finally what they have represented is clear to you. Interpreting these dreams can help to solve the riddle they represent; then they will stop coming.

## HEALING DREAMS

Healing dreams are indeed message dreams. They include messages that are meant to motivate you to take some specific action in regard to your health or a possible medical problem. The body has a natural ability to make problems known to us. Always heed the warnings dreams offer.

## PROPHETIC DREAMS

These dreams are also called precognitive dreams, in that they usually predict or foretell some aspect of your future. Some people do not believe that prophetic dreams exist, which is why these dreams are often referred to as psychic dreams. However, those who have them are adamant that they offer accurate direction.

## EPIC DREAMS

As the name implies, epic dreams are unforgettable to those who experience them, not just in length but also in vivid detail. These dreams are also known as cosmic dreams, because of the symbology and meaning they contain. If interpreted accurately, epic dreams have the power to change your life, especially because they usually reveal some profound inner clarity.

## LUCID DREAMS

A lucid dream occurs when you are in a state of knowing that you are dreaming. Though you remain asleep, you actively tell yourself that this is only a dream and you remain dimly or completely aware that this is so. Some people have developed the ability to take control of a lucid dream once they recognize that they're dreaming. If you can do this, you can become an active participant in your dream and can control where it is going and what you do in it. In a sense, you are scripting your own dream.

## DAYDREAMS

Researchers are still trying to determine where daydreams fit into the spectrum of dreaming, since daydreams happen somewhere between the wakeful state and a sound sleep. These "half dreams" often take on the tone of a fantasy or surreal experience. Research indicates that most of us can daydream for more than an hour a day. Some daydreamers use the fuzzy boundaries of the wakeful dream to shape their visions and visualize positive outcomes in their waking lives.

## HOW TO INTERPRET YOUR DREAMS

We suggest that you keep a pen and pad by your bed so that you can make a list of all the elements of your dream immediately upon waking. Dreams are quick to flee from the memory, and every element of a dream can add to its successful interpretation. Write as much down as you can remember. In this case, more is better; you can never have too much information.

We cycle through several dreams in the course of a night's sleep, so if you awaken during the night, try to jot down your impressions. Once you've passed through the dreaming state into a deeper, less active stage of sleep, you can no longer access the visions you had while dreaming. Thus, when sleeping soundly, we remember only those dreams that came immediately before our alarm jolted us awake. Some people actually wake themselves up so they can accurately remember the mid-sleep-cycle dreams that they normally would forget if they slept through until the morning.

Once you have written down everything you can remember, then you can uncover the real meaning of the words or elements that appeared in your dream. Start with one word at a time, probing your memory for any half-recalled associations or related elements. Record any additional aspects that occur to you; then look up in this dream dictionary the meaning of each element you've noted on your pad. Continue with this exercise until you have gathered information on everything you feel was pertinent in your dream.

Now the fun begins. As you go through the definitions you've discovered, most likely you will see a theme emerging. Do all the meanings point to an answer to a problem? Is there a birth or death coming in your life? Do you need to reconnect or reevaluate your friendships? Are there references to monetary loss or gain? If most of what you dreamed points in a certain direction, watch for and address these issues in your waking life.

There may be several themes within a dream. Divide up the dream into those themes that you perceive. Problems often have many layers, and so, too, will the dreams that untangle them. You may find that the dream is actually drawing a map of how several parts of your life will ultimately come together.

However, not everything is as it may first appear. As you will discover, some dream elements signify their own opposites. For instance, dreaming of death almost universally means a birth of some sort, either an actual birth of a person or the death of one aspect of your life and the birth of another. While unusual references to certain parts of the body in a dream can indicate an unknown ailment, dreaming explicitly of sickness often suggests good health. As you piece together all the symbols and emotions in a dream, you will see how it fits together to give you your dream story. And through the story of your dreams, you will uncover the story of your life.

We hope this book gives you the guidance you need to see your dreams more clearly, helping you to unlock their hidden meanings and understand the true messages of your subconscious.

## ABACUS

To dream of an abacus means you are taking an account of your life in an outdated way. You might need to reexamine your approach and reassess a situation in a whole new light.

## ABANDONMENT

To dream that you've been abandoned indicates that you will have difficulty in framing your plans for future success. If you dream of abandoning others, you will see unhappy conditions piled thick around you and you will despair of overcoming them.

If it is your house or business being abandoned, you will soon come to grief by taking too many risks.

If you abandon a lover, you will unexpectedly come into a sizable inheritance.

If it is religion that you abandon, you will come to grief through your attacks on prominent people.

If you dream of abandoning children, you may lose your fortune through lack of calmness and judgment.

Abandoning your business in a dream may warn of upcoming quarrels or suspicion.

## ABBESS

To dream of an abbess who is smiling and benign tells you that you will be surrounded by true friends and pleasing prospects.

## ABBEY*

To dream of an abbey in ruins foretells that your hopes and schemes will end badly.

To dream of an abbey not in ruins foretells of blessings.

*See *Church, Priest.*

## ABBOT*

To dream that you are an abbot augurs that plots are being laid for your downfall. To dream of an abbot in prayer forewarns you of flattery and deceit.

*See *Church, Priest.*

## ABDOMEN*

To see your abdomen in a dream indicates that you have great expectations, but you must curb excess and redouble your energies, for too much pleasure threatens to do you harm.

To see your abdomen shriveled means that you will be persecuted by false friends.

A swollen abdomen warns of tribulations—but you will overcome them and enjoy the fruits of your labor.

To see blood oozing from the abdomen foretells an accident or tragedy in your family.

*See *Belly.*

## ABDUCTION

To be abducted or kidnapped in a dream is a warning that you must leave a situation in your life that no longer serves you, and you should do so regardless of your desires at this time.

To be abducted by a stranger means that a current situation will end no matter what you do. You will be spirited away from the situation, person, event, or decision that is no longer in your best interest. This will occur at the hand of an unknown source.

To be abducted by someone you do know means that someone who is familiar to you will be instrumental in helping you get out of your situation.

Conversely, if you abduct someone, you are seeking help to clear up a problem or situation in your life. If you abduct someone you do not know, you are desperately seeking anyone who can help you.

To abduct someone you do know indicates the same need for help but in this case you know who it is you want that help from.

## ABHORRENCE

To dream that you abhor a person predicts that you will experience strong dislike for someone and your doubts about his or her honesty will prove correct.

To dream that you are abhorred by others foretells that your best intentions may devolve into selfishness.

## ABILITY

To dream that you have the ability to perform a task or duty—whether physical, mental, or otherwise—without any training or experience means that a situation is coming up in your life that you may not think you can master.

Conversely, to lack the ability to do something that you know you can do very well reminds you that it's time for you to reevaluate your skill and expand your current knowledge. Something is missing for you to be able to complete your task and bring a current situation to a logical and successful end.

## ABJECTNESS

To dream that you are abject suggests that you will be the recipient of bad news. You may be unsuccessful in your attempts to become prosperous.

To dream of others who are abject is a sign of bickering and false dealings among your friends.

## ABODE*

To dream that you can't find your abode means you may completely lose faith in the integrity of others.

If you have no abode in your dreams, you will be unfortunate in your affairs, and lose by speculation.

To dream of changing your abode signifies that you will undertake a sudden journey.

*See Home.

## ABORTION

To dream that you have had an abortion signifies that you are contemplating an enterprise that, if carried out, will bring disgrace and unhappiness.

## ABOVE

To dream of anything hanging above you, and about to fall, implies danger. If it falls on you, you may experience ruin or sudden disappointment. If it falls near you, but misses, it is a sign that you will narrowly escape losing your money or will avoid other misfortunes. Should it be securely fixed above you, so as not to imply danger, your condition will improve after a threat of loss.

## ABROAD (FOREIGN TRAVEL)

To dream that you are abroad, or going abroad, foretells that you will soon find it necessary to absent yourself from your native country or habitual state for a sojourn in a different place, either physical or mental.

## ABSCESS

To dream of an abscess that seems to have reached a chronic stage indicates that you will be overwhelmed by a misfortune of your own or that your deepest sympathies will be enlisted to help ease the misfortunes of others.

## ABSENCE

To grieve over the absence of anyone in your dreams indicates that repentance for some hasty action will be the means of repairing your friendships. If you rejoice over the absence of friends, you will soon be rid of an enemy.

## ABSENTMINDEDNESS

To dream of being absentminded or forgetful means that you have or will have a clear and precise grasp of a problem.

## ABSINTHE

To come under the influence of absinthe in dreams suggests that you are likely to waste your energies in pleasure.

## ABUNDANCE

To dream of abundance foretells that you will have no occasion to reproach fortune, and that you will not need her future favors.

## ABUSE

To dream of abusing a person indicates that you will be unfortunate in your affairs, losing good money through overbearing behavior in business.

To dream of yourself being abused suggests that you will be troubled in your daily pursuits by the ill will of others.

## ABYSS*

Looking into an abyss in a dream means that you will be confronted by threats of seizure of property. You may experience quarrels and reproaches of a personal nature that will render you unfit to meet the problems of life.

*See *Pit, Precipice.*

14

## ACADEMY

To visit an academy in your dreams suggests that you will regret allowing opportunities to pass you by through idleness and indifference.

To dream that you head an academy or are a member of one suggests that your aspirations are easily defeated. You will take on knowledge, but be unable to rightly assimilate and apply it.

To dream of returning to an academy after you've finished there signifies that demands will be made that you're unable to meet.

## ACCELERATION

To accelerate in a dream means you will be moving quickly into or out of a situation or event, and this quick movement will be beneficial to you.

## ACCENT

To dream that you speak with an accent means the words that are coming out of your mouth may not ring true to your ears.

## ACCEPTANCE

For a businessperson to dream that a proposition has been accepted foretells that he or she will succeed in making a trade that previously looked doomed.

To dream that you've been accepted by your sweetheart indicates that you will happily wed the object of your admiration.

## ACCIDENT

To dream of an accident warns that travel of any kind may, for a short period, put your life at risk.

## ACCLAIM

To dream that you are being honored or praised for something suggests that an event or situation in your life will bring you good fortune and recognition.

## ACCOMPLICE

To dream of being or needing an accomplice for any act, illegal or otherwise, means you fear you won't be able to complete the task on your own. You need someone's assistance to finish what is before you.

## ACCORDION

If you dream of hearing or playing the music of an accordion, expect to engage in amusement that will free you from sadness and remorse. You will thus be empowered to take up your burden more cheerfully.

## ACCOUNTS

To dream of having accounts presented to you for payment suggests that you will find yourself in a dangerous position. You may have to resort to the law to disentangle yourself. If you dream of paying these accounts, you will soon effect a compromise in some serious dispute.

To dream of holding accounts against others speaks of disagreeable contingencies arising in your business, marring its smooth management.

## ACCUSATION

To dream that you accuse anyone of a mean action indicates that you will quarrel with those under you, and your dignity will be compromised.

To dream you are accused means you may be gossiping in a sly or malicious way.

## ACHES

To dream that you have aches means that some other person is profiting by your ideas. If this dream has an actual physical cause, however, it is of little significance.

## ACID

To dream of drinking acid represents much anxiety.

To dream that you are taking psychedelic acid means you will soon have to account for a misdeed that you previously thought you could hide.

To see poisonous acids in your dream indicates that some treachery against you may come to light.

## ACORN

Acorns are a powerful portent of pleasant things ahead.

To dream of gathering acorns from the ground suggests success after weary labors. To dream of shaking them from the trees indicates that you will rapidly attain your wishes in business or love.

To see green-growing acorns or to see them scattered over the ground suggests that affairs will change for the better. In contrast, decayed or damaged acorns symbolize disappointments and reverses.

To dream of pulling them green from the trees indicates that you will injure your interests through haste and indiscretion.

## ACQUAINTANCE

To meet acquaintances in your dream and to converse pleasantly with them foretells that your business will run smoothly, as will your domestic affairs.

If you seem to be arguing or engaged in unpleasant talk, then humiliations and embarrassments will engulf you.

If you feel ashamed of meeting an acquaintance, or if you meet him or her at an inopportune time, this signifies that you will be guilty of illicit conduct, and other parties will let the secret out.

After dreaming of acquaintances, you may see or hear from them.

## ACQUITTAL

To dream that you are acquitted of a crime indicates that you are about to come into possession of valuable property, but there is danger of a lawsuit before you do so.

To see others acquitted foretells that your friends will add pleasure to your labors.

## ACROBAT

To dream of seeing acrobats suggests that you will be prevented from carrying out bold schemes by the foolish fears of others.

If see yourself as an acrobat, your existence will be made almost unendurable by the ridicule of your enemies.

## ACTOR

To see an actor in your dreams indicates that your present state will be one of unbroken pleasure and favor.

If you dream of yourself as an actor, you will have to work for subsistence, but your labors will be pleasant.

If you dream of being in love with one, your inclination and talent will be allied with pleasure and not toil.

To dream of a dead actor warns that your good luck will be overwhelmed by misery.

To dream of an unemployed actor foretells that your affairs will undergo a change from promise to failure.

## ADAM AND EVE

To dream of Adam and Eve tells you that many blessings are coming your way.

## ADAMANT BEHAVIOR

To dream of being adamant indicates that you will be troubled and defeated in some desire in your life.

## ADD (ATTENTION DEFICIT DISORDER)

To dream that you have ADD, or that a loved one does, predicts that you will be very focused when it comes to solving a current problem.

## ADDER

To dream of seeing an adder strike indicates that you will be greatly distressed over the ill luck of friends. It also threatens a loss to yourself.

## ADDICTION

To dream you are an addict means that no matter how hard you try to release yourself from a situation, you will always be enslaved by some quality of it. The situation is most likely a negative one and will be extremely difficult to overcome.

## ADDITION

To dream of pondering an addition problem indicates that you will struggle to overcome difficult situations. These will soon assume formidable dimensions in your business transactions.

To find some error in addition symbolizes overcoming enemies by discerning their intention before they have executed a plan.

Adding figures with a machine implies that you have a powerful ally who will save you from much oppression. If you fail to read the figures, however, you will lose a fortune by blind speculation.

## ADDRESS

To dream of a specific address, whether on a house, a letter, or otherwise, tells you to bet the numbers in the lottery.

## ADIEU

To dream of bidding cheerful adieus to people indicates that you will make pleasant visits and enjoy much social festivity; but if they have a sad or doleful tone, you will endure loss and sorrow.

If you bid adieu to home and country, you will travel as an exile from fortune and love.

To throw kisses of adieu to loved ones or children foretells that you will soon have a journey to make, but there will be no unpleasant accidents or incidents connected with this trip.

## ADMIRATION

If you dream that you are the object of admiration, you will retain the love of former associates though your position takes you above their circle.

## ADMONISHMENT

To dream that you admonish a person or a pet means that your generous principles will keep you in favor.

## ADOPTION

If you dream of yourself as adopted, and you're not, look for a birth announcement or a pregnancy that will seem like a miracle.

## ADORATION

To adore someone or something in a dream means that the object of your focus has a special place in your life and will bring you much happiness.

## ADULATION

To dream that you seek adulation indicates that you may pompously expect an unmerited position of honor.

If you offer adulation, you will deliberately part with some dear belonging in the hope of furthering material interests.

## ADULTERY

To dream of committing adultery foretells that you will be arraigned for some illegal action or will be embarrassed socially.

## ADVANCEMENT

To dream of advancing in any endeavor suggests a rapid ascendancy in career and in affairs of the heart.

To see others advancing foretells that friends will hold positions of favor near you.

## ADVENTURER

To dream that you are victimized by an adventurer augurs that you will be easy prey for flatterers and designing villains.

## ADVERSARY*

To dream that you meet or engage with an adversary suggests that you promptly defend yourself against any attacks. Sickness may also threaten you after this dream.

If you overcome an adversary, you will escape the effect of some serious disaster.

*See *Enemy*.

## ADVERSITY

To dream that you are in the clutches of adversity represents failures and continued bad prospects.

To see others in adversity portends gloom. Someone's illness may produce grave fears in you.

## ADVERTISEMENT

To dream that you are paying for advertisements indicates that you will have to resort to physical labor to promote your interests or establish a fortune.

To read advertisements means you will find stiff competition in labor.

## ADVICE

To dream that you receive advice tells you that you will raise your standard of integrity and strive, by honest means, to reach competence and a new moral altitude.

To dream that you seek legal advice suggests transactions of dubious merit and legality.

## ADVOCATING

Advocating any cause in your dreams speaks to being faithful to your interests, trying to deal honestly with the public, and being loyal to friends.

## AFFAIR

To dream you are having a romantic or sexual affair means you are being deceitful to yourself and those around you.

## AFFECTION

To dream you are lavishing affection on someone is an indication that you need to show more affection in some situation or to someone in your life.

Conversely, to be lavished with affection in your dream means you are in need of more displays of affection in your life.

## AFFIRMATION

To dream you are seeking affirmation for an idea you have means that it is something you will have to do alone. If you dream you are affirming something for someone else, you will have help.

## AFFLICTION

To dream that affliction lays a heavy hand upon you or others and brings your energy to a halt warns that some disaster is surely approaching you. You may soon have troubles to deal with.

## AFFLUENCE*

Dreaming of affluence suggests fortunate ventures and pleasant associations with people of wealth.

*See *Wealth*.

## AFFRONT

This is a bad dream. You are sure to shed tears and weep over a friendship.

## AFRAID, FEAR

Feeling afraid to proceed with an affair or journey implies that you will find trouble in your household, and enterprises will be unsuccessful.

To see others afraid means that a friend will be deterred from performing a favor for you due to his or her own difficulties.

## AFTERBIRTH

If you dream of an afterbirth, a death is coming in your life.

## AFTERNOON

To dream of a sunny afternoon corresponds to friendships that are lasting and entertaining. A cloudy, rainy afternoon implies disappointment and displeasure.

## AGATE

To see agate in a dream signifies a slight advance in business affairs.

## AGE

In dreams, age represents good health and vitality.

## AGONY*

This is not as good a dream as some would wish you to believe. It portends worry and pleasure intermingled, more of the former than of the latter.

To agonize over the loss of money or property indicates that disturbing and imaginary fears over your affairs or the illness of a dear relative will persist.

*See Weeping.

## AIR*

To dream of air denotes a withering state of things, and bodes no good to the dreamer.

To dream of feeling hot air suggests that you will be influenced to evil by oppression.

To feel cold air denotes discrepancies in your business and incompatibility in domestic relations.

If you feel oppressed with humid air, some curse will fall on you that will cloud your optimistic view of the future.

*See Humidity.

## AIRCRAFT*

To dream about aircraft means that you are trying to get from one place to another by flying, either spiritually or literally. This could also be a prophetic dream: you might be taking a trip by aircraft in the future.

*See *Airplane, Hang glider, Helicopter, Jet plane.*

## AIRPLANE

In dreams, an airplane symbolizes flying to loftier places.

## AIRPORT

To dream you are in an airport echoes the comings and goings of situations and events in your life. It can also be an anticipatory dream if you are planning to travel or take a trip.

## AISLE

To dream you are traveling down an aisle tells you—depending on the length of the aisle—how long it will take you to find an answer to a pending question.

## ALABASTER

To dream of alabaster foretells success in marriage and all legitimate affairs.

## ALARM BELL

To hear an alarm bell in your sleep indicates that you will have cause for anxiety.

## ALBUM

To dream of a photo album suggests you will have success and true friends.

## ALCOVE

When you dream of being in an alcove or crawling into one, you are trying to hide away and reassess a situation.

## ALEHOUSE*

Dreaming of an alehouse tells you to be very cautious of your affairs. Enemies are watching you.

*See *Bar, bartending.*

## ALGEBRA

If you dream of trying to solve an algebra problem and you have mastered it without difficulty, whatever is troubling you will also be resolved easily.

However, if your dream involves working at the problem diligently before you finally solve it, this means the answer will take time, but you will indeed have success.

To dream of an algebra problem you cannot solve means that you will have to get help with a problem or abandon it entirely.

### ALIEN/EXTRATERRESTRIAL

To dream of an alien from another planet foretells a visit from someone unknown to you.

### ALLEY

To dream of an alley tells you that your fortunes will not be as pleasing or promising as before. Many vexing cares will present themselves to you.

### ALLIGATOR

To dream of an alligator, unless you kill it, is unfavorable to all people connected with the dream. It is a dream of caution.

### ALLOY

To dream of an alloy means complications in your business.

### ALMANAC

To dream of an almanac indicates variable fortunes and elusive pleasures.

Studying an almanac's signs foretells that you will be harassed by small matters taking up your time.

### ALMOND

Almonds are a good omen that wealth is in store. However, sorrow will go with it for a short while.

### ALMS

Alms will bring evil if given or taken unwillingly. Otherwise, this is a good dream.

### ALPHABET

If you dream of writing specific letters of the alphabet or writing the entire alphabet, this means you are taking your time and being diligent and meticulous in events in your life.

### ALTAR

To dream of seeing a priest at the altar denotes quarrels and dissatisfaction in your business and home.

To see a marriage at an altar represents sorrow to friends, or succumbing to old age.

To witness a sacrificial offering on an altar denotes the coming of good fortune.

## ALUM

Alum seen in a dream portends frustration of well-laid plans.

Tasting alum suggests secret remorse over some evil you've done to an innocent person.

## ALUMINUM

To dream of aluminum represents contentment with any fortune, however small.

## AMATEUR

To dream of seeing an amateur indicates that you will see your hopes pleasantly and satisfactorily fulfilled.

If there is any indistinctness or distortion in the dream, you are likely to meet with quick and decided defeat in some enterprise apart from your regular business.

## AMBIGUITY

To be doubtful in your dreams means that in your wakeful state, you do not believe what you are seeing, hearing, and feeling.

## AMBUSH

To dream that you are attacked in ambush warns of a danger lurking secretly near you; you will soon be set upon and overthrown if you disregard this warning.

If you lie in ambush to avenge yourself, you will stoop to debasing actions to defraud your friends.

## AMERICA

High-ranking officials who dream of America should be careful in state affairs. Others can expect some trouble after this dream.

## AMETHYST

Amethyst represents contentment in business. It can also be a dream of healing.

## AMMONIA

Ammonia symbolizes the displeasure you feel at the conduct of a friend. Quarrels and the disruption of friendships will follow this dream.

## AMMUNITION

Dreaming of ammunition foretells the undertaking of some work that promises fruitful completion. To dream that your ammunition is exhausted denotes fruitless struggles and endeavors.

## AMNESTY

To be granted amnesty or to grant amnesty to someone else indicates a dream of promised forgiveness.

## AMOROUSNESS

To dream of being amorous warns you against personal desires and pleasures that threaten to engulf you in scandal.

## AMPLIFICATION

If you dream of amplifying anything, it means you want more of something or you need to see the larger picture.

## AMPUTATION

Partial amputation of limbs denotes small offices lost; the loss of entire legs or arms portends unusual economic depression.

## AMULET

If the amulet is sparkly and new, it means the power you have over a situation or person is for the good. If it is dull and old, this power is misguided.

## ANCHOR

To dream of an anchor indicates travel, change of residence, or good fortune. It's a favorable omen if the seas are calm.

## ANCIENT THINGS

If you dream of something very old or ancient and it's pleasing to you, the old way of doing things is just fine. But if it is disturbing, then you will have to rethink an approach to a situation or event in your life.

## ANDIRONS

If andirons seen in a dream support burning logs, they denote good will among friends; if they are in an empty fireplace, loss of property and death are signified.

## ANECDOTE

To dream of relating an anecdote signifies that you prefer cheerful companionship to intellectual effort; your affairs will prove as unstable as yourself.

## ANGEL

To dream of angels is prophetic of blessings, good fortune, and spiritual well-being.

## ANGER

To dream of anger implies disappointments in loved ones and broken ties. Enemies may make new attacks upon your property or character.

To dream that friends or relatives are angry with you suggests that you will mediate between opposing friends and gain their lasting favor and gratitude. To be angry or find someone angry at you in a dream predicts much happiness in a current relationship.

## ANGLING*

To dream of catching fish is good. If you fail to catch any, it will be bad for you.

*See *Fish*.

## ANGUISH

To be in anguish over a loved one or an event means you are feeling hamstrung in your waking life about helping someone or being able to do anything about a situation. You may need to find alternative ways to offer help.

## ANIMALS*

A dream about a friendly, calm animal is positive. However, to dream of an animal that you are afraid of, or you fear might attack you, is negative.

*See specific animals.

## ANKLE

If you dream of a healthy, normal ankle, your own or someone else's, you will be able to walk away from an event or person in your life that is bothersome to you.

If you dream of an unhealthy ankle, then the help being offered to you may not be to your benefit. Additionally, you may not be able to walk away from a difficult situation or person.

## ANNOYANCES

This dream suggests that you have enemies who are at work against you. Annoyances experienced in dreams are apt to find speedy resolution in the trifling incidents of the following day.

## ANSWER

To receive an answer in your dream to a question or dilemma you have in your waking life is usually a prediction. This answer should be heeded.

## ANT

The dreamer of ants should expect many petty annoyances during the day. You'll be chasing little worries and finding general dissatisfaction in all things.

## ANTAGONISM

To antagonize or be antagonized in a dream means that you are being pushed into something that you do not want to or should not do.

## ANTARCTICA

Dreaming of the Antarctic can have a positive meaning because of the pureness of the snow and vastness of the landscape, which would tell you that things are fresh and clean in your life. Alternatively, it could mean that your life is cold and sterile.

## ANTELOPE

Seeing an antelope in a dream foretells that your ambitions will leap high, but they may be realized only through great energy.

## ANTIBIOTICS

To dream of taking antibiotics means you are curing a sickness or a general feeling of being unwell in your life.

## ANTIDOTE

To dream of needing or taking an antidote for a poison means your problem will be solved just in the nick of time.

## ANTIQUES

To dream of buying or selling antiques implies dealing with reminders of the past. Buying antiques denotes the acquisition of things from the past that feel comfortable and secure. Selling them implies ridding yourself of reminders of the past that no longer serve a purpose.

## ANUS

To dream of this orifice means that you need to eliminate waste from your life.

## ANVIL

To dream of a hot anvil with sparks flying represents pleasing work; to the farmer, it suggests an abundant crop. It's a favorable dream for women.

To dream of a cold anvil predicts small favors may be expected from those in power. The means of success is in your hands, but to obtain it you will have to labor under difficulty.

If the anvil is broken, it foretells that you have, through your own neglect, thrown away promising opportunities that you cannot reclaim.

## ANXIETY

A dream of this kind is often a good omen of favorable circumstances coming your way.

## APARTMENT COMPLEX

To dream of an apartment complex tells you that you want to feel safe, surrounded by many people.

## APATHY

To dream of being apathetic about a situation, person, or event means that you need to make an important decision in your life.

## APE

This dream denotes fun and happiness; you can anticipate good times to come.

## APOLOGIZING

To apologize, or be apologized to, denotes a dream of forgiveness. It foretells that you will be forgiven or you will be forgiving of an ill committed against you.

## APPAREL*

In dreams, apparel represents enterprises that will succeed or fail, depending on whether the garments seem to be whole and clean or soiled and threadbare.

To see fine apparel that's out of date means you will find fortune but will scorn progressive ideas.

To see yourself or others clad in white denotes change, and you will nearly always find that the change involves sadness.

To walk with a person wearing white is a message of that person's illness or distress, unless it's a young woman or child. In that case, you will have pleasing surroundings for a season at least.

To see yourself or others dressed in black portends quarrels, disappointments, and disagreeable companions; or, if it refers to career, the business will fall short of expectations.

To see many colored garments foretells swift changes and the intermingling of good and bad influences in your future.

To dream of ill-fitting apparel suggests that you are likely to make a mistake.

*See *Clothes, Coat.*

## APPARITION

If you dream of an apparition of someone you know, it usually means that that person is thinking fondly of you in the afterlife or is giving you a heads-up regarding something to come in the near future. If you dream of an apparition of someone you don't know, analyze the rest of the dream to figure out the message from that unknown person.

## APPLAUSE

To be applauded in your dreams means that you will be honored for something you have done, big or small.

## APPLE

This is a very good dream. To see red apples on trees with green foliage is exceedingly propitious.

## APPLIANCE

To dream about an appliance that is running smoothly denotes an event in your life that will also run smoothly. To dream of one that is in need of repair or running poorly suggests that an upcoming event will have many twists and turns and will need to be fixed before it can unfold.

## APPRENTICE

Dreaming that you serve as an apprentice bespeaks your struggle to win a place among your companions.

## APPROPRIATION

To appropriate something in a dream means that you will be taking something for yourself that you justly deserve and are entitled to.

## APPROVAL

To seek approval from another in a dream tells you that you need to seek acceptance from yourself, not from those around you.

## APRICOT

Dreams of growing apricots denote that the future, though seemingly rosy-hued, holds bitterness and sorrow for you. To eat them signifies the near approach of calamitous influences. If others eat them, your surroundings will be unpleasant and disagreeable.

## APRIL

To dream of the month of April signifies that much pleasure and profit will be your allotment. If the weather is bad, it is a sign of temporary bad luck.

## APRON

To dream of an apron signifies security in your personal and business endeavors.

## AQUEDUCT

To see water flowing through an aqueduct means you will be creating channels to make your life easier and flow more smoothly.

## ARCADE

To dream of being in an arcade, with all its noise and lights, means you will be in a situation that is very festive and joyful.

## ARCH

An arch denotes your rise to distinction and the gaining of wealth through persistent effort. To pass under one predicts that many who formerly ignored your position will seek you out.

## ARCHBISHOP

To dream of seeing an archbishop suggests that you will have many obstacles to overcome in your attempt to master life or rise to public honor.

To see one in the everyday dress of a common citizen indicates that you will have aid and encouragement from those in prominent positions and will succeed in your enterprises.

## ARCHITECT

Seeing architects drawing plans presages a change in your business that is likely to result in loss to you.

## ARGUING

To argue with someone in your dreams means you will have a pleasant conversation with that person.

## ARM

To dream of seeing a healthy arm implies that ill health is coming to someone close to you. To dream of an unhealthy arm suggests that good health is on the horizon.

## ARMOR

In dreams, armor is protection against slander and vicious rumors.

## ARMY

A dream about an army means you will have many friends in your lifetime.

## AROMA

Dreaming of pleasant aromas indicates that the dreamer will be the recipient of something pleasurable. If the aroma is unpleasant, it's a warning that something displeasurable will be coming your way.

## AROUSAL

To be aroused in a dream, in any sense, means you need to take time off to relax.

## ARRANGING

To arrange things in your dream, physically or psychologically, indicates that things are being put in order for you—or need to be.

## ARREST*

Dreaming of an arrest, either yours or someone else's, means you will soon be making changes.

*See *Jail, Prison.*

## ARRIVAL

To arrive in a grand way in a dream tells you that you need more humility. To arrive inconspicuously means the opposite: you need to put yourself more in the forefront.

## ARROGANCE

If someone in your dream is being arrogant, you must face a trait in yourself or another that you have been unwilling to address but that has become problematic in the relationship.

## ARROW

Pleasure follows this dream. Entertainments, festivals, and pleasant journeys may be expected. Suffering will cease. An old or broken arrow, however, portends disappointments in love or business.

## ARSENIC

To dream of this poison means you will discover that someone has been dealing with you in an underhanded manner.

## ART GALLERY

To visit an art gallery portends an unfortunate relationship at home. You struggle to appear happy but secretly wish to be elsewhere.

## ARTERIES

Dreaming of a healthy blood vessel suggests that a health issue you are facing or are about to face will turn out fine. If it is damaged or has no blood pumping through it, expect to face a challenging health problem.

## ARTICHOKE

Dreams of this veggie mean that you are getting to the heart of a problem and can expect a sweet reward for the effort. As you peel away the outer, hard leaves (the issues), each layer reveals a solution.

## ARTIFICIALITY

When you dream of something artificial, something not real or that mimics the true thing, you have replaced something that was real in your life with a substitute.

## ARTIST

To dream of being an artist or watching an artist at work foretells to creating something pleasing in your life.

## ASCENT*

If you reach the extreme point of an ascent—the top of a staircase, for instance—without stumbling, this is a good sign.

*See Falling, Hill, Ladder.

## ASCETICISM

To dream of asceticism says that you will cultivate strange principles and views, rendering yourself fascinating to strangers but unappealing to people who know you well.

## ASHES

Dreaming of ashes warns of woe; many bitter changes are sure to come. In business, ashes represent unsuccessful deals.

## ASIA

To dream of visiting Asia means change. Good fortune will follow.

## ASKEW

If you dream of something that is askew, you may need to straighten your perception of a situation in your life.

## ASP

An unfortunate dream. Friends may be working against you.

## ASPARAGUS

To dream of asparagus indicates prosperous surroundings and success.

## ASPHALT

Standing on hot asphalt or seeing it being applied to the road means that a burning issue in your physical environment needs to addressed.

## ASPHYXIATION

To feel you are being suffocated or asphyxiated in a dream means that you need to stop, take a deep breath, and reevaluate an event in your life now or in the near future.

## ASPIRIN

To dream of taking aspirin or giving it to another person warns that you need help alleviating physical or emotional pain in your life.

## ASS*

To see a donkey in a dream implies that you'll have many annoyances and delays before receiving news or goods. To see donkeys carrying burdens indicates that, with patience and toil, you will succeed in your efforts in travel, and in love.

If a donkey pursues you and you are afraid of it, you will be the victim of scandal. If you unwillingly ride one, unnecessary quarrels may follow.
*See *Donkey*.

## ASSASSIN

To see an assassin is a warning of losses that may befall you at the hands of hidden enemies. If you are the one receiving the assassin's blow, you will not overcome your troubles. To see a bloodstained assassin standing nearby another person means that misfortune will come to you.

## ASSAULT AND BATTERY

To dream you are being assaulted warns that you need to watch your back. To dream that you are assaulting someone or being charged with assault and battery is a dream of strength.

## ASSEMBLAGE

To dream that you are assembling something physically means that in your waking life the pieces that must come together to solve a problem will do so.

## ASSEMBLY

To find yourself in an assembly among others in a happy environment means support and camaraderie from your friends and family.

## ASSISTANCE

Giving assistance to anyone in a dream foretells favor in your effort to rise to a higher position. If anyone assists you, you will be well-placed, and loving friends will be near you.

## ASSOCIATE

To be someone's associate in your dream speaks of a good partnership in your life, currently or soon.

## ASSORTMENT

If you dream of having an assortment of physical objects, you have limited options in solving a problem that has been vexing you.

## ASSUMPTIONS

Assuming that you already know an answer to a question implies that you do not have enough information to solve the problem.

## ASTER

This starlike flower of many colors foretells a wish soon to come true.

## ASTHMA

To dream of having asthma means you need to clean out the pollutants in your life.

## ASTONISHMENT

To be astounded in a dream suggests that you will be disappointed in the near future.

## ASTRAL, THE

Dreams of the astral mean that your efforts and plans will culminate in worldly success and distinction. A specter or picture of your astral self means you have reached a higher spiritual level.

## ASTROLOGY

To practice astrology, or work with someone who practices it, suggests that researching and understanding your astrological chart can bring answers and direction to your life.

## ASTRONOMY

To dream of studying the stars tells you to reach beyond your limitations and learn more about yourself spiritually.

## ASYLUM

To dream of an asylum denotes sickness and unlucky dealings that cannot be overcome without great mental struggle.

## ATHEISM

To dream of being an atheist, if you are religious in your waking life, warns you to examine your belief in yourself.

## ATHLETICS

To dream of being an athlete or of watching athletes foretells a period in your life when you will be physically very strong and agile.

## ATLAS

To dream you are looking at an atlas suggests that you should study your interests carefully before you make changes or journeys.

## ATONEMENT

Dreaming of atonement means you will be forgiven for any mistake or wrong you have done.

## ATROPHY

To witness the wasting away of a limb tells you to pay special attention to that body part.

## ATTACK

To witness an attack or to be attacked by an animal or a person indicates that you will need much strength in an upcoming situation. To attack someone or something in a dream warns that you might be on the verge of emotionally hurting another person in your waking life.

## ATTENTION

To dream of not receiving any attention in your life foretells the opposite: that you will be lavished with attention in the future to an extent that you might not want.

To dream of being lavished with attention means that you are not paying enough attention to the people who care most about you and to yourself.

## ATTIC

To dream that you are in an attic suggests you are entertaining hopes that will fail to materialize.

## ATTIRE

To see yourself in formal attire foretells an upcoming funeral.

## ATTORNEY*

To see an attorney indicates that serious disputes will arise between parties interested only in worldly things. Enemies will oppress you with false claims.

If you see an attorney defending you, your friends will assist you, but that assistance will cause you more stress than the trouble your enemies create.

*See Lawyer.

## AUCTION

To dream of an auction in a general way is good. If you hear the auctioneer, it means bright prospects and fair treatment in business ventures. To dream of buying at an auction signifies good luck.

## AUDIBILITY

To be able to hear something in your dream that you normally couldn't tells you to pay close attention to your instincts.

## AUDIENCE

To dream of standing stagestruck in front of an audience foretells that when you need the right words, you will have them.

If you dream of standing before an audience that isn't paying attention to you, you need to assert yourself more in certain aspects of your life.

To dream of receiving undying adoration from an audience warns you to be humble.

## AUDIT

To dream of having an audit conducted tells you that your finances are in very good order.

## AUDITORIUM

To dream of an auditorium filled with people implies personal loneliness. An empty auditorium means your life will be filled with many friends and family.

## AUGER

To see augers in your dreams suggests labor and toil.

## AUGMENTATION

To dream of having body parts augmented predicts that you will expand your thinking spiritually.

## AUGUST

In dreams, the month of August represents unfortunate deals and misunderstandings in love affairs.

## AUNT

If this relative appears smiling and happy, slight differences will soon give way to pleasure. If your aunt is upset, prepare for a coming quarrel among relatives or friends.

## AURA

To dream of auras denotes the coming of spiritual enrichment.

## AUTHENTICITY

To dream of seeking something authentic warns that something you believe to be real and true in your waking life may not be.

## AUTHOR

Dreaming that your manuscript has been rejected indicates that, after some doubt, the work will be accepted as authentic and original.

To dream of seeing an author poring over his or her work and perusing it with anxiety suggests that you are worried about a literary creation, your own or someone else's.

## AUTHORITY

To bend to authority in your dream indicates that you are not listening to those around you who truly have the experience to help guide you.

## AUTOGRAPH

A dream that you are giving autographs refers to an upcoming contract that will need your signature. Receiving an autograph or watching someone autograph something means you need someone else's signature to get what you want.

## AUTOMOBILE

To dream of riding in a car implies that you will be restless under pleasant conditions and will make a change in your affairs. If a car breaks down, your enjoyment of pleasure will not be as great as you hope.

To find yourself escaping from the path of a car tells you to avoid a rival.

To buy or sell a car heralds changes in your finances that you must observe carefully.

## AUTOPSY

To dream of conducting an autopsy or of watching one means that you need to examine, dissect, and cut out those parts of your life that no longer serve you.

## AUTUMN

To dream of this season means you can obtain property through inheritance or litigation.

## AVALANCHE

To dream of watching an avalanche foretells many changes in your life. To be caught in an avalanche is a prophetic dream of changes that you have not anticipated and do not want.

## AVENGING, VENGEANCE

To avenge a wrong done to you in a dream warns that you will have a wrong done to you in your waking life.

## AVIARY

Dreaming of an aviary full of birds tells you that your thoughts and ideas need to be contained. If the aviary is empty or if you see birds flying out, something you want in your life will be stolen.

## AVOIDANCE

To dream of avoiding a situation or person advises you of the need to meet something or someone directly, or a problem will never be resolved. To be avoided in a dream warns that you will not be recognized for your accomplishments.

## AWARD

Receiving an award in your dream means the opposite: Someone will steal recognition away from you in your waking life. To give an award, on the other hand, means that you will be recognized for your hard work and diligence.

## AWE

To dream of being in awe of a person, event, situation, or object means you are giving too much power to someone or something.

## AWKWARDNESS

To feel awkward in a situation or around a person means the opposite: you will have all the courage and confidence you need to face something that previously daunted you.

## AWNING

Standing under an awning in your dream represents being protected. If the awning is ripped or broken, the protection you think you have is just an illusion.

## AX

Seeing an ax in a dream foretells that any pleasure you find will depend on your struggles and energy. To see others using an ax indicates energetic, lively friends who are a pleasure to be with and who make life good.

A broken or rusty ax suggests illness and loss of money and property.

## AXLE

To dream of seeing yourself fixing a broken axle on a motor vehicle means that what you thought was broken will be whole again. To dream of an unfixable broken axle speaks of a goal that should be abandoned.

## AZALEA

To dream of an azalea bush or flower is to dream of hope.

## AZTECS

To dream of the ancient Aztecs is a spiritual dream. It means that you are balanced and centered in your spiritual life

### BABBLING

To babble in a dream, or feel that what you are saying isn't making sense, means you need to rethink your words before you speak.

### BABOON

If you dream of a baboon, you need to spend more time with family and friends or you need to get more serious about your life.

### BABUSHKA

To dream of a babushka or other kerchief means you are hiding your thoughts from other people.

### BABY

To dream of crying babies is indicative of ill health and disappointments. A happy baby denotes love requited and many warm friends.

### BABY CARRIAGE

To dream of a baby carriage suggests that a friend will devise many pleasurable surprises for you.

### BABYSITTING

To dream you are babysitting or being babysat means you need to be more playful; if you are being too childish, you need to develop an adult consciousness.

### BACHELORHOOD

If a man dreams of being a bachelor, and he isn't, there are problems in his love life.

### BACK

To dream of seeing a naked back denotes loss of power. Lending advice or money can be dangerous.

If you see a person turn and walk away from you, envy and jealousy are working to your detriment.

To dream of one's own back bodes ill for the dreamer.

## BACKGAMMON

To dream of playing backgammon portends unexpected meetings with strangers.

If you win the backgammon game, it means gain in your life. If you lose, unsettled business affairs will bother you.

## BACKSTABBING

Conditions will change from good to bad if you are joined by others in backstabbing. To dream of your friends stabbing you in the back means they will remain loyal.

## BACON

It is good to dream of eating bacon.

## BACTERIA

To dream of bacteria means that your health is in good shape.

## BADGE

To give or receive a badge bespeaks a need to develop more courage for an upcoming event.

## BADGER

To dream of a badger is a sign of success after battles with hardships.

## BAFFLEMENT

To feel baffled by a situation in your dream means you will find clarity with regard to a vexing event in your life. If you try to baffle someone in your dream, you will create confusion in an upcoming life event.

## BAGEL

If you dream of eating a bagel or making one, expect to go around in circles before you find a solution to a problem—but you will find one.

## BAGGAGE

To carry baggage means you must clear out emotional issues that are keeping you from seeing things as they truly are. To pack baggage foretells an upcoming trip. To unpack a bag signifies increased clarity regarding the future.

## BAGPIPES

Dreaming of bagpipes is not bad, unless the music is harsh and the player is in rags.

### BAIL BONDS

If the dreamer is seeking bail or is bailing someone out, unforeseen troubles will arise; accidents are likely to occur; unfortunate alliances may be made.

### BAILIFF

To dream of a bailiff implies that your goals may be too high to reach.

### BAKERY

To dream of a bakery tells you to be cautious if you're making changes in your career.

### BAKING*

In dreams, baking is a sign of good luck.

*See Bread, Crust, Custard.

### BALANCING

To dream of trying to stay balanced on an object tells you to seek more give-and-take in your view of a current situation. To be unable to balance means you're looking at things myopically; you need to broaden your outlook.

### BALCONY

Dreaming of a balcony suggests unpleasant news about friends.

### BALDNESS

If you see a bald person in a dream, expect a change that will benefit you.

### BALL

Catching or throwing a ball in your dreams represents giving or receiving someone's love.

Dreaming of a fête or ball is a very satisfactory omen if beautiful and well-dressed people are dancing to strains of entrancing music. If the party finds you gloomy and distressed by the inattention of others, expect a death in the family soon.

### BALLAD

To hear or sing a ballad in your dream means you will be singing with happiness in the future.

### BALLET

A dream about ballet indicates marital infidelity; quarrels, and jealousies between sweethearts; it can also suggest failures in business.

## BALLOONS

Blighted hopes and adversity come with a dream of balloons.

## BALLOT

To cast a ballot or vote in a dream means that someone values your opinion.

## BALSAM

In dreams, this evergreen, which suggests Christmas, symbolizes good health.

## BAMBOO

To dream of bamboo means great fortune is coming into your life. If a panda is eating the bamboo, it's double fortune.

## BANANA

To dream of bananas warns you to watch out in your business and personal life for setbacks and dishonesty.

## BANDAGE

To dream of a bandage means healing and good fortune. If you dream of sporting a bandage, your problem will have an easy solution. If someone else is wearing it, you will help another person solve a problem.

## BANDANNA

If you wear a bandanna in a dream, worries and hard work lie ahead of you. If someone else is wearing it, expect happy family news.

## BANDIT

To dream of being robbed, or to see other people being robbed, means you will be embarrassed.

## BANGING NOISE

If you dream of hearing someone make loud, banging noises—or if you are making the noise yourself—the message is that you need to speak up.

## BANGLE BRACELET

To dream of this wrist jewelry means you feel shackled by an event, decision, or person.

## BANISHMENT

To dream of being banished to a foreign land is a dream of great prosperity.

## BANISTER

To hold a banister while walking down the stairs in a dream means that you are very secure in your life.

To grab a banister while falling down the stairs predicts that you will be saved from unpleasantness at the last moment.

## BANJO

To dream of a banjo implies that pleasurable moments are on the horizon.

## BANK

To see an empty bank in a dream foretells of business losses.

Giving out money denotes carelessness; receiving it, great gain and prosperity.

## BANKRUPTCY

A dream of bankruptcy suggests partial collapse in business and weakening of the brain faculties. Consider it a warning to avoid speculation.

## BANNER*

To see your nation's banner or flag floating in a clear sky denotes triumph over foreign foes. To see it battered signifies war and loss of military prowess.

*See *Flag*.

## BANQUET

It is good to dream of a banquet. Friends want to do you favors.

To dream of yourself, together with many beautifully attired guests, eating from costly china and drinking old, expensive wine foretells enormous gain in enterprises of every nature, as well as happiness among friends.

## BANTAM CHICKEN

To see bantam chickens in your dream implies that while your fortune may be small, you will enjoy contentment. If the chickens appear sickly, or if they are exposed to wintry storms, your interests will be impaired.

## BAPTISM

To dream of baptism advises you to strengthen your character by showing restraint when offering your opinions. To dream that you are being baptized signifies that you will humiliate your inner self for public favor.

## BARB

To dream of being caught on a barb means that an unpleasant situation in your life will be very painful to get rid of.

## BARBARIAN

To encounter a barbarian in your dream suggests that you should deal with someone in your life very unconventionally if you hope to get your point across.

## BAR, BARTENDING

To dream of tending a bar warns that you may resort to some questionable mode of advancement.

Seeing a bar denotes community activity, quick improvement of finances, or the consummation of illicit desires.

## BARBECUE

To smell or eat barbecue in your dream means that your spiritual self is being nurtured.

## BARBED WIRE

To dream of being tangled in barbed wire means a situation in your life is so painful to dislodge from, you find it easier just to stay put.

## BARBER

To dream of a barber signifies that success will come through hard work and close attention to detail.

## BARBITURATE

To dream of taking a sedative or barbiturate means that your eyes are wide open to events unfolding in your life.

## BARE FLOOR

To walk on a bare floor in your dream tells you that you'll always be steady on your feet.

## BAREFOOT

To dream of being barefoot means overcoming difficulties in reaching your goals; it also suggests impending good luck.

## BARE NAKED*

To dream you are naked means you will suffer embarrassment in the near future. It can also refer to exposing some deception occurring in your life.
*See Nakedness.

### BARGAIN

To dream of finding a bargain suggests good fortune. To dream of haggling warns that something of value may be taken away from you.

### BARKING DOG

To hear an angry, menacing dog barking in your dream warns you to beware of a so-called friend.

### BARK OF A TREE

To feel the bark of a tree under your hand in your dream means that you have a sturdy character.

To see the bark of a tree in your dream advises you to go slowly with the opposite sex.

### BARLEY

If you dream of this grain, you need a fresh start in some aspect of your life.

### BARMAID

For a young woman to dream that she is a barmaid suggests an attraction to reckless men and a preference for illicit pleasures.

### BARN

Seeing a barn filled with ripe grain, perfect ears of corn, and fat livestock is an omen of great prosperity. If the barn is empty, the reverse may be expected.

### BARNACLES

To dream of barnacles means you will "scrape away" the negative in your life.

### BAROMETER

Seeing a barometer in a dream tells you that a profitable change will soon take place in your life.

If the barometer is broken, displeasing incidents in your business may arise unexpectedly.

### BARON

To dream of a baron suggests that your status will be elevated.

### BARRACKS

Dreaming of a military barracks full of soldiers means that you have much camaraderie in your life and never lack for friends to support you.

To dream of an empty barracks means your fight will be fought alone.

## BARREL, CASK

Dreaming of a full barrel denotes prosperous times and feastings. If it's empty, your life will be void of joy and consolation.

## BARTENDER

To dream of a bartender means you need to be more selective about your choice of partners.

To be a bartender in your dream means you will be called upon to give advice.

## BARTERING

If you are bartering in your dream, it's a warning sign that something you purchase will not be what you believe it is or that the deal is not fair to you.

## BASEBALL

If baseball is played in your dream, you are easily contented and your cheerfulness makes you a popular companion.

## BASEMENT*

To dream that you are in a basement warns that you will see lucrative opportunities sinking; with them, pleasure will dwindle into trouble and care.

*See *Cellar*.

## BASHFULNESS

To be bashful or shy in a dream means you will be quite sociable at an upcoming event.

## BASIN

To dream of bathing in a basin foretells a rise in social status.

## BASKET

To dream of seeing or carrying a basket signifies that you will meet unqualified success if the basket is full; empty baskets indicate discontent and sorrow.

## BASKETBALL

To participate in this sport in your dream means you will reach your goals.

To be a spectator watching a basketball game in your dream advises you to stop sitting on the sidelines in your waking life and participate more fully.

### BASS (FISH)

To dream of this colorful fish means that good fortune is coming your way.

### BASS VOICE

To dream that you have a bass voice suggests that you may detect some discrepancy in your business brought about by the deceit of someone in your employ.

Romantically, it foretells estrangements and quarrels.

### BASTARD

If you dream of being a bastard, it means you are an honorable person. If you dream of someone else being a bastard, expect an improvement in your social standing.

### BASTING

To dream of basting meats while cooking is a sign of prosperity and happiness.

### BAT

If you are frightened of these winged creatures in your dream, you need to be quiet about your personal affairs. If you are not afraid of the bats, you have an opportunity for financial gain in business.

### BATHING

To dream of bathing means good luck is coming your way.

### BATHROOM

To dream of a bathroom is an omen of good luck.

### BATTER

To dream you are making any kind of batter means something you have been trying to accomplish is not yet completed.

### BATTERY

To dream of replacing a battery suggests renewing a friendship with someone from your past.

### BATTLE

Dreaming of battle represents striving with difficulties and finally winning. If you are defeated in battle, bad deals made by others will mar your prospects.

## BAUBLE

To dream of a bauble means that social success and fortune are coming your way.

## BAYONET

To dream of a bayonet signifies that enemies hold you in their power, unless you get possession of the bayonet.

## BAY TREE

Dreams of bay trees are generally good for everybody. A verdant leisure awaits you in which you will have many pleasing diversions. You will reap much knowledge during this respite from labor.

## BAZAAR

Going to a bazaar in your dream means you have many choices. If you buy any item at a bazaar, you will spend money on an object or an event that brings joy.

## BEACH

If you dream you are on a sandy beach, your financial situation needs to be put in order.

## BEACON LIGHT

To dream of a beacon light means that your life is very balanced. If you're in distress, expect warm attachments to form with young people. If you're sick, this dream signifies speedy recovery and continued health. Business will gain new impetus.

To see a beacon light go out in time of storm or distress, however, suggests setbacks during a time when you thought fortune was smiling on you.

## BEADS

To dream of beads foretells attention from those in high places. Counting beads portends joy and contentment. Stringing them implies that you will obtain the favor of the rich.

## BEAGLE

To dream of this hunting dog suggests loyalty among your colleagues and peers in the workplace.

## BEAK

To dream of a bird's beak warns that someone's sharp words may ruin your day.

## BEAM

To dream of seeing a beam of light shining in your eyes means you will be left in the dark regarding a problem you are trying to solve. To dream of a beam showing you the way suggests that you will get guidance.

To dream of a wooden beam in good repair indicates that you are living in a stable, sturdy environment. If you dream of a broken beam, things in your life may need to be fixed.

## BEANS

To dream of uncooked beans means difficulties ahead; cooking them reveals that you will see financial gain.

## BEAR

Dreaming of a bear signifies overwhelming competition in pursuits of every kind. To kill a bear portends extrication from former entanglements.

## BEARD

To dream of seeing a beard suggests that an uncongenial person will oppose you. You may experience a fierce struggle for mastery and you are likely to lose money. A gray beard signifies hard luck and quarrels.

To see a beard on a woman foretells unpleasant associations and lingering illness.

If someone pulls your beard, you risk losing property.

To comb and admire a beard shows that your vanity will grow with prosperity. Former companions may come to despise you.

## BEAST

To dream of encountering and conquering a beast means you have been successful in conquering your lower self and baser emotions.

To be chased, attacked, and defeated by the beast advises you to assess what may be weak or negative in your character.

## BEATING

It bodes no good to dream of beating or being beaten by someone. Expect discord.

## BEAUTY

Dreaming of beauty in any form is preeminently good. A beautiful woman brings pleasure and profit. A lovely child represents love reciprocated and a happy union.

## BEAVER

To dream of seeing beavers means you will attain comfortable circumstances by diligent effort. If you dream of killing beavers for their skins, you may be accused of fraud and improper conduct toward the innocent.

## BECKONING

To beckon someone in a dream speaks of new friends and acquaintances on the horizon.

## BED

Dreaming of a bed, clean and white, denotes peace of mind. To dream of making a bed signifies a new friendship or business associate. To dream of being in bed in a strange room suggests that unexpected friends will visit you. If a sick person dreams of being in bed, complications will arise and, perhaps, death.

To dream that you are sleeping on a bed in the open air foretells delightful experiences and opportunities to improve your fortune.

To dream of a child wetting a bed implies unusual anxiety; those who are sick may not recover as quickly as might be expected. If you're the one wetting the bed, illness or tragedy may interrupt your daily routine.

## BEDBUGS

Seen in your dreams, they indicate continued sickness and unhappiness.

## BEDLAM

To dream of being in the midst of chaos and bedlam tells you that you're entering a quiet time in your life.

## BEDROOM

To see a newly furnished bedroom predicts a happy change involving journeys to distant places and pleasant companions.

## BEECH TREE

To dream of a beech tree means you will be chewing on an idea for longer than necessary.

## BEEF*

To dream of beef is an omen of pleasant surroundings and harmony in love and business. If it's raw and bloody, though, this means sadness and disappointment.

*See Meat.

### BEEHIVE

To dream of a beehive means prosperity and freedom from worry in the future. If you upset the beehive in your dream, you will suffer from financial trouble that you have created.

### BEER*

To dream of drinking at a bar portends disappointment. If you see others drinking, the work of schemers will displace your fondest hopes.

*See *Drunkenness*.

### BEES

Bees signify pleasant and profitable times. Those in positions of authority can expect obedient employees and a healthy environment. If a bee stings you, though, you could experience loss or injury.

### BEETLE

To dream of seeing beetles on your person denotes poverty and small ills. To dream of killing them is good.

### BEETS

If your dream features beets growing abundantly, peace and fruitful harvest will reign in the land; eating them with others is a sign full of good tidings.

### BEGGAR

To dream of an old, decrepit beggar is a sign of bad management and, unless you are economical, could signify the loss of property.

### BEGGING

To find yourself begging in a dream tells you that good fortune and wealth are on the horizon. To give money to a beggar in a dream advises you to be careful about how you are spending your money. To refuse to give to a beggar in your dream means you need to be more generous in your life.

### BEGRUDGING

In a dream, when you begrudge someone something that the person deserves, it suggests that in your waking life you will have something taken away from you.

When you are begrudging about making an effort to do something in your dream, it means the task will be fairly easy.

## BEGUILE

If you beguile another in your dream, you will be cheated and lied to. If you are the person being beguiled, the full truth is being spoken to you.

## BEHEADING

If you dream of being beheaded, overwhelming defeat or failure in an undertaking will soon follow. To see others beheaded means you may soon find yourself taking another direction in your personal or business life.

## BELCHING, BURPING

If you belch or burp in a dream, or someone else doess, you need to be more observant of situations and people around you.

## BELIEF

To dream of being steadfast in your beliefs warns that you will be questioned about something you have said. If you sway in your beliefs in your dream, you will have the courage and strength to stand up for what you believe.

## BELLADONNA

Strategic moves will bring success in business. If you dream of taking belladonna, however, debt problems loom.

## BELLE

To dream you are a belle at a social gathering denotes social embarrassment at an upcoming event.

## BELLMAN

Fortune is hurrying after you. Questions of importance will be settled amicably among friends and families.

## BELLOWS

Working a bellows in a dream suggests that while you may struggle, by your energy and perseverance, you'll achieve a lasting triumph over poverty and fate. To dream of seeing a bellows means distant friends long to see you.

## BELLS

To hear bells tolling in your dreams means death.

## BELLY*

It is bad to dream of seeing a swollen belly; this indicates sickness.

    To see a healthy belly denotes good health and well-being.

*See *Abdomen*.

## BELOVED

To dream that you are beloved means that the person or people in your dreams hold you in high regard; you are indeed loved very much.

## BELT

To dream of owning a stylish new belt suggests that you are soon to meet a stranger and make an engagement that may hurt your prosperity. If your belt is out of fashion, you will be censured for rudeness.

## BENCH

Distrust debtors and confidants if you dream of sitting on a bench. If you see others doing so, though, happy reunions between friends who have been separated through misunderstandings are suggested.

## BENDING

To bend an object in your dream means you will be straightforward in finding whatever answers you seek.

To bend a person to your will or your way of thinking strongly suggests that you must examine your conscience about something you have said to another that may have caused hurt.

## BEQUEST

After this dream, the knowledge of duties well performed and the health of the young are assured.

## BEREAVEMENT

To dream of grieving the loss of a child warns you that your plans will meet with frustration quickly; where you expect success, there will be failure.

The loss of relatives or friends denotes disappointment in well-formed plans and augurs a poor outlook for the future.

## BERRIES

To dream of berries on the vine, or of eating them, means that you have good social standing among your peers. This also signals material wealth and good fortune.

## BERTH

To dream of lying in a berth on a ship means you will have safe travel by water.

## BESIEGING

To witness the besieging of a castle or other building means that something may be stolen from you. It warns you to safeguard your home or business.

## BEST MAN

If you are a man dreaming of being the best man at a wedding, happiness and the love of family and friends are coming your way.

If you are a woman, your dream foretells future security.

## BETRAYAL

To dream of being betrayed by a loved one means the person will always be a steadfast and loyal companion. To dream you are betraying a loved one means you are not as loyal as you claim to be.

## BETROTHAL

Dreaming of being betrothed or engaged is a prediction of a broken relationship. If you dream of a betrothal being broken, this is actually a prediction of an upcoming marriage.

## BETTING

To dream of betting on races warns you to be cautious when engaging in new undertakings. Enemies are trying to divert your attention away from legitimate businesses.

Betting at gaming tables indicates that illegal tactics will be used to take money from you.

## BEVERAGE*

To dream of drinking a beverage speaks of your thirst for life being quenched; you find much joy in living. To give another person a beverage to drink means you will help that person meet a current goal.

*See *Punch*.

## BEWILDERMENT

If you dream of being bewildered or of trying to bewilder or confuse another in your dream, your honesty will always be strong.

## BEWITCHING

If you dream of being bewitched or of trying to bewitch someone, you are wasting time in your daily life.

## "BHAGAVAD GITA"

To dream of the "Bhagavad Gita" suggests a season of seclusion and rest for exhausted faculties. A pleasant journey for your benefit will be planned by your friends.

This is a dream of many blessings, although little financial advancement is promised.

## BIBLE

To dream of the Bible indicates blessings and good fortune.

## BICEPS

To dream of muscular biceps means protection. Scrawny-looking biceps indicate a health problem.

## BICKERING

To bicker or argue with someone in a dream means a happy relationship is on the horizon.

## BICYCLE

To dream of riding a bicycle uphill signifies bright prospects.

## BICYCLE HELMET

To dream of wearing a bicycle helmet or having one put on you indicates a false sense of security.

## BIDDING

If you find yourself bidding on an object in a dream, such as at an auction, you may lack funds to buy something for yourself in the near future.

## BIFOCALS

To dream of wearing or seeing someone wear these glasses suggests that you can see both sides of an issue.

## BIGAMY

For a man to commit bigamy in a dream denotes loss of manhood and failing intellect.

If a woman dreams of bigamy, she will suffer dishonor unless she is very discreet.

## BIKINI

To dream of seeing yourself in a bikini and being embarrassed by the way you look means you are taking very good care of yourself physically. To see someone else in a bikini warns you to take care of your physical health.

## BILL

To pay a bill in a dream warns you to make a careful accounting of your money.

To receive a bill in a dream means good fortune. If you can't pay the bill, something you are purchasing or paying for in your waking life will actually cost much less than you anticipated.

## BILLIARDS

Dreaming of playing billiards foretells coming troubles, lawsuits, and contention over property. Slander will work to your detriment. If the table and the billiard balls lie idle, deceitful comrades are undermining you.

## BINDING

To dream of binding any of your body parts hints at the release of inhibitions and insecurities.

To bind another person in any way indicates freeing yourself from a relationship.

## BINOCULARS

To use binoculars in your dream predicts a sudden, unexpected event that you will be able to examine closely and then take care of easily and quickly.

## BIOCHEMISTRY

To study biochemistry or see someone else studying biochemistry in a dream means you will hear of an event in the world of science that will shake you to your core.

## BIOGRAPHY

A dream of reading or writing a biography about someone is a warning not to spread rumors and to use your words wisely when talking about others.

## BIOLOGY

To study or see someone else studying biology in a dream suggests that a relationship in your life must be dissected in order for you to understand it better.

## BIRCH

To dream of this tree means you will shed your fears, becoming less thin-skinned and more flexible in the way you think.

## BIRD*

It is favorable to dream of birds with beautiful plumage. Flying birds signify prosperity for the dreamer. All disagreeable environments will vanish before the wave of prospective good.

To catch birds also indicates good fortune.

*See *Cardinal*. See also specific birds.

## BIRDS' NESTS

To dream of seeing birds' nests suggests that you will be interested in an enterprise that will prove profitable.

To see an empty nest denotes gloom in business or sorrow through the absence of a friend.

With eggs in the nest, good results will follow all engagements. If chicks are in the nest, expect successful journeys and satisfactory dealings. If they are lonely and deserted, however, your own folly will cause you anxiety.

To dream of a nest filled with broken or bad eggs portends disappointment and failure.

## BIRTH

For a married woman to dream of giving birth to a child foretells great joy and a substantial legacy; for a single woman, loss of virtue and abandonment by her lover.

## BIRTHDAY

To the young, to dream of a birthday is a signal of poverty and falsehood. To the old, it indicates long trouble and desolation.

## BIRTHDAY PRESENT

Receiving birthday presents means you have many accomplishments. Working people will advance in their trades. Giving birthday presents means you have found a new respect for those in your life.

## BISCUIT

Eating or baking biscuits indicates ill health and family peace ruptured over unimportant issues.

## BISHOP

To dream of a bishop means it will take hard work to accomplish your goals.

## BISON

To dream of a live bison means that your spirit will be strong in the face of coming adversity. A dead or a stuffed bison suggests losing faith in yourself and your ability to solve a vexing problem.

## BISQUE

To dream of bisque china warns of upcoming rough patches in an important relationship.

To dream of bisque soup means that your soul needs nourishment.

## BITCH

To dream of a female dog warns you to beware the women in your life.

To be called a bitch means a female loved one may cause you hurt.

### BITE MARK

A bite mark, whether from an insect, animal, or human, acts as a warning that someone wishes you ill. It also implies a wish to undo work that is past undoing. You are also likely to suffer losses through some enemy.

### BITTERNESS

To dream of having a bitter taste in your mouth or eating something bitter means you will soon find your life very sweet. To dream that you are bitter toward someone or something means that you will soon discover that your fears are actually unfounded.

### BIZARRE BEHAVIOR

To witness or display bizarre behavior means you are taking yourself too seriously.

### BLACK

In dreams, black represents the ending of one phase of life and the beginning of another and marks transitions, death, and rebirth.

### BLACKBERRIES

To dream of blackberries denotes many ills. To gather them is unlucky. Eating them suggests losses.

### BLACKBOARD

To see anyone writing in white chalk on a blackboard means your financial security is in question.

### BLACKMAIL

To be blackmailed or want to blackmail someone suggests that you're thought of as a trustworthy friend.

### BLACK MARKET

To find yourself purchasing something on the black market in a dream warns you to examine your future purchases for authenticity.

### BLACKOUT

If you dream of blacking out, your senses will be fully awake during an upcoming situation you need to resolve.

To dream of experiencing an electrical blackout suggests you use your five senses to solve problems in your life.

## BLACKSMITH

To see a blacksmith in a dream tells you that difficult projects will soon work to your advantage.

## BLADDER

To dream of your bladder hints that you will have serious trouble in your business if you are not careful with your health and the way you invest your energy.

## BLADE

To dream of sharpening a blade warns you to be wary of giving advice with a sharp tongue.

## BLANCHING

To dream of yourself or someone else blanching a food item means that even though a problem in your waking life might seem resolved, you need to dig deeper to find a true solution.

## BLANDISHMENTS

To dream of cajoling someone or performing an act of blandishment advises you to be more flexible in your thinking.

To be cajoled in a dream is a warning to stand strong about what you believe.

## BLANKET

Soiled blankets in a dream mean treachery. New and white blankets speak of success where you fear failure.

## BLASPHEMY*

Blasphemy in a dream warns that an enemy is creeping into your life. Feigning friendship, this person will do you great harm.

To dream you are cursing yourself means bad luck.

To dream you are being cursed by others signifies affection and prosperity.

*See Profanity.

## BLAST

To dream of hearing or feeling a blast of air or fire means you are protected from negativity in your waking life.

## BLAZING FIRE

To watch a blaze, big or small, in your dream warns that you must stay alert in a relationship.

If you are engulfed by a blaze and feel no fear, your relationships are strong and trustworthy.

## BLEATING

To hear young animals bleating in your dream suggests that you will have new responsibilities, but not necessarily pleasant ones.

## BLEEDING

To dream of bleeding signifies bad luck and financial loss.

## BLEMISH

To dream of seeing blemishes on yourself or someone else means that your friendships are pure and innocent.

## BLENDING

To dream of blending or combining different ingredients warns you to look at the issues in your life one at a time, not jumbled together, which could overwhelm you.

## BLESSEDNESS

To feel you are blessed in a dream means that you have a pleasant surprise coming.

## BLIGHT

To see blight or decay on a vegetable or other food suggests a fruitful harvest or a positive outcome to something.

## BLINDFOLD

To dream of a blindfold tells you to reexamine your plans and goals.

## BLINDMAN'S BLUFF

To dream of playing blindman's bluff suggests engaging in an enterprise that will likely humiliate you and cause you financial loss.

## BLINDNESS

To dream of being blind denotes a sudden change from affluence to poverty.
    To see others blind means that a worthy person will call on you for aid.

## BLINKING

Blinking normally in a dream means that your insights are clear.
    Blinking incessantly implies that you need to reexamine your thinking.

## BLISS

To dream of feeling blissful and happy foretells sadness.

## BLISTER

To dream of noticing a blister or feeling its pain warns you to watch your step in an upcoming adventure. To pop a blister and see it drain means that any misstep you take in a venture will correct itself immediately.

## BLIZZARD

If you dream of a snowstorm, it means you are being blinded by illusion.

## BLOATEDNESS

If you dream of someone looking bloated or swollen, good luck will come your way.

If you dream of being bloated, you will receive troubling news about your finances.

## BLOCKAGE

To dream that you have a blockage in your body means that you will have a spiritual epiphany or breakthrough.

## BLOCKS

Dreaming of cinder blocks suggests that you will soon experience money trouble.

Children's building blocks indicate that you are currently building toward your future, materially.

## BLOND HAIR

To dream of shiny blond hair (yours or someone else's) means you will soon outshine everyone around you in an upcoming project. To dream of unwashed blond hair is a warning to take precautions in this project.

## BLOOD

Bloodstained garments indicate enemies who seek to tear down a successful career that is opening up before you. Beware of uncomfortable friendships.

To see blood flowing from a wound predicts physical ailments and worry, or bad business caused by disastrous dealings with foreigners.

To dream of blood on your hands portends immediate bad luck if you are not careful.

## BLOODSTONE

To dream of seeing a bloodstone tells you that you will be unfortunate in your social engagements.

## BLOSSOMS

To dream of seeing trees and shrubs in bloom suggests that a time of prosperity is nearing.

## BLOT

If you dream of seeing a blot on something that is not of your making, you will soon solve a mystery that has been eluding you.

If you put a blot on something, look for unexpected improvements in your finances.

## BLOTCHES

To dream of seeing blotches on your skin warns that you need to make yourself clear in your communication and actions.

## BLOTTING PAPER

To dream of using blotting paper signifies that you may be tricked into betraying secrets that involve a friend.

To see worn blotting paper denotes continued disagreements in the home or among friends.

## BLOWS

Dreaming of blows portends injury to yourself. If you defend yourself, a rise in business will follow.

## BLUE

To dream of any shade of blue might warn of a bout of depression. It could also refer to an unexpected, positive event. Finally, blue might indicate that the sky's the limit in a current endeavor.

## BLUE JAY

To dream of this bird warns you to put things in perspective and examine your priorities.

## BLUNDERING

If you dream of making a blunder, great success awaits you.

## BLUSHING

To dream of blushing suggests worry and humiliation through false accusations.

## BOA CONSTRICTOR

To dream of this snake indicates stormy times and bad fortune. Disenchantment will follow. To kill one in a dream, however, is good.

## BOAR

If you dream of a boar chasing you, disappointment awaits you. If you kill it in your dream, you will have a corresponding gain in your life.

## BOARDINGHOUSE

To dream of a boardinghouse foretells that you will suffer entanglement and disorder and you are likely to change your residence.

## BOASTING

If you hear someone else boasting in your dreams, you will sincerely regret an impulsive act that causes trouble for your friends.

To boast to a competitor foretells that you will be unjust and will use dishonest means to win in competition.

## BOAT

Dreaming of a boat on clear water signals bright prospects. If the water is unsettled and turbulent, cares and unhappy changes threaten.

Unlucky is the dreamer who falls overboard while sailing on stormy waters.

## BOBBIN

To dream of a bobbin means that hard work lies ahead of you if you hope to complete a project.

## BODY

If you dream of your own body, it means that success is well within your reach.

To dream of someone else's body means you have a long way to go before you reach success.

If you dream of a cadaver or dead body, whether beautiful or deformed, great success is coming your way.

## BOG*

Bogs in dreams speak of heavy burdens. You may feel hopeless even trying to rise to the challenge. Illness and other worries may oppress you.
*See Swamp.

## BOIL

If you dream of a boil running pus and blood, expect unpleasant things in the immediate future. The insincerity of friends may cause you great inconvenience.

## BOILER

To dream of seeing a boiler in need of repair warns you of bad management or disappointment.

## BOLT

To dream of bolts signifies formidable obstacles that will impede your progress. If the bolts are old or broken, your expectations will be eclipsed by failures.

## BOMB

To see a bomb going off in your dreams, or to make one, tells you that a project demands meticulous attention to detail or it will blow up.

## BOMBSHELL

To dream of bombshells foretells anger and disputes ending in lawsuits. Many unpleasant incidents may follow such a dream.

## BONE

To see your bone protruding from your flesh cautions that treachery may ensnare you.

A pile of bones means a loss of finances.

## BONNET

For a woman to dream of a bonnet denotes gossip and slanderous insinuations, both of which call for careful defense.

If a man sees a woman tying her bonnet, this indicates unforeseen good luck shortly. His friends will be faithful and true.

A young woman is likely to engage in pleasant and harmless flirtations if her bonnet is new and any color except black.

## BONUS

Dreaming of receiving a bonus indicates unexpected financial gain.

## BOOK

To dream of studying suggests pleasant pursuits, honor, and riches.

For an author to dream of a work going to press is a dream of caution; there will be much trouble before the work reaches the public.

To dream of devoting great study and time to learning difficult subjects, and the hidden meaning of scholarly texts, indicates honors well earned.

To see children working at their books denotes harmony and good conduct of the young.

To dream of old books is a warning to shun evil in any form.

## BOOKCASE

To see a bookcase in your dreams means that you associate knowledge with your work and pleasure.

Empty bookcases imply that you will be upset because you lack the means or ability to work.

## BOOKKEEPING

Dreaming of a bookkeeper means that someone will soon hold you accountable for your recent actions.

To dream of being a bookkeeper means that you will soon be holding someone accountable for actions.

## BOOKSTORE

To visit a bookstore in your dream foretells that you will be filled with knowledge and unexpected interest.

## BOOMERANG

If you throw a boomerang and it comes back to you, someone is being dishonest with you.

If you dream of throwing one and it doesn't come back, expect a shift in some aspect of your life.

## BOOTH

The dream of being in a booth means you will soon be boxed in and need to make a decision. If you dream of being outside a booth, you can help someone make a decision that will be liberating.

## BOOTS

If you dream of wearing new boots, you will be lucky in your dealings.

Old and torn boots indicate sickness and snares.

## BORDER

To dream of planting or installing a border around your home, office, or other physical environment suggests a psychological need for boundaries to keep other people from interfering in your life.

If the border is a rock or other heavy material, you need to make your boundaries strong.

A border of flowers tells you that your boundaries are currently easy to maintain, which means that people naturally understand what you will and will not accept.

## BORROWING

Borrowing is a sign of loss and insufficient support.

If bankers dream of borrowing from other banks, this warns of a catastrophic run on their own banks.

If another person borrows from you in a dream, help in time of need will be extended or offered you. True friends will be there for you.

## BOSOM

A healthy bosom means coming prosperity, while an unhealthy one means loss, either financial or personal.

## BOSS

To dream of being a boss means that you will soon fail at your job or career.

Disliking your boss, on the contrary, means that in your waking life, you and your supervisor get along very well.

Liking your boss in a dream means you need to watch your back at work.

## BOTANY

To dream of this science or of being a botanist suggests many pleasant surprises in your lifetime.

## BOTTLE

Bottles are good to dream of if they're filled with transparent liquid. You will overcome all obstacles in affairs of the heart, and prosperity will ensue.

If the bottles are empty, though, trouble will enmesh you, but you will be able to disengage yourself by using strategy.

## BOUGH

To dream of sitting on the bough of a tree means you must seek ways to make your life more secure.

To watch a bough swinging in a breeze or moving means your security is rock-solid. If the bough breaks, your security has been breached.

## BOULDER

To come across a boulder in your dream that you can move or walk around with ease suggests that your problems are nearly insurmountable.

To face a boulder that you can't move or easily get around means your current problems will be overcome easily.

## BOUNCING

To watch yourself, someone else, or an object bouncing in a dream foretells great joy in your life.

## BOUNDARY

To dream of setting a boundary around yourself, regardless of what it's made of, counsels that you must establish rules in your life.

To dream of having a boundary destroyed also warns you to set rules.

## BOUNTY

To receive abundance in your dream warns you to be cautious of your financial situation.

## BOUQUET

To dream of a richly colored bouquet suggests a legacy from some wealthy and unknown relative; also, pleasant, joyous gatherings among young folks.

A withered bouquet signifies sickness and death.

## BOW

To tie a bow in your dream means you will soon tie up the loose ends of an affair.

## BOW AND ARROW

To dream of a bow and arrow tells you that you can achieve great gain from others' inability to carry out plans.

To make a bad shot means disappointed hopes in business affairs.

## BOWEL MOVEMENT

In dreams, having a bowel movement or watching someone have one represents great fortune or good luck.

## BOWL

To dream of an empty bowl means disappointment is on the horizon.

To dream of a full bowl means gain.

## BOWLING

To dream of bowling and knocking down pins foretells good fortune.

To dream of getting a gutter ball or missing the pins means that good fortune will soon be within your reach, but you will not be able to grasp it.

## BOX

Opening a box in your dream signifies untold wealth and suggests that delightful journeys to distant places may have happy results. If the box is empty, disappointment will follow.

## BOXING

If you are boxing or watching boxers in a dream, be careful of repeating past mistakes.

## BOY

If you dream of a boy, good fortune is coming in your near future.

## BOYCOTT

To find yourself or others boycotting something in a dream means that this same thing will become a part of your life soon.

## BRACELET

To see a bracelet encircling your arm in a dream assures you of an early and happy marriage.

The loss of a bracelet signifies loss and vexation. Finding one means that good property will come into your possession.

## BRAIN

To see your own brain in a dream warns that uncongenial surroundings will turn you into an unpleasant companion.

Seeing the brains of animals foretells mental trouble.

If you eat them, you will gain knowledge, and profit unexpectedly.

## BRAKING

To dream of braking a motor vehicle with ease means you will be offered a new opportunity.

If you cannot get the brakes on a vehicle to work in a dream, be wary of accepting any new offers or prospects.

## BRAMBLES

To dream of brambles entangling you suggests that lawsuits and legal problems lie ahead.

## BRANCH

Dreaming of a branch full of fruit and green leaves betokens wealth and many delightful hours with friends. If they are dried, it indicates sad news.

## BRANDY

To dream of brandy warns that while you may reach heights of distinction and wealth, you lack that ability to create true friendship from the people you are trying to please. In other words, there is an inauthenticity to those relationships that have carried you far.

## BRASS

To dream of brass indicates that you will rise rapidly in your profession.

## BRASSIERE

For a woman to dream of a bra means security.

If a man dreams of a bra, he needs to watch his back with his associates.

## BRAVERY

To see yourself or another performing an act of bravery in a dream means that you will not have the courage you need in an upcoming situation.

## BRAYING

Hearing an ass bray is significant of unwelcome tidings or intrusions.

## BREAD*

To dream of bread is a good indicator that your life, both personal and professional, is on the right track.

To dream of breaking bread with others indicates that you have an assured competence in your life.

*See *Baking, Crust*.

## BREAKAGE

Breakage is a bad dream. To dream of breaking any of your limbs denotes bad management and probable failures. To break furniture suggests domestic quarrels.

To break a window signifies bereavement. If you see a broken ring, order will be displaced by furious and dangerous uprisings, as the kind caused by jealousy and contentiousness.

## BREAKFAST*

To see a tasty breakfast indicates sudden, favorable changes.

If you are eating alone, it means you will fall into a trap set by your enemies. Eating with others is a good sign.

*See Meal.

## BREAKING WIND

To break wind in front of people means you are moving in the wrong direction with your ideas. To hear someone else break wind in a dream suggests unexpected travel.

## BREASTS

To dream of breasts means you will be nurtured in the near future—mentally, emotionally, spiritually, and physically.

## BREATH

If you come close to a person in your dream who has pure, sweet breath, your conduct will be commendable, and successful business deals will follow.

Fetid breath indicates sickness and snares.

Losing your breath signals failure where success seemed assured.

## BREEZE

To feel a breeze in your dream means that an upcoming project or event will go smoothly.

## BREWING

To dream of being in a vast brewing establishment implies persecution by public officials, but you will eventually prove your innocence and will rise above your persecutors.

Brewing in any way in your dreams denotes initial anxiety that usually gives way to profit and satisfaction.

## BRIARS

To see yourself caught among briars means a problem with your career. But if you disentangle yourself, you will find a solution.

## BRIBE, BRIBERY

To dream of being offered a bribe and accepting it warns of a possible problem with gambling.

If you don't accept the bribe in your dream, you will be lucky in games of chance.

## BRICKS

Seeing bricks in a dream indicates unsettled business and disagreements in love affairs. To make bricks means you will doubtlessly fail in your efforts to amass great wealth.

## BRIDE*

For a young woman to dream that she is a bride foretells that she will shortly come into an inheritance that will please her exceedingly—if she is happy making her bridal preparations. If she isn't, she will suffer disappointments.

To dream that you kiss a bride predicts a happy reconciliation between friends. For a bride to kiss others suggests many friends and pleasures for you; if she kisses you, you will enjoy health and find that your sweetheart inherits unexpected fortune.

To kiss a bride and find that she looks careworn and ill indicates that you will be displeased with your success and the actions of your friends.

If a bride dreams that she is indifferent to her husband, it foretells many unhappy circumstances.

*See *Marriage, Wedding.*

## BRIDEGROOM

If you dream of a bridegroom, either yourself or someone else, expect delays in your plans in the near future. To dream that you are a bridegroom means a temporary breakup of a relationship.

## BRIDESMAID

To dream of bridesmaids, either yourself or others, means difficulties in your love life.

## BRIDGE

If you see a long, dilapidated bridge mysteriously winding into darkness, then profound melancholy over the loss of possessions will befall you, and your life will be dismal.

To the young and those in love, bridges foretell disappointment in the heart's fondest hopes; loved ones will fall below expectations.

To cross a bridge safely suggests ultimately surmounting difficulties, though the means hardly seem safe. Any obstacle or delay threatens disaster.

If you see a bridge give way before you, beware treachery and false admirers.

## BRIDLE

To dream of a bridle means you will engage in an enterprise that will give you much worry, but will eventually result in pleasure and gain. An old or broken bridle suggests that you will encounter difficulties that will likely take you down.

## BRIDLE BIT

To see bridle bits in your dream implies that you can subdue and overcome any obstacle opposing your advancement or happiness. If they break or are broken, you may be surprised into making concessions to enemies.

## BRIEFCASE

To dream of a briefcase that is old and worn means great success in your business.

To dream of one that is new tells you to watch for unforeseen and unwanted changes in business.

## BRIMSTONE

To dream of brimstone foretells that disreputable dealings will lose you many friends if you fail to rectify mistakes you are making.

To see fire and brimstone warns that you are threatened with loss.

## BROADCAST

To dream of a broadcast indicates success through hard work.

## BROKER

To dream of a broker, yourself or someone else, means that you need to be careful in your financial dealings,

## BRONCHITIS

To dream that you have bronchitis signifies that you will be detained in your plans by complications of sickness at home.

## BRONZE

To dream of bronze means that your fortunes will be uncertain and unsatisfactory.

## BROOCH

To dream of a brooch that is shiny and new counsels you to watch your heart.

To dream of an antique brooch means that you can count on close relationships, and that the people around you are steadfast and loyal.

## BROOD

To see a fowl with her brood denotes accumulation of wealth.

## BROOK

To cross a clear brook in a dream foretells ease in solving an upcoming problem. To cross a muddy brook indicates that the problem will be solved, but only with hard work. To fall into a clear book means that current problems will be over soon. Conversely, a muddy brook indicates that the problem will demand time and resources.

## BROOM

To dream of new brooms denotes thrift and rapid improvement in your fortune. If they are seen in use, you will lose in speculation.

## BROTH

Broth represents the sincerity of friends who will stand by you. If you need financial aid, it will be forthcoming.

To lovers, it promises a strong and lasting attachment.

To dream of making broth means you rule your own and others' fate.

## BROTHEL

To dream of being in a brothel warns that you will encounter disgrace through pandering to your vanity by overindulgence and greed in acquiring material possessions that you can ill afford.

## BROTHER

To dream of seeing your brother(s) full of energy means that you will rejoice at your own or their good fortune; but if they are poor and in distress, or begging for assistance, you will be called to a deathbed soon, or some dire loss will overwhelm you or them.

## BROWN

In dreams, any shade of brown symbolizes stability and security in your life and connection with the planet and nature.

## BRUISING

To dream of bruising counsels you to be careful with your partying. Too much fun can lead to problems, and you need to slow down.

## BRUSH

To dream of using a hairbrush means you will suffer misfortune due to your mismanagement. Old hairbrushes denote sickness and ill health.

To see a clothes brush indicates that a heavy task is pending. If you are busy brushing your clothes, you will soon receive reimbursement for difficult work.

To see miscellaneous brushes foretells a varied line of work that is pleasing and remunerative.

### BRUSSELS SPROUTS

To dream of these vegetables—whether you are eating, cooking, or looking at them—indicates small gains in the future.

### BUBBLE

To dream of bubbles means your current problems will vanish into thin air.

To dream of blowing bubbles advises you to watch your finances.

### BUCKLE

To dream of buckles foretells that you will be beset by invitations to pleasurable events, and your affairs will be in danger of chaotic confusion.

### BUDDHA

To dream of the Buddha means abundant blessings.

### BUFFALO

To dream of buffalo forecasts large profits—unless you kill or injure a buffalo, in which case you need to be careful in new business ventures.

### BUGLE

If you hear joyous blasts from a bugle in a dream, prepare for happiness, as harmony and good things are being created for you by unseen powers.

Blowing a bugle denotes fortunate dealings.

### BUGS

To dream of bugs indicates that unpleasant complications will arise in your daily life.

### BUILDINGS*

To see large and magnificent buildings with green lawns stretching out before them signifies a long life of plenty and includes travel and exploration in foreign countries.

Small and newly built buildings denote happy homes and profitable undertakings; old and filthy buildings, however, warn of ill health and the loss of love and livelihood.

*See *House.*

## BULL

If you dream of a bull pursuing you, you will be beset by business trouble at the hands of envious and jealous competitors.

Dreaming of a bull goring a person suggests that misfortune will overtake you as a result of using another person's possessions.

## BULLDOG*

If you dream of entering strange premises and having a bulldog attack you, you are at risk of committing perjury to obtain your desires.

If one meets you in a friendly way, you will rise in life, regardless of criticism and the interference of enemies.

*See *Dog*.

## BULLET

To dream of a bullet means you are exposed to possible danger or vicious rumors.

To dream you are hit by a bullet warns you to get a medical checkup at once.

## BULLFROG

To dream of seeing or hearing a bullfrog means new friendships are on the horizon.

## BULL'S-EYE

To dream of hitting a bull's-eye means important news is coming your way.

To dream of someone else hitting a bull's-eye counsels you to reexamine your relationship with that person; he or she may not be trustworthy.

## BULLYING

To be bullied in a dream speaks of loyal and good friends in your waking life. If you do the bullying, you are not as good a friend as you should be.

## BUMPING

If you dream of being bumped or of bumping into someone or something, be very careful where you put your loyalties.

## BUNDLE

If you dream of receiving a wrapped bundle, an unexpected gift or invitation is coming your way.

If you dream of carrying a bundle, beware of being criticized.

## BUNION

To dream of having a bunion fixed means you will be steady on your feet in an upcoming challenge.

To have a painful bunion in a dream tells you that a project or upcoming event may need to be aborted.

## BUNK

Dreaming of sleeping in a bunk yourself, or of seeing others sleep there, symbolizes security.

To dream of an empty bunk hints at the need to find more security in your life.

## BURDEN

To dream that you carry a heavy burden signifies that you will be tied down by injustice due to favoritism shown your enemies by those in power. If you struggle free from the burden, you will climb to the heights of success.

## BURGLAR

If you dream that burglars are searching your person, you will have dangerous enemies to contend with. They may destroy you unless you're extremely careful in your dealings with strangers.

If you dream of your home or place of business being burglarized, your good standing in business or society will be assailed, but your courage will protect you.

## BURIAL*

To attend a burial is a sign of healthy relationships and happiness in your personal life.

*See Funeral.

## BURIED ALIVE

To dream that you are buried alive warns that you are about to make a great mistake, which your opponents will quickly turn to your disadvantage.

If you are rescued from the grave, your struggle will eventually correct your mistake.

## BURLAP

To dream of this coarse material means that you will find great satisfaction in the finer things around you.

## BURNS

Burns stand for good news, good tidings, and good health.

## BURRS

To dream of burrs indicates that you will struggle to free yourself from an unpleasant obstacle and seek a change of surroundings.

## BUS

To dream of a bus means you are heading toward your heart's desire and will indeed get what you want. However, waiting for a bus means a setback is ahead.

An accident involving a bus indicates financial worry.

## BUSH

To dream of a bush means that a change in location is on the horizon.

A dream of hiding in the bushes says you have no secrets.

To dream of cutting or burning a bush suggests that your secrets will be exposed.

## BUSINESS

To dream of your business flourishing means you will encounter hard times ahead. To dream of your business failing foretells unexpected gain.

To dream of documents regarding your business being signed warns you of dishonesty among your colleagues.

## BUSINESS CARDS

If you dream of handing someone your business card or receiving a business card from someone, expect introductions to people who will be beneficial to your finances.

## BUTCHER

If you dream of a butcher slaughtering cattle and being drenched with blood, you may expect a long and fatal illness in your family.

To see a butcher cutting meat suggests that your character will be dissected by society to your detriment. Beware of writing letters or documents.

## BUTTER

To dream of eating fresh butter is a sign of good health and plans carried out well; it will bring you possessions, wealth, and knowledge.

To eat rancid butter denotes competence acquired through manual labor.

Selling butter represents small gain.

## BUTTERFLY

To see a butterfly among flowers and green grass indicates prosperity.

To see them flying about denotes news from friends by letter or from someone who has seen them.

## BUTTERMILK*

Any dream of buttermilk denotes sorrow.

*See *Milk*.

## BUTTOCKS

If you dream of buttocks, prepare for good times ahead.

## BUTTON

To dream of sewing buttons tells you that emotional worries will soon be looming. To dream of buttons in general suggests losses or ill health.

## BUZZARD

To dream that you hear a buzzard foretells that some old scandal or gossip will resurface to disturb you.

## BYPASS

If you dream of a bypass in a road, it is warning you to be straight and honest in your dealings with others.

### CAB

To ride in a cab in dreams suggests pleasant avocations, prosperity, and comfort.

To ride in a cab at night with others says that you have a secret you keep from your friends.

### CABBAGE

It is bad to dream of cabbage. Green cabbage represents unfaithfulness in love and infidelity in marriage.

To dream of cutting cabbage implies that you are tightening the cords of calamity around you by lavish expenditure.

### CABIN*

To dream of a ship's cabin is rather unfortunate. Some mischief is brewing for you. You will most likely be engaged in a lawsuit, which you will lose due to the instability of your witness.

*For a log cabin, see *House*.

### CABINET

If you dream of putting items in a cabinet, you will soon be getting your disarrayed house in order.

To take items out of a cabinet in a dream advises you to discard unwanted items in your life.

### CABLE

To dream of a heavy metal wire cable foretells a decidedly hazardous project, which, if you successfully carry to completion, will reward you with riches and honor.

To dream of receiving cablegrams suggests that a message of importance will reach you soon, and will cause problems.

### CACHE

If you dream of hiding something in a cache, you might have property stolen.

## CACHET

To dream of applying a cachet (a distinguishing mark or seal) suggests that you will soon be facing legal problems.

## CACKLING

To hear the cackling of hens warns you of a sudden shock produced by the news of an unexpected death.

## CACTUS

To dream of cactus implies smooth sailing in your love affairs.

## CADDIE

If you dream of being a caddie, you are shouldering other people's burdens unnecessarily.

To dream of having a caddie counsels you to take responsibility for your own problems.

## CAFÉ

If you dream of a café, it may be time to slow down and relax more.

## CAFETERIA

To dream of a full cafeteria means that you have many friends and supporters.

An empty cafeteria warns that you need to focus more on your friends and nurture those relationships.

## CAFFEINE

If you dream of craving caffeine, you need to find peace in your relationships.

If you dream you are having too much caffeine, it's a warning that your relationships have become stale.

## CAGE

If you see a cage full of birds in your dream, you will be the happy recipient of immense wealth and will have many beautiful and charming children. If there is only one bird, you will have a happy and wealthy marriage. No birds in the cage indicates a member of the family lost to death.

To see caged wild animals indicates that you will triumph over your enemies and misfortunes. If you are in the cage with them, it suggests harrowing accidents while traveling.

## CAKE*

In dreams, cakes symbolize gain for the hardworking and opportunity for the enterprising. Those in love will prosper.

To dream you are making cake batter means that something you have been trying to accomplish in your life is not completed yet. Baking cakes is not as good an omen in dreams as seeing them or eating them. *See Pancakes.*

### CALCIUM

To dream that you are in need of more calcium in your diet means that you need more strength in your life.

### CALCULATING, CALCULATOR

If you are calculating something in your dream, it warns that you may not be able to count on someone or some event you've been anticipating.

### CALENDAR

To dream of marking a calendar indicates that you will be very orderly and systematic throughout the year.

To see a calendar denotes disappointment in your calculations.

### CALICO

In dreams, calico can symbolize old-fashioned ideas about love relationships.

### CALL GIRL

To dream of a call girl means that the woman in your life is faithful and true. To dream of being a call girl warns of misguided sexual activity.

### CALLIGRAPHY

Dreaming of doing calligraphy means you will be signing important papers. If you watch someone do calligraphy, you will be invited to an important social event.

### CALLING

If you dream of receiving a calling to go into religious life—or any kind of profession—a good career choice and financial well-being are on the way.

### CALLUS

If you dream of being callused, it is a dream warning you that those around you are too quick and hard in their dealings with you.

### CALMNESS

Dreaming of calm seas suggests a successful ending to a doubtful undertaking. Feeling calm and happy in your dream is a harbinger of a long and well-spent life and a vigorous old age.

## CALORIES

If you dream of calories, you are being warned to watch your eating habits, which might lead to health issues.

## CALVES*

To dream of calves peacefully grazing on a velvety lawn suggests that you will become a great favorite in society and win the heart of a loyal person. To the young, this dream indicates festive gatherings and enjoyment. To a businessperson, it speaks of profit from sales; to a lover, entering into a mutually respectful relationship. Those engaged in seeking wealth will see it rapidly increasing.

If the calves are scrawny, the object sought will be much harder to obtain.

*See *Cattle*.

## CALYPSO

A dream of hearing calypso music means joyful and fun times ahead.

## CAMCORDER

To dream of a camcorder prophesies that you will make pleasant memories in the near future.

## CAMEL

To see this beast of burden in a dream signifies that you will exercise great patience and fortitude in a time of almost unbearable anguish.

Such a dream may also suggest that you will be the recipient of unexpected beneficence and will wear your new honors with dignity and charity.

To lovers, this dream foretells congenial dispositions.

To see a herd of camels in the desert denotes assistance when aid seems unlikely. It may also involve a sickness from which you recover, contrary to all expectations.

## CAMEO BROOCH

If you dream of a cameo brooch, some sad occurrence claims your attention.

## CAMERA

To dream of a camera signifies changes to your environment.

## CAMISOLE

To dream of a camisole counsels you to pay attention to breast health.

## CAMOUFLAGE CLOTHING

If you are wearing camouflage in your dream, you are telling too many people too much about your business and dealings.

To see someone else wearing camouflage means you will be revealing secrets to others.

## CAMPAIGNING

To dream of embarking on a political campaign signifies your opposition to approved ways of conducting business. You will set up innovative plans for yourself even if enemies are working against you, and you will triumph over those in power.

## CAMPHOR

If you dream of camphor, you are being warned about unscrupulous and unfriendly people in your environment. If you are a woman, be aware that this could lead to scandal.

## CAMPING

If you dream of camping in the open air, expect a change in your affairs. You may need to prepare to make a long and tiring journey.

If you see campgrounds, many of your companions may move on to new places, and your own prospects will appear gloomy.

## CAMPUS

To dream that you are on a campus suggests that you will learn new things soon or will return to school.

## CANAL

To dream of a muddy and stagnant canal portends sickness, digestive disorders, and dark designs of enemies. But if its waters are clear, you can anticipate a placid life and the devotion of friends.

## CANARY

To dream of this sweet songbird denotes unexpected pleasures. To dream that one is given to you indicates a positive legacy. To give away a canary suggests disappointment in your dearest wishes. To dream that one dies warns of the unfaithfulness of dear friends.

## CAN, CANNING

To dream of canning or to see cans reminds you to save more money.

## CANCELLATION

To cancel or have something canceled in a dream is a warning to be careful in your love life.

## CANCER

If you dream of having cancer, have faith that you will be happy.

To dream that someone else has cancer means you will bring happiness to someone in the very near future.

## CANDLE

To dream of candles burning with a clear and steady flame implies both financial well-being and the trustworthiness of those around you.

If you see yourself molding candles, you may receive an unexpected offer of marriage or embark on a pleasant visit to distant relatives.

If you are lighting a candle, you will meet someone objectionable to your family and friends.

To see a candle flickering in a draft warns that enemies are circulating detrimental reports about you.

## CANDLESTICK

To see a candlestick bearing a whole candle denotes a bright future filled with health, happiness, and loving companions.

If it's empty, the reverse.

## CANDY

To dream of making candy suggests that profit will accrue from industry.

To dream of eating fresh candy implies social pleasure and romance.

Sour candy suggests illness. It also implies that annoyances will grow out of secrets kept too long.

If you dream of sending someone a box of candy, you will make an offer and meet with disappointment.

## CANE

To see cane growing in a dream suggests advancing favorably toward your goal. To see it cut denotes absolute failure in all undertakings.

A walking cane represents much success in future business dealings.

## CANINE*

In dreams, a canine tooth represents fortune; the longer the tooth, the greater the fortune.

To dream of a dog (canine) means loyalty.

*See Dog.

## CANISTER

Seeing a canister in a dream suggests that you're holding on to outmoded thoughts or possessions.

## CANKER

To dream of seeing a canker on anything is a bad omen. It foretells death and sorrow.

## CANNIBAL

If you dream of a cannibal or a tribe of cannibals, take care to avoid being taken advantage of in a business deal.

## CANNON

A cannon in a dream implies that your home and country are in danger of foreign invasion, perhaps war.

## CANNONBALL

This warns that secret enemies are uniting against you.

## CANOE*

Paddling a canoe in dreams reflects perfect confidence in your ability to conduct business profitably.

*See Water.

## CANONIZATION

Dreaming of someone or yourself being canonized warns you to beware of negative or evil forces in your life.

## CANOPY

To dream of a canopy or of being underneath one tells you that false friends are influencing you into unethical ways of securing gain. Protect those in your care.

## CANTALOUPE

If you dream of a field of cantaloupes, your future business dealings will go smoothly.

If you dream of holding a single cantaloupe, love, peace, and happiness are entering your life.

Eating a cantaloupe cautions you about false love.

## CANTEEN

Dreaming of a canteen says you have a sense of security in your life.

## CANTERING

Watching or riding a cantering horse in your dream means that your environment will be filled with luxury items and lovely things.

## CANVAS

A blank canvas in your dream foretells a clear and bright future.

Seeing yourself paint on a canvas speaks to creating the future you long for.

A ripped or torn canvas in your dream warns that an aspect of your love life needs repair.

## CAP

If a woman dreams of seeing a cap, she will be invited to take part in a festive event.

## CAPE

If you dream of wearing a cape, others think of you as masterful in what you do. If you put your cape on someone else, you will step aside and let someone else solve a problem.

## CAPITOL BUILDING

If you dream of seeing a capitol building, you want more control over the projects you're currently involved in.

## CAPPUCCINO

To drink or make cappuccino in a dream means that your friendships will turn cold.

## CAPSIZING

To dream of capsizing foretells that something will turn your world upside down.

## CAPSULE*

To dream of a capsule (pill) indicates that you need to contain your temper.
*See Pill.

## CAPTAIN

If you dream of seeing a captain, your noblest aspirations will be realized.

## CAPTIVE

To dream that you are a captive indicates that you may have treachery to deal with; if you cannot escape, injury and misfortune will befall you.

To dream of taking anyone captive portends joining pursuits and people of low status.

## CAR

To dream of seeing cars denotes journeys and changes in quick succession.

To get into one shows that the travel you've been contemplating will be made under circumstances different from what you thought.

To dream of a sleeping car on a train indicates that your struggle to amass wealth is animated by selfish and lewd desires that you must work to master and control.

To see streetcars in your dreams warns that some person is actively interested in causing you trouble.

## CARAMEL

To dream of this chewy candy means that words that come out of your mouth easily and sweetly will soon be used against you.

## CARAT

To dream of a carat means that a gift is on its way. The more carats the ring weighs, the bigger the gift.

## CARAVAN

To dream of a caravan suggests that in the near future you will be asked to be the leader of a project.

## CARAWAY

To dream of a caraway seed means that something new may be coming into your life.

## CARBON COPY

To dream of a carbon copy counsels you to think outside the box and not copy anyone else.

## CARCASS

To dream of a carcass denotes spiritual rebirth and enlightenment.

## CARDBOARD

To dream of cardboard tells you to beware losing physical strength. It indicates a possible health issue.

## CARDINAL

It is unlucky to dream of seeing a cardinal in his robes; a Catholic cardinal is a harbinger of bad news.

To dream of the bird, however, suggests family harmony, happy social events, and business expansion.

## CARDIOGRAM

To dream of a receiving a bad cardiogram warns of heartache.

To dream of a good one tells you that new love lies ahead.

## CARDS

If you dream of playing cards with others for fun, you will see the realization of hopes that have long buoyed you up. Small ills will vanish.

But playing professionally, or for high stakes, implies difficulties of a serious nature.

If you dream of losing at cards, you will encounter enemies.

If you win, you will justify yourself in the eyes of the law, but you may have trouble doing so.

## CAREER

To dream of a career change means you will be staying in your present career.

To dream of remaining in your present career indicates that you will be making a career change.

## CAREGIVING

If you are the caregiver in a dream, it's time to take care of your own affairs. This dream may also suggest that you are exercising too much control over others.

To dream of someone else offering care to you means that others have been too involved in your personal business.

## CARIBOU

To dream of caribou is a warning not to run with the herd.

## CARICATURE

To see a cartoon of yourself or someone else in your dream tells you that you're viewing yourself or others in a distorted way.

## CARJACKING

To dream of a carjacking means you will soon buy a new vehicle.

## CARNAGE

To dream of carnage predicts the announcement of a birth.

## CARNATIONS

To dream of carnations foretells death.

## CARNIVAL

To dream that you are participating in a carnival portends that you are soon to enjoy some unusual pleasure or recreation.

If masks are in use, or you see incongruous or clownish figures, expect discord in the home; business will be unsatisfactory and love unrequited.

## CAROLING

To dream of singing a carol means that good news will be coming your way soon.

## CARP

In dreams, this fish symbolizes good fortune and wealth.

## CARPENTER

To see a carpenter at work foretells honest endeavors to further your fortune, rather than engaging in time-consuming pastimes that squander your energy.

## CARPET

To see a carpet in a dream denotes profit; wealthy friends will come to your aid.

If you walk on a carpet, you will be prosperous and happy.

To dream that you buy a carpet suggests great gain. If you're selling them, you will go on a pleasant and profitable journey.

## CARPOOLING

To dream of a carpool suggests that you're afraid to be alone.

## CARRIAGE

To dream of a carriage implies that you will be gratified and that you will make visits. To ride in one suggests a sickness that will soon pass, leaving you to enjoy health and good fortune.

If you dream that you are looking for a carriage, you will work hard and eventually achieve success.

## CARRIER

To dream of a carrier foretells a gift or happy message.

## CARROT

To dream of carrots portends prosperity and health.

## CARSICKNESS

To dream of being carsick means that good health and safe travel await you.

## CART

If you dream of riding in a cart, bad luck and constant work will fill your time as you struggle to provide for your family.

Seeing a cart denotes bad news from kin or friends.

Driving a cart suggests that you will meet with success in business and other aspirations.

## CARTOON

To dream of a cartoon warns you that illusions can cloud the way you view yourself or others.

## CARTRIDGE

To dream of cartridges foretells quarrels and dissension. An unhappy fate threatens you or someone close to you.

If the cartridges are empty, you will be tempted to be irresponsible in your actions with your associates or friends.

## CARTWHEEL

To dream of a cartwheel suggests that problems in your life will turn around.

## CARVING

To dream of carving a cooked bird indicates you will be materially poor and will struggle with ill-tempered friends.

Carving meat denotes bad investments; but if you make changes, your prospects will be brighter.

## CASH*

If you dream that you have plenty of cash, but it's borrowed, you will be looked upon as worthy, but those who come in close contact with you may find you mercenary and unfeeling.

If you dream of seeing your pockets or purse filled with cash, you will have to spend money on an unexpected problem.

Looking for cash in a dream indicates a windfall in the near future.

*See Money.

## CASH BOX

To dream of a full cash box means that favorable prospects will soon open up.

If it's empty, you will experience meager remuneration.

## CASHEW NUTS

To dream of this nut foretells improving health.

## CASHIER

To see a cashier in a dream means that others will claim your possessions. If you owe anyone, you will be deceitful in your dealings with someone wealthy.

## CASHMERE

To dream of cashmere means you find much warmth in your friendships.

## CASINO

To dream of a casino means that you are gambling too much.

## CASKET

To dream of an empty casket indicates the loss of a friendship.

To dream of seeing yourself in a casket foretells good luck.

To dream of seeing someone else in a casket foretells sadness but not death.

## CASSEROLE

To dream of a casserole means that you will be able to combine many aspects of your life to create happiness in the near future.

## CASSETTE

If you dream of a cassette tape, you may need reassurance during a project or event.

## CASTANET

To dream of this musical instrument suggests happy times ahead.

## CASTAWAY

To dream of a castaway means you'll need to be alone in the future.

## CASTLE

If you dream of being in a castle, you have enough money to make the life you wish to live. You can be a great traveler, enjoying contact with people of many nations.

Seeing an old and vine-covered castle suggests romantic tastes; take care not to enter an undesirable marriage or engagement.

If you dream of leaving a castle, you will be robbed or will lose your beloved or other dear one to death.

## CASTOR OIL

To dream of castor oil indicates that you will discover that one of your friendships is insincere and the friend is actually betraying you. You will soon end this friendship.

## CAT*

To dream of a cat in general denotes bad luck, unless you kill it or drive it away. If the cat attacks you, enemies will go to any extreme to damage your reputation. But if you succeed in banishing the cat, you will overcome great obstacles and rise in fortune and fame.

Hearing the scream or the meowing of a cat warns you that a false friend is using everything at his or her command to do you harm.

If you dream that a cat scratches you, an enemy will succeed in wrenching from you the profits of a deal you worked hard to make happen.
*See Kitten.

## CATACOMBS

To dream of an underground burial chamber marks the need for direction and careful navigation in an upcoming situation.

## CATAPULT

To dream of a catapult augurs sudden and unforeseen change.

## CATCHING

To dream of catching something indicates financial gain.

To dream of someone else making a catch means financial loss.

## CATECHISM

To dream of the catechism foretells that you will be offered a lucrative position, but the terms will be difficult and you will be reluctant to accept it.

## CATERPILLAR

To see a caterpillar in a dream denotes hypocritical people in your immediate future; beware of deceitful appearances.

You may suffer a loss in love or business.

## CATFISH

To dream of catfish means it's time to clean your environment.

## CATHEDRAL

To dream of a cathedral indicates blessings and good fortune.

## CAT SCAN

To dream of a CAT scan suggests that you need to look more deeply at a problem.

## CATSUP

To dream of catsup warns that you should resist the desire to cover up a potential problem.

## CATTLE*

To dream of seeing good-looking and fat cattle contentedly grazing in green pastures denotes prosperity and happiness thanks to a congenial and pleasant companion.

If the cattle are lean, shaggy, and poorly fed, you will be likely to toil all your life because of misspent energy and dislike of details in work. Correct your habits after this dream.

To see cattle stampeding means you must exert power to keep your career profitable.

A herd of cows at milking time indicates that you will achieve wealth as a result of the work of many people.

If you dream of milking cows with full udders, good fortune is in store for you.

*See *Calves*.

## CAULDRON

Dreaming of a cauldron, empty or full, warns you to beware underhanded tricks from mean-spirited people.

## CAULIFLOWER

To dream of eating cauliflower means you will be taken to task for neglect of duty.

If you see it growing, your prospects will brighten after a period of loss.

## CAULKING

If you dream of caulking something in your home or business, you need to keep quiet.

## CAVALCADE

To dream of a cavalcade means you must resist the temptation to follow others.

## CAVALRY

To dream that you see a division of cavalry denotes personal advancement and distinction.

## CAVEMAN

To dream of a caveman suggests that you are embracing too many old-fashioned ideas.

## CAVERN OR CAVE

To dream of seeing a cavern yawning before you suggests that many problems will assail you; adversaries may hinder your advancement. Work and health are threatened.

To be in a cave foreshadows change.

## CAVIAR

To dream of caviar warns you to be careful of spending your money unwisely.

## CAVITY

To dream of having a cavity means you will soon have a wish fulfilled.

## CAYENNE

In dreams, this spicy pepper symbolizes heated arguments.

## CB RADIO

To dream of this type of radio means that you will soon be connecting with friends from the past.

## CCU

To dream of a critical care unit means you may have to deal with heartache in the near future.

## CD

To dream of a CD indicates the need to contain your emotions, especially in the near future.

## CD-ROM

To dream of a CD-ROM warns of repeating old mistakes.

## CEDAR

To dream of seeing green and shapely cedar boughs denotes success. To see them dead or blighted signifies despair.

## CEILING

To dream of a ceiling indicates that you are putting limitations on yourself or others.

## CELEBRATION

To celebrate in a dream means a death is in your future.

## CELEBRITY

To dream of a celebrity warns of pending social scandal.

## CELERY

If you dream of seeing fresh, crisp stalks of celery, you will be prosperous and influential beyond your highest hopes.

If it's decaying, a death in your family will soon occur.

If you dream of eating celery, boundless love and affection will be heaped upon you.

## CELESTIAL SIGNS (ANGELS AND ETHEREAL BEINGS)

Celestial signs represent good news about your personal and financial life.

## CELL

To dream of a jail cell advises you to delegate tasks at your job among co-workers.

## CELLAR

If you dream of being in a cold, damp cellar, you will be oppressed by doubts. You will lose confidence in all things and suffer gloomy forebodings from which you will fail to escape unless you control your will. This dream also indicates loss of property.

To see a cellar stocked with wine means profit.

## CELLOPHANE

To dream of cellophane warns that you need to beware of illusions in your relationships.

## CELL PHONE

To dream of a cell phone with good reception indicates clear thinking about a project.

If it has poor reception, you might be confused by other people's ideas.

## CELLULITE

To dream of having cellulite means you will have good health.

## CELT

To dream of being a Celt or of being in a clan of Celts means you will soon find your spiritual center.

## CEMENT

If you dream of solid cement, your life is solid for the near future.

If the cement is broken, you need to watch your dealings with others and avoid being weak.

## CEMETERY

To dream of being in a beautiful and well-kept cemetery suggests unexpected news of the recovery of someone you had mourned as dead. Or you may regain property to which you were rightfully entitled.

An overgrown, forgotten cemetery predicts that you will live to see all your loved ones leave you, and you will be left in a stranger's care.

If a mother dreams of carrying fresh flowers to a cemetery, she may expect the continued good health of her family.

If you see little children gathering flowers and chasing butterflies among the graves, expect prosperous changes and no graves of any of your friends to weep over. Good health will hold sway.

## CENSUS

To dream of taking a census means you will soon be made accountable for your actions, good, bad, and neutral.

## CENTAUR

To dream of this mythical half man/half horse indicates that you are living in two different realities.

## CENTERFOLD

To dream of being in a centerfold is a warning that you have become too self-absorbed.

## CENTERPIECE

To dream of making a centerpiece means you will soon be putting your affairs in order. Looking at a centerpiece suggests that your affairs are already in order.

## CENTIPEDE

To dream of this insect counsels you to move faster on a project or on making a change in your life.

## CENT, PENNY

To dream of counting pennies means you will be facing financial loss. If you're finding them, you'll find happiness; losing them suggests financial gain.

## CENTRAL NERVOUS SYSTEM

To dream of having an unhealthy central nervous system implies a time of calm in the near future.

To dream of a healthy CNS means you will be entering a period of great drama.

## CEO

To dream of being a CEO means that advancement in your career will come only through great effort.

If you dream of another person being a CEO, you will be recognized through your hard work.

## CERAMIC

To dream of whole, perfect ceramics suggests perfecting a craft. If they are damaged or broken, put aside new projects until later.

## CEREBRAL PALSY

To dream of having cerebral palsy indicates good health.

## CEREMONY

In dreams, ceremonies represent a death on the horizon.

## CERTIFICATE

To dream of a certificate indicates the signing of legal documents in the near future.

## CERVIX

To dream of a cervix foretells a pregnancy.

## CESSPOOL

To dream of a cesspool means great money luck, and financial gain in the near future.

## CHABLIS

If this white wine appears in a dream, new friends, new love, and happiness await you.

## CHAFF

Dreaming of chaff suggests an empty and fruitless undertaking and ill health that leads to much anxiety.

## CHAINS

Chains suggest calumny and treacherous designs of the envious. To dream of being bound in chains predicts that unjust burdens are about to be thrown upon your shoulders; if you succeed in breaking them, however, you will free yourself from some unpleasant business or social engagement. Seeing others in chains denotes bad fortunes for them.

## CHAIR

To see a chair in your dreams denotes failure to meet an obligation.

To see a friend sitting on a chair motionlessly signifies news of his or her illness or death.

## CHAIR MAKER

If you dream of seeing a chair maker, worry from apparently pleasant labor will confront you.

## CHAIRMAN

To see a chairman in dreams means you will seek recognition and be recompensed with a position of trust. If you are a chairman, you will be distinguished for your justice and kindness to others.

## CHALET

To dream of this mountain home means you will be advancing to high places at work.

## CHALICE

To dream of a chalice suggests pleasure for you, but sorrow for others. To break one foretells your failure to obtain power over someone.

## CHALK

If you dream of using chalk on a board, you will attain public honor. Handfuls of chalk foretell disappointment.

## CHALLENGES

If you are challenged to fight a duel, you will become involved in a socially difficult situation and will be compelled to apologize or else lose friendships.

To accept a challenge means that you will bear many sorrows as you work to shield others from dishonor.

### CHAMBER

To find yourself in a beautiful and richly furnished chamber implies sudden fortune, either through legacies from unknown relatives or through investment. If the chamber is plainly furnished, you will need to be frugal in the near future.

### CHAMBERMAID

In dreams, a chambermaid represents bad fortune and deleterious changes.

### CHAMELEON

Chameleons signify deceit and self-advancement; your success causes others to suffer.

### CHAMPION

To dream of a champion indicates that you will win the warmest friendship through your dignity and moral conduct.

### CHANCELLOR

To dream of being or dealing with a chancellor suggests that dealings with the law are on the horizon.

### CHANDELIER

To dream of a chandelier portends that unhoped-for success will make it possible for you to enjoy pleasure and luxury easily.

A broken or badly kept chandelier indicates that unfortunate speculation will diminish your seemingly substantial fortune.

To see the light in one go out foretells that sickness and distress will cloud a promising future.

### CHANTING

To hear a chant repeated over and over in your dream means that you must repeat your mistakes before you learn your lesson.

### CHAPEL

To dream of a chapel denotes dissension in social circles and unsettled business. To be in a chapel denotes disappointment and change of business.

### CHAPERONE

To dream of being a chaperone means you have the ability to go it alone and still be successful. To dream of being chaperoned suggests that you need guidance and help.

## CHARCOAL

To dream of unlighted charcoal signifies bleak situations and miserable unhappiness. If the coals are burning and glowing, however, expect great enhancement of fortune and joy.

## CHARIOT

To dream of riding in a chariot foretells that favorable opportunities will present themselves; if you use them well, they can lead to good. To fall from a chariot or see others fall from one denotes displacement from high positions.

## CHARITY*

To dream of giving to charity indicates that you will be harassed with supplications from the poor, and your business will be at a standstill.

If you dream of giving to charitable institutions, your right of possession to property will be disputed. Worries and ill health will threaten you.

If you dream that you are an object of charity, you will succeed in life after hard times.

*See Demands.

## CHASING

To dream of being chased suggests a comfortable life with new friends and family.

## CHASTISEMENT

To dream of being chastised suggests that you have not been prudent.

If you chastise someone else, you have an ill-tempered partner in either business or marriage.

## CHEATING

If you dream of being cheated in business, you will meet designing people who seek to close your avenues to fortune.

## CHECKERS

To dream of playing checkers suggests that you will be involved in serious difficulties. Strange people may come into your life and do you harm.

Dreaming that you win implies success in a doubtful enterprise.

## CHECKPOINT

To dream of being stopped at a checkpoint indicates ease and comfort in your life. Seeing yourself moving freely through your dreams warns you to check the motives behind the things you are doing.

## CHECKS

To dream of writing bad checks indicates that you will resort to subterfuge in order to carry forward your plans.

If you receive checks, you will be able to pay your bills and you will inherit money.

To dream that you are cashing checks denotes depression and loss in business.

## CHEERING

To cheer or hear others cheering in your dream foretells bad news.

## CHEESE

To dream of eating cheese denotes success in love.

## CHEETAH

To dream of this animal, either at rest or running, is a warning to move quickly in your projects and affairs. Do not waste time with indecision!

## CHEMICAL WARFARE

To witness chemical warfare in a dream is a prediction that problems will be solved for you in a very efficient and unconventional way.

## CHEMISE

To dream of a chemise means that you will hear unfavorable gossip about yourself.

## CHEMOTHERAPY

To go through or to witness this cancer treatment in your dreams is a warning to be careful about a health issue.

## CHERRY

To dream of cherries means that you will gain popularity through your amiability and unselfishness. To eat them portends possession of a much-desired object. To see green ones indicates approaching good fortune.

## CHERUB

Dreaming of cherubs is a prediction of upcoming joy that will leave a mark of lasting happiness on your life.

## CHESS

In dreams, playing chess represents stagnation in business, dull companions, and poor health.

If you dream of losing at chess, worries from small-minded sources will ensue; but if you win, expect to triumph over the negative influences.

## CHEST

To dream of someone with a bare chest means you will be free to enjoy the good things in life.

## CHESTNUT

To dream of handling chestnuts foretells losses in business, but may also indicate an agreeable companion in life. Eating them suggests a time of sorrow but ultimate happiness.

## CHEWING

To dream that you are able to chew and swallow is a good sign and means that you will have an easy time in upcoming events and projects. To have trouble chewing something means you may need to seek professional help in some area of your life very soon.

## CHICKEN*

To dream of seeing a brood of chickens suggests many areas of worry, some of which will prove profitable. Young or half-grown chickens signify fortunate enterprises, but to make them so you will have to exert physical strength.

If you see chickens going to roost, enemies are planning evil for you.

Eating chicken reminds you that selfishness will detract from your otherwise good name. Business and love will remain precarious.

*See *Hen, Rooster.*

## CHICKEN POX

Dreaming of this disease warns you to look closely at your friendships.

## CHIEF

To dream of a chief of any kind indicates advancement in your career.

## CHIFFONIER

To see a chiffonier or search through one in your dream suggests that you will have disappointments. To see an organized chiffonier indicates pleasant friends and entertainment.

## CHILBLAIN

To dream of suffering from chilblains indicates that you will be driven into bad dealings through the anxiousness of a friend or partner. This dream also portends your own illness or an accident.

## CHILDBIRTH

To dream of giving birth predicts fortunate circumstances and the safe delivery of a beautiful baby.

For an unmarried woman to dream of being in childbirth denotes unhappy changes from honor to disgrace.

It can also suggest an impending death if the person giving birth is physically too old to do so, or if you are.

## CHILDREN

To dream of seeing many beautiful children suggests great prosperity and blessings.

To see children working or studying denotes peaceful times and general prosperity.

To romp and play with children lets you know that your financial and romantic investments will lead to happiness.

## CHIMES

In dreams, chimes represent fair prospects for business.

## CHIMNEY

To dream of seeing chimneys indicates that a very displeasing incident will occur in your life.

A damaged chimney denotes sorrow and that a death is likely in your family.

One overgrown with ivy or other vines foretells that happiness will result after sorrow or loss of relatives. To see a fire burning in a chimney tells you that much good is approaching you.

## CHINA

To dream of painting or arranging china foretells a pleasant and financially secure home life.

## CHINA SHOP*

To buy china in your dream suggests problems in both business and personal life. But if someone buys it for you, look for prosperity and happiness.

*See Crockery.

## CHINESE

To dream of eating Chinese food means you will soon hear good news.

To see yourself as a Chinese person in a dream means you will change the way you look in the very near future.

To dream of being surrounded by Chinese people—if you are not Chinese—means good fortune and luck with money.

## CHIPMUNK

To dream of this animal indicates that you need to start saving for an upcoming trip or happy occasion that you have not yet planned.

## CHOCOLATE

To dream of chocolate suggests that you will provide abundantly for those who are dependent on you. Seeing chocolate indicates agreeable companions and employment.

If it's bitter, illness or other disappointments will follow.

Drinking chocolate foretells prosperity after a short period of unfavorable reversals.

## CHOIR

If you dream of a choir, expect cheerful surroundings to replace gloom and discontentment.

## CHOLERA

To dream of this dreaded disease portends that virulent sickness will rage, and that many disappointments will follow.

To dream that you are attacked by cholera foreshadows your own sickness.

## CHOWDER

To make or eat chowder in a dream means many new, meaningful friends are coming your way.

## CHRIST

To dream of beholding Christ signifies peaceful days full of wealth and knowledge, abundant with joy and contentment.

## CHRISTMAS TREE

To dream of a Christmas tree denotes joyful occasions and an auspicious fortune. To see one dismantled foretells that a painful incident will follow a festive occasion.

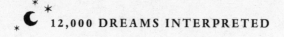 

## CHRYSANTHEMUM

Gathering chrysanthemums signifies loss. To see them in bouquets tells you that love will be offered.

## CHURCH*

To dream of seeing a church or other house of worship denotes disappointment in pleasures long anticipated.

*See *Chapel, Synagogue.*

## CHURCHYARD

To dream of walking in a churchyard means disappointments that you will surely overcome.

## CHURNING

If you dream of churning, you will have difficult tasks ahead of you, but through diligence and industry you will accomplish them and be very prosperous.

## CIA

To dream of this secretive branch of the government means you will be asked to do something illegal or against what you believe is right.

## CIDER

To dream of cider suggests that you may win a fortune, if you don't squander your time on material pleasure. To see people drinking cider suggests that you are under the influence of unfaithful friends.

## CIGAR

To dream of a cigar indicates a celebration in the near future.

## CIRCLE

To dream of a circle tells you that your affairs will deceive you in their potential for gain.

## CIRCUIT BREAKER

To dream of having to reset a tripped circuit breaker means you will have to redo something you thought you had finished.

## CIRCUMCISION

To dream of circumcision means you need to remove from your life people or things that do not matter to you.

## CIRCUS

To dream of a circus suggests that you have created an illusion about yourself that may be exposed in the near future.

## CISTERN

To dream of a cistern indicates that you are in danger of interfering with the pleasures and rights of your friends.

To draw from a cistern implies that you will increase your enjoyment of life in a questionable manner.

An empty cistern foretells change from happiness to sorrow.

## CITY

To dream that you are in a strange city means that an unhappy event may force you to change your abode or mode of living.

## CITY COUNCIL

To dream of a city council cautions that your interests will clash with public institutions, with discouraging results for you.

## CITY HALL

In dreams, city hall symbolizes contention and threats of lawsuits.

## CLAIRVOYANCE

To dream of being clairvoyant and seeing yourself in the future denotes significant changes in your present occupation.

To dream of visiting a clairvoyant suggests that you might seek advice for indecision.

## CLAM

To dream of clams suggests that you will have dealings with an obstinate but honest person. If you eat the clams, you will enjoy another's prosperity.

## CLARET

To dream of drinking claret suggests positive influences on your life.

## CLARINET

To dream of a clarinet hints that underneath your dignified appearance you are indulging in frivolity. If the clarinet is broken, you will incur the displeasure of a close friend.

## CLASSICAL MUSIC

To dream of classical music means happy times ahead.

## CLAY

To dream of clay denotes isolation and probable insolvency.

If you dream of digging in a clay bank, you will submit to extraordinary demands from your enemies.

## CLEANING

If something will not come clean in your dream, you are being lied to.

To dream of cleaning a place spotless says that you are being dealt with honestly.

## CLERGYMAN*

To dream of a clergyman suggests small disappointments that will prove to be blessings.

*See *Minister.*

## CLIMBING*

If you dream of climbing a hill or mountain and reaching the top, you will overcome the most formidable obstacles between yourself and a prosperous future; but if you fail to reach the summit, your dearest plans will be wrecked.

If you climb a ladder to the last rung, you will succeed in business; but if the ladder breaks, you will be plunged into unexpected straits, and accidents may happen to you.

To see yourself climbing the side of a house in some mysterious way in a dream, and to have a window suddenly open to let you in, foretells that you will make or have made extraordinary ventures against the advice of friends, but success will eventually crown your efforts, though there will be times when despair will almost enshroud you.

*See *Ascent, Hill, Mountain.*

## CLITORIS

To dream of this genital feature foretells pregnancy and birth.

## CLOCK

To dream that you see a clock denotes danger from a foe.

If you hear one strike, you will receive unpleasant news. The death of a friend is implied.

## CLOISTER

To dream of a cloister bodes dissatisfaction with present surroundings. You will soon seek a new environment.

## CLONING

To dream of cloning advises that you must see both sides of a problem before you can find a solution.

## CLOSET

To dream of an empty closet means money problems. A full closet indicates business profits.

To dream of being locked in a closet means you will have to reveal something of yourself to those around you soon.

## CLOTHES*

To dream of seeing soiled and torn clothes denotes deceit that will harm you. Beware of friendly dealings with strangers.

Clean, new clothes symbolize prosperity.

To dream that you own an assortment of clothes is a good omen.

*See *Apparel*.

## CLOUDS

To dream of seeing dark, heavy clouds portends misfortune and bad management. If rain is falling, anticipate trouble and sickness.

If you see bright, transparent clouds with the sun shining through them, you will be successful after much struggle.

To see clouds and stars suggests fleeting joys and small advancements.

## CLOVEN FOOT

To dream of a cloven foot portends that some unusual ill luck is threatening you. Avoid the friendship of strangers.

## CLOVER

Walking through fields of fragrant clover is a propitious dream. It brings all objects desired into your reach.

To dream of clover suggests that prosperity will soon enfold you.

## CLUB

To dream of being approached by someone bearing a club suggests that you will be assailed by your adversaries, will overcome them, and will be unusually happy and prosperous. If you club anyone, however, you will undergo a rough and profitless journey.

## COACH

To dream of riding in a coach denotes continued losses in business. Driving one implies business changes.

## COAL

Coals blazing in the fire represent pleasure and many pleasant changes. To dream you handle them speaks of unmitigated joy. To see dead coals implies trouble and disappointment.

## COAL MINE, COLLIERY

To dream of being in a coal mine or colliery and seeing miners reveals that evil will assert its power for your downfall. If you dream of holding shares in a coal mine, however, it denotes your safe investment in some deal.

## COAST

To see the coast or to stand on or near a large body of water in your dream means that good news is coming. You may also be the one giving good news to someone else.

## COAT*

To dream of wearing another's coat signifies that you will ask a friend to give you security. A torn coat represents the loss of a close friend and dreary business. If you lose your coat, you will have to rebuild your fortune lost through overconfidence in speculations.

A new coat portends for you some literary honor.

*See *Apparel, Clothes.*

## COAT OF ARMS

In dreams, a coat of arms symbolizes loyalty among friends and associates.

## COCA-COLA™

To dream of this soft drink means upcoming health issues or relationship problems.

## COCAINE

To dream of being addicted to cocaine or to use it means sorrow is coming your way.

## COCKADE

To dream of this ornament or adornment suggests you beware of seeking titles or special recognition for yourself.

## COCK CROWING

To dream of hearing a cock crowing in the morning is significant of good. If you are single, it denotes an early marriage and a luxurious home.

To hear one at night means despair and cause for tears.

If you dream of seeing cocks fighting, you will leave your family because of quarrels and infidelity. This dream usually announces some unexpected and sorrowful events.

## COCKPIT

To dream of sitting in a cockpit, either flying or stationary, means you will have better control of a problem in the very near future.

## COCKROACH

To dream of this insect is to be warned that your friends are playing you for a fool.

## COCKTAIL

To drink a cocktail while dreaming indicates that you will be deceived by your friends.

## COCOA

To dream of cocoa indicates that you will cultivate distasteful friends for your own advancement and pleasure.

## COCONUT

Coconuts in dreams warn you of sly enemies encroaching on your rights in the guise of ardent friends. Dead coconut palm trees are a sign of loss and sorrow. The death of someone near you may follow.

## C.O.D.

To dream that an item you are receiving needs to be paid for by C.O.D. foretells an unexpected expense.

## COFFEE

To dream of drinking coffee indicates that your friends disapprove of your marriage plans. If you're married, disagreements and frequent quarrels are implied.

To dream of dealing in coffee portends business failure. Selling coffee portends loss. Buying it is less ominous.

Ground coffee foretells successful struggles with adversity.

## COFFEE GRINDER

To see a coffee grinder in your dreams tells you that you are approaching serious danger; you need all your energy and alertness to avert possibly disastrous consequences.

To hear it grinding means it will be hard for you to recognize someone who doesn't have your best interests at heart.

## COFFEEHOUSE

To see or visit a coffeehouse in your dreams foretells that you will unwisely attempt friendly relations with people you know to be your enemies.

## COFFIN

This dream is unlucky. To businesspeople, a coffin represents debts and the inability to avoid accumulating them. To see your own coffin in a dream tells you to expect business failure and domestic sorrow.

To dream of a coffin moving by itself suggests sickness and marriage in close conjunction, sorrow and pleasure intermingled. Death may follow, but there will also be good.

To see your own corpse in a coffin signifies that brave efforts will end in defeat and ignominy. To dream of being in a coffin in a moving hearse denotes desperate, possibly fatal illness of you or someone close to you. Quarrels with the opposite sex are also indicated. You will consider your conduct toward a friend remorsefully.

## COINS

To dream of gold coins denotes great prosperity.

## COLD CUTS

Slicing cold cuts in a dream predicts separation. To dream of eating cold cuts means you will solve a problem in a relationship.

## COLD SORE

To dream of having a cold sore means you may have to reveal something you would rather keep to yourself.

## COLLAR

If you dream of wearing a collar, you will have high honors thrust upon you that you will hardly be worthy of.

## COLLECTOR

To be a collector in your dream warns that you will be spending too much money soon.

## COLLEGE

To dream of a college means that you'll soon advance to a position you've long sought. To dream that you are back in college foretells distinction through well-favored work.

## COLLIE*

To dream of this dog suggests that you will be rescued from a unpleasant situation in the near future.

*See *Dog*.

## COLLISION

If you dream of a collision, you will meet with a serious accident or with disappointment in business.

## COLOGNE

To dream of applying or buying cologne indicates happy times ahead.

## COLONEL

To dream of seeing or being commanded by a colonel suggests that you will fail to reach any prominence in social or business circles. If you are a colonel, it means you will attempt to hold positions above those of friends or acquaintances.

## COLUMN

To dream of any kind of structural columns means you will be recognized by your peers for your work.

## COMA

To see someone else in a coma in a dream predicts that you will soon "awaken" to a new idea that will improve your life.

To see yourself in a coma means that you will experience a setback on your way toward a goal.

## COMBAT

Combat represents the struggle to stay on firm ground.

If you dream of engaging in combat, you seek to ingratiate yourself romantically with someone whom you know to be another person's partner, and you will run great risks of losing your good reputation.

## COMBING HAIR*

To dream of combing hair suggests the illness or death of a friend or relative. Damage to friendship and loss of property are also indicated.

*See *Hair*.

## COMEDY

To dream of seeing a comedy suggests simple pleasures and easy tasks.

## COMET

In dreams, these awe-inspiring objects sailing through the skies speak of good change and happy times.

## COMFORTER

To be wrapped in a comforter for warmth in a dream means that a friendship or love relationship will start to turn cold and confusing.

To wrap another in a comforter means you will be of aid to someone experiencing confusion in a relationship.

## COMIC SONG

To sing or hear comic songs in dreams foretells that you will enjoy much pleasure for a time, but difficulties will overtake you.

## COMMANDER

To dream of being commander of a ship means you will soon travel to places you never thought you would go.

To take orders from a commander suggests unexpected business travel.

## COMMANDING

To dream of being commanded says that you will be humbled in some way by your associates due to scorn you've shown your superiors.

If you dream of giving a command, you will have some honor conferred upon you, but if you give the commands in a tyrannical or boastful way, disappointments will follow.

## COMMANDMENT

To dream of receiving commandments suggests you can be unwisely influenced by those of stronger will than your own.

To read or hear the Ten Commandments read is a sign of blessings.

## COMMERCE

To dream that you are engaged in commerce indicates that you will handle your opportunities wisely and advantageously.

To dream of failure and a gloomy outlook in commercial circles warns of business trouble in waking life.

## COMMERCIAL

To dream of being in a commercial or to see someone you know making or acting in a commercial suggests that you will receive social recognition.

## COMMITTEE

To form a committee in your dreams means you need to follow the advice of others for a while. To be a member of a committee implies that you will be giving advice.

## COMMON COLD

If you dream of suffering from a cold, you are warned to examine the issues in your life that need attention. Enemies are at work to destroy you. Your health is also at risk.

## COMMUNE

To find yourself or a loved one living in a commune in your dreams suggests you need to get back to basics for your health.

## COMPANION

To dream of seeing a wife or husband signifies small anxieties and probable sickness.

To dream of social companions tells you that frivolous pastimes may engage your attention, keeping you from your work.

## COMPANY

A dream of buying or selling a company, or having one go bankrupt, predicts good fortune in business.

## COMPASS

To dream of a compass suggests that you will be forced to struggle within narrow limits, thus making success harder, but more deserving of honor.

To see one pointing in the wrong direction threatens loss.

## COMPLETION

To dream of completing a task implies that you actually will soon be completing something in your waking life sooner than expected, something that will finally give you an opportunity to relax.

If you dream of completing a journey, it means you will soon have the financial means and opportunity to go somewhere you had not thought possible.

## COMPLEXION

To dream that you have a beautiful complexion is lucky. You will have many pleasing experiences in life.

To dream that you have a bad complexion denotes disappointment and sickness.

### COMPUTER*

To dream of working at a computer suggests a time of learning.

If you can't understand what's on the screen, you need to rethink your goals for the future.

*See *Deletions*.

### COMPUTER VIRUS

To dream that your computer is infected with a virus and crashes is a sign that bad times will clear up and you will develop a new outlook on life.

To give a virus to another through a computer program warns that you will be lied to in an important business matter.

### CONCERT

To dream of a successful concert denotes seasons of success and pleasure. If you are an author, the success will be with your literary work. If you are a businessperson, it portends successful trade. To the young it signifies romantic bliss and faithfulness.

Ordinary concerts suggest disagreeable companions and ungrateful friends. Business will show a falling-off.

### CONCUBINE

For a man to dream that he is in the company of a concubine warns that he is in danger of public disgrace, striving to keep the world unaware of his true character and the state of his business.

For a woman to dream that she is a concubine indicates that she will degrade herself by her own impropriety.

### CONDOM

To use or wear a condom in your dreams means you will soon need to pay close attention to business dealings.

To remove a used condom means you are well protected in business.

### CONDOR

To dream of witnessing the flight of this amazing bird means you will be "flying high" in the future with money luck and much love in relationships.

### CONDUCTOR

To dream of seeing yourself as a train conductor means you will enjoy safe travel by land in the near future.

To have your money taken by a train conductor suggests you've found a great travel bargain.

To dream of being a musical conductor predicts money gain in the near future.

## CONFECTION

To dream of confections indicates that someone's words may sound sweet but be untrue.

## CONFESSIONAL

To dream of being in a confessional means you have secrets that will be exposed.

## CONFETTI

To dream of confetti obstructing your view in a crowd of merrymakers indicates that you will lose much by seeking enjoyment before completing your work.

## CONJURER

To dream of a conjurer suggests that unpleasant experiences will beset you in your search for wealth and happiness.

## CONJURING

To dream that you are in a hypnotic state or under the power of others portends disaster, because your enemies will enthrall you; if you hold others under a spell, you will assert your willpower and stand up to them.

To dream of seeing hypnotic and sleight-of-hand performances signifies worries and perplexities in government, business, and at home.

## CONSCIENCE

To dream that your conscience bothers you for deceiving someone implies that you may be tempted to commit wrongdoing. You should be mindful of this tendency.

To dream of having a clear conscience means you stand in high esteem.

## CONSPIRACY

To dream that you are the object of a conspiracy foretells you will make a wrong move in your life choices.

## CONSTELLATION

To look at or be able to pick out a constellation in the night sky portends dreams coming true in the near future.

## CONSTITUTION

To see or read this legal document suggests winning a legal battle in court.

## CONSUMPTION

To dream that you have consumption (tuberculosis) means that you are exposing yourself to danger. Remain with your friends.

## CONTACT LENS

To lose a contact lens in your dream recommends that you open your eyes to deception.

To remove lenses or put them in your eyes means you will see problems at work or in a relationship more clearly.

To help someone else put in contacts predicts that you will be asked to help someone clear out the drama from his or her life.

## CONTEMPT

If you dream of being in contempt of court, you have committed business or social indiscretions.

If you dream that you are held in contempt by others unreasonably, you will succeed in winning their highest regard, and will find yourself prosperous and happy. But if the contempt is merited, your exile from business or social circles is intimated.

## CONTRACT

The signing or writing of contracts in your dream tells you to beware of legal matters ahead.

If you refuse to sign a contract, or someone else refuses, it means a big promotion in business is coming.

## CONVENT

To dream of seeking refuge in a convent indicates that your future will be free from care and enemies—unless on entering the building you encounter a priest. If so, you will seek often and in vain for relief from stress and strife.

## CONVENTION

To dream of a convention suggests unusual activity in business affairs and relationships.

## CONVICT

To dream of seeing convicts suggests disasters and sad news.

To dream that you are a convict indicates that you will worry over something, but will eventually clear up all mistakes.

## COOKIE

A dream of cookies foretells minor arguments.

## COOKING

To dream of cooking a meal tells you that some pleasant duty will fall to you. Many friends will visit you in the near future. If there is discord or a lack of cheerfulness, you may expect harassment and disappointment.

## COOP

To dream of a chicken coop filled with chickens foretells prosperity. To see an empty coop indicates money problems arising from deception.

## COPPER

To dream of copper suggests oppression from your superiors.

## COPPERPLATE

Copperplate seen in a dream warns that discordant views may cause unhappiness among members of a household.

## COPPERSMITH

To dream of a coppersmith suggests small returns for labor, but overall contentment.

## COPYING

To dream of copying denotes an unfavorable outcome to plans that are usually successful.

## CORAL

In dreams, coral symbolizes enduring friendships that will benefit you greatly, especially in times of trouble.

## CORDLESS ITEM

To dream of any item run cordlessly means that your business dealings will seem effortless.

## CORK

To dream of corks signifies that you will soon enter a state of prosperity and will revel in happiness.

## CORKSCREW

To dream of seeing a corkscrew indicates an unsatisfied mind. Heed this as a warning to curb your desires, which may put you on dangerous ground.

To dream of breaking a corkscrew while using it indicates perilous surroundings. To the best of your ability, use your willpower (or the power of intentionality) to steel yourself against your unhealthful inclinations.

## CORN

If you dream of husking ears of corn, you will enjoy success and pleasure.

To see others gathering corn suggests that you will rejoice in the prosperity of friends or relatives.

## CORNER

This is an unfavorable dream if you see yourself as frightened and hidden in a corner for safety.

If your dream involves seeing people talking in a corner, enemies are seeking to destroy you. The chances are that someone whom you consider a friend will prove a traitor.

## CORNET

A cornet seen or heard in a dream suggests kind attention from strangers.

## CORNFIELD

To dream of passing through a green and luxurious cornfield, seeing full ears hanging heavily, speaks of great wealth, happiness, and true friendship. Fine crops, rich harvest, and harmony in the home are yours.

Young corn newly plowed represents favor with the powerful and upcoming success. Ripe corn denotes fame and wealth.

To see it cribbed signifies that your highest desires will be realized.

Shelled corn denotes wealth and unstinting favors.

Eating green corn suggests harmony among friends.

## CORNMEAL

Dreaming of cornmeal foretells the consummation of ardent wishes.

Eating corn bread in your dream implies that you will unwittingly throw obstacles in the way of your own advancement.

## CORNS

To dream that corns hurt your feet says that enemies are undermining you and you will have much distress; but if you succeed in clearing your feet of corns, you will inherit a large estate from an unknown source.

## CORONATION

To dream of a coronation foretells that you will enjoy friendships with prominent people.

## CORPSE

To dream of a corpse means a full and happy life—if the corpse is a stranger. If it is someone you know, that suggests estrangement and unhappiness in love affairs.

To see a battlefield strewn with corpses indicates war and general dissatisfaction within countries and among political factions.

An animal corpse represents an unhealthy situation, whether in business or health.

## CORPULENCE

To dream of being corpulent indicates a bountiful increase of wealth. To see others corpulent denotes unusual activity and prosperous times.

## CORSAGE

To wear a corsage or put one on someone else in a dream is a warning of illness or death.

## CORSET

To dream of a corset indicates that you will be perplexed as to the meaning of the attention you may be receiving.

## CO-SIGNER

To add your name to a document or to be a co-signer on a document in a dream foretells that help will be available when you need it.

## COSMETICS

For a woman to use or buy cosmetics is good luck. For a man to use women's cosmetics warns of bad business dealings.

## COSSACK

To dream of a Cossack denotes personal humiliation brought about by dissipation and extravagance.

## COSTUME

To wear a costume or see others wearing one in a dream foretells an unusual turn of events. Make sure to see things as they really are, not as you want them to be.

## COT

To dream of a cot foretells an affliction, either through sickness or accident. Cots in rows signify that you will not be the only one in trouble; friends will be afflicted also.

## COTTAGE

To dream of a cottage in the woods or a cottage on the shore is a dream of happy family gatherings in the future.

## COTTON

To dream of fields growing young cotton denotes great business and prosperous times. For farmers to see cotton ready for gathering suggests wealth and abundance.

If manufacturers dream of cotton, they benefit. For merchants, it denotes a change for the better in business.

To see cotton in bales is a favorable indication of better times.

## COTTON CAP

To dream of wearing this nightcap is a good dream denoting many sincere friends.

## COTTON CLOTH

To see cotton cloth in a dream suggests easy circumstances. No great changes follow this dream.

## COTTON GIN

To dream of a cotton gin foretells advancement that is very pleasing.

To see a broken or dilapidated gin signifies that misfortune and trouble will overthrow success.

## COUCH

To dream of reclining on a couch implies the entertaining of false hopes. Be alert to every change, for only in this way will your hopes be realized.

## COUGHING

To dream that you are aggravated by a constant cough indicates poor health; but you will recuperate if you take care and exercise good habits.

To dream of hearing others cough indicates unpleasantness from which you will ultimately emerge.

## COUNSELOR

If you dream of a counselor, you are likely to be possessed of some ability yourself, and you will usually prefer your own judgment to that of others. Be careful not to be judgmental.

## COUNTENANCE

If you dream of a beautiful countenance, you may safely look for some pleasure in the near future; but to behold an ugly and scowling visage portends unfavorable transactions.

## COUNTER

To dream of counters foretells that active interest will prevent idleness from infecting your life with unhealthful desires.

To dream of empty and soiled counters suggests unfortunate engagements that bring great uneasiness of mind.

## COUNTERFEIT MONEY

If you dream of counterfeit money, you will have trouble with some unruly and worthless person.

## COUNTERPANE

A counterpane is very good to dream of, if it's clean and white, but if it's soiled you may expect harassing situations. Sickness usually follows this dream.

## COUNTING

To dream of counting money means you will be lucky and always able to pay your debts; but if you're counting out money to another person, you will meet with loss of some kind. Such will be the case, also, in counting other things: If you count for yourself, good; for others, bad luck will attend you.

## COUNTRY

To dream of being in a beautiful and fertile country suggests that good times are at hand. Wealth will pile in on you, and you will be able to reign in any field or endeavor.

If the country is dry and bare, you will see and hear of troublesome times. Famine and sickness will be in the land.

## COURTSHIP

To dream of being courted signifies that disappointments will follow false hopes and fleeting pleasures.

For a man to dream of courting implies that he is not worthy of a companion.

## COUSIN

Dreaming of a cousin denotes disappointments and afflictions. Saddened lives are indicated.

To dream of an affectionate correspondence with your cousin predicts a fatal rupture between families.

## COW*

To dream of seeing cows waiting for the milking hour promises abundant fulfillment of hopes and desires.

*See Cattle.

## COWSLIP

To dream of gathering cowslips portends the unhappy ending of seemingly close and warm friendships; seeing them growing and in full bloom denotes a crisis.

## COXCOMB

To dream of a coxcomb suggests a low state of mind. Work to elevate your mind to nobler thoughts.

## CRAB

To dream of crabs indicates that you will have many complicated affairs and will need to exert sound judgment if you hope to solve them. This dream portends a long and difficult courtship.

## CRADLE

To dream of a cradle with a beautiful infant occupying it portends prosperity.

To rock your own baby in a cradle denotes the serious illness of a family member.

## CRANBERRY

To dream of this fruit means the coming together of family and friends for a celebration.

## CRANE

To dream of seeing a flight of cranes means a joyful meeting with lost friends and faithful close friends. To see cranes fly to the ground means unexpected joy and prosperity.

## CRAWFISH, CRAYFISH

Deceit is sure to assail you in your affairs of the heart after dreaming of this backward-crawling crustacean.

To dream of this bottom-feeding crustacean means you will be on the top of your game in an upcoming project.

## CRAWLING

If you dream that you are crawling on the ground, you may expect humiliating tasks.

Crawling over rough places and stones indicates that you have not taken proper advantage of your opportunities.

To crawl in mire with others suggests depression in business and loss of credit. Your friends will have cause to censure you.

## CREAM

To dream of seeing cream served suggests that you will be associated with wealth, provided you are engaged in a business other than farming.

To drink cream denotes immediate good fortune.

## CREDIT

To dream of asking for credit cautions that you have cause to worry, although you may be inclined sometimes to think things look bright.

To credit another warns you to be careful of your affairs, as you are likely to trust those who will eventually do you harm.

## CREEK

To dream of a creek denotes new experiences and short journeys. If it is overflowing, you will have serious trouble briefly. If the creek is dry, not only will you feel disappointment, but you will see someone else obtain the things you worked hard to achieve.

## CREMATION

To dream of seeing bodies cremated indicates that enemies will reduce your influence in business circles.

If you dream that you are being cremated, it portends failure if you listen to other people's opinions rather than your own.

## CREPE

To dream of seeing crepe hanging from a door indicates that you will hear of the sudden death of a relative or friend.

To see someone dressed in crepe indicates that sorrow, but not death, will come your way. Seeing crepe in a dream is bad for business.

## CREW

To dream of seeing a work crew means a canceled trip.

## CRIB DEATH

This is a dream of an upcoming pregnancy or birth.

## CRICKET

To hear a cricket in your dream indicates melancholy news, perhaps the death of a distant friend.

If you see crickets, expect to struggle with poverty.

## CRIES

If you dream of hearing cries of distress, you will be engulfed by serious trouble, but by being alert you will be able to emerge from these distressing straits eventually and will rise above them successfully.

If the cry is of surprise, you will receive aid from unexpected sources.

Hearing the cries of wild beasts foretells a serious accident.

To hear a cry for help from relatives or friends warns you of their sickness or distress.

## CRIMINAL

To dream of associating with a person who has committed a crime indicates that you will meet unscrupulous people who will try to use your friendship for their own advancement.

## CRIPPLED★

To dream of being handicapped means you will soon find help from an associate or friend. If you dream of others who are maimed and physically challenged, you will soon be called upon to help a friend or colleague.

★See *Lameness, Limping.*

## CROCHETING

To dream of doing crochet foretells entanglement in a basically unimportant incident springing from too much curiosity about other people's affairs.

## CROCKERY

To dream of having nice, clean crockery indicates that you will be a tidy and economical housekeeper.

If you dream of being in a crockery store, mind the details of your business. An untidy store with empty shelves implies loss.

## CROCODILE

If you dream of this creature, you will be deceived by your warmest friends.

## CROISSANT

To dream of this flaky, crusty baked item indicates that carefree, happy times are upon you.

## CROSS

To dream of seeing a cross indicates joy and triumph after a hard struggle.

## CROSSBONES

To dream of crossbones is not a good omen. It foretells financial loss and trouble with relationships.

## CROSSBOW

To dream of firing this weapon means that you will soon be on your mark regarding your goals.

To dream of having one fired at you warns you of so-called friends.

## CROSSROADS

To dream of a crossroads suggests that you will be unable to complete a previously favorable opportunity to reach your goals. If you are undecided which road to take, you are likely to let unimportant matters irritate you. You will be better favored by fortune if you decide on your route and plan in advance. After this dream you may have an important matter to decide about in business or love.

## CROUP

To dream that your child has the croup denotes slight illness, but it is no reason to fear. This is generally a good omen of health and domestic harmony.

## CROW*

To dream of seeing a crow betokens misfortune and grief.

If you hear crows cawing, you will be influenced by others to make a bad deal disposing of property.

*See Raven.

## CROWD

To dream of a large crowd of well-dressed people at an event suggests pleasant involvement with friends; but anything occurring in the dream that mars the pleasure of the guests in the crowd denotes distress and loss of friendship; unhappiness will be found where you expected profit and congenial interactions. This can also denote dissatisfaction in government and dissension within the family.

To see a crowd in a church indicates that a death may affect you, or some slight unpleasantness may develop.

To see a crowd in the street indicates unusually brisk trade and a general air of prosperity.

If you dream of trying to be heard in a crowd, you will push your own interests ahead of everyone else's.

### CROWN

To dream of a crown prognosticates change in your life habits. You will travel a long distance from home and form new relationships. Fatal illness may also be the sad subject of this dream.

To dream that you wear a crown signifies loss of personal property.

To dream of crowning a person denotes your own worthiness.

### CRUCIFIX

To see a crucifix in a dream is a good omen and a blessing.

### CRUCIFIXION

If you chance to dream of the Crucifixion, you will see your opportunities slip away, tearing your hopes from your grasp and leaving you wailing over the frustration of desire.

### CRUELTY

To dream of cruelty being shown to you foretells trouble and disappointment. If it is shown to others, you will set a disagreeable task for others, which will contribute to your own loss.

### CRUST*

To dream of a crust of bread indicates that the incompetence of elected officials threatens to bring misery.

*See *Bread, Baking.*

### CRUTCHES

To dream that you are on crutches implies that you depend largely on others for support and advancement.

To see others on crutches suggests unsatisfactory results from labors.

### CRYING

To dream of crying means happy times ahead.

To hear and see others crying warns that they may unexpectedly call on you for aid.

To see or hear babies crying predicts good news.

## CRYOGENICS

To dream of a body being preserved cryogenically—including your own—means you will be freed of financial burden.

## CRYSTAL

To dream of crystal in any form is a sign of coming depression, either social or financial.

## CUB

To dream of a baby animal with its parent hints at expansion in your family.

To dream of a baby animal alone predicts problems with your children and their ability to learn.

## CUBICLE

To dream of a cubicle means your ideas need to be expanded.

## CUCKOO

To dream of a cuckoo prognosticates a painful illness, the death of a loved one, or an accident to someone in your family.

## CUCUMBER

This is a dream of plenty, denoting health and prosperity.

## CULT

To find yourself in a cult or trying to escape from one warns that you need to examine your spiritual awareness.

## CUNNING

To dream of being cunning warns that you are being dishonest in the way you present yourself to your friends and those around you. If you are associating with cunning people, you are being deceived for other people's advancement.

## CUP

In dreams, an empty cup symbolizes financial gain; a full cup, financial loss. To drink from a cup suggests sorrow.

## CUPBOARD*

To see a cupboard in your dream signifies pleasure and comfort, or penury and distress, depending on whether the cupboard is clean and full, or empty and dirty.

*See *Safe*.

129

## CURBSTONE

To dream of stepping on a curbstone suggests your rapid rise in business circles. You are held in high esteem by your friends and the public.

## CURRYCOMB

To dream of a currycomb foretells that you must endure much hard work to obtain wealth and comfort.

## CURRYING A HORSE

To dream of currying a horse suggests that you will have a hard time in doing so, but you will indeed reach the height of your ambition.

## CURTAIN

To dream of curtains foretells unwelcome visitors who cause you worry and unhappiness. Soiled or torn curtains mean disgraceful quarrels and reproaches.

## CUSHION

To dream of reclining on silk cushions suggests that your ease will be at the expense of others; but if you dream of seeing the cushions, you will prosper in business and love.

## CUSTARD*

To dream of making or eating custard indicates that you will be called upon to entertain an unexpected guest.

*See *Baking*.

## CUSTOMER

To wait on customers means you will get an unexpected gift. To dream of being a customer means you will give a gift to someone in the future.

## CUSTOMS

To dream of practicing a custom warns against closed-mindedness.

To dream of going through customs implies that you will have rivalries and competition at work. If you can't get through customs in a dream, you are not being honest with yourself or others.

## CUT

To dream of a cut means that sickness or the treachery of a friend may cause you great unhappiness.

## CUTICLE

To dream of having your cuticles worked on—or needing to be worked on—means you will be very creative in the future.

## CYANIDE*

To dream of this poison is a sign of good health.

*See *Poison*.

## CYCLONE

To dream of a cyclone foretells big changes at home.

## CYCLOPS

To see one-eyed creatures in your dreams portends an overwhelming intimation of secret intrigue against your fortune and happiness.

## CYMBAL

Hearing a cymbal in your dreams predicts the death of a very aged person of your acquaintance.

## CYST

To dream of having this growth is a warning about hidden meanings in people's words.

## DAGGER

Seeing a dagger in a dream suggests threatening enemies. If you remove the dagger from the hand of another, you will be able to counteract the influence of your enemies and overcome misfortune.

## DAHLIA

To see fresh and bright dahlias in a dream signifies good fortune for the dreamer.

## DAIRY*

To dream of dairy products means you will be nurturing a hobby or outside activity that brings you much pleasure.

To dream of a dairy means that there is money and/or prosperity coming your way.

*See *Churning, Butter.*

## DAISY

To dream of a bunch of daisies implies sadness, but if you dream of being in a field where these lovely flowers are in bloom, with the sun shining and birds singing, happiness, health, and prosperity will lead you through the pleasantest avenues of life.

## DAMASK ROSE

To dream of seeing a damask rosebush in full bloom foretells that a wedding will soon take place in your family, and great hopes will be fulfilled.

## DAMSON PLUMS

It's a particularly good dream if you are so fortunate as to see damson plum tree branches laden with rich purple fruit and dainty foliage; expect riches.

To dream of eating damsons forebodes grief.

## DANCING*

To the married, to dream of seeing a crowd of merry children dancing signifies loving, obedient, and intelligent children and a cheerful and comfortable home. To young people, it denotes easy tasks and many pleasures.

To see older people dancing suggests a brighter outlook for business.

If you dream of dancing by yourself, unexpected good fortune will come to you.

*See Ball, Quadrille.

## DANCING MASTER

To dream of a dancing master warns that you are neglecting important affairs to pursue frivolities.

## DANDELION

To see dandelions blossoming and green foliage foretells happy unions and prosperity.

## DANGER

To dream of being in a perilous situation where death seems imminent indicates that you will emerge from obscurity into distinction and honor; but if you should not escape the impending danger, and if you die or are wounded, you will suffer in business and be troubled at home and by others. If you are in love, or if you seek love, your prospects will grow dim.

## DARKNESS

To dream of darkness overtaking you on a journey augurs ill for any work you may attempt, unless the sun breaks through before the journey ends, in which case, difficulties will be overcome.

## DATE*

To dream of seeing dates on trees signifies prosperity and happy relationships; but if you eat the dates, it augurs want and distress.

*See Fruit.

## DAUGHTER

To dream of your daughter suggests that displeasing incidents will give way to pleasure and harmony. If in the dream she disappoints you for any reason, you will suffer vexation and discontent.

## DAUGHTER-IN-LAW

To dream of your daughter-in-law indicates that an unusual event will add to your happiness or discontent. The difference depends on whether she is pleasant or unreasonable in the dream.

## DAVID

To dream of the biblical David means the coming of blessings.

## DAY

To dream of the day portends improvement and pleasant associations. A gloomy or cloudy day foretells loss and disappointment in new enterprises.

## DAYBREAK

To watch the daybreak in a dream augurs success, unless the scene is indistinct and unusual; then it may imply disappointment when success in business or love seems assured.

## DEAD

To dream of the dead means rebirth and new beginnings.

## DEATH*

To dream of your own death means the release of worries. To dream of someone else's death often foretells news of a birth.

*See Corpse, Dead, Ghost, Phantom.

## DEBT

Debt in a dream is rather challenging and foretells worries in business and love, as well as feelings of incompetency; but if you have enough funds to meet all your obligations, things will improve.

## DECEMBER

To dream of December foretells the accumulation of wealth, but the loss of friendship. A stranger will capture the heart of someone who loved you.

## DECK*

If you dream of being on a ship while a storm is raging, disasters and unfortunate alliances will plague you; but if the sea is calm and the light distinct, your way to success is clear. For lovers, this dream augurs happiness.

*See Boat, Ship.

## DECORATING

To dream of decorating signifies a favorable outlook in business and continued success socially and educationally.

## DEED*

To dream of seeing or signing deeds foreshadows a lawsuit. Be careful in selecting counsel, to avoid being the loser.

*See Mortgage.

## DEER

This is a favorable dream, denoting pure, deep friendships and a quiet and uneventful life. To dream of hunting deer denotes failure in your pursuits.

## DEFROSTING

To dream of defrosting something or needing to defrost something counsels you to be patient with an upcoming project that will take more time than you anticipated.

## DÉJÀ VU

To dream of having the same thing happen to you over and over, or of seeing the same person again and again, suggests that you will need to deal with a problem several times before it is solved.

## DELAY

To be delayed in a dream warns you of enemies scheming to prevent your progress.

## DELEGATING

To delegate power to another or to have someone else take over your job means you will soon be rewarded for a job well done.

## DELETIONS*

To dream of deleting words (or files from your computer) warns you to be careful of deception and dishonesty around you.

*See *Computer*.

## DELICATESSEN

To dream that you work in a deli means you will have a pleasant time on vacation. To dream that you shop at a deli tells you that dreams are starting to come true.

## DELIGHT

To dream of experiencing delight over something signifies a favorable turn of events. For lovers to be delighted with the conduct of their sweethearts suggests pleasant greetings.

To feel delight when looking at beautiful landscapes speaks of great success and warm relationships.

## DELIVERY

To deliver anything or have it delivered to you means good fortune is coming your way.

## DELUGE

To dream of much water at one time means that good fortune and prosperity await you—if the water is clear. If the water is muddy, money troubles lie ahead.

## DEMANDS★

To dream that you are hit with a demand for charity suggests being placed in embarrassing situations, but fully restoring your good name by sheer persistence. If the demand is unjust, you will become a leader in your profession.

★See *Charity*.

## DEMENTIA

To find yourself suffering from this disease means you will be very sharp in future business dealings. To find someone else suffering from this in a dream warns you to read the fine print on contracts.

## DEMOCRAT

To dream of being a Democrat when you are not means you will be seeking advice from someone you never thought you would look to for help.

## DEMOLITION

To watch something being demolished in a dream indicates that you will be moving. If you are unhappy as you watch, the unexpected move is unwelcome.

## DEMON

To be in the presence of a demon in your dream warns you of evil doings around you. To fight and defeat a demon suggests that you will have many blessings in family, home, and work.

## DENIAL

To find yourself in a state of denial in a dream means you are taking your responsibilities too seriously and need to lighten up.

## DENIM

To dream of this material means you have a few tough times ahead. To see and feel the denim softened implies the tough times are over.

To wear or make clothing from denim in a dream indicates security in your life.

## DENT

To put a dent in a vehicle in your dream means you may be the target of theft if you are not careful. To fix a dent means a problem that seemed very large will turn out to be an easy fix.

## DENTIST

To dream of a dentist working on your teeth suggests that you will doubt the sincerity and honor of someone you have dealings with.

## DENTURES

To wear dentures in a dream, or prepare to, means you may find yourself lying to escape a problem. To find or lose someone else's dentures warns that you will be lied to about an important matter in the near future.

## DEODORANT

To dream that you need to put this on means good health. To refuse to wear it in your dream means you will soon have a health problem that needs immediate attention.

## DEPARTURE

To dream of waiting for your means of transportation to depart means that your time will be wasted on trivial matters. To watch a departure suggests that you will finish a project with time to spare.

## DEPORTATION

To find yourself being deported from your country in a dream means you will soon be traveling for business.

## DEPOSIT

Depositing money in a bank in a dream warns you to watch your spending. To dream that someone else is depositing money into your account is a sign of good fortune.

## DERAILMENT

To dream that you see, or are in, a train derailment that does not lead to any injuries means your current health issues will get better quickly. To have or see injuries in your dream means that an unexpected health issue will soon emerge.

## DERELICT

To deal with one or more derelicts in your dream means that you and several colleagues will soon brainstorm for ideas. If you are a derelict, the dream is a warning that you are being too lazy at work and need to take more responsibility.

### DERMATOLOGIST

To dream that you are a dermatologist means someone will be getting under your skin and giving you trouble soon. To dream that you go to one to clear up skin problems suggests that your friends are loyal and true.

### DERRICKS

In dreams, derricks symbolize strife and obstruction on your way to success.

### DESECRATION

To dream that you see something desecrated means your priorities are not what they should be. To dream that you are responsible for the desecration means you will honor someone for a good deed.

### DESERT

To dream of wandering through a gloomy and barren desert predicts famine, racial strife, and great loss of life and property.

### DESIRE

To find yourself desiring something in a dream that's never interested you before predicts an upcoming adventure to an unexpected place. To have no desire for the things you love means you are in need of a change in your work, home, family, or friendships.

### DESK

To be using a desk in a dream implies unforeseen ill luck. To see money on your desk implies unexpected extrication from private difficulties.

### DESPAIR

To be in despair indicates that you will have many cruel vexations in the working world. To see others in despair foretells the distress and unhappy situation of some relative or friend.

### DESPERATION

To find yourself desperate to solve a problem or get rid of something in your dream means you will have the means to take a pleasant vacation or purchase an item you've been longing for.

## DESPONDENCY

To dream that everyone around you is despondent means fun and happy times are coming. If you are the despondent one, expect a vacation or a good time in the near future.

## DESSERT

To dream that you are eating dessert is a good omen, unless you're eating it alone; then it warns of the ending of a friendship. To make or bake a dessert means good luck.

## DESTITUTION

To find yourself destitute is a dream of money luck coming in the near future.

## DESTROYING

To see something destroyed in your dream means you will soon rebuild your life for the better. To destroy things in a dream warns you to examine your life and make sure you are really making the right decisions for the change you want.

## DETAINING

To be detained in a dream suggests that you will have the freedom to do what you want in an upcoming project. To detain another means that you will have to stick to the rules in this project.

## DETECTIVE

To dream of being followed by a detective when you are innocent indicates that fortune and honor are drawing nearer to you each day; if you feel yourself guilty, however, you are likely to find your reputation at stake, and friends will turn from you.

To hire a detective is a warning of dishonesty among your friends.

To be a detective means you will soon discover a hidden secret that will bring you good fortune.

## DETERGENT

To buy or use detergent in a dream means you will come clean about something you have been keeping secret. You will feel refreshed and renewed afterward.

## DEVICE

To dream of a device being in working order means you will soon be purchasing something that will give you pleasure. To dream of a device in need of repairs counsels that something mechanical will soon break down.

## DEVIL*

If the dream involves fighting the devil, you will outwit those who want to harm you. If you speak to him, you will find temptations hard to resist. This dream can also portend ill health and mental stress.

*See *Dragon, Satan*.

## DEVOTION

To dream of devotion implies prosperity, peace, and adoration from your associates.

## DEW

To feel the dew falling on you in your dreams portends that you will be attacked by fever or some malignant disease; but if you see dew sparkling through the grass in the sunlight, great honors and wealth are about to be heaped upon you. If you are single, a wealthy marriage will soon be your portion.

## DIABETES

To dream that you have diabetes means good health.

## DIADEM

To dream of a diadem implies that some honor will be tendered you for acceptance.

## DIAGNOSIS

To dream you are getting a good diagnosis for an ailment you are having in your dream warns you to be wary of health issues. If it is a bad diagnosis, your health is good.

## DIAGRAM

To draw or see a diagram in your dream suggests that you should pay close attention to upcoming legal matters in your life.

## DIAL

If you dream of a dial on the clock and you can't read it, you are wasting time. If you can read it, you have more control in your life than you thought. Dialing a telephone in a dream portends good fortune, especially if you can remember the numbers you dialed.

## DIALYSIS

To dream of being on kidney dialysis foretells that you will soon be clearing out toxic relationships in your life.

## DIAMOND

To dream of owning diamonds is a very propitious dream, signifying great honor and recognition from high places.

For a speculator, it denotes prosperous transactions. Diamonds are omens of good luck, unless they are stolen from the bodies of the dead, in which case they suggest that your own unfaithfulness will be discovered by your friends.

## DIAPER

To dream of wearing a diaper implies that you are ashamed of something you have done or will be shamed publicly for it.

To dream of putting a diaper on someone means you will find yourself protecting another person's integrity.

## DIARRHEA

Dreams of having or seeing diarrhea foretell excellent fortune and good luck.

## DIARY

To dream of writing in a diary means you need to be careful in what you are thinking, because it may become reality.

To dream that you are reading someone else's diary suggests renewed or new friendships.

## DICE

To dream of dice indicates unfortunate speculations and consequent misery. It can also foretell contagious sickness.

## DICTIONARY

To dream that you are referring to a dictionary signifies that you depend too much on the opinions and suggestions of others for the clear management of your own affairs; you could do this yourself by giving your will free rein.

## DIESEL FUEL

To dream of this petroleum product is a warning not to feed or pass on a vicious rumor.

## DIET

To dream that you are on a diet and can't lose weight foretells a health problem. To dream that you are on a diet and *are* losing weight means good health is on the horizon.

## DIETITIAN

To dream of being a dietitian suggests that you need to eat more healthily.

## DIFFERENCES

To dream that you differ with someone means that in your waking life you will actually be "on the same page" with someone else.

## DIFFICULTY

This dream signifies temporary embarrassment for businesspeople of all classes, including soldiers and writers. But if you extricate yourself from difficulties, expect prosperity.

## DIGESTION

To have problems digesting food in your dream means that you will find an upcoming situation very hard to stomach.

## DIGGING

To dream of digging indicates that although you will never be in want, life will be an uphill affair.

If you dig a hole and find any glittering substance, expect a favorable turn in fortune; but if you open up a vast area of hollow mist, you will be harassed with real misfortunes and filled with gloomy forebodings.

If water fills the hole you dig, events will not bend to your will, despite your most strenuous efforts.

## DIGIT

To dream you are writing digits means you will have good luck.

To dream you are missing a digit on a hand or foot means that a project you are currently working on needs help so you can complete it.

## DIGITAL CLOCK

Looking at a digital clock in a dream predicts good fortune, especially if you can remember the numbers.

## DIKE, DAM

To dream of a dam that is breaking or leaking—whether the water is clear or muddy—suggests dishonesty coming into your life.

To dream of being able to fix a dike that is broken indicates good fortune if the water is clear. Muddy water betokens hard times ahead, but all will turn out fine.

## DILAPIDATION

To dream of seeing a building that is dilapidated means you will be moving to a home whose worth is beyond your wildest imagination.

## DIMES*

To dream of seeing or collecting dimes means good fortune. To dream of losing them warns you to watch your money in an upcoming business deal.
*See *Cash, Money.*

## DIMPLE

To dream of a dimple foretells pleasant surprises coming into your life.

## DINER

To dream of eating in a diner suggests that you need to watch your food intake and the way you are eating.

## DINNER

To dream of eating dinner alone indicates that you will often have cause to think seriously of the necessities of life.

If you are one of many invited guests at a dinner, you will enjoy the hospitality of those who are able to extend many pleasant courtesies to you.

## DINOSAUR

To dream of these ancient animals recommends that you rethink an idea that may be outdated.

## DIPLOMA

To dream you are receiving or giving a diploma means you will be learning a new skill in the near future.

## DIPLOMAT

To dream of a diplomat (yourself or someone else) suggests that you be very careful in what you say to people and how you say it.

## DIRECTIONS

To dream that you are asking for directions reminds you to be careful with your driving skills. If you dream that you are giving directions, you will be able to find an easy solution to an upcoming problem.

## DIRECTOR

To be a director in your dream means it's time to lead rather than follow.

## DIRECTORY ASSISTANCE

To ask for a phone number through directory assistance in a dream foretells an unexpected phone call coming your way.

## DIRT

To dream of seeing freshly stirred dirt around flowers or trees means that thrift and healthful conditions abound.

Dreaming that someone throws dirt on you warns of enemies trying to injure your character.

## DISABILITY

To dream that you are disabling something means you will receive a pleasant surprise in the mail.

To dream you are disabled assures you that you have the ability to stand on your own two feet in an upcoming problem, even though you may not believe it.

## DISAGREEMENT

To dream that you are having a disagreement means that your friends are extremely loyal to you as you work through a problem.

## DISAPPEARING

To dream of something, someone, or yourself disappearing suggests that you will have clarity with an upcoming problem, making it very easy for you to solve.

## DISAPPOINTMENT

To find that you are disappointed in a dream predicts a coming gift.

## DISARRAY

To find your life or environment in disarray means your life is actually very settled and balanced.

## DISASTER

To dream of being in any disaster involving public transportation warns that you are in danger of losing property or of being harmed by a disease.

Other disasters may signify loss by death; but if you dream that you are rescued, you will be placed in trying situations and come out unscathed.

If you dream of a train wreck in which you are not a participant, you will eventually be interested in some accident when a relative or friend is hurt, or you will have trouble of a business nature.

### DISBARMENT

To be a lawyer and dream you are being disbarred means you will gain recognition with your peers. To dream of knowing a lawyer who is disbarred warns of legal problems.

### DISBURSEMENT

To dream that you have money disbursed to you cautions you to be careful of theft. To disburse money in your dream means you will soon see monetary gain.

### DISCARDING

To discard anything is a dream of gain.

### DISCHARGE

To be discharged from military service, a military hospital, or a military job in a dream implies good change coming to your life.

### DISCIPLE

To dream of one of Jesus's disciples, or that you are one, is a dream of many blessings.

### DISCO

If you dream of dancing in a disco, look for good times ahead. To watch others dancing suggests that you will be overlooked at a special event or party.

### DISCOMFORT

To feel discomfort in a dream foretells good health. To cause discomfort to others is a warning of an upcoming health problem.

### DISCONNECTION

To dream of having your phone disconnected means you will be making a new friend soon. To disconnect someone's phone in a dream indicates that you will be dealing with a lie or rumor about yourself.

### DISCONTINUING

To have a favorite thing discontinued in a dream means a big surprise is coming.

## DISCOUNT

To ask for a discount means you should watch how you are spending your money.

## DISCOURAGEMENT

To feel discouraged over anything in a dream indicates that your wishes are coming true.

## DISCOVERY

To dream you make a discovery of any kind means you will soon lose a treasured item. This warning dream reminds you to be careful of your things.

## DISCREDITING

To dream that you have discredited another person means you will soon be called upon to help prove someone's honesty. To be discredited in a dream suggests that your friends will prove to be loyal and true when faced with a rumor about you.

## DISCRIMINATION

To dream that you are being discriminated against means that you will gain the respect of your peers. To dream that you are discriminating against someone suggests that you will have an opportunity to help a fellow worker.

## DISCUSSION

To find yourself dreaming that you are in a long discussion, heated or otherwise, means that you will soon have to prove yourself at work.

## DISEASE

To dream that you are diseased denotes a slight attack of illness, or it could denote unpleasant dealings with a relative.

## DISEMBARKATION

To dream of disembarking from any mode of transportation—ship, plane, car—indicates that you will soon be traveling.

## DISEMBODIMENT

To feel or see yourself disembodied in a dream asks you to examine your spiritual self.

## DISEMBOWELMENT

To perform an act of disembowelment in a dream is a sign of health issues on the horizon. To watch it suggests a good report about a current health concern.

## DISFIGUREMENT

To be disfigured means you will be complimented on your beauty from an unlikely source. If you dream you are going to disfigure someone else, you will be surprised by someone's integrity.

## DISGRACE

To fret in a dream over disgraceful conduct will bring you unsatisfied hopes, and worries will harass you.

To be in disgrace yourself indicates that you hold morality in low esteem; you are in danger of harming your reputation.

## DISGUISE

To dream that you are in disguise warns you not to lie in your relationships. To see another in disguise suggests that you are being lied to.

## DISH*

To dream of handling dishes denotes good fortune; but if they should be broken, fortune will be short-lived for you.

To see shelves of polished dishes implies success in marriage.

Dreaming of dishes portends success, and you will be able to fully appreciate your good luck. Soiled dishes represent dissatisfaction and an unpromising future.

*See Crockery.

## DISHONESTY

To uncover dishonesty in a dream means that the truth will be revealed about a friend, surprising you. If you yourself are dishonest in a dream, you will be truthful in your waking life: you need to watch your words, for they may hurt someone else.

## DISHWASHER

To dream of buying, selling, loading, or unloading a dishwasher foretells happy times ahead.

## DISINFECTING

To disinfect anything in your dream cautions you to look closely at a contract before signing it.

### DISINHERITED

To dream that you are disinherited warns you to look well at your business and social standing.

### DISK

To see a disk in your dream suggests that you will be making fond memories in a new relationship.

### DISLOCATION

To dislocate a bone in your dreams is a warning that a broken friendship is coming.

### DISLODGEMENT

To dislodge something from your throat in a dream lets you know that you will indeed be heard when you speak the truth about someone or something.

If you're unable to dislodge it, the dream is warning you to watch your words, for they might be misrepresented or misunderstood.

### DISMANTLING

To dismantle anything in a dream indicates a project being finished ahead of time.

### DISMEMBERING

To find yourself dismembering another in a dream predicts a broken engagement or love relationship. To have one of your own body parts removed warns of upcoming health issues.

### DISMISSAL, TERMINATION

To dream of being dismissed from a job portends upcoming fame.

### DISMOUNTING

To see yourself in a dream dismounting from an animal means you will soon travel. If you help another dismount, you will soon have to travel unexpectedly.

### DISOBEDIENCE

To have your commands disobeyed in your dream advises you to be clear on what you ask for in the future. To disobey someone else suggests that you will have a clear mind during an upcoming trouble or issue.

## DISORGANIZATION

To find yourself very disorganized in a dream, you must find a way to change a current relationship or it will fail.

## DISOWNING

To disown someone in a dream means that a lasting friendship is currently in your life. To be disowned means you will soon start a new friendship that will last a lifetime.

## DISPLAY

To dream that you put something or someone on display suggests that you will soon face shame for an act of yours. To be on display means you will have to explain your actions.

## DISPUTE

To dream of disputes over trifles indicates bad health and unfairness in judging others.

To dream of disputing with learned people shows that you have some latent ability but are a little sluggish in developing it.

## DISQUALIFICATION

To dream that you are disqualified from a sporting event or contest means you will win in a similar endeavor in your waking life. To disqualify someone else warns that you may not be able to finish an upcoming sporting event, competition, or contest.

## DISSECTING

If you dissect anything in a dream, you will soon have to face a problem that you have been trying to hide from.

## DISSOLVING

To dream of something dissolving in a liquid means your troubles will soon end.

## DISTAFF

To dream of a distaff denotes frugality, with pleasant surroundings. It also signifies that you are cultivating a devotional spirit.

## DISTANCE

To dream of being a long way from home implies that you will make a journey soon in which you may meet many strangers who will be instrumental in changing your life from good to bad.

To dream of friends at a distance suggests slight disappointments. To dream of distance itself signifies travel and a long journey.

### DISTILLING

To distill alcohol in a dream foretells problems with your love life. To drink anything that has been distilled means that new love is on the horizon.

### DISTORTIONS

To dream of something in a distorted way means you will have to take a closer look at the things you plan to buy.

### DISTURBANCES

To disturb someone in your dream tells you that people are talking behind your back. To be disturbed in a dream is a sign of good friendships.

### DITCH*

To dream of falling in a ditch denotes degradation and personal loss; but if you jump over a ditch, you will live down any suspicion of wrongdoing.
*See *Trench*.

### DIVA

To see yourself as a diva in your dreams means you will be humiliated in front of your peers. To notice another acting as a diva suggests that you will soon humiliate someone.

### DIVISION

To do this type of math or to physically divide something yourself in your dreams means you will soon have time for more pleasure in your life. If you see someone else doing this, you will have more than enough to share with others.

### DIVIDEND

In dreams, dividends symbolize successful speculations or prosperous harvests. Failure in securing hoped-for dividends proclaims failure in management or love affairs.

### DIVING

To dream of diving into clear water signifies a favorable end to some embarrassment. If the water is muddy, you will suffer anxiety at the turn your affairs seem to be taking.

Watching others diving indicates pleasant companions. For lovers to dream of diving marks the consummation of happy dreams and passionate love.

## DIVINING ROD

To see a divining rod in your dream foretells ill luck and dissatisfaction with present surroundings.

## DIVORCE

To dream of being divorced indicates that you are not satisfied with your companion and should cultivate a more congenial atmosphere at home. It is a dream of warning.

## DIXIELAND

To dream that you are hearing this jazz music foretells happy times ahead.

## DIZZINESS

This dream indicates possible blood-pressure problems. It also can predict an upset from a new love interest.

## DJ

To be a DJ spinning records in your dreams means you will soon be entertaining unexpectedly. To watch a DJ in your dream portends an upcoming invitation from a surprising person.

## DNA

If you hear the term *DNA* in your dream or are looking at a model of DNA, this is a dream of pregnancy and birth.

## DOA (DEAD ON ARRIVAL)

To dream of hearing someone being pronounced dead on arrival—or hearing it said of yourself—means you will be receiving good news about a health issue, either yours or that of someone you love.

## DOCK

To dream of being on a dock indicates that you are about to make an unpropitious journey. Accidents will threaten you. If you are wandering alone on a dock and darkness overtakes you, you will meet with deadly enemies; but if the sun is shining, you will escape the dangers.

## DOCTOR

It is a most auspicious dream, denoting good health and general prosperity, if you meet a doctor socially, for you will not then spend your money on his or her services.

To dream of a doctor professionally signifies discouraging illness and disagreeable differences between members of a family.

To dream that a doctor makes an incision in your flesh without there being any blood indicates that you will be tormented and injured by some evil person, who may try to make you pay out money for his or her debts. If the doctor cuts you and there is blood, you will be the loser in some transaction.

## DOCUMENT

To read, sign, or get signed documents of any kind in a dream warns of legal problems or poor money speculations.

## DOG*

To dream of a vicious dog suggests enemies and unalterable misfortune. To dream that a dog nuzzles you indicates great gain and constant friends. A dog with fine qualities lets you know that you will be possessed of solid wealth.

If you dream that a bloodhound is tracking you, you are likely to fall into some temptation that threatens your downfall.

To dream of small dogs indicates that your thoughts and chief pleasures are of a frivolous order.

If you dream of dogs biting you, expect a quarrelsome companion either in marriage or business. Lean, filthy dogs indicate failure in business, as well as sickness among children.

A dog show symbolizes many and varied favors from fortune.

To hear the barking of dogs foretells news of a depressing nature. Difficulties are more than likely to follow. To see dogs chasing foxes or other large game suggests an unusual briskness in all affairs.

To see fancy pet dogs reveals a love of show—and an owner who is selfish and narrow. For a young woman, this dream foretells a fop for a sweetheart.

To feel much fright upon seeing a large mastiff implies that you will experience inconvenience because of efforts to rise above mediocrity.

To hear the growling and snarling of dogs indicates that you are at the mercy of designing people and you will be afflicted with unpleasant home surroundings.

To hear the lonely baying of a dog foretells a death or a long separation from friends.

To hear dogs growling and fighting portends that you will be overcome by your enemies and that your life will be filled with depression.

If you dream of dogs and cats seemingly on friendly terms suddenly turning on each other, showing their teeth, and a general fight ensuing, you will meet with disaster in love and worldly pursuits unless you succeed in quelling the row.

If you dream of a friendly white dog approaching you, it portends for you a victorious engagement, whether in business or love. For a woman, this is an omen of an early marriage.

To dream of a many-headed dog warns that you are trying to maintain too many branches of business at one time. Success always comes with concentration of energies. A man who wishes to succeed in anything should take heed of this dream.

If you dream of a mad dog, your most strenuous efforts will not bring desired results, and a fatal disease may even be clutching at your vitals. If a mad dog succeeds in biting you, it is a sign that you or some loved one is on the verge of insanity, and a tragedy may occur.

To dream of traveling alone with a dog following you foretells staunch friends and successful undertakings.

Swimming dogs represent an easy stretch to happiness and fortune.

To dream that a dog kills a cat in your presence is significant of profitable dealings and some unexpected pleasure.

For a dog to kill a snake in your presence is an omen of good luck.

*See Bulldog, Collie, Mad dog, Puppy.

## DOGWOOD

To dream of this tree is a dream of blessing coming in your life, especially if it is in bloom out of season.

## DOLL

To dream of a doll suggests social and familial happiness.

## DOLLAR

To dream of a silver dollar or dollars means good luck.

## DOLPHIN

If you dream of a dolphin, you're liable to come under a new government. It is not a very good dream.

## DOME

To dream that you are in the dome of a building, viewing a strange land-scape, signifies a favorable change in your life. You will occupy honorable places among strangers.

To behold a dome from a distance portends that you will never reach the height of your ambition; if you are in love, the object of your desires will scorn your attention.

## DOMINOES

If you dream of playing at dominoes and you lose, you will be affronted by a friend, and your family will feel much concern for your safety, because you are not discreet romantically or in other matters.

If you are the winner of the game, you will be courted and admired by certain dissolute characters, bringing selfish pleasures to you but much distress to your relatives.

## DONKEY*

To dream of a donkey braying in your face indicates that you are about to be publicly insulted by a lewd and unscrupulous person.

If you hear distant braying filling space with melancholy, you will receive wealth and release from unpleasant bonds by the death of someone close to you. If you see yourself riding on a donkey, you will visit foreign lands and explore many places that are difficult to reach.

To see others riding donkeys suggests a meager inheritance for them and a life of toil.

To drive a donkey signifies that all your energies and pluck will be brought into play against desperate efforts by your enemies to overthrow you. If you drive a donkey while you are in love, evil people will cause you trouble.

If you are kicked by this little animal, it shows that you are carrying on illicit affairs and are anxious about the possibility of betrayal.

If you lead a donkey by a halter, you will be master of every situation, leading others into your way of seeing things by flattery. To see children riding and driving donkeys suggests that they will be both healthy and obedient.

To fall or be thrown from a donkey denotes ill luck and disappointment. Lovers will quarrel and separate.

To see a donkey that is dead denotes satiety resulting from licentious excesses.

To dream of drinking the milk of a donkey suggests that frivolous desires will be gratified at the expense of responsibility.

If you see a strange donkey among your stock, or on your premises, you will inherit some valuable things.

To dream of coming into the possession of a donkey by gift or purchase portends that you will attain enviable heights in the business or social world; if you're single, you will enter into a successful marriage. *See *Mule*.

## DONOR

Organ donation in your dreams warns of upcoming health problems.

## DOODLING

To find yourself doodling on something in your dreams cautions you to step back from a problem and rethink how you are going to solve it.

## DOOMSDAY

To dream that you are looking forward to doomsday is a warning for you to give substantial and material affairs close attention, or you will find that the artful and scheming friends you are entertaining will get what they desire from you, which is your wealth and not your heart.

## DOOR*

To dream of entering a door suggests slander and enemies, people you are trying in vain to escape from. If the door you dream of entering is your childhood home, your days will be filled with plenty and with congeniality.

To see others go through a doorway denotes unsuccessful attempts to get your affairs in order. It also foreshadows changes for farmers and in the world of politics.

For authors, it suggests that the reading public will refuse to read their new works.

If you dream that you attempt to close a door and it falls from its hinges, injuring someone, evil threatens a friend through your unintentional wrong advice. If you see another attempt to lock a door, and it again falls from its hinges, you will have knowledge of some friend's misfortune and be powerless to help.

*See *Dutch door*.

## DOORBELL

To dream you hear or ring a doorbell foretells unexpected tidings, or a hasty summons to business or to the bedside of a sick relative.

## DORMITORY

To see yourself living in a dormitory implies a possible move to another location. To visit a dormitory in your dream means that travel is on the horizon.

## DOUBLE

To dream of seeing two of an item foretells good luck with money. To dream that you see double means you need to look again at something or someone to totally understand a problem you are having.

## DOUGHNUT

To dream of doughnuts means travel, sometimes unexpected.

## DOVE

Dreaming of doves mating and building their nests indicates a peaceful world and joyous homes where children are obedient and mercy is extended to all.

To hear the lonely, mournful voice of a dove portends sorrow and disappointment through the death of one to whom you looked for aid. Often it portends the death of a father.

Dreaming of a dead dove portends a separation of husband and wife, through either death or infidelity.

White doves suggest bountiful harvests and the utmost confidence in the loyalty of friends.

To dream of seeing a flock of white doves denotes peaceful, innocent pleasures and fortunate developments in the future.

If one brings you a letter, pleasant news from absent friends is intimated, as is a lover's reconciliation. If the dove seems exhausted, a note of sadness will pervade the reconciliation, or a sad touch may be given the happy tidings by mention of an invalid friend; a slight drop in business affairs may follow. If the letter bears the message that you are doomed, it foretells that a desperate illness, either your own or that of a relative, may cause you financial misfortune.

## DOWNPOUR

To dream that you are caught in a downpour is an omen of great fortune coming your way.

## DOWNSIZING

To dream that you have been fired because your company has downsized is a great predictor of advancement at work.

## DOWN SYNDROME

To dream that you have Down syndrome, or someone else does, indicates good mental health and clarity.

## DOWRY

To dream that you fail to receive a dowry suggests poverty and a cold world to depend on for a living. If you do receive one, your expectations for the day will be fulfilled.

## DOZEN

To dream that you have a dozen of anything represents abundance, whether you keep things or give them away.

## DRAFT

To dream that you are sitting or standing in a draft means you will learn a good lesson. To dream of being drafted into the army indicates peaceful times in your life.

## DRAGON*

To dream of a dragon suggests that you allow yourself to be governed by your passions; you are likely to place yourself in the power of your enemies through those outbursts of sardonic tendencies. You should be warned by this dream to cultivate self-control.

*See *Devil, Satan.*

## DRAGONFLY

To dream of a dragonfly means monetary gain—though it may just be fleeting.

## DRAMA

To dream of seeing a drama signifies pleasant reunions with distant friends. If you are bored at the performance, you will be forced to accept an uncongenial companion at some entertainment or secret affair.

To write a drama portends that you will be plunged into distress and debt, to be extricated as if by a miracle.

## DRAPES

To dream of drapes on a window or to find yourself or someone else draping a cloth over something suggests that you're trying to cover up a financial problem from those around you.

## DRAWBRIDGE

To dream of a drawbridge either closing or opening means that exciting times are coming—but you will need to take everything slowly to keep healthy.

## DRAWING

To dream that you are drawing a picture of yourself or someone else means you will go through a time of questioning your spiritual self.

## DREADLOCKS

To dream that you have this hairstyle means you will be thinking in a totally different way about a love relationship. To see dreadlocks on another signifies new love coming into your life. To cut or have your dreadlocks cut implies a coming problem that could change a love relationship.

## DRESS REHEARSAL

To dream of being in a dress rehearsal reveals your ability to take your time to figure out an upcoming problem or confusing situation in your life.

## DRESSING

To experience trouble dressing in a dream means that evil people will worry you and keep you from happiness. If you have trouble getting dressed on time, this means you will have many annoyances through the carelessness of others. Depend on your own efforts, as much as possible, for contentment and success.

## DRILLING

To dream of drilling anything warns you to look at how you might be wasting time on trivial matters.

## DRINKING

To be given to drinking in your dream suggests ill-natured rivalry and contention over small possessions. To think you have quit drinking or find that others have done so shows that you will rise above your present state and will prosper.

## DRIVEWAY

To pave a driveway or see one being paved tells you that extreme luck with money is coming your way. To sit in your car in a driveway means the same thing.

### DRIVING

To dream of driving signifies unjust criticism of your seeming extravagance. You will be compelled to do things that appear undignified.

To dream of driving a public cab denotes menial labor with little chance for advancement. If it is a wagon, you will remain in poverty and unfortunate circumstances for some time.

If you are driven by others, you will profit by superior knowledge of the world and will always find some path through difficulties.

### DROPPING

To dream that you find yourself dropping things suggests good health.

### DROPPING OUT

To drop out of anything in a dream—a play, a school, an event, what have you—means you will soon be in a position to learn something new.

### DROUGHT

To experience a drought in a dream means you will have more than enough and will share your wealth.

### DROWNING

To dream of drowning denotes loss of property and life; but if you are rescued, you will rise from your present position to one of wealth and honor.

If you see others drowning and go to their relief, you will aid your friend in high places and will bring deserved happiness to yourself.

### DRUGS*

To take a drug in a dream suggests that you will learn of a loved one's poor health. To give a drug in your dream means a problem with your own health. If you buy or sell drugs, there is dishonesty among your friends, family, or co-workers; you need to stay away from them.

*See specific drugs.

### DRUM

To hear the muffled beating of a drum indicates that an absent friend is in distress and is calling on you for aid.

To see a drum foretells amiability and a great aversion to quarrels and dissension.

### DRUMSTICK

To dream of eating a drumstick is a sign of good fortune.

To use drumsticks to play a drum is a sign of happy times ahead. To use them to play on something other than drums means you will be deceived in a contract if you are not careful.

## DRUNKENNESS*

Drunkenness in all forms is unreliable as a good dream. Everyone is warned by this dream to shift thoughts into more healthful channels.

This is an unfavorable dream if you are drunk on heavy liquors, indicating profligacy and loss of employment. You will be disgraced by stooping to forgery or theft.

To see others in a drunken condition foretells for you, and probably others, unhappy states.

However, if drunk on wine, you will be fortunate in business and in love and will scale exalted heights in literary pursuits. This dream always foretells aesthetic experiences.

*See Beer, Intoxication.

## DRY CLEANING

To dream of bringing clothing to a dry cleaner means you will soon be "cleaning" up past relationships that have ended. To pick up items from the dry cleaner in your dream suggests that new friendships are coming your way.

## DRY ICE

To handle dry ice with gloves in a dream cautions you about deception among your co-workers. To dream that you handle it without gloves means you will be asked to be deceitful to someone. This is a warning that you must say no or you will be blamed and another will go free.

## DUCK

To dream of seeing wild ducks on a clear stream signifies fortunate journeys, perhaps across the sea. White ducks around a farm indicate thrift and a fine harvest.

To hunt ducks denotes displacement in employment and the carrying out of plans.

To see them shot reveals that enemies are meddling in your private affairs.

Flying ducks foretell a bright future for you. This also denotes marriage and children in a new home.

## DUCT TAPE

To dream of using this in any manner means you will soon solve a problem, but it will surface again and you will have to solve it differently the next time.

## DUEL

To dream of fighting a duel means people around you may try to get you into trouble.

## DUET

To dream of hearing a duet played suggests a peaceful existence for lovers. Businesspeople carry on a mild rivalry.

To musical people, dreaming of a duet denotes competition and wrangling for superiority.

To hear a duet sung augurs unpleasant tidings; but this will not last, as some new pleasure will displace the unpleasantness.

## DULCIMER

To dream of a dulcimer lets you know that the highest wishes in life will be attained by exalted qualities of mind.

## DUMBNESS, MUTENESS

To dream of being dumb indicates your inability to persuade others into your mode of thinking, and to use them for your profit by your glib tongue.

To the dumb, it denotes false friends.

## DUMP

To dream of a dump means you will be asked to help someone get out of trouble.

## DUMPLING

If you dream of eating or making dumplings, you will soon find yourself stress-free for a while.

## DUNNING NOTICE

To dream that you receive a dunning notice warns you to look after your affairs and correct a tendency toward neglect in business and love.

## DUNE

To climb a dune in your dream means you will have an easy time with an upcoming problem. To run down or fall down a dune in a dream means trouble ahead that will not be easily solved.

## DUNGEON

To dream of being in a dungeon foretells struggles with the vital issues of life—but by wise dealing, you will disengage yourself from obstacles and the designs of enemies. For a woman this is a dark dream; willful indiscretions cause the loss of status among honorable people.

To see a dungeon lighted up portends threats of entanglement that your better judgment warns you against.

## DUNGHILL

If you dream of a dunghill, you will see profits coming in through the most unexpected sources. This is a dream of good luck.

## DUPLEX

To live in, own, or visit someone residing in a duplex means you will have to share something you thought would be all yours, such as money from an inheritance.

## DUPLICATING

To duplicate anything in your dream advises you to look twice at things before you make a major life decision.

## DUSK

This is a dream of sadness; it portends an early decline and unrequited hopes and suggests a dark outlook for trade and pursuits of any kind.

## DUST

To dream of dust covering you suggests that you will be slightly injured in business by the failure of others. If you free yourself of the dust with judicious measures, you will clear up the loss.

## DUTCH DOOR*

To see this door in your dream means you will have several ways to solve a problem and you will feel protected while doing so.

*See Door.

## DUTCH OVEN

To cook in your dream with this pot means you will have a fun time coming to you with friends and family.

## DVD

If you see a DVD in your dream, you will be faced with memories that cause you either joy or pain.

## DWARF

This is a very favorable dream. Health and good constitution will be yours.

## DYEING

If you dream of seeing the dyeing of cloth or garments in process, it suggests luck—either bad or good, depending on the color. Blues, reds, and golds indicate prosperity; black and white, sorrow in all forms.

## DYING*

To dream of dying implies that you are facing big changes ahead in your life on many levels.

*See Death.

## DYNAMITE

To see dynamite in a dream is a sign of approaching change and the expansion of your affairs.

To be frightened by it indicates that a secret enemy is at work against you. If you are not careful of your conduct, he or she will pop up at an unexpected and helpless moment.

## DYSENTERY

To dream of having dysentery suggests that a desperate or fatal illness will overtake you or some member of your family. To see others thus afflicted implies disappointment in carrying out some enterprise through the neglect of others. Inharmonious states will vex you.

## DYSLEXIA

To dream you have dyslexia means that you are going to be very clear in what you want in the near future when it comes to making contracts.

If you dream of helping someone learn how to overcome dyslexia, you will have to read between the lines in what people are saying to you in order to understand their true meaning.

## EAGLE

To see an eagle soaring above you denotes lofty ambitions that you will struggle fiercely to realize; regardless of the struggle, you will gain your desires.

To see an eagle perched on distant heights suggests that you will possess fame, wealth, and the highest position attainable in your country.

Young eagles in their aerie symbolize your association with people of high standing; you will profit from their wise counsel. You will in time come into a rich legacy.

To dream that you kill an eagle portends that no obstacles whatever are allowed to stand between you and the utmost heights of your ambition. You will overcome your enemies and be possessed of untold wealth.

Eating the flesh of one indicates a powerful will that does not turn aside in ambitious struggles, even for death. You will soon come into valuable possessions.

To see a dead eagle killed by others signifies that high rank and fortune will be wrested from you ruthlessly.

To ride on an eagle's back means that you will make a long voyage into almost unexplored countries in your search for knowledge and wealth, which you will eventually gain.

## EAR

If you dream of seeing ears, an evil and designing person is keeping watch over your conversation to harm you.

## EARMUFF

To dream of wearing earmuffs indicates that you will be well provided for against the vicissitudes of fortune.

## EARRING

To see earrings in dreams reveals that good news and interesting work are coming up.

To see broken earrings indicates that gossip of a low order will be directed against you.

## EARTH

To be in space looking at Earth is a dream foretelling great travel in your future.

## EARTHQUAKE

To see or feel an earthquake in your dream denotes business failure and much distress from turmoil and wars between nations.

## EARTHWORM

To see or touch this worm in your dream means you will be enriched with new learning in the near future.

## EASEL

To dream of a painting on an easel, or of the act of painting, suggests being able to create your own life in the near future. You will make major changes to your life that will be wonderful.

## EATING*

To dream of eating alone signifies loss and melancholy spirits.

To eat with others denotes personal gain, cheerful environments, and prosperous undertakings.

*See *Meal*.

## EAVESDROPPING

To dream of eavesdropping on a conversation means you will soon find yourself the center of false rumors. If someone else eavesdrops in your dream, you will soon discover a friend to be disloyal.

## EBONY

If you dream of ebony furniture or other articles of ebony, you will have many distressing disputes and quarrels in your home.

## ECHO

To dream of an echo portends that distressful or ill times are upon you. Because of your sickness, you may lose your employment, and friends will desert you in time of need.

## ÉCLAIR

To dream of making or eating this pastry is a sign of good fortune coming your way.

## ECLIPSE

To dream of an eclipse of the sun denotes temporary failure in business and other affairs, as well as disturbances in families. An eclipse of the moon foretells contagious disease or death.

## ECSTASY

To dream of feeling ecstasy implies that you will enjoy a visit from a long-absent friend. But if you experience ecstasy in *disturbing* dreams, you will be subjected to sorrow and disappointment.

## ECZEMA

To have this skin condition in a dream augurs good news in a health matter. To see someone else with the condition means you need to be alert for health problems in the near future.

## EDGE

To dream that you are on the edge of anything—a chair, stairs, a bluff, or a cliff—reveals that you will soon be taking a chance, which will turn out very well for you.

To dream that you are *falling off* the edge of something is even better. It means the chance you will take will better your life.

## EDITING

If you find yourself editing a document or anything similar in a dream, there will be changes in your job or career, usually for the better.

## EDUCATION

To dream that you are anxious to obtain an education shows that whatever your circumstances in life may be, you have a keen desire for knowledge, which will place you on a higher plane than your associates. Fortune will also be more lenient with you.

To dream that you are in places of learning foretells many influential friends for you.

## EEL

To dream of an eel is good if you can maintain your grip on it. Otherwise, fortune will be fleeting.

To see an eel in clear water denotes, for a woman, new but evanescent pleasures.

To see a dead eel signifies that you will overcome your most maliciously inclined enemies. For lovers, the dream denotes an end to a long, hazardous courtship or marriage.

## EFFIGY

To dream that you are making or seeing an effigy of someone you know warns that you will soon see another side of someone that you didn't know was there.

## EGG

To dream of finding a nest of eggs denotes wealth of a substantial character, and happiness and many children among the married.

To eat eggs implies that unusual disturbances threaten you in your home.

If you see broken eggs and they are fresh, fortune is ready to shower upon you her richest gifts. A lofty spirit and high regard for justice will make you beloved by the world.

To dream of rotten eggs suggests loss of property and degradation. An entire crate of rotten eggs, however, indicates that you will engage in profitable speculations.

If you dream of being spattered with eggs, you will sport riches of doubtful origin.

To see birds' eggs in your dream signifies legacies from distant relations, or gain from an unexpected rise in staple products.

## EGGNOG

To dream that you are making or drinking eggnog portends good health.

## EGGPLANT

To dream that you grow eggplant means a gain in fortune. To prepare or eat eggplant is double good fortune.

## EGRET

To dream of this waterfowl indicates that great luck is heading your way.

## EGYPT

To dream you are in Egypt or are Egyptian is a powerful spiritual dream. You will soon be examining your beliefs about religion.

## EJACULATION

To ejaculate in your dream warns that you are spending too much money on unneeded things.

## ELASTIC

To dream of this material in any way means that you will receive aid when you need it during an upcoming problem.

### ELBOWS

To see elbows in a dream signifies that arduous labors will devolve upon you, for which you will receive small reimbursement.

### ELDERBERRIES

To dream of seeing elderberries on bushes, with their foliage, suggests domestic bliss and an agreeable country home with resources for travel and other pleasures. Dreaming of elderberries is generally a good sign.

### ELDERLY

To be with the elderly, or to see yourself as elderly in your dream if you are not, means a long life with many happy moments is in your future.

### ELECTION

To dream that you are at an election predicts that you will engage in some controversy that will prove detrimental to your social or financial standing.

### ELECTRICITY

To dream of electricity implies that there will be sudden changes about you that will not afford you either advancement or pleasure. If you are shocked by electricity, you will face a deplorable danger.

Seeing a live electrical wire foretells that enemies will disturb your plans, which you have had much anxiety forming.

### ELEPHANT

To dream of riding an elephant indicates that you will possess wealth of the most solid character and honors that you will wear with dignity. You will rule absolutely in all your business affairs, and your word will be law in the home.

To see many elephants denotes tremendous prosperity. One lone elephant signifies that you will live in a small but solid way.

If you dream of feeding an elephant, you will elevate your standing in your community by your kindness to those who are socially below you.

### ELEVATOR

To dream of ascending in an elevator means that you will swiftly rise to position and wealth; but if you descend in one, your misfortunes will crush and discourage you. If you see one descending without you, you will narrowly escape disappointment in some undertaking.

A standing elevator foretells threatened danger.

## ELITE

To find that you are among the elite in a dream means you will soon lose money because of poor speculation.

## ELIXIR OF LIFE

To dream of the elixir of life indicates that new pleasures and new possibilities will come into your environment.

## ELM

To dream of this tree suggests continued growth in your personal life.

## ELOPEMENT

To dream of eloping is unfavorable. To the married, it indicates that you hold places you are unworthy to fill; if you don't mend your ways, your reputation will be at stake.

To the unmarried, it foretells disappointments in love and the unfaithfulness of men.

To dream that your lover has eloped with someone else denotes his or her unfaithfulness.

To dream of a friend eloping with someone you do not approve of means that you will soon hear of his or her entering into a disagreeable marriage.

## ELOQUENCE

If you think you are eloquent of speech in your dreams, there will be pleasant news for you concerning someone in whose interest you are working.

If you fail to impress others with your eloquence, there will be much disorder in your affairs.

## EMACIATION

To find yourself emaciated in a dream foretells a good outcome of an upcoming medical test. To see others emaciated means that an upcoming health issue will need to be taken care of immediately.

## E-MAIL

To send or receive e-mail in a dream augurs good news coming your way. To be unable to open your e-mail in the dream means you will have to find a way to communicate with someone who is giving you trouble, or things will not end in your favor.

## EMBALMING

To see embalming in process foretells altered positions in social life and threatens poverty.

To dream that you are looking at yourself embalmed portends unfortunate friendships that will force you into social circles lower than you are accustomed to moving in.

## EMBANKMENT

To dream of driving along an embankment suggests threats of trouble and unhappiness. If you continue your drive without unpleasant incidents, you will succeed in turning these forebodings to your advantage in your social or employment status.

To ride on horseback along an embankment means that you will fearlessly meet and overcome all obstacles on your way to wealth and happiness.

If you walk along one, you will have a weary struggle to elevate your status but will finally reap a reward.

## EMBARRASSMENT

The greater your embarrassment in a dream, the larger your success. If you embarrass others, you need to learn to trust your own judgment more.

## EMBASSY

To dream of working at an embassy, or going to one, is a dream of travel.

## EMBELLISHMENT, ADORNMENT

To find yourself embellishing anything in your dream—especially with jewels—is a dream of great luck. To dream of wearing something that has been embellished with anything that sparkles foretells the winning of a prize or lottery.

## EMBERS

To dream you have been burned by a hot ember implies hard times ahead in relationships. To put out burning or smoldering embers means you may soon be ending a friendship or love relationship.

## EMBRACING

To dream of embracing your spouse sorrowful or indifferent indicates that you will have dissension and accusations in your family. Sickness may also be threatened.

To embrace relatives signifies their sickness and unhappiness. For lovers to dream of embracing foretells quarrels and disagreements arising from infidelity. If these dreams take place under auspicious conditions, the reverse may be expected. If you embrace a stranger, it signifies that you will have an unwelcome guest.

## EMBROIDERY

If you dream of embroidery, you can create personal happiness on your own.

## EMBRYO

To see an embryo is a dream of good health. A dead embryo foretells a pregnancy, unless you are already pregnant; then it has no meaning at all.

## EMCEE

To be an emcee at an event in a dream suggests that you will soon be recognized for your hard work.

## EMERALD

If you dream of an emerald, you will inherit property that will involve trouble with other people.

To dream that you buy an emerald signifies unfortunate dealings.

## EMERGENCY

To feel that something in your dream is cause for emergency action means that you will soon be called upon to help solve a big problem at work or in your family.

## EMIGRATION

To find yourself emigrating from your country in a dream indicates an upcoming change of residence.

## EMPEROR

To dream of going abroad and meeting the emperor of a nation suggests that you will make a long journey that will bring neither pleasure nor much knowledge.

## EMPIRE

To dream of being a part of a great empire, rich or poor, portends good luck with money.

## EMPLOYEE

To see one of your employees in your dream denotes disturbances if he or she assumes a disagreeable or offensive attitude.

If the employee is pleasant and interesting, you will find no evil or embarrassing conditions upon awakening.

### EMPLOYMENT

This is not an auspicious dream. It implies financial depression and, if you're salaried, loss of employment. It also denotes physical illness.

To dream of being out of work suggests that you have nothing to fear, as you are always sought out for your conscientiousness, which makes you a desirable employee. Giving employment to others indicates loss for yourself.

### EMPRESS

To dream of an empress indicates that you will be exalted to high honors, but you will let pride make you very unpopular.

### EMPTINESS

To look inside something and see it empty foretells changes that will make your life more fulfilled. To empty something in a dream means you will soon have to watch your money and your spending.

### EMT

To be an EMT in a dream means you will receive good health news.

### ENCASING

To find yourself encased in anything in your dream suggests that you will soon be alone with your problems and will have to solve them yourself.

### ENCHANTMENT

To dream of being under the spell of enchantment means you may be hoodwinked in some way.

To resist enchantment predicts that you will be much sought after for your wise counsel and open-mindedness.

Dreaming of trying to enchant others portends bad luck.

### ENCHILADA

To make or eat this Mexican food in your dream means good fortune and luck.

### ENCLOSURE

If you dream that you find yourself enclosed in anything, you will soon find a way out of a problem you thought had no solution.

### ENCOURAGEMENT

To be encouraged to do something in your dream foretells an idea that may advance you at work. If you encourage someone else, you will soon be part of a team whose ideas will make money.

## ENCYCLOPEDIA

To dream of seeing or searching through encyclopedias portends that your literary ability will be at the expense of prosperity and comfort.

To dream of looking something up in an encyclopedia suggests furthering your education—if you find what you're looking for. If you don't, you will have to work much harder to learn something new.

## ENEMA

To get or give an enema in a dream portends great monetary luck.

## ENEMIES

To dream of overcoming enemies indicates that you will surmount all difficulties in business and enjoy the greatest prosperity. If you are defamed by your enemies, you will be threatened with failure in your work. Use the utmost caution while proceeding in affairs of importance.

To overcome your enemies in any form signifies gain. For them to get the better of you augurs adverse fortunes.

## ENERGY

To find yourself trying to save energy in a dream foretells a time of rest coming after much hard work.

To waste energy in your dream means you must repeat your work if you hope to complete it.

## ENGAGEMENT

To dream of a business engagement denotes dullness and worry at work.

To become engaged to be married in a dream foretells a broken relationship. To break an engagement means someone you know will soon become engaged, or you will receive an invitation to a wedding. It can also denote a hasty and unwise action in some important matter.

## ENGINE

To dream of an engine suggests that you will encounter grave difficulties and journeys, but will have many friends to uphold you. Disabled engines stand for misfortune and loss of relatives.

## ENGINEER

To dream of an engineer forebodes weary journeys but joyful reunions.

### ENGRAVING

If you dream of seeing something being engraved and you can read what it says, you will soon be signing important papers.

### ENLARGEMENT

To find yourself enlarging something in your dream, such as a picture, means you will soon expand your circle of friends.

### ENLISTMENT

To be enlisted in the military in a dream means you will soon be traveling outside your home country.

### ENSHRINING

To see a religious figure enshrined in your dream foretells many blessings in money and personal matters.

### ENSLAVEMENT

To be enslaved in your dream foretells that you will have the means to do the things you want to do. To enslave someone else in your dream warns you to be careful of being stolen from.

### ENTANGLEMENT

To dream that you are entangled, either physically or emotionally, means you have the freedom to choose a new direction in your life.

### ENTERTAINMENT

To dream of entertainment where there is music and dancing means that you will have pleasant tidings and will enjoy health and prosperity.

To the young, this is a dream of many and varied pleasures and the high regard of friends.

### ENTRAILS*

To dream of human entrails denotes misery and despair, shutting out all hope of happiness. To dream of the entrails of a wild beast signifies the overthrow of your mortal enemy.

If you tear the entrails of another in your dream, you may engage in cruel persecutions to further your own interests. If you dream of your own entrails, the deepest despair will overwhelm you.

*See *Intestines*.

### ENTRANCE*

To dream of an entrance to a building foretells the end of a relationship.

*See *Door*.

## ENTREPRENEUR

To dream you are an entrepreneur means advancement in your career. To dream you are dealing with an entrepreneur suggests a job loss.

## ENVELOPE

Envelopes seen in a dream are omens of sorrowful news.

## ENVY

To dream that you envy others indicates that you will make warm friends through your unselfish deference to the wishes of others. If you dream of being envied by others, you will suffer some inconvenience from friends overanxious to please you.

## EPAULET

To dream of wearing epaulets implies coming honors and the respect of your peers.

## EPICURE

If you dream of sitting at the table with an epicure, you may enjoy some fine distinction, but you will be surrounded by people of selfish principles.

If you dream that you are an epicure yourself, you will cultivate your mind, body, and taste to the highest degree.

## EPIDEMIC

To dream of an epidemic signifies mental prostration and worry caused by distasteful tasks. Contagion among relatives or friends is foretold by dreams of this nature.

## ERASURE

To dream of erasing something from a piece of paper or a blackboard suggests that rumors will cause you social embarrassment.

## ERMINE

To dream that you wear this beautiful and costly fur implies exaltation, lofty character, and wealth forming a barrier against want and misery.

If you see others thus clothed, you will be associated with wealthy people, polished in literature and art.

## ERRAND

To go on errands in your dreams indicates congenial associations and mutual agreement in the home circle.

## ERUPTION

To dream of something erupting, like a volcano, means a sudden change for the better.

## ESCALATOR

To dream of going up an escalator is a dream of good success; to go down an escalator is a dream of possible defeat, but this can be reversed.

## ESCAPING

To dream of escape from injury or accident is usually favorable. If you escape from a place of confinement, it signifies your rise in the world by diligently applying yourself to business.

To escape from any contagion denotes your good health and prosperity. If you try to escape and fail, you will suffer from the designs of enemies who slander and defraud you.

## ESKIMO

To dream of being among the Eskimos means you need to watch your spending; if you find yourself in financial trouble, you will not have any help.

## ESTATE★

To dream that you have come into the ownership of a vast estate suggests that you will receive a legacy some distant day, but one quite different from your expectations.

★See *Inheritance*.

## ETCHING

If your dream includes etchings, you will be seeking out artistic endeavors that you never expected.

## EULOGY

To dream of giving a eulogy means that you may say something in the near future that will embarrass you.

If someone is delivering *your* eulogy, a pleasant surprise is coming in the future, usually a gift.

## EUROPE

To dream of traveling in Europe foretells that you will soon go on a long journey, gaining knowledge of the manners and customs of foreign people. This will also enable you to improve your financial standing.

## EVACUATION

To dream of evacuation indicates a possible home move.

## EVANGELIST

To dream of being an evangelist means you will undertake a spiritual journey that will open your mind.

To listen to an evangelist advises you to examine your spiritual beliefs.

## EVE

To dream of this biblical character offers blessings to the dreamer and can be interpreted as a portent of pregnancy and birth.

## EVENING

To dream of evening closing in about you suggests unrealized hopes; you may commit to unfortunate ventures.

To see stars shining clearly speaks of present distress, but a brighter fortune is behind your trouble.

If the evening is lovely, good health is indicated; a stormy evening foretells a health problem that needs to be addressed.

## EVERGLADES

To dream that you are in the Everglades indicates that you will discover many new aspects of your personality in the near future.

## EVERGREEN

Dreaming of evergreen trees denotes boundless resources and wealth, happiness, and learning.

## EVIDENCE

To give evidence in a dream means you will be asked to help someone. If you hear someone else giving evidence, someone will give you help.

## EVIL

To be involved in an evil atmosphere or see evil spirits in your dream predicts obstacles to your goals.

## EXAM

To dream of taking an exam and failing suggests that you are aiming too high; there is something you probably won't be able to accomplish.

If you pass the test, your goals are achievable.

## EXAMINING

To find yourself examining something in your dream means that most of your problems will have clarity and be easy to solve.

If you are the one being examined, you will need to learn to keep your mouth shut about your problems.

## EXCAVATION

To dream of an excavation predicts that you will receive a surprise gift.

## EXCHANGING

To dream of an exchange suggests profitable dealings in all classes of business.

## EXCOMMUNICATION

To dream that you have been excommunicated warns you that lies and deceit exist in your friendships.

## EXECUTION*

To dream of seeing an execution signifies that you will suffer some misfortune through the carelessness of others.

To dream that you are about to be executed and some miraculous intervention occurs tells you that you will overthrow enemies and succeed in gaining wealth.

*See *Hanging*.

## EXERCISING

If you dream that you are enjoying exercise, it's a dream of good luck. If you are tired and don't want to exercise, the dream advises you to watch your money.

## EXHAUSTION

If you dream of being exhausted, you need to exercise more caution in your body movements.

## EXHIBITION

If you dream of being in or witnessing an exhibition, one of your problems may require more patience on your part.

## EXILE*

To dream that you are exiled suggests that you will be taking an unwelcome journey.

*See *Banishment*.

## EXPERT

To dream of an expert—whether it's yourself or someone else—means you will recover something that you have lost.

## EXPLORATION

If you see yourself as an explorer on an adventure in dreams, you soon will be quarreling with friends and relatives.

## EXPLOSION

To dream of explosions portends that the disapproval of those connected with you will cause you transient displeasure and loss. Business will also displease you.

To dream that your face, or the face of someone else, is blackened or mutilated in an explosion signifies that you will be unjustly accused of indiscretion, and circumstances may convict you even though the accusation is not true.

To see the air filled with smoke and debris from an explosion indicates unusual dissatisfaction in business circles and much social antagonism.

If you dream of being enveloped in the flames from an explosion, or if you are blown into the air, unworthy friends will infringe on your rights and abuse your confidence.

## EXTERIOR

To find yourself changing the exterior of your home or a building in a dream means that you will be moving soon.

## EYE

To dream of seeing an eye warns you that watchful enemies are seeking the slightest chance to cause injury to your business.

To dream of brown eyes denotes deceit and perfidy; blue eyes, weakness in carrying out any intention; gray eyes, a love of flattery.

To dream of losing an eye, or that your eyes are sore, portends trouble.

## EYEBROWS

A dream of eyebrows suggests that you will encounter sinister obstacles in your immediate future.

## EYEGLASSES

To dream of seeing or wearing eyeglasses indicates that you will be afflicted with disagreeable friendships from which you will strive vainly to disengage yourself.

## EYELASHES

To dream of long, beautiful eyelashes means happiness in your love and social life. If they are false, you will discover a secret about a relationship that will stun you.

To be without eyelashes in a dream warns you to watch your back with certain friends or colleagues.

## EYEWITNESS

To be an eyewitness to a situation or crime in your dream means you will soon be presented with a proposal for expanding your finances.

## FABLE

To dream of reading or telling fables suggests pleasant tasks and a literary turn of mind. To the young, it signifies romantic attachments.

To hear or to tell religious fables predicts that you will become very pious.

## FABRIC

To dream of cutting or sewing fabric foretells financial gain.

## FACELESSNESS

To dream of a faceless person means that a new friendship, or help from a stranger, is on the horizon.

To dream that you are faceless cautions you to start thinking on your own, not to depend on other people's opinions.

## FACELIFT

To dream of having a facelift predicts much joy and happiness coming into your life.

## FACES

This dream is favorable if you see happy and bright faces, but it signifies trouble if they are disfigured, ugly, or frowning at you.

To a young person, an ugly face foretells lovers' quarrels; or for a lover to see the face of his or her sweetheart looking old warns of separation and the breakup of happy associations.

To see a strange and weird-looking face tells you that enemies and misfortunes surround you.

To dream of seeing your own face denotes unhappiness; to the married, threats of divorce will be made.

To see your face in a mirror suggests displeasure with yourself for not being able to carry out plans for self-advancement. You will also lose the esteem of friends.

## FACIAL

To dream of receiving or giving a facial tells you that there is much calm and serenity coming into your life.

## FACTORY

To own or work in a factory in your dream means you will experience financial gain through unusual circumstances. To dream of a large factory denotes unusual activity in business circles.

## FADING

To dream of something fading warns that you need to be careful of losing something.

## FAILURE

For a lover, a dream of failure is sometimes of contrary significance—a dream in which the dreamer suffers fear, not injury. If a man dreams that he fails in his pursuit of marriage, this signifies that he only needs more mastery and energy, as he has already the love and esteem of his sweetheart.

For a young woman to dream that her life is going to be a failure denotes that she is not applying her opportunities to good advantage.

For a businessperson to dream of failure forebodes loss and bad management. This should be corrected, or failure threatens to materialize in earnest.

## FAINTING

To dream of fainting signifies illness in your family and unpleasant news of those who are absent.

## FAIR

To dream of being at a fair means that you will someday have a pleasant and profitable business and a congenial companion.

## FAIRY

To dream of a fairy is a favorable omen.

## FAITHLESSNESS

To dream that your friends are faithless implies that they hold you in worthy esteem. For a lover to dream that his sweetheart is faithless signifies a happy marriage.

## FAKIR

To dream of an Indian fakir indicates uncommon activity and phenomenal changes in your life. Such dreams may sometimes be gloomy.

## FALCON

To dream of a falcon cautions you that your prosperity will make you an object of envy and malice.

## FALLING*

To dream that you sustain a fall and are frightened means that you will undergo some great struggle but will eventually rise to honor and wealth. If you are injured in the fall, you will encounter hardships and loss of friends.
*See *Edge*.

## FAME

To dream of being famous suggests disappointed aspirations. To dream of famous people portends your rise from obscurity to places of honor.

## FAMILY

To dream of your family as harmonious and happy signifies health and easy circumstances; but if there is sickness or contention, it forebodes gloom and disappointment.

## FAMINE

To dream of a famine augurs that your business will be unremunerative, and sickness will prove a scourge. This dream is generally bad. If you see your enemies perishing by famine, however, you will be successful in competition.

## FAMISHMENT

To dream that you are famished suggests that you are meeting disheartening failure in an enterprise that once seemed promising.

To see other people famished brings sorrow to them as well as to yourself.

## FAN

To see a fan in your dreams tells you that pleasant news and surprises are awaiting you in the near future.

## FANTASY

To have a fantasy dream foretells good fortune; fame may be coming your way.

## FAREWELLS

To dream of bidding farewell is not particularly favorable; you are likely to hear unpleasant news of absent friends.

## FARM*

If you dream that you are living on a farm, you will be fortunate in all undertakings.

To dream of buying a farm denotes abundant crops to the farmer, a profitable deal of some kind to the businessperson, and a safe voyage to the traveler and sailor. Visiting a farm signifies pleasant associations.

*See Estate.

## FASHION

To dream of being concerned about fashion or what you are wearing means you soon will be examining your thoughts about your female friends and deciding whether or not they are loyal to you.

## FAST FOOD

To dream of eating, buying, or selling fast food means you must develop more patience in your life to achieve a specific goal.

## FATAL ACCIDENT

To witness or experience a fatal accident in a dream suggests that something you thought was a mistake will actually be of benefit to you.

## FATES, THE

To dream of the Fates foretells disagreements and unhappiness.

## FATHER*

To dream of your father signifies that you are about to be involved in a difficulty and will need wise counsel if you hope to extricate yourself. If your father is dead, the dream suggests that your business is affecting you negatively; you will have to use caution in conducting it.

*See Parents.

## FATHER-IN-LAW

To dream of your father-in-law implies contentious relations with friends or relatives. To see him well and cheerful foretells pleasant family relations.

## FATIGUE

To feel fatigued in a dream foretells ill health or oppression in business.

## FATNESS*

To dream that you are getting fat indicates that you are about to make a fortunate change in your life. To see others being fat signifies prosperity.

*See Corpulence.

## FAUCET

To dream of turning on or shutting off a faucet with clear running water or liquid betokens good luck and money.

If the water is murky or polluted, you will experience troubles with your finances.

To dream of not being able to turn off the faucet implies extreme financial gain or loss, depending on the clarity of the water.

## FAVORITE

To dream of being a favorite among friends or family means you will be called upon to help in a project that will better your financial position.

## FAVORS

To dream that you are asking favors of anyone indicates that you will enjoy abundance and that you will not especially need anything.

To grant favors means you are about to suffer a loss.

## FAWN, FAWNING*

To dream of seeing a fawn indicates that you have true and upright friends. To the young, it indicates faithfulness in love.

To dream that a person fawns over you or cajoles you is a warning that enemies are about you in the guise of interested friends.

*See Deer.

## FAX

To send or receive faxes in your dream means that you will receive a message that will prove very important in your career.

## FBI

To dream of dealing with the FBI warns you to watch what you say to people about your finances and your career; if you're not careful, what you say may be used against you.

## FDA

To dream of dealing with this government agency advises you to watch your health in the very near future.

## FEAR

To dream that you feel fear, from any cause, suggests that your future engagements will not prove as successful as you expect.

## FEAST

To dream of a feast foretells pleasant surprises planned for you. To see disorder or misconduct at a feast suggests quarrels or unhappiness through the negligence or sickness of some person.

Arriving late at a feast indicates that vexing affairs will occupy you.

## FEATHER

To dream of seeing feathers falling around you means your burdens in life will be light and easily borne.

To see eagle feathers indicates that your aspirations will be realized; but seeing chicken feathers leads to small annoyances. To dream of buying or selling goose or duck feathers speaks of thrift and fortune; black feathers, disappointments and unhappy amours.

## FEBRUARY

To dream of February suggests continued ill health and general gloom. If you happen to see a bright, sunshiny day in this month, you will be unexpectedly and happily surprised by some good fortune.

## FECES

To dream of bodily waste portends extremely good luck with money.

## FEE

To find you need to pay a fee for something in a dream means that you will receive money unexpectedly.

## FEEBLE

To dream of being feeble suggests unhealthful occupation and mental worry. Seek to make a change for yourself after this dream.

## FEEDING

To dream of feeding yourself, someone else, or animals implies that you will receive an unexpected invitation to a party or social affair.

## FEET

To dream of seeing your own feet forewarns of despair. You will be overcome by the will and temper of another.

To see others' feet indicates that you will maintain your rights in a pleasant but determined way and will win for yourself a place above the common walks of life.

To dream of washing your feet means that you will let others take advantage of you.

To dream that your feet are hurting you portends troubles of a humiliating character, as they usually are family quarrels.

If you see that your feet are swollen and red, you will make a sudden change in your business by separating from your family.

## FEMALE

For a male to dream that he is a female predicts career advancement.

## FENCE

To dream of climbing to the top of a fence predicts that success will crown your efforts.

To fall from a fence signifies that you will undertake a project for which you are unqualified and will see your efforts come to naught.

To be seated on a fence with others and have it fall under you denotes an accident in which some person will be badly injured.

To dream that you climb through a fence signifies that you may employ means that are not altogether legitimate to reach your desires.

To push a fence down and walk to the other side indicates that you will, by enterprise and energy, overcome the most stubborn barriers between yourself and success.

To see livestock jumping a fence *into* your enclosure means that you will receive aid from unexpected sources; if the animals are jumping *out* of your lot, loss in trade and other affairs may follow.

To dream of building a fence indicates that you are, by economy and industry, laying a foundation for future wealth.

## FENDER

To dream of having the fender of your car fall off means that a joyful time is coming.

To see a damaged fender in a dream indicates a happy time, but with a small problem attached to it.

Dreams of replacing the fender on your car foretell an unexpected vacation.

## FERN

To see ferns in dreams foretells that pleasant hours will break up gloomy forebodings.

If the ferns are withered, though, that indicates that varied illnesses of your family members will cause you grave unrest.

## FERRET

To dream of this weasel-like animal suggests that you have the ability to get out of a very tight spot in an upcoming situation.

## FERRIS WHEEL

To dream of being on a Ferris wheel and being afraid cautions you that a problem you've tried to put behind you requires another look. If you enjoy the ride in your dream, however, happy times are coming to your life.

## FERRY

If you dream of a ferry over waters swift and muddy, you will be baffled in your highest wishes by unforeseen circumstances.

To cross on the ferry while the water is calm and clear suggests that you will be very lucky in carrying out your plans, and fortune will crown you.

## FERTILIZER

To dream of applying—or even seeing—fertilizer tells you that good fortune, in the form of money, is coming your way.

## FESTERING SORE

To dream of a festering sore means that good health is yours.

## FESTIVAL

To dream of being at a festival suggests indifference to the cold realities of life and a love for those pleasures that make you old before your time. You will never want, but you'll be largely dependent on others.

## FEUD

To be caught up in an ongoing feud in a dream means you will find many trustworthy friends coming to your aid in times of trouble.

## FEVER*

To dream that you are stricken with fever signifies that you are worrying over trifling affairs while the best of life is slipping past you. Pull yourself into shape and engage in profitable work.

To dream of seeing some of your family sick with fever denotes temporary illness for them.

*See *Illness*.

## FIANCÉ

If you know that someone is your fiancé in a dream, even if you don't know who the person is in real life, beware of a divorce or broken relationship.

## FIBERGLASS

To dream of handling or working with this material predicts that a long-lost friend will soon appear.

## FIBER OPTICS

To work with fiber optics in a dream means that you will open career doors through communication.

## FIDDLE*

To dream of a fiddle foretells harmony in the home and many joyful occasions abroad.

*See *Violin*.

## FIELD*

To dream of dead corn or of stubbled fields indicates dreary prospects for the future.

Fields ripe with corn or grain denote great abundance and happiness to all classes.

To see newly plowed fields in a dream suggests early wealth and fortunate advancement to places of honor.

If you dream of fields freshly harrowed and ready for planting, you are soon to benefit from your long struggles for success.

*See *Cornfield, Land, Wheat*.

## FIEND

To dream of encountering a fiend forebodes reckless living and loose morals. For a woman, this dream signifies a blackened reputation.

To dream of a fiend warns you of attacks from false friends. If you overcome a fiend, you will be able to intercept the evil designs of enemies.

## FIESTA

To be part of this Mexican party in a dream is a sign that good times are coming soon in your love life.

## FIFE

To dream of hearing a fife predicts an unexpected call for you to defend your honor or that of some person near to you.

If you dream of playing a fife yourself, whatever else may be said of you, your reputation will remain intact.

## FIG

Dreaming of eating figs signifies an unhealthy condition of your body.

Seeing figs growing in a dream usually betokens health and profit.

## FIGHTING

To dream that you engage in a fight implies that you will have unpleasant encounters with your business opponents, and lawsuits will threaten you. To see fighting among others means you are squandering your time and money.

If you dream that you are defeated in a fight, you will lose your right to property. Whipping your assailant, on the other hand, indicates that you will, by courage and perseverance, win honor and wealth despite opposition.

To dream that you see two men fighting with pistols suggests many worries and perplexities. While no real loss is involved in the dream, only small profit is predicted, and some unpleasantness may be involved.

## FIGURES (NUMBERS)

To dream of figures indicates great mental distress and a wrong being committed. You will be the loser in a big deal if you're not careful in your actions and conversation.

## FILBERTS

To dream of seeing filberts is favorable, denoting a peaceful and harmonious domestic life and profitable business ventures.

To dream of eating filberts signifies, to the young, delightful associations and many true friends.

## FILES, FILING

To dream of seeing a file folder signifies that you will transact some business that will prove unsatisfactory in the extreme.

To see yourself filing bills and other important papers foretells animated discussions over significant matters, and these will cause you much unrest and disquiet. Unfavorable predictions for the future are also implied in this dream.

## FILIGREE

To see filigree on a piece of jewelry in your dream means you will soon find something that was lost long ago and had deep meaning in your life.

## FILLETING

If you dream of filleting meat or fish, you will soon be examining your future goals and choosing the ones that will work best for your financial gain.

## FILM

To handle film or to load film into a camera in a dream means you will soon experience something that will leave a lasting impression on your life.

## FILTH

To dream of living in filth suggests that you have a very clear head when it comes to your business matters. To clean away filth means you will soon win money.

## FIN

If you dream that your body has grown fins like a fish, you will change residence soon. To touch fins with another with fins suggests that someone will ask to live with you.

## FINCH

To dream of this little bird tells you that good friends and happy times lie ahead.

## FINGERNAILS

To dream of soiled fingernails forebodes disgrace in your family through the wild escapades of the young. Well-kept nails indicate scholarly tastes and some literary attainments, and also thrift.

## FINGERPRINTS

To see fingerprints in a dream indicates minor financial stress. If you are fingerprinted, or someone else is, you will soon receive help from a friend.

## FINGERS

To dream of seeing your fingers scratched and bleeding implies much trouble and suffering. You will despair of making your way through life.

Beautiful hands with clean fingers suggest that your love will be requited and that you will become renowned for your benevolence.

If you dream that your fingers are cut clean off, you will lose wealth and a legacy through the actions of enemies.

## FIRE

Dreaming of fire is favorable, unless you get burned. To dream of seeing your home burning suggests a loving companion and obedient children.

If business owners watch their stores burning in dreams, a great rush in business and profit can be expected. To dream that they are fighting the fire and do not get burned denotes that they will suffer many worries about business. Seeing the ruins of the business after a fire forebodes ill luck. Owners will be almost ready to give up the effort, but some unforeseen good fortune will bear them up again.

If you dream of kindling a fire, you may expect many pleasant surprises. You will have distant friends to visit.

### FIREBRAND

To dream of a firebrand suggests favorable fortune, if you are not burned or distressed by it.

### FIRE ENGINE

To see a fire engine denotes worry under extraordinary circumstances that will nevertheless result in good fortune. To see one broken down foretells accident or serious loss.

### FIRE ESCAPE

To climb down a fire escape in your dream means you will have an easy time with a work project. To climb up suggests a hard time with a work project.

### FIRE EXTINGUISHER

To use this to put out a fire in a dream means you will soon have to deal with an issue that cannot be avoided any longer.

### FIREFIGHTER

To see a firefighter in your dreams signifies the constancy of your friends.

### FIREFLY

To dream of these bugs foretells happy and joyous news.

### FIREWORKS

Dreaming of fireworks indicates enjoyment and good health.

### FIRMAMENT*

To dream of a firmament filled with stars denotes many trials and almost superhuman efforts before you reach the pinnacle of your ambition. Beware the snares of enemies in your work.

To see the firmament illuminated and filled with heavenly hosts denotes great spiritual research, but a final pulling back on nature for sustenance and consolation. You will also often be disappointed in fortune.

*See *Celestial signs, Heaven, Sky.*

## FIRST AID

A dream of giving or getting first aid indicates that you will be rewarded for your hard work in the future.

## FISH

To dream that you see fish in clear-water streams indicates that you will be favored by the rich and powerful. Dead fish signify the loss of wealth and power through some dire calamity.

To dream of catching a catfish suggests that you will be embarrassed by the evil designs of enemies, but your luck and presence of mind will tide you safely over.

To wade in water, catching fish, portends that you will acquire wealth through your own ability and enterprise.

To dream of fishing denotes energy and economy; but if you do not succeed in catching any, your efforts to obtain honor and wealth will be futile.

Eating fish speaks of warm and lasting attachments.

## FISHERMAN

If you dream of a fisherman, you are nearing times of greater prosperity than you have yet known.

## FISH HOOK

If you dream of fish hooks, you have opportunities to make for yourself a fortune and an honorable name.

## FISH MARKET

To visit a fish market in a dream brings competence and pleasure.

To see decayed fish in a market tells you that distress may come in the guise of happiness.

## FISHNET

To dream of a fishnet portends numerous small pleasures and gains, but a torn one represents vexatious disappointments.

## FISHPOND

To dream of a muddy fishpond denotes illness through dissipation. To see one clear and well stocked with fish portends profitable enterprises and extensive pleasures.

## FIST

To shake or clench your fist in a dream suggests satisfying events in personal and business matters.

## FITS

To dream of having fits indicates that you will fall prey to ill health and will lose your employment.

If you see others in this plight, you will experience much unpleasantness in your circle caused by quarrels from those under you.

## FLAG

To dream of your national flag portends victory if at war, prosperity if at peace.

To dream of foreign flags suggests ruptures and breaches of confidence between nations and friends.

If you dream of being signaled by a flag, be careful of your health and name, as both are threatened.

## FLAKES

Seeing any kind of flakes in a dream implies that you will be in an embarrassing situation that will take some doing to get out of.

## FLAMES*

To dream of fighting flames foretells that you will have to put forth your best efforts and energy if you are to succeed in amassing wealth.

*See *Fire.*

## FLAMINGO

A dream about this pink bird signals travel to new and exciting places.

## FLANNEL

To dream of this warm material means you will soon be hearing of a pregnancy or birth.

## FLASHLIGHT

To use a flashlight or to see its beam in your dream implies that you will soon make new friends.

## FLAX

In dreams, flax symbolizes prosperous enterprises.

To dream of flax spinning foretells that you will be given to industrious and thrifty habits.

## FLEAS

To dream of fleas indicates that you will be provoked to anger and retaliation by the evil machinations of those close to you.

## FLEET

If you see a large fleet of ships moving rapidly in your dreams, expect a hasty change in the business world.

## FLESH

To dream of healthy flesh suggests upcoming medical issues. To see rotting flesh in a dream signals monetary gain.

## FLIES

In dreams, flies represent sickness and contagious maladies. They also indicate that enemies surround you.

## FLIGHT, FLEEING

To dream of flight (fleeing) signifies disgrace and unpleasant news regarding those who are absent.

If you dream of seeing anything flee from you, you will be victorious in some contentious matter.

## FLIRTATION

To flirt, or to be flirted with, in a dream means you will have social success.

## FLOATING

To dream of floating indicates that you will overcome obstacles that seem overwhelming. But if the water you are floating in is muddy, your victories will not be gratifying.

## FLOOD*

To dream of floods destroying vast areas of the landscape and carrying you off with the muddy debris denotes sickness, loss in business, and a most unhappy and unsettled situation in marriage.

*See *Water*.

## FLOOR

To dream of cleaning or improving the looks of a floor foretells financial success. To sit or lie on a floor in a dream is good luck.

## FLORIST

If you are married, to dream of a florist portends trouble in your relationship. For the single, a new romance is on the way.

## FLOSSING

To dream of flossing your teeth warns you to be careful of what you say to others, for they may use it against you in the future.

## FLOUR

To dream of flour denotes a frugal but happy life.

## FLOWERS*

To dream of seeing flowers blooming in gardens signifies pleasure and gain, if they're bright-hued and fresh; white denotes sadness. Withered and dead flowers portend disappoint and gloom.

If you dream of flowers blooming in barren soil with no vestige of foliage, you will have some grievous experiences, but your energy and cheerfulness will enable you to climb through these to prominence and happiness.

*See *Bouquet*. See also individual flowers.

## FLUTE

To dream of hearing notes from a flute signifies a pleasant meeting with friends from far away, and profitable engagements.

## FLYING (ON YOUR OWN)

To dream of flying high over the earth denotes marital calamities. To fly low, almost to the ground, indicates sickness and uneasy states from which you will recover.

To fly over muddy water warns you to keep close with your private affairs, as enemies are watching to enthrall you.

To fly over broken places signifies ill luck and gloomy surroundings. If you notice green trees and vegetation below you, you will suffer temporary embarrassment followed by a flood of prosperity.

To dream of seeing the sun while you fly suggests useless worries, for you will succeed despite any fears of evil.

To dream of flying through the firmament, passing the moon and other planets, foretells famine, wars, and troubles of all kinds.

To fall while flying portends your downfall. If you wake during your fall, however, you will succeed in reinstating yourself.

## FLYPAPER

To dream of flypaper signifies ill health and disrupted friendships.

## FLYTRAP

To see a flytrap in a dream warns of malicious designs against you. If it's full of flies, small embarrassments will ward off greater ones.

## FOAL

To dream of a foal indicates new undertakings in which you will be rather fortunate.

## FOG

To dream of traveling through a dense fog suggests trouble and business worries. To emerge from the fog foretells a journey that's wearisome but profitable.

## FOGHORN

To hear a foghorn in your dream is a caution; perhaps your subconscious is warning you to be prepared for sudden change. To hear one continually suggests that you are experiencing extreme stress.

## FOLIAGE

To dream of new foliage hints at new romance. Decaying foliage suggests the ending of a relationship.

## FOOD

Eating fresh food in a dream is a sign of good luck. Dreaming of eating spoiled or rotting food warns you to expect setbacks in something you are planning.

Selling food in a dream means good monetary luck, while buying it signifies a happy family celebration on the horizon.

To just taste food means you may soon have a monetary loss.

## FOOLISHNESS

If you feel like a fool in a dream, it means you will soon have lots of fun with friends and family.

## FOOTBALL

To dream of playing signals monetary gain. Watching football advises you to watch who you make friends with.

## FOOTBRIDGE*

To dream of crossing a clear stream of water on a log or similar footbridge denotes pleasant employment and profit. If the water is thick and muddy, however, it indicates loss and temporary disturbance.

To fall from a footbridge into clear water suggests a short widowhood terminating in an agreeable marriage; but if the water is not clear, your prospects are gloomy.

*See Bridge.*

## FOOTPRINTS

To see a woman's footprints in your dream is a sign of success in new opportunities. A man's footprints warn you to be careful about what changes you make to your life right now. And a child's footprints foretell the end of worries over a situation or problem.

To see your own footprints in a dream means much success is on the way for you.

## FOREHEAD

To dream of a fine, smooth forehead indicates that you will be thought well of for your judgment and fair dealings. An ugly forehead hints at displeasure in your private affairs.

## FOREIGN PLACE, FOREIGNER

To dream of being someplace foreign means you will soon be able to fulfill a wish or dream.

To see a foreigner in a dream suggests good luck.

## FOREST

To dream of finding yourself in a dense forest denotes loss in trade, unhappy home influences, and quarrels among families. If you are cold and hungry, you will be forced to make a long journey to settle an unpleasant affair.

To see a forest of stately trees decked out in foliage denotes prosperity and pleasures.

## FORGERY

Be careful of new friendships if you see your name forged on a document in a dream. To forge a name yourself means unexpected money.

## FORK

To dream of a fork suggests that enemies are working for your displacement.

## FORMS, SHAPES

To dream of anything ill formed denotes disappointment. A beautiful form implies favorable conditions to health and business.

## FORSYTHIA

To dream of this shrub foretells peace and happiness coming into your life.

## FORT

To dream of defending a fort indicates that your honor and possessions will be attacked, causing you great worry.

To dream of capturing a fort denotes victory over your worst enemy, and fortunate engagements.

## FORTRESS

To dream that you are confined in a fortress suggests that enemies will succeed in placing you in an undesirable situation. To put others in a fortress denotes your ability to rule in business.

## FORTUNE

The greater the fortune you make in a dream, the smaller will be your financial success in waking life.

## FORTUNE-TELLING

To dream of a fortune-teller means you will need help with your indecision in a career or personal matter. If you dream of *being* a fortune-teller, you have good judgment.

## FOUNTAIN

To dream that you see a clear fountain sparkling in the sunlight denotes vast possessions, ecstatic delights, and many pleasant journeys. A clouded fountain suggests the insincerity of associates and unhappy engagements and love affairs. A dry and broken fountain indicates death and cessation of pleasures.

## FOWL*

To dream of seeing fowl suggests temporary worry or illness.

*See *Chickens.*

## FOX

To dream of chasing a fox implies that you are engaging in doubtful speculations and risky love affairs.

If you see a fox slyly coming into your yard, beware of envious friendships; your reputation is being slyly assailed.

Killing a fox indicates that you will win in every engagement.

## FRACTIONS

To dream of fractions reveals that someone close to you will annoy you and create disturbance in your life.

## FRAMING

To dream of framing something or seeing something framed betokens success in upcoming projects.

## FRAUD, DEFRAUDING

To dream that you are defrauding a person indicates that you will deceive your employer for gain, indulge in degrading pleasures, and fall into disrepute. If you are defrauded, it signifies the unsuccessful attempt of enemies to defame you and cause you loss.

If you accuse someone of defrauding you, you will be offered a place of high honor.

## FRECKLES

To dream that your face is freckled implies that many displeasing incidents will insinuate themselves into your happiness. If you see the freckles in a mirror, you may be in danger of losing your love to a rival.

## FREEDOM

To feel free in a dream reveals that you are happy and content with your partner. To long for freedom suggests that you'll soon be parting ways with your partner.

## FREIGHT

To dream of freight being handled or shipped, or seeing a freight train in a dream, suggests improvement and advancement at work.

## FRIENDS

To dream of friends being well and happy denotes pleasant tidings of them. You may soon see them or some of their relatives.

To see friends troubled and haggard means that sickness or distress is upon them.

If you dream that you are sorrowfully taking your departure from someone who has wronged you, you will have differences with a close friend; alienation will perhaps follow.

## FRIGHT

To dream that you are frightened of anything suggests temporary and fleeting worries.

## FROG

To dream of catching frogs implies carelessness in watching your health; this may cause distress in your family.

To see frogs in the grass indicates that you will have a pleasant and even-tempered friend as your confidant and counselor.

Seeing frogs in low, marshy places foretells trouble, but you will overcome it through the kindness of others.

To dream of eating frogs signifies fleeting joys and very little gain from associating with certain people.

Hearing frogs portends that you will go on a visit to friends, but it will in the end prove profitless.

## FROST

In dreams, seeing frost on a gloomy morning symbolizes exile to a strange country. Still, your wanderings will end in peace.

To see frost on a sunlit landscape suggests guilty pleasures from which you will be glad to turn away later in life. Your exemplary conduct will succeed in making your circle forget past escapades.

## FROWNING

To see a frown on yourself or someone else in a dream marks new and exciting friendships coming into your life.

## FROZEN FOOD

To eat or make frozen food in a dream suggests a pleasant time or an unexpected trip.

## FRUIT*

To dream of seeing fruit ripening on a tree with the foliage visible usually foretells a prosperous future. Green fruit signifies disappointed efforts or hasty action.

To buy or sell fruit denotes much business, but it's not very remunerative To see or eat ripe fruit signifies uncertain fortune and pleasure.

*See specific fruit.

## FRUIT SELLER

To dream of a fruit seller means that you will endeavor to recover a loss too rapidly and will engage in unfortunate speculation.

## FRUSTRATION

To be frustrated in a dream or to wake up frustrated means the coming of events that will be very pleasing and easy to accept.

### FRYING

To fry anything in a dream means your present love relationship will soon become unhappy.

### FUDGE

Eating, making, buying, or selling fudge in dreams represents taking your present love relationship for granted. If you do not learn to appreciate your partner, you may soon be alone.

### FUGITIVE

To dream of being a fugitive suggests trouble with your family. To dream of helping a fugitive means unexpected money problems.

### FUN

To have fun in a dream means that good times lie ahead. To be made fun of suggests problems with a business matter.

### FUNERAL

To see a funeral in your dream denotes an unhappy marriage and sickly offspring.

If this is the funeral of a stranger, it suggests unexpected worries. If it's your child's, it may denote health among your family, or it may suggest very grave disappointments from a friendly source. To dream of the funeral of any relative implies psychological or emotional issues and family worries.

To attend a funeral in black foretells an early widowhood.

### FUNGUS (MOLD)

To see fungus on anything in your dream warns you against being intimidated by your co-workers.

### FUNNEL

To dream of a funnel means you will soon experience confusion regarding an issue you thought you understood clearly.

### FUR

To dream of dealing in furs denotes prosperity and an interest in many concerns.

To be dressed in fur signifies your safety from want and poverty.

To see fine fur implies honor and riches. If a young woman dreams that she is wearing costly furs, she will marry a wise man.

## FURNACE

To dream of a working furnace foretells good luck. If it needs repair, you will have trouble with children or hired help.

To fall into one augurs that an enemy will overpower you in a business struggle.

## FURNITURE

To dream of broken furniture indicates love troubles; nice furniture, future happiness. To dream of buying furniture means an unexpected change you may not like. To sell furniture in a dream suggests a small financial problem in the future.

## FUSE (OR CIRCUIT BREAKER)

To change or fix a fuse or circuit breaker in your dream suggests that you'll waste energy on a project you never complete.

## FUTURE

To dream of the future suggests careful reckoning and avoidance of detrimental extravagance.

## GADGET

To dream of playing with or making some kind of gadget means you will be facing a decision about changing your job.

## GAG

To be gagged or to gag someone or something in your dream suggests that you'll soon be asked to help someone cover up a lie.

## GAIN

The greater the gain in your dream, the worse your finances will be in the near future. But if you were dishonest in your gain, the dream portends a successful business deal.

## GAITER

To dream of gaiters, whether you are wearing them or not, foretells pleasant amusements and rivalries.

## GALAXY

To dream you are traveling to, from, or through a galaxy foretells unexpected travel to a faraway, exotic place.

## GALE

To dream of being caught in a gale signifies business losses and trouble for working people.

## GALLERY

To dream of seeing an art gallery hung with artwork means new friends are coming into your life.

To look down from a balcony-type gallery in your dream suggests a good outcome to a current project. To fall from a gallery warns of an argument with a friend or loved one.

## GALLOWS

To dream of seeing a friend on the gallows warns you to meet desperate emergencies with decision, or a great calamity will befall you.

If you dream that *you* are on a gallows, you will suffer from the maliciousness of false friends. If you rescue anyone from the gallows, it portends desirable acquisitions.

To dream that you hang an enemy denotes victory in all spheres.

## GAMBLING

To dream that you are gambling and win suggests low associations and pleasure at the expense of others. If you lose, it foretells that your disgraceful conduct will be the undoing of someone near you.

## GAME*

To dream of killing game animals implies fortunate undertakings, but selfish emotions; failing to kill any game on a hunt denotes bad management and loss.

*See *Hunting*.

## GANG

To dream of being in a gang means that you are not taking a leadership role in your relationships.

Being afraid of or threatened by a gang in your dream suggests that you're in a time of depression that only you can overcome.

To dream of being beaten by a gang or one of its members warns of financial troubles that may embarrass you.

## GANGRENE

To dream that you see anyone afflicted with gangrene foretells the death of a parent or near relative.

## GARAGE

A dream of a public garage indicates changes in your business affairs. If the garage is empty, the dream warns of being cheated by someone you trust.

To dream of parking in your own garage refers to security in your business affairs.

## GARBAGE

To see heaps of garbage in your dream indicates thoughts of social scandal and unfavorable business of all kinds.

## GARDEN

To dream of a garden filled with evergreens and flowers denotes great peace of mind and comfort. Vegetables in a garden suggest misery or calumny and loss of fortune.

## GARDENIA

In dreams, the gardenia represents a new love affair or the rekindling of a past one.

## GARGLING

A dream about gargling suggests that changes in the offing will benefit you even if they seem problematic at the start.

## GARGOYLE

A dream of a gargoyle is a warning about being silly and being taken for a fool.

## GARLAND

To dream of wearing a garland of flowers predicts victory in a trying situation. Be careful if you are given a garland in your dream, however, because you will find that your friendships may be dishonest.

## GARLIC

To dream of passing through a garlic patch denotes a rise from penury to prominence and wealth. To eat garlic in your dreams implies that you take a sensible view of life and leave its ideals to take care of themselves.

## GARRET

To dream of climbing to a garret suggests that you tend to run after theories while leaving the cold realities of life to others less able to handle them than you are.

## GARTER

For a lover to find his lady's garter foretells that he will soon find rivals for her affections.

For a woman to dream that she loses her garter signifies that her lover will be jealous and suspicious of someone more handsome.

If a married man dreams of a garter, his wife may hear of his clandestine attachments and may fight with him over it.

For a woman to dream that she is admiring beautiful jeweled garters on her limbs suggests that she will be betrayed in her private moments, and her reputation will hang in the balance. If she dreams that her lover fastens them on her, she will hold his affection and faith through all criticism.

## GAS

To dream of gas implies that you entertain harmful opinions of others and deal with them unjustly, and then suffer consequent remorse.

To think you are asphyxiated in a dream indicates that you will incur trouble through your own wastefulness and negligence.

To try to blow gas out signifies that you will unwittingly entertain enemies who can destroy you.

To extinguish gas in your dream means that you will ruthlessly destroy your own happiness.

If you light it, you will easily find a way out of oppressive ill fortune.

## GAS LAMP

In dreams, a gas lamp represents progress and pleasant surroundings.

If you see one explode or otherwise fail to work, this dream foretells distress.

## GASOLINE

To dream of gasoline indicates that after a short struggle, there will be a successful completion of a task.

## GAS STATION

To dream of buying or selling gas warns that you will experience a period of slow business. To dream of buying anything other than gas at a gas station means some of your business associates will turn out to be dishonest. To dream of running out of gas implies that you will soon find creative ways to make money.

## GATE

To dream of seeing or passing through a gate warns that you'll soon receive alarming tidings about absent people. Business affairs will not be encouraging.

Dreaming of a closed gate portends an inability to overcome present difficulties. To lock one suggests successful enterprises and well-chosen friends. A broken one signifies failure and discordant surroundings.

To find opening or passing through a gate troublesome implies that your most engrossing labors will fail to be remunerative or satisfactory.

To swing on one foretells that you will engage in idle and dissolute pleasures.

## GATHERING

To gather items in your dreams means you will find much satisfaction in your life.

To be at a gathering of people predicts pleasant family relationships in the near future.

## GAUZE

To dream of being dressed in gauze denotes uncertain fortune.

## GAVEL

If you dream of a gavel, you will be burdened with an unprofitable yet not unpleasant pursuit. To use one suggests that you are displaying officiousness toward your friends.

## GAZEBO

To dream of a gazebo, no matter what the weather, speaks of security in your life.

## GEARSHIFT

To dream of yourself or someone else shifting gears in a vehicle foretells changes coming to your love life, either good or bad.

## GEESE*

To dream that you are annoyed by the quacking of geese denotes a death in your family. To see them swimming means your fortune is gradually increasing.

To see them in grassy places assures success. If you see them dead, you will suffer loss and displeasure. If you are picking them up, you will come into an inheritance.

To eat them suggests that your possessions are disputed.

To dream of one goose warns you to watch your health and perhaps schedule a checkup. If the goose is flying or swimming, you will experience an unexpected trip and much social happiness.

*See *Animals*.

## GEISHA

To be a geisha in your dream means you will be honored for your integrity. If you see a geisha in a dream, you will need to prove your integrity in a sticky situation.

## GELATIN

To make or eat gelatin in your dream foretells the fast coming and going of happiness.

## GEMS*

To dream of gems foretells a happy fate in both love and business affairs.

*See *Jewelry*.

## GENEALOGY, FAMILY TREE

To dream of your genealogical tree suggests that you will be burdened with family cares or will find pleasure in domains other than your own.

If you see others studying your family tree, you may be forced to yield your rights to others. If any of the branches are missing, you will ignore some of your friends because of their straitened circumstances.

## GENIE

To dream of a genie foretells the unexpected granting of a big wish.

## GENITALS

To dream of healthy genitals, either male or female, means a good love life is in the future. If the genitals in your dream are diseased or deformed, however, the dream is warning that you are being too forward and possibly promiscuous in your sex life.

If someone exposes their genitals to you in a dream, you may be in need of counseling for your sex life in your waking life.

## GEOGRAPHY*

To dream of studying geography suggests that you will travel much and visit places of renown.

*See *Atlas*.

## GERANIUM

To see this flower in your dream predicts unexpected wealth. To smell it increases that fortune.

## GERMS

To see, be aware of, or worry about germs in a dream foretells the renewal of energy and vitality in your life.

## GEYSER

To dream of a geyser suggests that your life will be taking some twists and turns, but you will find happiness in the end.

## GHETTO

A dream featuring a ghetto means you will have to tighten your money belt and start to save for a rainy day.

## GHOST*

To dream of a ghost is normally good news, unless it frightens you or makes you uncomfortable. In that case, you should see a medical doctor for a checkup.

*See *Death, Dead*.

## GHOUL

Ghouls in a dream represent coming disappointments.

## GIANT

To dream of a giant appearing suddenly before you suggests a great struggle between you and your opponents. If the giant succeeds in stopping your journey, you will be overcome by your enemies.

If the giant runs from you, prosperity and good health will be yours.

## GIFT

To dream that you receive gifts tells you that you will not fall behind in payments, and you'll be unusually fortunate in speculations or love matters.

To send a gift portends that displeasure will be shown to you, and ill luck will surround your efforts.

## GIG*

If you run a gig (a one-horse carriage) in your dream, you will have to forgo a pleasant journey to entertain unwelcome visitors. Sickness also threatens you.

*See *Cart*.

## GIGGLING

To find yourself giggling in a dream warns of troubled finances. To see others giggle tells you that a fun social life is in your near future.

## GIGOLO

To see yourself as a gigolo is a dream of good fortune, but you will have to pay a price for it. To be taken in by a gigolo in your dream, on the other hand, is a sign of good fortune that comes with no price attached.

## GILDING

If you dream of yourself gilding something, you will have a stroke of monetary luck. To dream of seeing gilding on something suggests that your luck is changing for the better.

## GINGERBREAD

To dream of making or eating this dessert predicts a very happy love life.

## GINGHAM*

To dream of wearing, sewing, seeing, or just touching this fabric foretells a time coming in your life when you will have to turn away from the past in order to move forward.

*See *Fabric.* See also specific fabric.

## GIRAFFE

To dream of this long-necked animal means you need to mind your own business and keep out of other people's affairs.

## GIRDLE

If you dream of wearing a tight girdle, you will be influenced by designing people.

To see others wearing velvet or jeweled girdles foretells that you will strive for wealth more than honor.

## GIRL

To dream of seeing a healthy-looking girl predicts pleasing prospects and domestic joy. If she is thin and pale, you will have sickness in your family.

## GLADIOLUS*

To dream of this flower means you will soon be very busy in your social life.

*See *Flower.* See also specific flowers.

## GLASS*

To dream of looking through glass suggests that bitter disappointments will cloud your brightest hopes.

To break glass dishes or windows foretells the unfavorable termination of enterprises.

To receive a gift of cut glass suggests that you will be admired for your brilliance and talent. To be the giver of cut-glass ornaments signifies that you will fail in your undertakings.

If you dream of seeing clearly through a glass window, you will have employment but will have to work as a subordinate. If the glass is clouded, you will be situated badly.

*See *Looking glass, Mirror, Pane of glass.*

## GLASSBLOWER

If you dream that you see glassblowers at work, you will contemplate business changes that seem to be for the better but will involve a loss to yourself.

## GLASS HOUSE

To see a glass house foretells that you are likely to be injured by listening to flattery.

## GLIDER

To dream of flying through the air in a glider predicts an upcoming business proposition. Make sure you know all the facts before you act on it.

## GLOBE

In dreams, a globe represents new interests and adventures.

## GLOOM*

To be surrounded by gloomy situations in a dream warns you of rapidly approaching unpleasantness and loss.

*See *Despair.*

## GLOVES

To dream of wearing new gloves suggests that you will be cautious and economical in your dealings with others, but not mercenary. You will experience lawsuits or business troubles, but will settle them satisfactorily to yourself. Wearing old or ragged gloves predicts that you will be betrayed and will suffer loss. If you dream of losing your gloves, you will be deserted and will need to support yourself.

Finding a pair of gloves in your dream denotes a marriage or new love affair. If you pull your gloves off, you will meet with poor success in business or love.

## GLOWING

To see anything glowing in your dream means good changes to your life.

## GLUE

In general, glue symbolizes money investments in your dreams. To get glue on yourself or your clothing in a dream implies that you have very loyal friends. Gluing something together suggests advancement and recognition in your professional life.

## GOAL

For yourself or someone else to score a goal in a dream means that new friends and new opportunities are coming.

## GOAT*

To dream of goats wandering around a farm signifies seasonable weather and a fine yield of crops. To see them otherwise speaks of cautious dealings and a steady increase of wealth. If a billy goat butts you, be wary lest enemies get possession of your secrets or business plans.

*See *Animals*.

## GOATEE

If you dream of seeing a goatee on yourself or someone else, be careful not to take chances with your health.

## GOBLET

If you dream of drinking water from a silver goblet, you will meet unfavorable business results in the near future.

To see goblets of ancient design suggests that you will receive favors and benefits from strangers.

## GOD

If you dream of God, you will achieve rare contentment, peace of mind, and abundant blessings.

## GOGGLES

To dream of goggles warns you of disreputable companions who will wheedle you into lending your money foolishly.

## GOLD

If you handle gold in a dream, you will be unusually successful in all enterprises.

To find gold indicates that your superior abilities will place you easily ahead in the race for honors and wealth. If you lose gold, you will miss the grandest opportunity of your life through negligence.

To dream of finding a gold vein indicates that some uneasy honor will be thrust upon you. If you dream that you contemplate working a gold mine, you will endeavor to usurp the rights of others, and you should beware of domestic scandals.

To dream of the color gold indicates good fortune and wealth, as well as loyalty among friends.

### GOLDFISH

To dream of goldfish foretells many successful and pleasant adventures.

### GOLD LEAVES

To dream of gold leaves signifies a bright future.

### GOLF

To be playing or watching golf suggests indulging yourself in pleasant daydreams.

If you dream of any unpleasantness connected with golf, however, you will be humiliated by a thoughtless person.

### GONDOLA

To dream of a romantic gondola ride means you are in need of a change in your love life. A vacation may help you rekindle romance with your partner.

### GONG

In dreams, the sound of a gong represents a false alarm of illness, or a vexing loss.

### GOOSEBERRIES

To dream of gathering gooseberries is a sign of happiness after trouble, and a favorable indication of brighter prospects in business affairs. If you are eating green gooseberries, you will make a mistake along your route to pleasure and will be catapulted into the vortex of sensationalism. Bad results are sure to follow the tasting of green gooseberries.

To merely see gooseberries in a dream foretells that you will escape some dreaded work.

### GOOSEBUMPS

Having goosebumps in a dream warns you to show gratitude to your friends before you lose them.

### GORILLA

If a gorilla in your dream frightens you, you are being warned about a painful misunderstanding coming in a relationship. If the gorilla is calm and friendly, you will be making new friends soon.

## GOSSIP

To dream of being interested in gossip suggests humiliating trouble caused by overconfidence in transient friendships. If you are the subject of gossip, expect a pleasurable surprise.

## GOURD

Dreaming of a gourd signals that happy relationships will abound.

## GOUT

If you dream of having gout, you are sure to be exasperated beyond endurance by the silly conduct of a relative, and you may suffer a small financial loss through the same person.

## GOVERNMENT

To dream of being involved in government predicts a period of uncertainty in your life.

## GRACE

To dream of saying or hearing this type of prayer means you will soon receive an unexpected gift.

## GRADUATION

To dream of a graduation in any form implies a rise in business or social status.

## GRAIN

Grain makes for a most fortunate dream, betokening wealth and happiness.

## GRAMMAR

To dream that you are studying grammar implies that you are soon to make a wise choice among momentous opportunities.

## GRAMOPHONE, PHONOGRAPH

To dream of hearing an old-fashioned gramophone foretells the appearance of a new and pleasing comrade who will lend himself willingly to advance your enjoyment. If the gramophone is broken, some fateful occurrence will thwart and defeat any delights that you hold in anticipation.

## GRANDPARENTS

If you dream of meeting your grandparents and conversing with them, you will meet with difficulties that will be hard to surmount. Following good advice will allow you to overcome many obstacles.

# GRAPES

If you eat grapes in a dream, you will be burdened with many cares; but if you see them hanging in profusion among the leaves, you will soon attain an eminent position and be able to impart happiness to others.

# GRASS

This is a very propitious dream indeed. It promises a happy life to the tradesman, rapid accumulation of wealth, fame to literary and artistic people, and a safe voyage through the turbulent sea of love.

To see a rugged mountain beyond a green expanse of grass signifies trouble in the future. If, in passing through green grass, you pass withered places, expect sickness or embarrassment in business.

To be a perfect dream, the grass must be clear of obstruction or blemishes. If you dream of withered grass, the reverse is predicted.

# GRASSHOPPER

To dream of seeing grasshoppers on green vegetables suggests that enemies threaten your best interests. If you see them on withered grasses, you face ill health and disappointing business.

# GRAVEL

In dreams, gravel represents fruitless schemes and enterprises. If you see gravel mixed with dirt, you will speculate poorly and lose good property.

# GRAVES

Dreaming of graves is unfortunate. Ill luck in business transactions will follow, and sickness is threatened.

If you dream of seeing a newly dug grave, you will have to suffer for the wrongdoings of others. Visiting a new grave reveals that danger of a serious nature is hanging over you.

To dream of walking on graves predicts an early death or unfortunate marriage. Looking into an empty one denotes disappointment and loss of friends. If you see a live person in a grave covered by earth except for the head, some distressing situation will take hold of that person; you yourself may experience a loss of property.

To see your own grave suggests that enemies are warily seeking to engulf you in disaster; if you are not watchful, they will succeed.

To dream of digging a grave speaks of uneasiness over some venture, as enemies will seek to thwart you, but if you finish the grave you will overcome opposition. If the sun is shining, good will come out of seeming embarrassments. If you return to bury a corpse and it has disappeared, trouble will come to you from obscure quarters.

To see a graveyard barren except for the tops of the graves signifies a season of much sorrow and despondency. Still, greater benefits and pleasure await you if you properly shoulder your burden.

To see your own corpse in a grave foreshadows hopelessness and oppression.

### GRAVESTONE

To dream of a gravestone predicts a pregnancy or birth. To dream that you see your name on it predicts much happiness coming through a family celebration.

### GRAVY

To dream of eating gravy portends failing health and disappointing business.

### GREASE

To dream of grease suggests travels in the company of disagreeable but polished strangers.

### GREEK LANGUAGE

To dream of reading Greek indicates that your ideas will be discussed and finally accepted and put into practical use. If you try to read Greek but can't, technical difficulties lie in your way.

### GREEN

To dream of this color indicates monetary flow, as well as mental and physical healing.

### GREENHOUSE

To dream of seeing or being in a greenhouse suggests that much love, success, and happiness will come to you soon.

### GREYHOUND*

A greyhound is a fortunate animal to see in your dream. If you own this dog, it signifies friends where enemies were expected.

*See Animals.

### GRILLING

If you dream of grilling food, you should not bother friends right now with your problems.

## GRILLWORK

To dream of a decorative grillwork warns you to be careful in affairs of the heart.

## GRINDSTONE

Turning a grindstone in your dream prophesies a life of energy and well-directed efforts bringing handsome rewards. If you are using the grindstone to sharpen tools, you will be blessed with a worthy helpmate.

Dreaming of being a grindstone dealer signifies small but honest gain.

## GRITS

To dream of eating or making grits predicts that someone from your past will be in contact with you soon.

## GROANING

If you hear groans in your dream, decide quickly on your course, for enemies are undermining your business. If you are the one groaning with fear, you will be pleasantly surprised at a turn for better in your affairs, and you may look for pleasant visiting among friends.

## GROCERIES

To dream of groceries, if they are fresh and clean, is a sign of ease and comfort.

## GROOMING

To dream of an animal being groomed suggests that you will soon be dealing with legal issues.

## GROTTO

To see a grotto in your dreams implies incomplete and inconstant friendships.

## GROUND

If you dream you are lying on the ground, it is a warning to watch your back with so-called friends.

## GROWTH

To dream of things growing implies advancement, either at work or in a relationship.

## GUARDIAN

To dream of a guardian means that you will be treated with consideration by your friends.

## GUARDING

To dream of someone or something being guarded warns you that you might soon be the victim of a theft. To be guarded by someone else suggests financial gain.

## GUESSING

If you find yourself guessing in a dream, it suggests that you will find a solution to a troubling situation. If someone else is doing the guessing, beware of false friendships.

## GUEST

To dream of being a guest means you will soon suffer a falling-out in a friendship. To dream that you have guests at your home predicts a renewal of friendships.

## GUILLOTINE

Dreaming of a guillotine is a warning to watch what you say before you lose a valued friendship.

## GUILT

To dream of others being guilty means that some of your friends are untrustworthy. Be careful. To dream of feeling guilty predicts renewed friendships.

## GUITAR

Dreaming of a guitar signifies a merry gathering. If you play it, your family life will be harmonious.

## GULLS

To dream of gulls prophesies peaceful dealings with ungenerous people. Seeing dead gulls suggests separation from friends.

## GUM-CHEWING

To chew gum in a dream cautions you against telling new friends too much about your life.

## GUMS

To dream of healthy gums suggests that good relationships abound in your life. If they are unhealthy, a problem may be coming in your relationships.

## GUN

This is a dream of distress. Hearing the sound of a gun denotes loss of employment; to proprietors of establishments, bad management. If you shoot anyone with a gun, you will fall into dishonor. If you are shot, you will be annoyed by evil people and perhaps suffer an acute illness.

## GUTTER

In dreams, a gutter symbolizes degradation. You will be the cause of unhappiness to others.

If you dream of finding articles of value in a gutter, your right to certain property will be questioned.

## GYMNASIUM

If you dream you are in a gymnasium, you will suffer an embarrassing situation in the near future.

## GYMNAST

To dream of a gymnast suggests that you will suffer misfortune in speculation or trade.

## GYPSY

In dreams, a gypsy represents good luck and financial gain.

## HABIT

If you dream of having a bad habit, you will be coming into a difficult time socially.

To dream you are wearing a riding or a religious habit counsels you to be firm in the breakup of a relationship.

## HAGGARDNESS

To see a haggard face in your dreams suggests misfortune and defeat in love matters.

To see your own face haggard and distressed denotes trouble over love affairs, which may render you unable to meet business engagements in a healthy manner.

## HAIL

If you dream of being in a hailstorm, you will meet poor success in any undertaking. If you watch hailstones fall through sunshine and rain, you will be harassed by cares for a time, but fortune will soon smile upon you. To hear hail beating the house indicates distressing situations.

## HAIR

To see your hair turning gray foretells death and contagion in the family of some relative or friend.

To see yourself covered with hair is an omen of indulgence in vices to an extent that will disbar you from the society of refined people. If you see well-kept and neatly combed hair, your fortune will improve.

To dream you've cut your hair close to the scalp indicates that you will be generous to the point of lavishness toward a friend.

To see hair growing out soft and luxuriant signifies happiness and luxury. If you see tangled and unkempt hair, life will be a veritable burden, business will fall off, and the marital yoke will be troublesome to carry.

To dream of having your hair cut suggests serious disappointments.

If you dream that your hair is falling out and baldness is apparent, you will suffer financial loss.

To dream that a lock of your hair turns gray and falls out is a sign of trouble and disappointment in your affairs. Sickness will cast gloom over bright expectations.

To dream that you are washing your hair means your troubles will soon go down the drain.

## HAIRDRESSER

Should you visit a hairdresser in your dream, this is a warning against repeating gossip. Mind your own business.

## HAIRPIN

To dream of a hairpin predicts good fortune in the near future.

## HAIRY HANDS

To dream that your hands are covered with hair like that of a beast signifies that you will create intrigue against innocent people. Alert enemies are working to forestall your designs.

## HALL

To dream of walking down a hallway means small annoyances on the horizon in business matters.

To dream of being in a concert hall suggests a delay in business that you must act on quickly.

## HALLOWEEN

In dreams, this holiday represents recognition in community affairs.

## HALLUCINATION

If your dream involves a hallucination, a friend will call upon you for help—but he or she may not be entirely truthful about the difficulties. Try not to get involved personally.

## HALO

To dream of someone else wearing a halo is sad news. To dream of yourself with a halo predicts blessing and travel. A halo of light seen around an object in your dream means that you will be praised for your accomplishments.

## HALTER

To dream that you put a halter on a young horse means that you will manage a very prosperous and clean business. Love matters will shape themselves to suit you.

To see other things haltered indicates that fortune will be withheld from you for a while. You will win it, but with much toil.

## HAM

To dream of a ham suggests that you are in danger of being treacherously used. Cutting large slices of ham means that you'll successfully meet all opposition.

To dress a ham signifies that you will be leniently treated by others.

If you dream of dealing in hams, prosperity will come to you. Also good health is prophesied.

If you eat ham, you will lose something of great value.

If you smell ham cooking, you will be benefited by the enterprises of others.

## HAMBURGER

To dream of eating or making a burger means that abundance and happiness are on the way in your home.

## HAMMER

If you dream of seeing a hammer, you will have some discouraging obstacles to overcome in order to firmly establish your fortune.

## HAMMOCK

An empty hammock in your dream means that loss is on the horizon.

If you are in a hammock, be careful not to be self-centered in your waking life.

To be in a hammock with someone of the opposite sex suggests that a good social life is unfolding around you.

If you fall out of a hammock, you are taking your friends for granted.

## HAMPER

To dream of an empty laundry hamper foreshadows emotional upset. A full hamper indicates happy news.

## HAMSTER*

To dream of this creature means that you are entering an abundant period in your life. If you see it running around the wheel in its cage, repeated good fortune is coming.

*See Animals.

## HAND*

If you see beautiful hands in your dream, you will enjoy great distinction and rise rapidly in your calling; but ugly and malformed hands point to disappointments and poverty.

To see blood on hands denotes estrangement and unjust censure from members of your family. If you have an injured hand, some other person will succeed in what you are striving most to obtain.

A detached hand indicates a solitary life; people will fail to understand your views and feelings.

If you burn your hands, you will overreach the bounds of reason in your struggle for wealth and fame and you will lose.

To see your hands covered with hair suggests that you will not become a solid and leading member of your circle.

To see your hands enlarged implies quick advancement. If you see them smaller, the reverse is predicted.

To see your hands soiled indicates that you will be envious and unjust. Washing your hands foretells participation in some joyous festivity.

To dream that your hands are tied indicates that you will be involved in difficulties. In loosening them, you will force others to submit to your dictates.

*See Fingers.*

## HANDBAG

For a woman to dream of an empty handbag foretells monetary luck in the near future. For a man to dream this suggests the coming of a big purchase. A full handbag warns you to watch your money speculation.

To dream that you can't find something in your handbag means a lost object will soon be found.

## HANDBALL*

To dream of watching or playing handball means you will have competition in your career advancement.

*See Racquetball.*

## HANDBILL

To dream of distributing handbills portends contentiousness and possible lawsuits. If you dream of printing handbills, you will hear unfavorable news.

## HANDCUFFS

Finding yourself handcuffed in your dreams means that you will be annoyed and vexed by enemies. You may also be menaced with sickness and danger.

To see others thus means that you will subdue those oppressing you and rise above your associates.

To dream of handcuffs suggests that formidable enemies are surrounding you with objectionable conditions. To break the handcuffs is a sign that you will escape toils planned by enemies.

## HAND GRENADE

To dream of throwing a hand grenade means you will be the center of social embarrassment.

## HANDICAP

To dream of being handicapped indicates good health. To dream of seeing someone else handicapped warns you to see your doctor soon. Helping a handicapped person—or being helped if you are handicapped—suggests that dealing with a health issue will have an excellent outcome.

## HANDKERCHIEF

In dreams, handkerchiefs represent flirtations and affairs. To lose one suggests a broken engagement through no fault of your own. Seeing torn handkerchiefs foretells that lovers' quarrels will reach such straits that reconciliation will be improbable, if not impossible. Soiled handkerchiefs suggest that you will be corrupted by indiscriminate associations.

## HAND-ME-DOWNS

To dream of having hand-me-down clothing predicts that amazing good fortune is on the horizon.

## HANDSHAKE

To dream of offering or receiving a handshake tells you that loyalty and honor exist among your friends.

## HANDSOMENESS

If you see yourself looking handsome in your dreams, you will prove an ingenious flatterer.

To see others so appearing indicates that you will enjoy the confidence of jet-setters.

## HANDWRITING

To dream that you see and recognize your own handwriting foretells that malicious enemies will use your expressed opinion to foil you in advancing to some contested position.

## HANDYMAN

To dream of being a handyman means you will soon encounter a problem that will be very hard to fix. If you dream of hiring a handyman, a strong and clear solution is waiting in the wings.

## HANGER

Dreaming of putting anything on a hanger means that you will soon be carefree.

## HANG GLIDER

To dream of being in a hang glider suggests you will be worry-free in your business dealings.

## HANGING*

To see a large group of people gathering for a hanging suggests that many enemies will band together to try to demolish your position.
*See *Execution*.

## HANGOVER

To dream that you are experiencing a hangover, if you are single, warns against being morally loose and promiscuous. For a married person to dream of being hungover implies a release from familial problems.

## HANUKKAH

To be a Gentile and dream of celebrating Hanukkah foretells many financial blessings.

## HAPPY HOUR

Dreaming of happy hour warns you that something in your life will bring you sadness.

## HARBOR

To dream of coming into a harbor suggests future financial security. To dream of leaving a harbor is a warning about friendships.

## HARDWARE

To dream of tools and other things one buys in hardware stores predicts good luck in the future.

## HARE*

If you see a hare escaping from you in a dream, you will lose something valuable in a mysterious way. If you capture a hare, you will be the victor in a contest. If you make pets of hares, you will have an orderly but unintelligent companion. A dead hare betokens death to some friend; existence will be a commonplace, prosaic affair.

To see hares chased by dogs suggests trouble and contentiousness among your friends, and you will attempt to bring about friendly relations. If you dream that you shoot a hare, you will be forced to use violent measures to maintain your rightful possessions.

*See *Rabbit*.

## HARELIP

If you dream of a having a harelip, be careful deciding whether or not to share secrets with your friends. To dream of seeing someone else with a harelip foretells a new friendship coming into your life.

## HAREM

To dream that you maintain a harem indicates that you are wasting your best energies on low pleasures. Life holds fair promise if your desires are rightly directed.

If a woman dreams that she is in a harem, she will seek pleasure where pleasure is unlawful, as her desires will be toward married men as a rule. If she dreams that she is a favorite, she will be preferred before others in material pleasures, but the distinction will be fleeting.

## HARLEQUIN

If you dream of a harlequin, trouble will beset you.

To be dressed as a harlequin suggest passionate error and unwise attacks on strength and purse.

## HARMONICA

Dreaming of this instrument, whether playing it or just hearing it, predicts an invitation to a party.

## HARNESS

If you dream of possessing a bright new harness, you will soon prepare for a pleasant journey.

## HARP

To hear the sad, sweet strains of a harp foretells the sad ending to what seems a pleasing and profitable enterprise.

To see a broken harp betokens illness or broken troth between lovers.

To play a harp yourself signifies that your nature is too trusting and you should be more careful in giving your confidence and love.

## HARPOON

To dream of harpooning a large fish or a whale predicts an increase in income. To be injured by a harpoon warns that you need to watch your credit.

## HARVEST

To dream of harvest time is a forerunner of prosperity and pleasure. If the harvest yields are abundant, the indications are good for country and state, as political machinery will grind to advance all conditions. A poor harvest is a sign of small profits.

## HASH

To dream you are eating hash, many sorrows and vexations are foretold. You will probably be troubled with various little jealousies and contentions over mere trifles, and your health will be menaced through worry.

## HASHISH

Dreaming of smoking or buying hashish foretells a pleasant experience at making new friends in the near future. To sell hashish warns of future legal problems.

## HASSOCK

To dream of a hassock forebodes the yielding of your power and fortune to another.

## HAT

If you dream of losing your hat, you may expect unsatisfactory business and the failure of others to keep important engagements.

For a man to dream that he wears a new hat predicts change of place and business, which will be very much to his advantage. For a woman this denotes the attainment of wealth; she will be the object of much admiration.

To see the wind blow your hat off in a dream suggests sudden changes in affairs, somewhat for the worse.

## HATBOX

Dreaming of a hatbox indicates a pleasant surprise coming into your life.

## HATCH

To find yourself going through a hatch in your dream marks the beginning of an unexpected adventure coming your way.

## HATCHET

A hatchet, seen in a dream, implies that wanton wastefulness will expose you to the evil designs of envious persons. If it is rusty or broken, you will come to grief over wayward people.

## HATCHING

To dream of watching a chick hatch from an egg foretells a pregnancy or birth announcement.

## HATRED

To dream that you hate someone suggests that if you are not careful, you will cause this person an inadvertent injury; or that a spiteful action will bring business loss and worry. If you are hated for unjust causes, you will find sincere and obliging friends, and your associations will be most pleasant. Otherwise, the dream forebodes ill.

## HAUNTING

To be haunted by a ghost in your dream foretells an unexpected gift. To find yourself in a haunted house or building suggests an unexpected move.

## HAWK

To dream of a hawk foretells good prospects in personal and business life.

## HAY

If you dream of mowing hay, you will find much good in life. If you are a farmer, your crops will yield abundantly.

To see fields of newly cut hay is a sign of unusual prosperity. If you are hauling hay and putting it into barns, your fortune is assured, and you will realize great profit from some enterprise.

If you see loads of hay passing through the street, you will meet influential strangers who will add much to your pleasure.

To feed hay to stock indicates that you will offer aid to someone who will return the favor with love and advancement.

## HAY FEVER

To dream of having this allergy indicates that mental clarity is coming your way.

## HDTV

Dreaming of watching a program in HDTV means you will find yourself balanced in your emotional life.

## HEAD

If you see a person's head in your dream, and it is well shaped and prominent, you will meet people of power and vast influence who will lend you aid in enterprises of importance.

If you dream of your own head, you are threatened with nerve or brain trouble.

If you see a head severed from its trunk, and the head is bloody, you will meet sickening disappointments and the overthrow of your dearest hopes and anticipations.

To see yourself with two or more heads foretells phenomenal and rapid rise in life, but the probabilities are that the rise will not be stable.

To dream that your head is aching indicates that you will be oppressed with worry. It also indicates that you need to see a doctor.

A swollen head suggests that you will have more good than bad in your life.

To dream of the head of a beast implies that the nature of your desires will run on a low plane; only material pleasures will concern you.

If you wash your head, you will be sought after by prominent people for your judgment and good counsel.

## HEADACHE

To dream of having a headache indicates that you need to see a doctor.

## HEADGEAR

If you dream of seeing rich headgear, you will become famous and successful. If the headgear is old and worn, you will have to yield up your possessions to others.

## HEADLIGHTS

To dream you are blinded by headlights foretells recognition for an upcoming project.

## HEADLINE

To dream of your name in a headline predicts social embarrassment. To see someone else's name in a headline predicts social embarrassment for someone else.

## HEADPHONES

To dream of wearing headphones means you will soon be told a secret that will shock you.

## HEALER

To dream of going to a healer suggests that you are in good health.

## HEARSE

To dream of a hearse means a lightening of your burdens and worries. If you ride with the driver or are the driver, an increase in responsibilities is foretold. If you are inside the hearse, an upcoming change will be important for your future.

## HEART

If you dream of your heart hurting and suffocating you, there will be trouble in your business. Some mistake of your own will bring loss if not corrected. Seeing your own heart foretells sickness and failure of energy.

If you see the heart of an animal, you will overcome enemies and merit the respect of all.

## HEART ATTACK

To dream of having a heart attack means happiness in a love affair in the near future. If you see someone else having a heart attack, expect a rocky love affair.

## HEARTBURN

To dream of having heartburn predicts heartache on the horizon.

## HEARTH

To dream of a hearth means a happy home life. If you dream of cooking on an open hearth, you will be nurturing your friendships.

## HEAT

To dream that you are oppressed by heat denotes a failure to carry out designs on account of a friend betraying you. Heat is not a very favorable dream.

## HEATER

To dream of a heater suggests that financial gain is on the horizon.

## HEATSTROKE

Dreaming of having heatstroke predicts the coming of a storm that may cause you material ruin.

## HEAT WAVE

To dream of a heat wave indicates that a financial problem is on the horizon due to a mechanical problem or breakdown out of your control.

## HEATHEN

To dream of being a heathen foretells a spiritual awakening.

## HEATHER

To dream of heather foretells joyous occasions in happy succession.

## HEAVEN

To dream of heaven predicts colossal change that will prove to be a blessing even though you may not think so at the time.

## HEDGEHOG

To dream of this little animal means you may have to make a choice against what you believe in.

## HEDGES

In dreams, evergreen hedges symbolize joy and profit. Bare hedges suggest distress and unwise dealings.

If you dream of being entangled in a thorny hedge, you will be hampered in your business by unruly partners or people working under you.

## HEEL

Dreaming of the heel of a foot—particularly if it feels uncomfortable or painful—warns against dishonest associates or family members in your life. To break a heel off your shoe predicts a broken relationship.

## HEIGHT

To dream of being taller than you are signals that your problems are not as bad as they appear to you. To dream of being smaller foretells a social embarrassment that will make you feel small.

To dream of being at a scary height above the ground means security in your love relationships.

## HEIR

To dream that you inherit property or valuables indicates that you are in danger of losing what you already possess and warns of coming responsibilities. Pleasant surprises may also follow this dream.

## HEIRLOOM

To dream of an heirloom suggests personal recognition in your social circle or with your business associates.

## HELICOPTER

To dream of being in or flying a helicopter means that you will have to make choices regarding your career.

## HELIUM

To dream of this gas betokens good business investments in the future.

## HELL

If you dream of being in hell, you will fall into temptation that will almost wreck you financially and morally.

To see your friends in hell indicates distress and burdensome cares. You will hear of the misfortune of a friend.

To dream of crying in hell suggests that friends are powerless to extricate you from the snares of enemies.

## HELMET

To dream of seeing a helmet counsels you that threatened misery and loss can be avoided by wise action.

## HEM

Dreaming of repairing a hem on a garment means that you will be satisfied with the outcome of a business project.

## HEMORRHAGING

For yourself or someone else to hemorrhage in your dream warns you that you need more relaxation in your life; do not overtax yourself.

## HEMORRHOID

To dream of this painful condition signifies that a mental disturbance in your life needs to be taken care of.

## HEMP

To dream of hemp indicates that you will be successful in all undertakings, especially major engagements.

To see hemp seeds in dreams denotes the approach of a deep and continued friendship. To the businessperson, it betokens favorable opportunity for moneymaking.

## HEN*

To dream of hens denotes pleasant family reunions joined by new members.

*See Chicken.

## HEPATITIS

Dreaming of having this disease warns that you need to express your true feelings to a loved one.

## HERBS

To dream of herbs indicates that you will have vexatious cares, though some pleasures will ensue.

To dream of poisonous herbs warns you of enemies.

Balm and other useful herbs suggest satisfaction in business and warm friendships.

## HERD

To dream of a herd of animals means that you will be soon following the good advice of friends and family for your financial gain.

## HERMIT

To dream of a hermit suggests sadness and loneliness caused by the unfaithfulness of friends. If you are a hermit yourself, you will pursue research into intricate subjects and will take great interest in the discussions of the hour.

To find yourself in the abode of a hermit betokens unselfishness toward enemies and friends alike.

## HERO

If you play the part of the hero in your dream, you will find yourself under criticism from your associates and old friends. If someone else in your dream is the hero, it foretells a profitable new business offer.

## HEROIN★

To dream that you or others are using this drug counsels you to seriously consider the people you associate with.

*See Drugs.

## HERRING

To dream of seeing a herring indicates a tight squeeze to escape financial embarrassment, but you will have success later.

## HETEROSEXUALITY

To dream you are heterosexual when you are not means that your love is pure and well intentioned.

## HICCUPS

Dreaming of having hiccups is a warning against drinking too much alcohol in your waking life.

## HICKORY

To dream of this wood foretells hard work with much success.

## HIDE

To dream of the hide of an animal denotes profit and permanent employment.

## HIDING

To dream that you have hidden away any object denotes embarrassment in your circumstances.

If you find hidden things, you will enjoy unexpected pleasures.

To dream of yourself hiding warns you not to be hasty in upcoming decisions. But if you dream that you are hiding something, it means that a secret needs to be brought to the forefront so you can get help for it.

## HIEROGLYPHS

Hieroglyphs seen in a dream suggest that wavering judgment in some vital matter may cause you great distress and monetary loss.

If you are able to read them, your success in overcoming some evil is foretold.

## HIGHCHAIR

To dream of yourself or someone else in a highchair means that you need to have more fun: you are being far too serious.

## HIGHLIGHTING

To dream of highlighting passages in a book or other printed material is a warning to pay close attention to your credit or finances in the future.

## HIGH SCHOOL

To dream of a high school foretells ascension to more elevated status in love, social, and business affairs.

## HIGH TIDE

To dream of high tide is indicative of favorable progress in your affairs.

## HIGHWAY

To dream of a busy highway means an increase in difficulties at work. To dream of an empty highway means smooth sailing with no worries at work. Crossing a highway warns that things will get worse before they get better.

## HILL*

To dream of climbing hills is good if the top is reached; but if you fall back, you will have much envy and contrariness to fight against.
*See Ascent.

## HINGE

To dream of a rusty or squeaky hinge suggests problems with family and personal affairs through gossip.

## HIPPOPOTAMUS*

To dream of this large animal foretells rivalry and competition in the workplace.
*See Animals.

## HIPS

For a woman to admire her own hips shows that she will be disappointed in love.

For a woman to dream that her hips are too narrow is an omen of sickness and disappointments. If too fat, she is in danger of losing her reputation.

To notice fat hips on animals foretells ease and pleasure.

## HISSING

To dream of people hissing is an omen that you will be displeased beyond endurance at the discourteous treatment shown you while among new acquaintances. If the people in the dream are hissing at you, you will be threatened with the loss of a friend.

## HISTORY

To dream that you are reading history indicates a long and pleasant recreation.

## HITCHHIKING

To dream that you are hitchhiking means that you are very self-reliant and have no need to depend on anyone else to solve your problems. To dream of picking up a hitchhiker predicts financial embarrassment.

## HITTING

To be hit in a dream tells you that good friendships abound in your life. If you hit someone, watch your back with your friends.

## HIV

To dream that you have this disease foretells good news about a current health issue. But if you dream of someone else having HIV, you may have a health problem that shouldn't be ignored.

## HIVES

To dream of being affected with hives denotes good health.

## HOARSENESS

To dream that your voice is hoarse warns you to be careful about possible thievery.

## HOBBY

To dream of a hobby implies that annoying changes are coming up in your life, but they are inconsequential.

## HOCKEY

Whether it be ice or field hockey, this dream reminds you that success will be achieved through your hard work.

## HOE

To dream of seeing a hoe indicates that you will have no time for idle pleasures: others depend on your work for subsistence.

If you dream of using a hoe, you will enjoy freedom from poverty by directing your energy into safe channels.

If you dream of a foe striking at you with a hoe, your interests will be threatened by enemies, but with caution you will stay away from real danger.

## HOG

To dream of seeing fat, strong-looking hogs foretells brisk changes in business and safe dealings. Lean hogs predict vexatious affairs and trouble with servants and children.

To see a sow and litter of pigs predicts abundant crops to the farmer and advances in the affairs of others.

To hear hogs squealing denotes unpleasant news from absent friends and foretells disappointment, death, or failure to realize the amounts you expected in deals of importance.

To dream of feeding your own hogs suggests an increase in your personal belongings.

If you dream that you are dealing in hogs, you will accumulate considerable property, but you will have much rough work to perform.

## HOLE

To dream of stepping or falling into a hole means you need to worry about dishonest friendships. To dream that you have a hole in a garment suggests financial luck. If you dig a hole in your dream, a sudden trip is in the offing. And if you observe holes, easier times are ahead.

## HOLIDAY

To dream of a holiday suggests that interesting strangers will soon partake of your hospitality.

## HOLLY

If your dream features any holly, you will be lucky in both money and friendship, unless you are pricked by the holly leaves, in which case you need to be careful about gossip.

## HOLOCAUST

To dream of being a victim of the Holocaust tells you that prosperity and good health are on the way. If you dream that you were a perpetrator, however, this is a dream of financial ruin.

## HOLOGRAM

To picture a hologram in a dream means you are not being true to yourself and your personality.

## HOLY COMMUNION

To dream that you are taking part in the Holy Communion implies blessings and peace of mind. If you give Holy Communion, spiritual awakening is on the horizon.

## HOLY GRAIL

To dream of having or seeking this holy cup suggests copious blessings.

## HOLY LAND

If you dream of being in the Holy Land or taking a trip to the Holy Land, extraordinary blessings are coming your way.

## HOME*

To dream of visiting your old home suggests that you will have good news to rejoice over.

*See Abode.

## HOMEOPATHY

To dream of this type of natural medicine means you may need to see a doctor.

## HOMESICKNESS

To dream of being homesick indicates that you will lose opportunities to enjoy travel or have pleasant visits.

## HOMICIDE*

To dream of committing homicide suggests that you will suffer great anguish and humiliation through the indifference of others, and that your gloom will cause perplexing worry to those close to you.

*See Killing.

## HOMINY

To dream of hominy suggests that romance will furnish you interesting diversion from absorbing study and planning for future progress.

## HOMOSEXUALITY

To dream you are homosexual when you are not means that your love is pure and well intentioned.

## HONEY

If you dream that you see honey, you will be possessed of considerable wealth.

Strained honey represents wealth and ease, but there will be an undercurrent in your life of unlawful gratification of material desires.

To dream of eating honey betokens wealth and love. To lovers, this indicates a swift rush into marital joys.

## HONEYCOMB

To dream of a honeycomb means that words you have spoken will sour in your mouth. Beware of spreading rumors.

## HONEYMOON

To dream of taking a honeymoon or of someone else taking a honeymoon signifies disappointments in love or personal relationships.

## HONEYSUCKLE

To see or gather honeysuckle implies that you will be contentedly prosperous and your marriage will be singularly happy.

## HOOD

To dream of wearing a hood warns you of deception from someone you trust.

## HOOF

To dream of an animal's hoof predicts financial gain.

## HOOK

To dream of a hook suggests that you'll assume unhappy obligations.

## HOOP

If you dream of a hoop, you will form influential friendships. Many will seek your counsel.

To jump through or see others jumping through hoops suggests that you will have discouraging outlooks, but will overcome them decisively.

## HOPS

In dreams, hops represent thrift, energy, and the power to grasp and master almost any business proposition. This is a favorable dream for all classes, lovers, and tradesmen.

## HORIZON

If you dream that the horizon is far away, success is predicted. Dreaming that the horizon is near means that you will still be successful, but that there may be a delay.

## HORN

To dream that you hear the sound of a horn indicates sudden news of a joyful character.

A broken horn denotes death or accident.

## HORNET

To dream of a hornet signals disruption to lifelong friendship and loss of money.

## HOROSCOPE

To dream of having your horoscope drawn by an astrologer foretells unexpected changes in affairs and a long journey; associations with strangers will probably happen.

If the stars are pointed out to you in an astrological way while your fate is being read, you will find disappointment where fortune and pleasure seemed to await.

## HORSE*

To dream of horses suggests that you will amass wealth and will enjoy life to its fullest extent.

If you dream of riding a runaway horse, your interests will be injured by the folly of a friend or employer. To see a horse running away with others warns that you will hear of the illness of friends.

To see fine stallions is a sign of success and high living; undue passion may master you. Broodmares suggest congeniality and an absence of jealousy for married couples and sweethearts.

If you dream of fording a stream on horseback, you will soon experience good fortune and will enjoy rich pleasures. If the stream is unsettled or murky, your anticipated joys will be somewhat disappointing.

If you swim on a horse's back through a clear and beautiful stream of water, your conception of passionate bliss will be swiftly realized. To those in business, this dream portends great gain.

To see a wounded horse foretells the trouble of friends. A dead horse signifies disappointments of various kinds.

To dream of riding a horse that bucks suggests that your desires will be difficult to reach. If you dream that he throws you, you will have a strong rival, and your business will suffer slightly through competition. If the horse kicks you, you will be repulsed by the one you love and your fortune will be diminished by ill health.

To dream of catching a horse to bridle and saddle, or harness, means that you will see a great improvement in business of all kinds. If you fail to catch the horse, fortune will play you false.

Spotted horses signify that various enterprises will bring you profit.

If you dream of having a horse shod, your success is assured. To dream that you yourself shoe him implies that you will work to make possibly dubious property your own.

To dream of racehorses means that you will be surfeited with fast living, but to the farmer this dream denotes prosperity. If you dream of riding a horse in a race, you will be prosperous and enjoy life.

To dream of killing a horse warns that you may injure your friends through selfishness.

If you mount a horse bareback, you will gain wealth and ease by struggle.

If you curry a horse, your business interests will not be neglected for frivolous pleasures. To dream of trimming a horse's mane or tail suggests that you will be a good financier.

To see horses pulling vehicles denotes wealth with some encumbrance, and love will find obstacles.

If you are riding up a hill and the horse falls but you reach the top, you will win fortune, though you will have to struggle against enemies and jealousy. If both the horse and you get to the top, your rise will be phenomenal and substantial. If you ride a horse downhill, your affairs will undoubtedly disappoint you.

To see a horse with a tender foot implies that some unexpected unpleasantness will insinuate itself into your otherwise propitious state. *See Mare.*

## HORSERADISH

To dream of horseradish foretells pleasant associations with intellectual and congenial people. Fortune is also expressed in this dream. For a woman, it indicates a rise above her present station.

If you eat horseradish, you will be the object of playful teasing.

## HORSESHOE

To dream of a horseshoe indicates advance in business and lucky engagements for women. Broken horseshoes bode ill fortune and sickness.

To find a horseshoe hanging on the fence suggests that your interests will advance beyond your expectations.

If you pick one up from the road, you will receive profit from an unknown source.

## HORSE TRADER

The appearance in dreams of a horse trader signifies great profit from perilous ventures.

If you dream that you are trading horses, and the trader cheats you, you will lose in trade or love. If you get a better horse than the one you gave up, you will better yourself in fortune.

## HOSE

To dream of a hose that is on means an adventure is coming. A dream of using a hose on a fire suggests exciting new love relationships and sexual satisfaction. To see a sprinkler on a lawn indicates the coming of new friends and social events.

### HOSPITAL*

If you dream that you are a patient in a hospital, a contagious disease may strike your community and you will narrowly escape affliction. If you visit patients there, you will hear distressing news of those who are absent.

*See *Infirmary*.

### HOST, HOSTESS

To dream of being a host or hostess at a party means that your life is improving.

### HOSTILITY

To dream of someone being hostile to you means you will soon have to admit something that you have done wrong. For you to be hostile means you need to watch what you say and be careful of how you treat others.

### HOTEL

To dream of living in a hotel implies ease and profit.

To dream of seeing a fine hotel foretells wealth and travel. If you dream that you are the proprietor, you will earn all the fortune you will ever possess.

If you dream of working in a hotel, you could find more remunerative employment than what you have.

### HOUND*

To dream of hounds on a hunt suggests coming delights and pleasant changes.

*See *Dog*.

### HOURGLASS

To dream of sand running through an hourglass suggests that you are wasting your time in pursuing either a love interest or a career path.

### HOUR, THE

To dream of seeing the hour on a clock or hearing a clock strike the hour means you are headed in the right direction.

### HOUSE*

If you dream of building a house, you will make wise changes in your present affairs.

To dream that you own an elegant house indicates that you may soon be leaving your home for a better one, and fortune will be kind to you.

Old and dilapidated houses denote failure in business or any effort, and declining health.

*See Buildings.

## HOUSEBOAT

To dream of a houseboat suggests that you have the security of a home—but also the luxury of being able to move around.

## HOUSEKEEPER

To dream that you are a housekeeper indicates that work occupies your time, making pleasure an ennobling thing.

To employ a housekeeper signifies that comparative comfort could be within your reach.

## HUGGING

If you dream of hugging someone, you will be disappointed in love and business.

## HULA DANCE

To dream of this dance suggests that exotic romantic adventure is coming your way.

## HUMANITARIANISM

To dream of being a humanitarian means you will be recognized socially for your accomplishments.

## HUMIDITY*

To dream that you are overcome by humidity foretells that you will combat enemies fiercely, but that their superior force will submerge you in overwhelming defeat.

*See Air.

## HUMMING

To dream of the sound of humming portends that you will soon hear news from someone who lives far away. To dream of humming bodes an improved social life.

## HUMMINGBIRD

In dreams, this tiny hovering bird symbolizes blessings, happiness, and pleasure coming your way.

## HUNCHBACK

To dream of a hunchback suggests unexpected reverses in your prospects.

## HUNGER

To dream that you are hungry is an unfortunate omen.

## HUNTING*

If you dream of hunting, you will struggle for the unattainable. If you dream that you hunt game and find it, you will overcome obstacles and gain your desires.

*See *Game.*

## HURDLE

If you dream of anyone jumping hurdles, you need to look at your personal behavior. You may be giving others a false impression about yourself.

## HURRICANE

To hear the roar and see a hurricane heading toward you with its frightful force predicts that you will undergo torture and suspense, striving to avert failure and ruin in your affairs. If you are in a house that is being blown to pieces by a hurricane and you struggle in the awful gloom to extricate someone from falling timbers, your life will suffer a change. You will move to distant places and still find no improvement in domestic or business affairs.

If you dream of looking at the debris and havoc wrought by a hurricane, you will come close to trouble, which will be averted.

To see a hurricane's dead and wounded suggests that you will be much distressed over the troubles of others.

## HURRYING

If you dream you need to hurry to do something for yourself, this foretells of a coming worry. To dream that you must hurry for someone else suggests an upswing in your social affairs.

## HURTING*

If you hurt a person in your dreams, you will do ugly work, avenging and injuring. If you yourself are hurt, you will have enemies who will overcome you.

*See *Injury.*

## HUSBAND

If you dream that your husband is leaving you, and you do not understand why, there will be bitterness between you, but an unexpected reconciliation will follow. If he mistreats you and upbraids you for unfaithfulness, you will have his regard and confidence, but other worries will ensue; you are warned to be more discreet in receiving attention from men. If you see him dead, disappointment and sorrow will envelop you.

To see him pale and careworn suggests that sickness will tax you heavily, and some of the family will linger in sick bay for a time.

If you see him contented and handsome, your home will be filled with happiness and bright prospects will be yours. If he is sick, he may mistreat you or be unfaithful.

If you dream that he is in love with another woman, he will soon tire of his present surroundings and seek pleasure elsewhere.

To be in love with another woman's husband in your dreams indicates that you are not happily married, or that you are not happy unmarried, but the chances for happiness are doubtful.

If you see your husband depart from you, and as he recedes from you he grows larger, inharmonious surroundings will prevent congeniality. If disagreeable conclusions are avoided, harmony will be reinstated.

For a woman to dream that she sees her husband in a compromising position with an unsuspected party indicates that she will have trouble through the indiscretion of friends. If she dreams that he is killed while with another woman, and a scandal ensues, she will be in danger of separating from her husband or losing property. Unfavorable conditions follow this dream, though the evil is often exaggerated.

### HUT

To dream of a hut denotes indifferent success. If you are sleeping in a hut, expect ill health and dissatisfaction. A hut in a green pasture predicts prosperity but fluctuating happiness.

### HYACINTH

If you dream that you see or gather hyacinths, you are about to undergo a painful separation from a friend, which will ultimately result in good for you.

### HYBRID

To dream of something that is a hybrid indicates transformation and change coming into your life.

### HYDRANT

To dream of a fire hydrant spewing water means your worries will soon be fading.

## HYDROPHOBIA

To dream that you are afflicted with hydrophobia suggests enemies and changes in business.

If you see others thus afflicted, your work will be interrupted by death or ungrateful dependence.

## HYENA

If you see a hyena in your dreams, you will meet much disappointment and ill luck, and your companions will be very uncongenial. If lovers have this dream, they will often be involved in quarrels. If a hyena attacks you, your reputation will be set upon by busybodies.

## HYGIENE

To have poor personal hygiene in a dream portends you will soon move up socially and acquire influential friends. To observe someone else's poor hygiene warns you against backstabbing friends.

## HYMN*

To dream of hearing hymns sung denotes contentment in the home and average prospects in business affairs.

*See *Singing*.

## HYPERVENTILATION

To dream you are hyperventilating means good fortune is in the offing.

## HYPOCRITE

If you dream that anyone has been a hypocrite with you, you will be turned over to your enemies by false friends.

Dreaming that you are a hypocrite suggests that you will prove yourself a deceiver and be false to friends.

## HYSSOP

To dream of hyssop suggests you will have grave charges incurred against you; if you are a woman, your reputation will be endangered.

## HYSTERECTOMY

To dream you are having or have had a hysterectomy foretells a pregnancy, either your own or someone else's.

## IBUPROFEN

To dream of this painkiller, either taking or giving it, means that a happy event is in the offing.

## ICE*

To dream of ice betokens much distress. Evil-minded people will seek to injure you in your best work.

To see ice floating in a stream of clear water indicates that your happiness will be interrupted by ill-tempered and jealous friends.

If you dream of walking on ice, you risk much solid comfort and respect for evanescent joys.

If you dream of making ice, you will make a failure of your life through egotism and selfishness. Eating ice foretells sickness. If you drink ice water, you will suffer ill health from dissipation.

Bathing in ice water means that anticipated pleasures will be interrupted by an unforeseen event.

*See *Icicle*.

## ICEBERG

In dreams, an iceberg represents obstacles you must overcome in order to move ahead in your career.

## ICE CREAM

To dream that you are eating ice cream foretells success in affairs already undertaken.

To see children eating it suggests that prosperity and happiness will attend you most favorably. If it is melted, though, your anticipated pleasure will stagnate before you can realize it.

## ICE CUBE

To dream of making or using ice cubes foretells a pleasant surprise or lovely gift coming into your life.

## ICE-SKATING

To dream that you are skating on ice implies that you are in danger of losing employment or something of value.

If you break through the ice, you will have unworthy friends to counsel you.

To see others skating suggests that disagreeable people will connect your name in scandal with someone who admires you.

To see ice skates denotes discord among your associates.

## ICICLE*

To see icicles falling from trees means that some distinctive misfortune or trouble will soon vanish. To see icicles on the eaves of houses suggests misery and want of comfort. Ill health is foreboded. To see icicles on a fence denotes suffering bodily and mentally. If you see them on trees, despondent hopes will grow gloomier; on evergreens, a bright future will be overcast with the shadow of doubtful honors.

*See *Ice*.

## ICING

To dream of icing on a confection means that you are not being told the whole story. Something is being sugarcoated for your benefit.

## ICON

To dream of an icon foretells many blessings in your life.

## IDEA

To dream of having a great idea predicts frustration, unless you can recall the idea when you wake up, in which case your dream indicates unusual good luck.

## IDEAL

For a young woman to dream of meeting her ideal foretells a season of uninterrupted pleasure and contentment.

A bachelor who dreams of meeting his ideal will soon experience a favorable change in his affairs.

## IDLENESS

If you dream of being idle, you will fail to accomplish your designs. If you see your friends in idleness, you will hear of some trouble affecting them.

## IDOL

Should you dream of worshiping idols, your progress toward wealth or fame will be slowed by petty issues.

To break idols signifies a strong mastery over yourself. No work will deter you in your upward rise to positions of honor.

If you see others worshiping idols, great differences will rise up between you and warm friends.

To dream that you are denouncing idolatry suggests that great distinction is in store for you through your understanding of the natural inclinations of the human mind.

## IGLOO

To dream of building or living in an igloo indicates unexpected financial expenditures regarding your home.

## IGNITING

To dream that you are igniting something, such as a firecracker or bomb, cautions you to be clear and specific about your business dealings. To dream that someone else is igniting something suggests that a business idea will soon catch fire.

## IGUANA

To dream of this animal betokens surprise social events or interesting new friends coming into your life.

## ILLEGALITY

To dream of performing something illegal portends good luck.

## ILLITERACY

To feel you are illiterate or to be aware of illiterate people in a dream implies an increase in career responsibilities that will be well rewarded.

## ILLNESS*

To dream of illness suggests upset.

*See *Sickness*.

## ILLUMINATION

In dreams, illumination is an omen of great good fortune.

## ILLUSION

To dream of an illusion, or to be aware of one in a dream, suggests that valuable information coming into your life will further your career or personal goals.

## IMITATION

To dream of imitations means that people are working to deceive you.

## IMMIGRANT

To dream of being a immigrant suggests a move in the near future, in either your career or your residence.

## IMMORTALITY

To dream that you are immortal warns you to watch your health issues in the future.

## IMP

To see imps in your dream signifies trouble from what seems a passing pleasure. To dream that you are an imp indicates that folly and vice will bring you to poverty.

## IMPALEMENT

To dream of being impaled on something means that you will soon be experiencing confusion and frustration in a relationship.

## IMPATIENCE

To dream of being impatient, or of someone else being impatient, warns you not to judge a person or situation hastily.

## IMPERIALISM

To dream of something that is imperial or that you are a member of royalty foretells a career advancement.

## IMPERSONATION

To dream of impersonating someone means you are not being truthful about a current problem in your life. If you are impersonated by someone in your dream, you will make new and interesting friends.

## IMPLANT

To dream of having an implant in your body betokens good health, social rewards, and financial gain.

## IMPLEMENTS

To dream of implements denotes an unsatisfactory means of accomplishing some work. If the implements are broken, you will be threatened with death or the serious illness of relatives or friends, or with failure in business.

## IMPOLITENESS

To dream of being impolite to someone else portends financial gain and social recognition. To dream of someone being impolite to you means that a change in relationships or career is in the offing.

## IMPOSTER

To dream that you are being cheated by an imposter suggests that a business deal may fail if you are not careful.

## IMPOTENCE

To dream of being impotent indicates that you will have a successful love life.

## INAUGURATION

To dream of an inauguration indicates that you will rise to a higher position than you have yet enjoyed.

## INCANTATION

To dream of using incantations suggests unpleasantness between husband and wife, or between sweethearts. To hear others repeating them implies dissembling among your friends.

## INCENSE

To dream of smelling incense or burning incense foretells the lightening of burdens. Whatever has been troubling you recently will be lifted.

## INCEST

To dream of incestuous practices means that you will fall from honorable places and will also suffer loss in business.

## INCISION

To dream of an incision foretells legal problems coming, unless you are a surgeon, in which case the dream is meaningless.

## INCOHERENCE

To dream of incoherence usually suggests extreme nervousness and excitement through the stress of changing events.

## INCOME

To dream of getting paid indicates that you may deceive someone and cause trouble to your family and friends.

To dream that a member of your family inherits an income predicts success for you.

To dream that your income is insufficient to support you suggests trouble to relatives or friends.

To dream of a portion of your income remaining signifies that you will be very successful for a short time, but you may expect more than you receive.

## INCOME TAX

To dream of filing or paying your income tax implies that you will soon be assisting a friend with a problem.

## INCREASE

To dream of an increase in your family may denote failure in some of your plans and success in others.

To dream of an increase in your business signifies that you will overcome existing troubles.

## INCUBATOR

To dream of animals, such as chickens and turkeys, in an incubator means upcoming financial gain. To dream of a small baby in an incubator foretells a pregnancy or birth.

## INDEPENDENCE

To dream that you are very independent indicates that you have a rival who may do you an injustice.

If you dream that you are independently wealthy, you may not be as successful at that time as you expect, but good results are promised.

## INDIAN (AMERICAN)

To dream of Native Americans is considered a good-luck dream.

## INDIFFERENCE

To dream of indifference signifies pleasant companions for a very short time.

## INDIGESTION

To dream of indigestion indicates unhealthy and gloomy surroundings.

## INDIGO

To see the color indigo in a dream suggests that you will deceive people to cheat them out of their belongings.

To see indigo water foretells an ugly love affair.

## INDISTINCTNESS

If in your dreams you see objects indistinctly, it portends unfaithfulness in friendships, and uncertain dealings.

## INDULGENCE

To dream of indulgence means you need to be aware of frivolous spending on unnecessary items so you can begin to save your money.

## INDUSTRIOUSNESS

To dream that you are industrious indicates that you will be unusually active in planning and working out ideas to further your interests, and that you will be successful.

To see others busy is favorable to the dreamer.

## INDUSTRY

To dream of heavy industry indicates an advancement in your business or career.

## INFANT

To dream of seeing a newborn infant suggests that pleasant surprises are nearing you.

## INFECTION

Dreaming of having an infection indicates the loss of a friendship or a job.

## INFERNO

To see an inferno in your dream foretells good fortune and good health.

## INFIDELITY

To dream of being unfaithful is a warning that you are making poor choices in your relationships.

## INFIRMARY*

To dream that you leave an infirmary denotes your escape from wily enemies who will cause you much worry.

*See Hospital.

## INFIRMITY

To dream of infirmities implies misfortune in love and business.

To dream that you see others infirm indicates various troubles and disappointments in business.

## INFLATING

To inflate or see something inflated in a dream warns against becoming cocksure in your life.

## INFLUENCE

If you dream of seeking rank or advancement through the influence of others, your desires will fail to materialize; but if you are in an influential position, your prospects will take shape.

If you see friends in high positions, your companions will be congenial, and you will be free from vexations.

## INFOMERCIAL

To dream of being in or watching an infomercial, and wanting to buy the product, warns against upcoming financial loss.

## INFRARED

To dream of seeing something in infrared suggests that a career choice will be more lucrative than you ever imagined.

## INGESTION

To dream of ingesting anything means that a period of learning will soon be coming.

## INGREDIENTS

Dreaming of mixing ingredients together means you will soon be incorporating different ideas and a different way of living into your current lifestyle.

## INHALER

If you dream of having to use an inhaler, a surprise gift will take your breath away.

## INHERITANCE*

To dream that you receive an inheritance foretells that you will easily obtain your desires.

*See *Estate*.

## INITIATING

To find you are initiating something into your life signals new beginnings in a relationship.

## INJECTION

To dream you are injecting something into yourself or someone else warns against upcoming health issues.

## INJURY*

To dream of an injury being done to you signifies that an unfortunate occurrence will soon grieve and vex you.

*See *Hurting.*

## INK

If you see ink spilled over your clothing, many small and spiteful meannesses will be dealt you through envy.

To dream that you have ink on your fingers suggests that you will be jealous and seek to injure someone unless you exercise your better nature. If it is red ink, you will be involved in serious trouble.

If you dream that you make ink, you will engage in low and debasing business and will fall into disrepute.

To see bottles of ink in your dreams indicates enemies and unsuccessful interests.

## INKWELL

An empty inkwell implies that you will narrowly escape public denunciation for some supposed injustice.

To see one filled with ink warns that if you are not cautious, enemies will succeed in calumny.

## IN-LAWS

To dream of your in-laws foretells family harmony. To dream that you are an in-law means that a family problem is on the horizon.

## INLET

To dream of sailing vessels coming into or going out of an inlet suggests material gain through new associates in your workplace.

## INMATE

To dream of being an inmate in a prison means you will have the freedom and finances to do the things you love.

## INN

To dream of an inn denotes prosperity and pleasure, if the inn is commodious and well furnished.

To be at a dilapidated and ill-kept inn implies poor success, mournful tasks, or unhappy journeys.

## INQUEST

To dream of an inquest foretells unfortunate friendships.

## INQUISITION

To dream of an inquisition bespeaks an endless round of trouble and great disappointment.

If you are brought before an inquisition on a charge of willfulness, you will be unable to defend yourself from malicious slander.

## INSANITY

To dream of being insane forebodes disastrous results to some newly undertaken work; ill health may also work sad changes in your prospects.

To see others insane denotes disagreeable contact with suffering and appeals from the poverty-stricken. Take the utmost care of your health after this dream.

## INSCRIPTION

To dream that you see an inscription foretells unpleasant communications. If you are reading inscriptions on tombs, you will be distressed by sickness of a serious nature.

If you write one, you will lose a valued friend.

## INSECT*

To dream of killing insects means that difficulties are on the horizon, but they will be easily overcome.

To dream that you have an insect in your ear suggests that unpleasant news will affect your business or family relations.

*See specific insects.

## INSIGNIA

To dream of an insignia suggests tough competition in business dealings. To dream of wearing an insignia means you will embark on an exciting new love affair.

## INSISTENCE

To find yourself insisting that something be done your way in your dream means you will soon have many happy, fun times with friends and family. To dream of someone insisting that you do something his or her way suggests a quarrel with a friend or family member.

## INSOLVENCY

If you dream that you are insolvent, you will not have to resort to bankruptcy to square yourself with the world: your energy and pride will enable you to transact business successfully. But other worries may sorely afflict you.

If you dream that others are insolvent, you will meet with honest men in your dealings, but by their frankness they may harm you.

## INSPECTING

To dream of yourself or someone else inspecting something closely portends that you will need to be careful in what you say to others; it may be misunderstood and cause problems.

## INSTANT REPLAY

To dream that you see something happening over and over warns that you may need to change your thoughts and ideas about an upcoming project or event.

## INSTITUTIONALIZING

To dream of yourself in any institution, for either physical or mental treatment, suggests good health and mental clarity.

## INSTRUCTIONS

When you are following instructions in a dream, a happy event will soon be coming with friends and family. To be giving instructions indicates a career advancement.

## INSTRUMENT

To dream of medical instruments foretells family quarrels. To dream of any other kind of instrument, including musical, suggests family unity.

## INSULT

Either getting or giving insults in a dream is a sign of loyalty among your friends and business associates.

## INSURANCE

To collect on an insurance policy in your dream means a financial setback. To buy an insurance policy in your dream bodes a good financial future.

## INTEMPERANCE

If you dream of being intemperate in the use of your intellect, you will seek after foolish knowledge, fail to benefit yourself, and give pain and displeasure to your friends. If you are intemperate in love or other passions, you will reap disease or loss of fortune and esteem.

## INTERCESSION

To intercede for someone in a dream shows that you will be able to secure aid when you need it most.

## INTERCOURSE*

To dream of having sexual intercourse and enjoying it portends a happy change in your love life. To dream of watching others suggests happiness in a relationship. To have or watch sexual intercourse that is uncomfortable or unpleasant implies that your way of thinking about a relationship will change, but not for the better.

*See *Sex*.

## INTEREST (FINANCIAL)

To dream that you must pay interest on money owed warns you to take hold of your spending. To receive interest on money portends a change in finances and may be very fortuitous.

## INTERIORS

To change the interior of any structure in your dream means that life is good, but that making changes right now may not be good for you.

## INTERNET

To dream that you are trying to connect to the Internet and cannot indicates that you have trouble getting your ideas across in a project at work. To be able to connect predicts that you will have an easy time in the same project.

## INTERNSHIP

To dream you are interning for a job means you might face a setback in your career and perhaps be looking for another job soon.

## INTERPRETER

To dream of an interpreter suggests that your business affairs often fail to show a profit.

## INTERSECTION

If you dream of yourself at an intersection and you are not sure which way to go, you will be very determined in how you achieve your goals and will be very happy with the result.

## INTERVIEW

To dream of preparing for, or going on, an interview foretells the coming of money. To dream that you are being interviewed and do not get the job implies a small financial loss that you'll soon recover from. To dream that you do get the job means a surprise gift or unexpected monetary gain in the near future.

## INTESTINES

To dream of seeing intestines signifies that you are about to be visited by a grave calamity that will remove a friend from your life.

To see your own intestines suggests that very serious situations are closing in around you; sickness that affects you in your daily life with others threatens you. Probable loss, with much displeasure, is also indicated.

## INTOXICATION*

To dream of intoxication indicates that you are cultivating the desire for illicit pleasures.

*See *Drunkenness*.

## INTRODUCTIONS

To dream that you are being introduced to someone means that you will soon be questioning whether some friendships are loyal and true. To dream that you are making the introduction betokens new friends.

## INUNDATION

To dream of seeing cities or country submerged in dark, seething waters denotes great misfortune and loss of life through some dreadful calamity.

To see human beings swept away in an inundation portends bereavement and despair, making life gloomy and unprofitable.

To see a large area inundated with clear water suggests profit and ease after seemingly hopeless struggles.

## INVALIDS

To dream of invalids is a sign of displeasing companions interfering with your interest. If you dream that you yourself are an invalid, you may be threatened with displeasing circumstances.

## INVECTIVE

To dream of using invective warns you against passionate outbursts of anger, which may estrange you from close companions.

If you hear others using invective, enemies are closing in on you.

## INVENTION

To find yourself inventing something in a dream means that you will soon change your residence or home.

To dream that you are admiring the invention of someone else warns you to keep your life just where it is; don't make any changes right now.

## INVENTOR

To dream of an inventor suggests that you will soon achieve some unique work, which will add honor to your name.

If you dream that you are inventing something, or are interested in some invention, you will aspire to fortune and will be successful in your designs.

## INVENTORY

To be taking inventory in your dream foretells problems that will be easy to solve.

## INVESTMENTS

To invest your own money in a dream means a financial setback. To invest someone else's money in your dream means financial gain.

## INVINCIBILITY

To feel you are invincible in a dream is a warning of health problems that should not be ignored.

## INVISIBILITY

To be invisible in a dream means you will not be taken seriously about an important matter having to do with changes you want to make in your life.

To know that someone is in your dream, but he or she is invisible, means you should listen to advice that may help to change some part of your life for the better.

## INVITATION

To dream that you invite people to visit indicates that an unpleasant event will cause worry and excitement in your otherwise pleasant surroundings. If you are invited to visit someone, you will receive sad news.

## IRIDESCENCE

To dream of something that looks iridescent predicts happiness and contentment coming into your life.

## IRIS

A dream about this flower signals happiness and prosperity.

## IRON

To dream of iron is a harsh omen of distress.

To feel an iron weight bearing you down signifies mental perplexities and material losses. To strike with iron denotes selfishness and cruelty to those dependent upon you.

To dream that you manufacture things of iron suggests that you use unjust means to accumulate wealth. If you sell iron, you enjoy dubious success and your friends may not be of noble character.

If you dream that the price of iron goes down, you will realize that money is a very unstable factor in your life. If iron goes up instead, you will see a gleam of hope in a dark prospect.

To dream of old, rusty iron signifies poverty and disappointment. Red-hot iron denotes failure for you through misapplied energy.

## IRONING

To dream of ironing denotes domestic comfort and orderly business.

## IRREGULARITY

To dream of asymmetrical shapes implies that you will find a solution to a problem in a very unusual way.

## ISLAND

To dream that you are on an island in a clear stream signifies pleasant journeys and fortunate enterprises. A barren island indicates forfeiture of happiness and money through intemperance.

To see an island denotes comfort and easy circumstances after much striving and worrying to meet obligations honorably.

If you see people on an island, expect a struggle to raise yourself higher in prominent circles.

## ITCHING

If you dream of seeing people with an itch, and you try to escape contact, you will stand in fear of distressing results. If you dream you have an itch yourself, you will be harshly used and will defend yourself by incriminating others.

To dream that you itch suggests unpleasant avocations.

## ITINERARY

If you find yourself making an itinerary in your dream, you will soon be putting your life in order for the better. To dream of reading someone else's itinerary means you will have to be more organized to achieve your goals.

## IVORY

To dream of ivory is favorable to the fortune of the dreamer.

To see huge pieces of ivory being carried denotes financial success and pleasures unalloyed.

## IVY

To dream of seeing ivy growing on trees or houses predicts excellent health and increase of fortune. Innumerable joys will succeed this dream.

Withered ivy speaks of broken engagements and sadness.

### JACK

To dream of a jack for a car marks an unexpected change to a problem. Conditions will get better.

### JACKAL

If you dream of this wild dog, a friend may persuade you to do something that you feel is wrong.

### JACKDAW

In dreams, jackdaws symbolize ill health and quarrels. If you catch one, you will outwit enemies. If you kill one, you will come into possession of disputed property.

### JACKET

If you dream of a nice jacket that is well fitted and comfortable, trouble lies ahead. A shabby or ripped jacket suggests financial gain.

### JACKHAMMER

To dream of operating a jackhammer, or of seeing someone else do so, implies a huge career leap.

### JACK-O'-LANTERN

To dream of a jack-o'-lantern or of carving a pumpkin foretells a mystery in your life that will soon be solved.

### JACKPOT

To dream of winning a jackpot suggests financial loss. The size of the jackpot foretells the relative size of the loss.

### JACUZZI

If you dream of sitting in a Jacuzzi and the water is clear, happiness and prosperity lie ahead. If the water is murky and dirty, this foretells much trouble. To dream of an empty Jacuzzi means that an invitation to a fun event in your life is in the offing.

## JADE
To dream of jade signals prosperity and social protection.

## JAGUAR
To dream of this animal means that you will have the agility and flexibility to perform a physical task that you weren't sure you could do.

## JAIL*
If you dream of being confined in jail, you will be prevented from doing profitable work by the intervention of envious people; if you escape, however, you will enjoy a season of favorable business.

If you see others in jail, people will urge you to grant privileges to those you deem unworthy.

*See *Prison*.

## JAILER
To dream of a jailer suggests that you are feeling controlled in some way.

To see a mob attempting to break out of jail is a forerunner of misfortune for you: desperate measures will be used to extort money from you.

## JALAPEÑO
To dream of eating this tiny hot pepper without feeling its heat warns that you need to watch what you say in the near future: it could come back to haunt you. To dream of a jalapeño that burns your mouth implies much success in a business dealing.

## JAM
To dream of eating jam, if pure, denotes pleasant surprises and journeys.

To dream of making jam foretells a happy home and appreciative friends.

## JANITOR
To dream of a lazy janitor denotes bad management and possible financial setbacks. To dream of one who is busy means the opposite.

If you look for a janitor and fail to find him or her, petty annoyances will disturb your otherwise placid existence. If you do find the janitor, you will have pleasant associations with strangers, and your affairs will have no hindrances.

## JANUARY
To dream of this month signifies loss, most likely of a person in your life with whom you find love or companionship.

## JAR

To dream of empty jars denotes impoverishment and distress. If you see them full, you will be successful. If you buy jars, your success will be precarious and your burden heavy. If you see broken jars, distressing sickness or deep disappointment awaits you.

## JASMINE*

To dream of this flower or this smell predicts success in romance and personal affairs.

*See *Jessamine.*

## JASPER

To dream of seeing jasper is a happy omen, bringing success and love.

## JAUNDICE

To dream that you have jaundice denotes prosperity after temporary embarrassments. If you see others with jaundice, you will be worried by unpleasant companions and discouraging prospects.

## JAVELIN

If you dream of defending yourself with a javelin, your most private affairs will be searched into to establish claims of dishonesty, and you will only be able to prove your innocence after much wrangling.

If you are pierced by a javelin, enemies will succeed in giving you trouble.

If you see others carrying javelins, your interests are threatened.

## JAW

To dream of seeing heavy, misshapen jaws denotes disagreements; ill feeling may be shown between friends.

If you dream that your jaws are clenched, you have been holding on to negative emotion for too long; it is time to release it.

If you dream of your own jaw, you might need to develop more strength of character to solve an issue.

To be in the jaws of an animal or monster suggests that a hasty judgment might cost you in the end.

## JAYBIRD

To dream of a jaybird foretells pleasant visits from friends and interesting gossip.

To catch a jaybird denotes pleasant, though unfruitful, tasks.

Seeing a dead jaybird suggests domestic unhappiness and many vicissitudes.

## JAYWALKING

To dream of people jaywalking predicts upcoming humiliation. To see yourself jaywalking warns of difficulty in a legal matter.

## JAZZ

To dream of hearing or playing this type of music cautions you that you are living beyond your means and will have to watch your credit.

## JEALOUSY

To dream that you are jealous indicates that you may be harboring those same feelings in your waking life. You may also need to look more closely at your self-esteem and see where it is lacking.

To dream that you are jealous of your spouse or partner means people in your environment bear you ill will.

To be the target of jealousy suggests that you will soon meet with some hostility but will overcome it; all will turn out to your advantage.

## JEANS

To wear brand-new blue jeans in a dream means that small difficulties will soon be overcome. To dream of well-worn jeans signals comfort and easy times ahead.

## JEEP

To dream of this vehicle predicts an argument with a family member or friend.

## JELLY

If you dream of eating jelly, many pleasant interruptions will take place. Making jelly indicates a reunion with friends.

## JELLYFISH

To dream of a jellyfish warns you not to lie in order to get what you want.

## JESSAMINE*

To dream of jessamine implies that you are approximating some exquisite pleasure, but it will be fleeting.

*See *Jasmine*.

## JESTER

If you dream of a jester, you will ignore important things while looking after silly affairs.

## JESUS

To dream of Jesus denotes fortitude and consolation during an adversity that will be arising in your life. If you dream that you speak to, pray to, touch, or are touched by Jesus, you will be blessed beyond your imagination: all your dreams will come true.

## JET PLANE

To dream of flying on this form of transportation indicates upcoming, unexpected travel. To watch a jet fly overhead advises you to prepare for an unexpected visitor. To see a jet crash portends financial prosperity.

## JET SKI™

A dream of a Jet Ski represents a journey of self-discovery. You will be looking at aspects of your unconscious life soon. This dream can also suggest that you will soon embark on a sexual adventure or relationship.

## JETTY

To dream of walking or sitting on a jetty warns that you are being too lazy in your personal and business affairs. If you are fishing from a jetty, however, you will be receiving a surprise gift soon.

## JEWELRY

To dream of broken jewelry denotes keen disappointment in attaining your highest desires.

## JEWELRY BOX

To dream of a full jewelry box predicts a possible theft in the future. An empty jewelry box foretells future gifts.

## JEWELS

To dream of jewels denotes pleasure and riches. To wear them brings status and satisfied ambitions. If you see others wearing them, distinguished places will be held by you or a friend.

To dream of jeweled garments betokens rare good fortune: inheritance or speculation will raise you to high positions. If you inherit jewelry, your prosperity will be unusual, but not entirely satisfactory.

To dream of giving jewelry away warns that some vital estate is threatening you. To find jewels denotes rapid and brilliant advancement in affairs of interest. If you give jewels away, you will unconsciously do harm to yourself. If you buy them, you will be very successful in momentous affairs, especially those pertaining to the heart.

### JEW'S HARP, JAW HARP

If you dream of a Jew's harp, you will experience a slight improvement in your affairs. To play one is a sign that you will fall in love with a stranger.

### JIG

In dreams, dancing a jig represents cheerful occupations and light pleasures.

### JIGSAW

If you dream of doing a jigsaw puzzle and find the task very hard, you will find that obstacles in your life are easily overcome. If the puzzle is easy to put together, more obstacles lie between you and the solution to your problems. To dream of a jigsaw, the tool, means you will soon be very creative in your home.

### JILTING

To be jilted in a dream suggests success in your love affairs and a possible marriage.

### JINGLE

To dream of a commercial jingle means that you will soon have new love interests. To dream of hearing bells jingle suggests good times ahead socially. Hearing the jingle of coins betokens a financial loss.

### JOB

To dream of looking for a job, or dream that you have lost one, implies that you will soon get a promotion. To be offered a job warns against a possible job loss.

### JOCKEY

To dream of a jockey suggests that you will receive a gift from an unexpected source. To see one thrown from a horse signifies that you will be called on for aid by strangers.

### JOGGING

To be jogging or see someone jogging in a dream predicts good mental and physical health.

### JOINTS

To dream of pain in your joints predicts an increase in material wealth.

## JOKE

To dream of laughing at a joke speaks of a disagreement with a friend. To dream of telling a funny joke implies good business success in the future. Telling dirty or offensive jokes means large profits.

## JOKER

To dream of the joker in a deck of playing cards means that your laziness may cost you money.

## JOLLITY

If you dream that you feel jolly and are enjoying the merriment of companions, you will realize pleasure from your current situation and have satisfying results in business. If there comes the least rift in the merriment in your dream, however, worry will intermingle with the success of the future.

## JOLT

To dream of receiving an electrical jolt warns that a surprise is coming that you will not like.

## JOSHUA TREE

In dreams, a Joshua tree symbolizes spirituality, purity, natural achievement, strength, and courage.

## JOURNAL

To dream of writing in a journal foretells correspondence from someone you haven't heard from in a while. To dream of reading someone else's journal implies dishonest and disloyal friendships.

## JOURNEY

To dream that you go on a journey signifies profit or disappointment, depending on whether the travels are pleasing and successful or whether accidents and disagreeable events intrude.

To see your friends start cheerfully on a journey indicates delightful change and harmonious companions. If you see them depart looking sad, it may be a long time before you see them again. Power and loss are implied.

To make a long-distance journey in a much shorter time than you expected means that you will complete some work in a surprisingly short time, and your reimbursement will be satisfactory.

## JOURNEYMAN

To dream of a journeyman suggests that you are soon to lose money in useless travels.

## JOWL

If your dreams feature large jowls, a friend or relative will soon tell you a lie.

## JOY

To dream that you feel joy over any event denotes harmony among friends.

## JOYSTICK

To dream of a joystick or video controller means that you may not have the control over something in your life that you thought you did. You should ask for help.

## JUBILEE

To dream of a jubilee suggests your participation in many pleasurable enterprises.

A religious jubilee denotes close but comfortable environments.

## JUDAS

If you dream of this fallen disciple, beware new friendships.

## JUDGE*

To dream of coming before a judge signifies that disputes will be settled by legal proceedings. Business or divorce cases may assume gigantic proportions.

To have the case decided in your favor denotes a successful termination to the suit; if it's decided against you, then you should seek to right an injustice.

To dream that you are being judged indicates that you are being put through some test in your waking life. You are seeking acceptance in order to move forward.

*See Jury, Law, lawsuit, Magistrate.

## JUDGMENT DAY

To dream of the Judgment Day foretells that you will accomplish some well-planned work, if you appear resigned and you are hopeful of escaping punishment. Otherwise, your work will prove a failure.

## JUG

If you dream of jugs filled with transparent liquids, your welfare is important to more than just yourself. Many true friends will unite to please and profit you. If the jugs are empty, your conduct will estrange you from friends and station. Broken jugs indicate sickness and failure in employment.

If you drink wine from a jug, you will enjoy robust health and find pleasure in all circles. Optimistic views will characterize you. If you take an unpleasant drink from a jug, disappointment and disgust will follow pleasant anticipations.

## JUGGLING

To dream of juggling advises you to jump on a business offer. Do not hesitate.

## JUGULAR VEIN

To dream of the jugular vein pulsing in someone's neck means good health. To see someone bleeding from this vein in your dream foretells a good prognosis for a health problem.

## JUICE

To dream of drinking or serving juice means financial help will be available to you when needed.

## JUKEBOX

To dream of a jukebox foretells a happy social event.

## JULY

If you dream of this month, you may be depressed or have a gloomy outlook, but just as suddenly your spirits will rebound; you will have unimagined pleasure and good fortune.

## JUMPING*

If you dream of jumping over any object, you will succeed in every endeavor; but if you jump and fall back, disagreeable affairs will make your life hard to deal with.

To jump down from a wall suggests reckless speculation and disappointment in love.

If you are just jumping up and down, you need to take a risk and move forward in your life; otherwise, you will continue to stay in one place.

*See Leaping.

## JUMPING JACKS

To dream of doing jumping jacks suggests that idleness and trivial pastimes will occupy your thoughts to the exclusion of serious and sustaining plans.

## JUNE

To dream of June foretells unusual gains in all undertakings.

## JUNE BUG

To dream of June bugs denotes an ill-tempered companion where a congenial one was expected.

## JUNIPER

To dream of seeing a juniper tree portends happiness and wealth arising from sorrow and depression. To eat or gather the berries of a juniper tree foretells trouble and sickness.

## JUNK

If you dream of junk, you need help in making a very big decision in your life. Seek it out.

## JUNKYARD

To dream of a junkyard indicates that there is much in your current life that you should discard, whether it be attitudes, outdated dreams, or personal characteristics that do not serve you well.

## JURY*

To dream that you are on a jury denotes dissatisfaction with your life; you will seek to materially change your position. It also may mean that you fall sway to what others think of you rather than relying on your own sense of self.

If you are cleared of a charge by a jury, your business will be successful and affairs will move your way; but if you should be condemned, bad influences will overpower and harass you.

*See *Judge, Law, lawsuit, Magistrate.*

## JUSTICE

To dream that you demand justice from a person indicates that you are threatened with embarrassment through the false statements of those eager for your downfall. If someone demands the same of you, you will find that your conduct and reputation are being assailed, and it will be extremely doubtful whether you can refute the charges satisfactorily.

## JUSTICE OF THE PEACE

To dream of this person foretells divorce or separation in a relationship.

## KALEIDOSCOPE

In dreams, kaleidoscopes portend changes with little good promise.

## KANGAROO

If you see a kangaroo in your dreams, you will outwit a wily enemy who seeks to place you in an unfavorable position before the public and the person you are striving to win over.

If a kangaroo attacks you, your reputation will be in jeopardy. If you kill one, you will succeed despite enemies and obstacles.

## KARAOKE

To dream of karaoke foretells an upcoming invitation. It may also be a warning that you are acting too overconfidently; watch your pride.

## KARATE

To dream of this martial art suggests that an obstacle to a long-term goal may arise, but you will be able to overcome it. If you direct and focus your energy, you will have a strong chance of success.

## KATYDID

To dream of hearing katydids is a prognostication of misfortune and unusual dependence on others.

## KAZOO

To play or hear this musical instrument foretells a happy social affair.

## KEEPSAKE

To dream of a keepsake advises you to take stock of how well loved you are.

## KEG

To dream of a keg indicates that you must struggle to throw off oppression. Broken kegs signify separation from family or friends.

## KELP

To dream of this sea plant means you can look forward to better times ahead.

## KENNEL

To dream of a kennel warns you that people you think are important truly have no significance at all.

## KEROSENE

To dream of this fuel means new interests are coming into your life.

## KETTLE

To see kettles in your dream denotes great and laborious work before you. A kettle of boiling water means your struggles will soon end and a change will come to you. A broken kettle denotes failure after a mighty effort to work out a path to success.

## KEY

To dream of keys in general denotes unexpected changes. If the keys are lost, unpleasant adventures will affect you, and a general sense of losing control of a situation may afflict you. If you are giving them to someone, beware that those around might be trying to steal your power; or you might be too ready to hand over control to something that you should not.

To find keys brings domestic peace and brisk turns to business, and often indicates that you are close to finding a solution to a problem. Broken keys portend separation from something or someone. You will no longer have access to something that you once did. Jangling keys suggest that you have taken decisive action, which will reap reward.

## KEYBOARD

To dream of using a keyboard on a computer means you will soon be sending and receiving papers about legal matters. To dream of playing at a musical keyboard, such as a piano, foretells a happy social time.

## KEYHOLE

To dream that you spy upon others through a keyhole means you will damage some person by disclosing confidences. If you catch others peeping through a keyhole, false friends may be delving into your private matters to advance themselves over you.

To dream that you cannot find a keyhole when you're trying to unlock a door suggests that you will unconsciously injure a friend.

## KHAKI

To dream of a uniform made of this material foretells a change in job or position. To dream of wearing khaki pants means an advancement in social standing.

## KICKING

To be kicked by someone in a dream means you have strong competition in your business or personal life. To kick someone implies an improvement or advancement in your career or serves as a gentle reminder not to be so aggressive with someone. To kick a ball for pleasure indicates happy times ahead.

## KID (BABY GOAT)

To dream of a kid suggests that you are not scrupulous in your morals. You will likely bring grief to someone's loving heart because of it.

## KIDNAPPING*

To dream of witnessing a kidnapping, or hearing or reading about one, means an important change is in the offing.
*See Abduction.

## KIDNEY

To dream about your kidneys foretells a serious illness or trouble in your marriage. It indicates a need to cleanse something from your life.

## KIDNEY STONE

To dream of this painful physical condition indicates that good health is on the way.

## KILLING*

To dream of aggressively killing a defenseless man prognosticates sorrow and failure. If you kill someone in self-defense or kill a ferocious animal that is attacking you, it denotes victory and a rise in position.
*See Homicide.

## KILT

To dream of wearing a kilt implies an unexpected trip.

## KINDERGARTEN

To dream of kindergarten means good luck and fortune are on the way.

## KING

If you dream of a king, you are struggling with your might, and ambition is your master. To dream that you are crowned king indicates that you will rise above your comrades and co-workers. If you are censured by a king, you will be reproved for a neglected duty.

## KISSING

To dream that you see children kissing denotes happy reunions in families and satisfactory work.

If you dream of kissing your mother or father, you will be very successful in your enterprises and will be honored and beloved by your friends. To kiss a brother or sister suggests much pleasure and good in your association.

To kiss your sweetheart in the dark denotes danger and immorality. To kiss her in the light shows that honorable intentions occupy your mind in connection with romance.

To dream of kissing illicitly denotes dangerous pastimes. Indulging in an unsavory relationship may bring tragedy.

If you dream of kissing an enemy, you will make advances toward reconciliation with an angry friend. Kissing a hand indicates respect and kissing a stranger reveals your need to develop more self-love, rather than seeking approval from those around you.

## KITCHEN

To dream of a kitchen denotes a need for spiritual or emotional nourishment or suggests that this need is being met. To dream that your kitchen is clean and orderly means that your personal life is in order.

## KITE

To dream of flying a kite denotes a great show of wealth or business, but with little true soundness to it all. To see the kite thrown upon the ground foretells disappointment and failure.

If you dream of making a kite, you will speculate much with little and will seek to win the one you love by misrepresentation.

To see children flying kites denotes pleasant and light occupation. If the kite ascends out of your vision, high hopes and aspirations will resolve themselves into disappointment and loss.

## KITTEN*

To dream of kittens is to dream of little cats, which tend to symbolize independence, magic, and control. Perhaps it is time to examine your lifestyle to see if you are keeping part of your life private and shaded from others. White kittens indicate that friends may turn on you. Soiled or dirty kittens are an unfortunate omen and can foretell troubled times ahead.

*See Cat.

## KKK (KU KLUX KLAN)

To dream of participating with or watching this white supremacist group suggests social embarrassment in the future.

## KLUTZ

To dream of being very uncoordinated tells you that social grace, achievement, and respect are on the way.

## KNAPSACK

To see a knapsack while dreaming indicates that you will find your greatest pleasure away from friends.

## KNEADING

To dream of kneading dough advises you to stay out of other people's business.

## KNEE

To dream of knees indicates your concern over support you are receiving from those around you. Feelings of inadequacy and issues of power or control also come into play. You may have more than you can handle.

## KNEELING

To dream that you are kneeling indicates that you might be falling under the control of those around you.

## KNIFE

To dream of a knife is bad for the dreamer: It portends separation, quarrels, and losses in business affairs.

To see rusty knives suggests dissatisfaction and complaints from those in the home, and separation of lovers. A dull knife indicates that hard work is getting you nowhere. Sharp and highly polished knives denote worry. Foes are ever surrounding you. Broken knives speak of defeat, whether in love or business.

To dream that you are wounded with a knife foretells domestic troubles. To the unmarried, it suggests that disgrace may follow. To dream that you stab another with a knife denotes baseness of character, and you should strive to cultivate a higher sense of right. An electric knife indicates getting to the root of a problem quickly.

### KNIFE GRINDER

To dream of a knife grinder implies that unwarranted liberties will be taken with your possessions.

### KNIGHT

To see a knight in your dream signifies honor, protection, and security, either from this plane or in the unseen world. Forces are coming together to protect you.

### KNITTING

To dream of knitting indicates that you possess a quiet and peaceful home.

### KNOB

To see doorknobs in a dream indicates that conditions are turning around. You need to get a handle on things.

### KNOCKER

If you dream of using a knocker, you will be forced to ask aid and counsel from others.

### KNOCKING

To hear knocking in your dreams suggests that you may soon hear tidings of a grave nature; or the dream could be putting you on notice that a significant change is on the horizon. If you are awakened by the knocking, the news will affect you more seriously.

### KNOT

To dream of seeing knots denotes much worry over the most trifling affairs.
To tie a knot reveals an independent nature.

### KOALA

In dreams, this animal represents your link to the unconscious realm. It can also symbolize protection and feminine nurturing qualities.

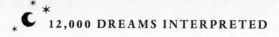 

## KRISHNA

To see Krishna in your dreams suggests that your greatest joy is in pursuit of spiritual knowledge, and you have cultivated a philosophical bearing toward life and sorrow.

## KUMQUAT

In dreams, kumquats symbolize luck and prosperity.

## KUNG FU

To dream of this martial art foretells an argument or disagreement with a close friend.

## LABEL

To dream of reading labels suggests that you have unknowingly let someone see your private affairs and you will suffer from the negligence.

To dream you are labeling things indicates that you are trying to make sense of something in your daily life.

To dream that something is mislabeled means you are not looking at things the right way. If you look for a label, you are working to make sense of a situation.

## LABOR

To dream that you watch domestic animals laboring under heavy burdens indicates that you will be prosperous but perhaps unjust to someone who works for you.

To see men toiling signifies profitable work and robust health. To see yourself labor implies a favorable outlook for any new enterprise and bountiful crops if you are interested in farming.

To dream that you are in labor with a baby means you will soon be successfully completing a project or aspect of your life and will be happy with the result. It doesn't foretell pregnancy.

## LABORATORY

To dream of being in a laboratory denotes great energies wasted in unfruitful enterprises when you might succeed at more practical efforts. If you think of yourself as an alchemist, you are trying to entertain far-reaching and interesting projects, but you will fail to reach the apex of your ambition.

## LABYRINTH

If you dream of a labyrinth, you will find yourself entangled in intricate and perplexing business conditions.

Dreaming of being in a labyrinth of night or darkness foretells passing but also agonizing sickness and trouble. A labyrinth of green vines and timbers denotes unexpected happiness from what seemed to be a cause for despair.

Dreaming of a network or labyrinth of railroads assures you of long and tedious journeys. You will meet interesting people, but no financial success will aid you on these journeys.

## LACE

Wearing lace in a dream about a wedding indicates fidelity in love and a rise in status.

If you dream of making lace, you will live a useful, industrious life and will never want for necessities. Selling lace indicates that your personal desires and material wants will exceed what you can afford. A dream of buying lace means you will become wealthy.

## LACQUER

To dream of applying lacquer means you soon will be tying up loose ends in a business or personal matter that is beneficial to you.

## LADDER*

To descend a ladder indicates disappointment in business and unrequited desires. Ascending one suggests prosperity and unstinting happiness. If you grow dizzy as you ascend, however, you will not wear new honors serenely. You are likely to become haughty and domineering in your newly acquired position.

To dream of a ladder being raised for you to ascend to some height means that your energetic and nervy qualifications will raise you to prominence in business affairs. To fall from one denotes despondency and unsuccessful transactions for tradespeople, and withered crops for farmers.

If you escape from captivity or confinement by means of a ladder, you will be successful, though many perilous paths may intervene. A broken ladder betokens failure in every instance.

*See *Ascent, Falling, Hill*.

## LADLE

To see a ladle in your dreams indicates that you will be fortunate in the selection of a companion, and that children will prove sources of happiness. If the ladle is broken or dirty, you will suffer a grievous loss.

## LADYBUG

To dream of this insect means success and happiness.

## LAGOON

To dream of a lagoon means that you will be drawn into a whirlpool of doubt and confusion through misapplication of your intelligence.

## LAIR

If you dream of an animal's lair and it is empty, problems loom. If the animal is in the lair, these problems may be easily overcome.

## LAKE

Lakes in general signify state of mind, but much of this dream has to do with the clarity of the water. Clear water is the best omen, dirty water is the worst.

To dream of being in a boat on a calm, serene lake indicates that you have peace and happiness coming your way. If the lake is stormy, you will take a turn for an emotional upheaval and possible loss. A dirty lake indicates that you are entering a period where circumstances beyond your control will test you.

## LAMAZE METHOD

If you dream of this breathing and relaxation method for childbirth and you are not pregnant, you will soon find a way to put your troubles behind you and relax. If you are pregnant, the dream is insignificant.

## LAMB*

Dreaming of a lamb foretells many good things.

To see a lamb playing in a green field indicates many friendships. Carrying one in your arms denotes an increase in wealth through hard work. It can also indicate vulnerability, either yours or another's, that needs to be considered when taking future action. Cooking, eating, or serving lamb is a good omen for finances.

*See Sheep.

## LAMENESS*

Seeing someone who is lame in a dream suggests that your hopes may not be realized at this time. Unless you can pinpoint who or what is holding things back, you will be disappointed.

*See Crippled.

## LAMENTING

To dream of bitterly lamenting the loss of friends or property signifies great struggles and much distress. From this, however, will spring joy and personal gain.

To lament the loss of relatives denotes sickness or disappointment, which will bring you into closer harmony with companions and will result in brighter prospects for the future.

## LAMP

To see lamps filled with oil denotes business activity from which you will receive gratifying results. Empty lamps represent depression and despondency.

To see lamps turned on indicates merited rise in fortune and domestic bliss. If they are dull, you will have jealousy and envy, coupled with suspicion, to combat, and you will find the person responsible and bring the matter to a successful conclusion.

To drop a lamp means your plans and hopes will abruptly turn into failure. If an oil lamp explodes, former friends will unite with enemies in damaging your interests. Broken lamps indicate the death of relatives or friends.

To light an oil lamp suggests that you will soon make a change that will lead to profit.

To carry a lamp portends that you will be independent and self-sustaining, preferring your own convictions to others'. If the light goes out, you will meet with an unfortunate end.

## LAMPPOST

To see a lamppost in your dreams means a stranger will prove your staunchest friend in time of pressing need.

If you fall against a lamppost, you will have deception to overcome or enemies will ensnare you.

If a lamppost lies across your path, you will have adversity in your life.

## LAMP SHADE

To see a lamp shade in your dream means you will soon be in need of protection.

## LANCE

To dream of a lance indicates formidable enemies and injurious experiments. To be wounded by a lance means an error of judgment will cause you annoyance. To break a lance means that seeming impossibilities will be overcome and your desires will be fulfilled.

## LAND*

To dream of fertile land bodes well; but if it's barren and rocky, failure and despondency are prognosticated.

To see land from the ocean indicates that vast avenues of prosperity and happiness will disclose themselves to you.

*See Field.

## LANDFILL

To dream of a landfill marks surprise gifts or monetary gain.

## LANDLORD

To dream of having a pleasant experience with a landlord foretells a change of residence. An unpleasant experience means a change of residence will fall through.

## LANDSLIDE

To dream of watching a landslide foretells the arrival of a large sum of money. To be caught in a landslide means an enormous sum of money.

## LANE

To dream of walking down a lane or narrow path warns you to be more discreet in your love affairs.

## LANGUAGES

To dream you hear someone speaking in a foreign language means that you are having a hard time understanding the motives or actions of another.

If someone is using foul language, you will find yourself in an embarrassing situation brought on by another.

## LANTERN

To dream of seeing a lantern before you lighting the darkness signifies unexpected affluence. If the lantern is suddenly lost to view, your success will take an unfavorable turn.

To carry a lantern in your dreams indicates that your benevolence will win you many friends. If it goes out, you will fail to gain the prominence you wish. If you stumble and break it, you will seek to aid others but in so doing lose your own station or be disappointed in some undertaking.

To clean a lantern signifies that great possibilities are open to you. To lose one means business trouble and disquiet in the home. If you buy a lantern, it signifies fortunate deals.

## LAP

To dream of sitting on someone's lap suggests pleasant security from vexing engagements.

## LAPDOG

To dream of a lapdog predicts that you will be succored by friends in an approaching dilemma. If it is thin and ill looking, distressing occurrences may detract from your prospects.

## LAP ROBE

To dream of a lap robe indicates that suspicious engagements will place you under the surveillance of others. If you lose one, your actions will be condemned by enemies, to your detriment.

## LARD

To dream of lard signifies a rise in fortune.

## LARK

To dream of larks flying suggests that through attaining your high aims and purposes, you will throw off selfishness and cultivate kindly graces of mind.

If you hear the larks singing as they fly, you will be very happy in a new change of abode, and your business will flourish. If you see them fall to the earth, singing as they fall, despairing gloom will overtake you in pleasure's bewildering delights.

A wounded or dead lark suggests sadness or death. To kill one portends injury to innocence through wantonness. If they fly around and alight on you, fortune will turn her promising countenance toward you. If you catch them in traps, you will win honor and love easily. To see them eating denotes a plentiful harvest.

## LARYNGITIS

To dream of having laryngitis warns that you may need to keep your opinions quiet. To dream of someone else having laryngitis means you will soon be offered good advice, which you should take.

## LASAGNA

To dream of eating or making lasagna foretells a solid financial gain or business advancement.

## LASER

If your dream features a laser, you will soon pinpoint a problem and find a solution.

## LASSO

To dream of a lasso is a happy omen for love and family affairs. However, being tangled or caught in a lasso means you will soon suffer embarrassment.

## LATCH

To dream of a door latch indicates that you will meet urgent appeals for aid and will respond unkindly. A broken latch foretells disagreements with your dearest friend. Sickness is also presaged in this dream.

## LATENESS

Any dream of you or someone else being late cautions you to avoid financial irresponsibility.

## LATEX

To dream of this rubberized material means you will soon be covering up a mistake that will be found out anyway.

## LATHER

To dream of lathering anything suggests that you will find a solution to a problem.

## LATIN

To dream of studying this language denotes victory and distinction in your efforts to sustain your opinion on subjects of vital interest to the public welfare.

## LATTICE

To dream of a lattice suggests that you may not clearly see a solution to a problem until someone else points it out to you.

## LAUGHING

To dream that you laugh and feel cheerful predicts success in your undertakings and bright companions socially.

Laughing insanely marks disappointment and a lack of harmony in your surroundings.

To hear the happy laughter of children means joy and health to the dreamer.

To laugh at the discomfort of others indicates that you will willfully injure your friends to gratify your own selfish desires. Mocking laughter suggests illness and disappointing affairs.

## LAUNCHPAD

If you dream of seeing or standing on a launchpad, you need to reevaluate your goals; they may be beyond your reach.

## LAUNDROMAT

To dream of washing your clothes in a Laundromat foretells happy times and festivities.

## LAUNDRY

To dream of laundering clothes suggests struggles, but a final victory in winning fortune. If the clothes are done satisfactorily, then your endeavors will bring complete happiness. If they come out unsatisfactorily, your fortune will fail to procure pleasure.

## LAUREL

Dreaming of laurel brings success and fame. You will acquire new possessions and love. Enterprises will be laden with gain.

## LAVA

To see lava flowing from a volcano means an exciting time in your social life.

## LAW, LAWSUIT*

To dream of engaging in a lawsuit warns you of enemies who are poisoning public opinion against you. If you know that the suit is dishonest on your part, you will seek to dispossess others for your own advancement.

*See *Judge, Jury.*

## LAWN

To dream of walking on a well-kept lawn indicates occasions of joy and great prosperity. Joining a merry party on a lawn suggests many happy times; business engagements will be successfully carried on.

## LAWN MOWER

To push or ride a lawn mower means you are cutting out unnecessary drama from your life.

## LAWYER*

To dream you are a lawyer when you're not means that you must seek help from another to solve a current dilemma. If you dream you see a lawyer, you will soon be involved in a scandal.

*See *Attorney*.

## LAXATIVE

To dream of taking a laxative means a job you have to do that may seem difficult will reap amazing benefits.

## LAYOFFS

To dream of layoffs means you will soon receive a promotion at work. To dream that you are laying people off warns you to watch for unexpected job changes.

## LAZINESS

To dream of feeling lazy, or acting so, indicates that you will make a mistake in the formation of enterprises and suffer keen disappointment.

## LEAD

To dream of lead foretells poor success in any engagement.

To dream of lead ore foretells distress and accidents. Business will assume a gloomy cast.

To melt lead cautions that by impatience you will bring failure upon yourself and others.

## LEAF

To dream of leaves that are green means abundance, good health, and happiness. If they are dry or wilted, expect financial loss. Falling leaves predict a change in friendship. And leaves that are blowing in the wind augur family arguments.

## LEAKING

To dream of seeing a leak in anything is usually significant of loss and vexations. It can also mean that your efforts will be fruitless.

## LEAPFROG

To dream of playing this game means that you may have stiff competition in a business project; you must stay on your toes throughout.

## LEAPING*

To dream of leaping over an obstacle indicates that you will gain your desires after much struggle and opposition.

*See *Jumping*.

## LEARNING

To dream of learning suggests that you will take great interest in acquiring knowledge, and, if you are economical with your time, you will advance far.

To enter halls or places of learning foretells a rise from obscurity.

To see learned men indicates that your companions will be interesting and prominent.

## LEASE

To dream of signing a lease means you will soon make a decision about changing your residence.

## LEATHER

To dream of leather denotes successful business and favorable engagements. You will enter into lucky speculations if you dream that you are dressed in leather. Ornaments of leather suggest faithfulness in love and at home. Piles of leather imply fortune and happiness.

To deal in leather signifies that no changes in your engagements are necessary for you to successfully accumulate wealth.

## LEDGE

To dream of standing on the ledge of a building and feeling no fear means that you will be willing to take a risk in business that will profit you. To jump or fall from a ledge suggests that you can overcome a problem you thought didn't have a solution.

## LEDGER

If you dream of keeping a ledger, you will have perplexities and disappointing conditions to combat. If you dream that you make wrong entries in your ledger, you will endure small disputes and a slight loss will befall you.

If you put a ledger into a safe, you will be able to protect your rights under adverse circumstances. A misplaced ledger suggests that your interests will go awry through neglect of duty. If you dream that your ledger gets destroyed by fire, you will suffer through the carelessness of friends. If it has worthless accounts, bad management and losses are implied; but if the accounts are good, then your business will improve.

## LEECH

To dream of leeches foretells that enemies will run over your interests. If the leeches are applied to you for medicinal purposes, you or someone in your family will have a serious illness. To see leeches applied to others denotes sickness or trouble to friends. If they should bite you, danger lurks in unexpected places, and you should heed well this warning.

## LEFTOVERS

To dream of eating leftovers foretells financial problems that can be overcome easily.

## LEGERDEMAIN

To dream of practicing legerdemain, or seeing others doing so, signifies that you will be placed in a position that will demand all your energy and power of planning if you hope to extricate yourself.

## LEGISLATURE

To dream that you are a member of a legislature suggests that you are vain about your possessions and will treat members of your family unkindly. You will have no real advancement.

## LEGS

If you dream of admiring someone's legs, you admire qualities, in this person, that it would behoove you to adopt in your own character.

To see misshapen legs denotes an inability on your part to stand on your own two feet. A wounded leg foretells losses.

To dream that you have a wooden leg indicates that you will demean yourself to your friends.

If ulcers are on your legs, it signifies a drain on your ability to aid others financially.

To dream that you have three or more legs suggests that more enterprises are planned in your imagination than will ever benefit you. If you can't use your legs, it portends poverty.

To have a leg amputated suggests the loss of valued friends. The home atmosphere will render life unbearable.

If your own legs are clean and well shaped, you have a happy future and devoted friends. If you are a woman and dream that your legs are hairy, you may be domineering in relationships.

To dream that one of your legs is shorter than the other suggests that there is imbalance in some aspect of your life.

## LEGUMES

In dreams, beans symbolize good fortune and gain in your life.

## LEMON

To dream of seeing lemons on their native trees among rich foliage denotes jealousy toward some beloved object, but demonstrations will convince you of the absurdity of the jealousy.

To eat lemons foretells humiliation and disappointments; it may also suggest a need for cleansing and healing. Green lemons suggest sickness. To dream that you are squeezing a lemon suggests the need to be more economical.

To see shriveled lemons implies divorce or separation.

## LEMONADE

If you drink lemonade in a dream, you will go to great lengths to please others at your own expense.

## LENDING

To dream that you are lending money foretells difficulties in making debt payments and unpleasant influence in private. Lending other articles denotes impoverishment through generosity.

If you refuse to lend things, you are awake to your own interests and maintain the respect of friends. For others to offer to lend you articles, or money, denotes prosperity and close friendships.

## LENS

To dream of any type of lens warns that you need to keep your eyes open to avoid trouble in relationships.

## LENTILS

In dreams, lentils represent quarrels and unhealthy surroundings.

## LEOPARD

To dream of a leopard attacking you suggests that while the future looks good, many difficulties loom through misplaced confidence.

To kill a leopard intimates victory in your affairs. To see one caged implies that enemies will surround you but will fail to injure you.

To see leopards in their native habitat trying to escape from you indicates that you will be embarrassed in business or love, but by persistent efforts you can overcome difficulties.

To dream of leopard skin indicates that your interests will be endangered by a dishonest person who will win your esteem.

## LEPROSY

To dream that you are infected with this dreaded disease foretells a sickness by which you will lose money and incur the displeasure of others. It can also mean you are not utilizing your potential; if you continue on this path, it will waste away. If you see others afflicted thus, you will meet discouraging prospects, and love will turn into indifference.

## LESBIANISM

To dream that you are a lesbian, if you are not in your waking life, signifies a union with aspects of yourself. It is symbolic of self-love, self-acceptance, and passion. You are comfortable with your sexuality and femininity. If in your dream you abhor the notion of lesbianism, this represents your fears and rejection of parts of your own sexuality.

## LETTER*

Letters indicate new opportunities or challenges.

To dream that you see a registered letter suggests that money matters will disrupt long-established relations.

To dream of an anonymous letter indicates that you will be annoyed by an unsuspected source. To write one suggests that you are jealous of a rival.

To dream of getting letters bearing unpleasant news denotes difficulties or illness. If the news is of a joyous character, you will have many things to be thankful for. If the letter is affectionate but is written on colored paper, you will be slighted in love and business. Blue ink denotes constancy, affection, and bright fortune. Red implies estrangements through suspicion and jealousy, but this may be overcome by wisely maneuvering the suspected party. If you fail to read the letter, you will lose something in either your business or social life.

If your letter is intercepted, rival enemies are working to defame you.

To dream of trying to conceal a letter from a sweetheart or spouse intimates that you are interested in unworthy occupations.

To dream of a letter with a black border signifies distress and the death of a relative.

To receive a letter written on black paper with white ink denotes that gloom and disappointment will assail you, and friendly intervention will render small relief. If such a letter passes between husband and wife, it suggests separation and scandal. To businesspeople, it denotes envy and avarice.

To dream that you write a letter predicts that you will be hasty in condemning someone, and regrets will follow. A torn letter means that mistakes may ruin your reputation.

To receive a letter by hand indicates that you are acting ungenerously toward your companions or sweetheart, and that you also are not upright.

To dream often of receiving a letter from a friend foretells his or her arrival. You may also hear from this friend by mail.

*See *Writing*.

## LETTER CARRIER

If you dream of a letter carrier coming with your letters, you will soon receive news of an unwelcome and unpleasant character. If the carrier passes without leaving you any mail, disappointment and sadness will befall you.

If you give him or her letters to mail, you will suffer injury through envy or jealousy.

If you converse with a letter carrier, you will implicate yourself in scandalous proceedings.

## LETTER FILE

To see a letter file in your dream is significant of important news that will cause you an irksome journey.

## LETTUCE

To see lettuce growing green and healthy suggests that you will enjoy some greatly desired good after an unimportant embarrassment.

If you eat lettuce in a dream, illness or petty jealousy will separate you from your lover or friends.

To gather it speaks of superabundant sensitivity and reminds you that your jealous disposition will cause you distress and pain.

To buy lettuce indicates that you will court your own downfall.

## LIAR

If you believe people to be liars in your dream, you may lose faith in a scheme that you have urgently put forward. For someone to call you a liar means that you will experience vexations through deceitful people.

## LIBRARY

To dream that you are in a library suggests that you will grow discontented with your environment and associations and will seek companionship in study and the exploration of ancient customs. To find yourself in a library for another purpose than study implies that your conduct may deceive your friends.

To dream that you cannot find a book in the library indicates that some aspect of yourself is lacking.

## LICE

A dream of lice contains much waking worry and distress. It often implies offensive ailments. Seeing lice on livestock foretells famine and loss; an enemy may also give you exasperation and vexation.

To have lice on your body foretells that you will conduct yourself unpleasantly with your acquaintances. To dream of catching lice predicts sickness; you may also cultivate morbidity.

## LICENSE

In a dream, a license symbolizes disputes and loss.

## LICENSE PLATE

If you dream about a license plate and are able to discern the numbers and letters, play them in a lottery.

## LICKING

To dream of being licked by an animal means that a friend will soon ask you for advice, which you should freely and thoughtfully give. If you dream that you are licked by someone, or you are licking yourself or something or someone else, expect satisfaction in overcoming difficulties.

## LICORICE

To dream of this candy or flavor warns against possible physical injury.

## LID

To dream of placing a lid on anything warns you that you should try to contain your emotions in an upcoming disagreement.

## LIES

If you dream of telling a lie, you can expect trouble in your friendships. If someone else is telling you a lie, help is coming your way from unexpected sources.

## LIFEBOAT

To dream of being in a lifeboat denotes escape from threatened turmoil. If you see a lifeboat sinking, friends will contribute to your distress. If you dream of being lost in a lifeboat, you will be overcome with trouble and your friends will be included, to some extent. If you are saved, you will escape a great calamity.

## LIFEGUARD

To dream that you are a lifeguard suggests that someone will rescue you from a problem at the eleventh hour. To dream of a lifeguard saving someone else suggests that you will soon come to the aid of a friend or family member.

## LIFE INSURANCE

To dream of a life-insurance policy predicts a death. To dream of cashing in on a life-insurance policy predicts a pregnancy announcement.

## LIFE INSURANCE SALESPERSON

To see life-insurance salespeople in a dream means that you will meet a stranger who will contribute to your business interests. Change in your home life is also foreshadowed. If the salesperson seems distorted or unnatural, the dream is more unfortunate than good.

## LIFE PRESERVER

To dream of a life preserver suggests that a friend or family member will help you out with a personal problem. If you are rescued by a life preserver, you may experience a personal problem with a friend or family member.

## LIFE SUPPORT

To dream of someone else on life support foretells good news about a health issue. To dream of being on life support yourself suggests good health and well-being for the immediate future.

## LIFTING

To dream of lifting someone or being lifted predicts happiness and personal gain.

## LIGHT

If you dream of light, success will attend you. If the light is weird, or if it goes out, you will be disagreeably surprised when an undertaking results in nothing.

To dream of a dim light indicates partial success.

## LIGHTER

To dream of using a lighter for good suggests that spiritual enlightenment is coming into your life. To dream of setting something on fire reveals that dishonesty and deceit are part of your personal life.

## LIGHTHOUSE

If you dream of seeing a lighthouse through a storm, difficulties and grief will assail you, but they will give way to prosperity and happiness.

To see a lighthouse from a placid sea denotes calm joy and congenial friends.

## LIGHTNING

Lightning in your dream foreshadows happiness and prosperity of short duration. If the lightning strikes an object near you, and you feel the shock, you will be damaged by the good fortune of a friend, or you may be worried by gossipers and scandalmongers.

If you see furious lightning parting black clouds, sorrow and difficulties will follow close upon fortune.

If lightning strikes you, unexpected sorrows will overwhelm you in business or love. To see lightning above your head heralds joy and gain. If the lightning is in the south, fortune will hide herself from you for a while. Lightning from dark and ominous-looking clouds is always a forerunner of threats, loss, and disappointment.

## LIGHTNING ROD

To see a lightning rod in your dream suggests that threatened destruction of a cherished work will confront you. If lightning strikes the rod, an accident or sudden news may bring you sorrow. If you are having one put up, beware how you begin a new enterprise, for you will likely be overtaken by disappointment.

To have a lightning rod taken down means that you will change your plans and thereby further your interests.

To see many lightning rods indicates a variety of misfortunes.

## LILAC

To dream of this fragrant flower predicts a broken friendship that will cause you heartache, but will turn out to be a blessing in disguise.

## LILY

To dream of this flower means you are seeking a level of purity in your life. This could come through the letting go, or dying, of certain aspects of your life, which will help with the cleansing and rebirth.

## LIMBO

To dream of doing the limbo predicts that you will overcome difficulties in a business matter.

## LIME (CHEMICAL)

To dream of this lawn additive foretells that disaster will prostrate you for a time, but you will revive to greater prosperity than before.

## LIME (FRUIT)

To dream of eating limes foretells continued sickness and rocky straits.

## LIMEKILN

To dream of a limekiln indicates that the immediate future holds no favor for speculations in love or business.

## LIMOUSINE

To dream of being driven in a limousine foreshadows an unexpected gift of money. To be the driver of a limo warns against possible future financial loss.

## LIMPING*

To dream of limping means that a small worry will unexpectedly confront you, detracting much from your enjoyment.

To see others limping signifies that you will be offended by the conduct of a friend. Small failures attend this dream.

*See *Crippled, Lameness.*

## LINEN

To see linen in a dream augurs prosperity and enjoyment. If a person appears to you dressed in linen garments, you will shortly be the recipient of joyful tidings in the nature of an inheritance. If you are wearing clean, fine linen in the dream, your fortune and fullest enjoyment of life are assured; if it is soiled, sorrow and ill luck will be met with occasionally, mingled with the good in your life.

## LINGERIE

If you dream about lingerie and you are a woman, expect a new love interest or the rejuvenation of a current love affair. If you are a man, you will be deceived by a friend whom you previously believed was thoughtful and honest.

## LINSEED OIL

To see linseed oil in your dream indicates that your impetuous extravagance will be held in check by the kind involvement of a friend.

## LION

To dream of a lion suggests that a great force is driving you. If you subdue the beast, you will be victorious in any engagement. If it overpowers you, then you will be open to the successful attacks of enemies.

To see caged lions indicates that your success depends on your ability to cope with opposition. To see someone controlling a lion in or out of its cage implies great mental power and success in business.

Dreaming of young lions hints at new enterprises, which will bring success if properly attended.

The roar of a lion signifies unexpected advancement.

If you see a lion looming over you, showing its teeth by snarling, you are threatened with defeat in your rise to power. Dreaming of a lion's skin suggests a rise to fortune and happiness.

To ride a lion speaks of courage and persistence in surmounting difficulties.

## LIP-READING

If you dream of reading someone's lips or having your lips read, you will be misunderstood in a current business affair. Be clear in your expression.

## LIPS

To dream of unsightly lips signifies disagreeable encounters, hasty decisions, and ill temper in marriage. Full, sweet, cherry lips indicate harmony and affluence. Thin lips signify mastery of the most intricate subjects. Sore or swollen lips suggest privations and unhealthy desires.

## LIPSTICK

If a woman dreams of wearing or applying lipstick, she can expect happiness and joy in her love relationships in the near future. For a man, the same dream foretells possible problems with a work associate.

## LIQUIDATION

If you are a business owner and you dream of liquidating your inventory and assets, look for solid financial gain from your business. If you are buying items from a liquidation sale in your dream, this hints at the loss of an important item in your life.

## LIQUOR

To dream of buying liquor denotes selfish usurpation of property upon which you have no legal claim. If you sell liquor, you will be criticized for benevolence. To dream of drinking liquor suggests that you will come into something of dubious value, but your generosity will draw convivial friends around you. To see liquor in barrels denotes prosperity, but also an unfavorable home life. If the liquor is in bottles, fortune will appear in a very tangible form.

## LISPING

To dream that you have a lisp means that your words will be taken as gold and that your advice will be recognized as worthwhile. To dream that someone else has a lisp suggests that dishonesty and lies are coming from a friend or trusted source.

## LIST

To make a list in your dream warns that you need more organization in your life. To be given a list in a dream suggests that you will soon be helping a friend.

## LIVER

To dream of your own liver counsels you to seek advice from a medical doctor.

To dream of eating liver indicates that some deceitful person has installed him- or herself in the affections of your sweetheart.

## LIZARD

To dream of lizards foretells attacks on you by enemies. If you kill a lizard, you will regain your lost reputation or fortune; but if it should escape, you will meet vexations and crosses in love and business.

## LOAD

To dream that you carry a load signifies a long life filled with labors of love and charity.

To fall under a load denotes your inability to attain the comforts that are necessary for those looking to you for subsistence.

To see others falling under a load denotes trials for them in which you will be interested.

## LOAF

In a dream, loaves of bread symbolize frugality.

Broken loaves bring discontent and bickering among lovers. To see loaves multiply phenomenally prognosticates great success; lovers will be happy with their chosen partners.

## LOBBY

To find yourself standing in the lobby of a hotel predicts an unexpected business trip that will bring you financial gain.

## LOBSTER

To dream of seeing lobsters suggests great favors and riches. If you eat them, you risk contamination by associating too freely with pleasure-seeking people. If the lobsters are made into a salad, success will not change your generous nature, but you will enjoy to the fullest your ideas of pleasure.

If you dream of ordering a lobster, you will hold prominent positions and will command many subordinates.

## LOCK

To dream of a lock denotes bewilderment. If the lock works at your command or as a result of your efforts, you will discover that someone is working you injury. If you are in love, you will find the means to overcome a rival; you will also make a prosperous journey. If the lock resists your efforts, you will be derided and scorned in love, and perilous voyages will bring to you no benefit.

## LOCKET

In a dream, a locket symbolizes a longstanding love relationship.

## LOCKJAW

To dream that you have lockjaw suggests that trouble lies ahead for you, as someone is going to betray your confidence.

To see others with lockjaw reveals that friends may unconsciously detract from your happiness by assigning you unpleasant tasks.

## LOCKSMITH

To dream of employing a locksmith warns you that you may need legal expertise to straighten out a personal or family matter. If you yourself are a locksmith in your dream, legal matters will go very smoothly in the near future.

## LOCOMOTIVE

To dream of a locomotive running at great speed implies a rapid rise in fortune, or perhaps foreign travel. If the locomotive is disabled, then many vexations will interfere with business affairs, and anticipated journeys will be laid aside through the want of means.

To see a completely demolished locomotive signifies great distress and loss of property.

To hear one coming augurs news of a foreign nature; business will assume changes that mean success to all involved.

If you hear a locomotive whistle or a horn, you will be pleased and surprised at the appearance of a friend who has been absent, or at an unexpected offer that will benefit you.

## LOCUSTS

To dream of locusts suggests that discrepancies will be found in your business, and you will worry and suffer.

## LODESTONE

If you dream of a lodestone, you will create favorable opportunities for your own material advancement.

## LODGER

If you dream that you have lodgers, you will be burdened with unpleasant secrets. If someone goes away without paying his bills, you will have unexpected trouble. For someone to pay his bill heralds favor and the accumulation of money.

## LOG

To saw a log in your dream means improvement in matters at home. To dream of logs on the ground is a favorable omen. Loading logs in a dream marks new opportunities in the offing. And a brightly burning log means family joy.

## LOG CABIN

To dream of a log cabin means satisfaction after hard work.

## LOGJAM

To dream of a logjam predicts obstacles in business affairs.

## LOINCLOTH

To dream of wearing a loincloth predicts a satisfying sex life. To dream of someone else wearing one suggests frustration in your sex life.

## LOLLIPOP

To dream of this confection means that you will need patience in order to complete an upcoming project—and you will find that you have it.

## LONELINESS

To dream of being lonely means that you will never be lonely.

## LONG DISTANCE

To dream of making a long-distance phone call predicts an upcoming trip. To receive a long-distance phone call from someone in your dream hints at an unexpected visit from an old friend or acquaintance.

## LOOKING

To dream of looking around or looking intently at an object predicts that you will need to take action to clear up a personal matter.

## LOOKING GLASS*

If a woman dreams of a looking glass, she will soon be confronted by shocking deceitfulness and discrepancies, which may result in tragic scenes or separations.

*See *Mirror*.

## LOOM

To dream of standing by and seeing a loom operated by a stranger denotes much vexation and unecessary irritation from the conversation of those around you. Some disappointment is coupled with this dream.

To see an idle loom suggests a sulky and stubborn person who will cause you much anxiousness.

## LOPSIDEDNESS

To dream of trying to right something lopsided advises that you will need patience with yourself in order to learn something new.

## LORD'S PRAYER, THE

To dream of repeating the Lord's Prayer reveals that you are threatened with secret foes and will need the alliance and support of friends to tide you over difficulties.

To hear others repeat it warns of danger from a friend.

## LOSS

To lose or misplace something in a dream indicates that you will have to overcome an obstacle soon in a personal matter. To lose something of great value means that the obstacle will be something you need assistance with.

## LOST*

To dream that you've lost your way warns you to disabuse your mind of a belief that luck will get you through. Your enterprises threaten failure unless you are painstaking in your management of affairs.

*See Path, Road.

## LOTTERY

If you dream of taking great interest in a lottery, you will engage in a worthless enterprise that will cause you to make an unpropitious journey. If you hold the lucky number, you will gain in a speculation that will perplex you and offer much anxiety.

To see others winning a lottery suggests convivialities and amusements bringing many friends together.

If you lose in a lottery, you will be the victim of schemers. Gloomy depression will result.

## LOTUS

In a dream, this floating flower that roots in swamps represents good luck.

## LOUDSPEAKER

To dream of hearing someone over a loudspeaker lets you know that troubles will soon come your way. But if the sound you are hearing isn't unpleasant or too loud, the troubles will be small.

## LOVE

To dream of loving any object implies satisfaction with your present environment.

If you dream that the love of others fills you with happy anticipation, success will give you contentment and freedom from the anxious cares of life. If you find that your love fails or is not reciprocated, you will become despondent over something.

To dream of the love of parents speaks of uprightness in character and a continual progress toward fortune. The love of animals indicates contentment with what you possess, though you may not think so. For a time, fortune will crown you.

## LOVELINESS

Dreaming of lovely things brings favor to all those connected with you. For lovers to dream that the other is a lovely person foretells for them a speedy and favorable marriage.

## LOZENGES

To dream of lozenges implies success in small matters.

## LSD

To dream of this hallucinogenic drug means you need a reality check; you are not seeing certain things in your life in the proper perspective.

## LUBRICATION

To lubricate anything in your dream means you will complete a project with ease.

## LUCK

To dream of being lucky is highly favorable to the dreamer. Fulfillment of wishes may be expected, and pleasant duties will devolve upon you.

To the despondent, this dream heralds an uplifting and a renewal of prosperity.

## LUGGAGE

To dream of luggage suggests unpleasant cares. You will be encumbered by people whose presence will prove distasteful to you. If you are carrying your own luggage, you are so full of your own distress that you are blinded to the sorrows of others.

To lose your luggage denotes unfortunate speculation or family dissension. To the unmarried, this dream foretells broken engagements.

## LUMBER

To dream of lumber suggests many difficult tasks and but little remuneration or pleasure. To see piles of lumber burning indicates profit from an unexpected source. To dream of sawing lumber denotes unwise transactions and unhappiness.

## LUNAR ECLIPSE

To dream of observing a lunar eclipse means change in the way you see yourself.

## LUTE

To dream of playing a lute augurs joyful news from absent friends. Pleasant activities follow this dream.

## LUXURY

To dream that you are surrounded by luxury indicates much wealth, but dissipation and self-indulgence will reduce your income.

## LYE

To dream of this harsh soap means that your credibility will soon be challenged.

## LYING

To dream that you are lying to escape punishment predicts that you will act dishonorably toward an innocent person. Lying to protect a friend from undeserved chastisement suggests that you will receive many unjust criticisms for your conduct, but you will rise above them and enjoy prominence.

To hear others lying means that they are seeking to trap you.

## LYME DISEASE

To dream of this disease means you are in good health.

## LYNX

To dream of seeing a lynx warns you that enemies are undermining your business and disrupting your home life.

## LYRE

To dream of listening to the music of a lyre suggests innocent pleasures and congenial companionship. Business will run smoothly.

## LYRICS

To dream of reading the lyrics of a song as you sing them means a happy time will be coming your way. To dream of writing lyrics foretells an unexpected joyous event.

## MACADAM

To dream that you see or travel on a macadam road signifies pleasant journeys from which you will derive much benefit. For young people, this dream suggests noble aspirations.

## MACARONI

In dreams, eating macaroni represents abundance. To see it in large quantities means that you will save money through the strictest economy.

## MACE

To dream of spraying someone with Mace™ predicts new friends and business acquaintances in your life. To dream of being sprayed implies dishonesty among friends or business associates.

To dream of using mace, the nutmeg spice, in your cooking foretells financial gain.

## MACHINERY

To dream of machinery suggests that you will undertake a project that occasions great anxiety but will finally result in good for you.

If you see old machinery, you will overcome enemies as you work to build your fortune. To become entangled in machinery foretells loss in your business; much unhappiness will follow.

Loss from bad deals generally follows this dream.

## MAD DOG*

To dream of seeing a mad dog suggests that enemies will make scurrilous attacks on you and your friends. If you succeed in killing the dog, however, you will overcome the negative opinions and will prosper greatly financially.

*See *Dog*.

## MADNESS

To dream of being mad reveals trouble ahead for the dreamer and threatens sickness, by which you will lose property.

To see others suffering under this malady denotes inconstant friends and gloomy endings to bright expectations.

### MADONNA, THE

To dream of the mother of Christ means many blessings are coming your way.

### MAGAZINE

To dream of reading a magazine means that the opportunity to learn something new will soon appear. To write or publish a magazine means you will soon be teaching someone something new.

### MAGGOTS

To dream of maggots foretells difficulties on the horizon in your personal or business life—yet you will easily overcome them and find much fortune and happiness.

### MAGI

To dream of these three wise men means many blessings are coming your way.

### MAGIC

To dream of accomplishing anything by magic indicates pleasant surprises. To see others practicing magic suggests profitable changes. To dream of seeing a magician implies interesting travel.

### MAGISTRATE★

To dream of a magistrate suggests that you will be harassed with threats of lawsuits and losses in business.

*See *Judge, Jury.*

### MAGNET

To dream of a magnet warns that evil influences may draw you from the path of honor.

### MAGNIFYING GLASS

To look through a magnifying glass in your dream speaks of a failure to accomplish your work in a satisfactory manner.

### MAGPIE

To dream of a magpie denotes dissatisfaction and quarrels. Guard your conduct and speech well after this dream.

# MAHOGANY

To dream of this type of wood implies inheritance or unexpected financial gain.

# MAID

To dream of having a maid means that good fortune is coming. To be a maid in your dream suggests advancement in your social standing and status.

# MAILBOX

To see a mailbox in a dream denotes that you are about to enter into transactions that will be claimed to be illegal. If you put a letter in one, you will be held responsible for some irregularity of another.

# MAKEUP

For a woman to dream of putting on her makeup is an omen of good fortune and happiness. For a man, it's a warning against deception in business.

# MALARIA

To dream that you have this illness indicates good health.

# MALICE

To dream of feeling malice toward anyone suggests that you stand low in the opinion of friends because of a disagreeable temper. Seek to control your passion. If you dream of people maliciously using you, an enemy in friendly garb is working to harm you.

# MALIGNANCIES

To dream that you have a malignancy portends good news about a health concern.

# MALL

To dream that you are in a mall means you need to watch your spending.

# MALLET

To dream of a mallet means that you will meet unkind treatment from friends on account of your ill health. Disorder in the home is also indicated.

# MALNUTRITION

This is a dream of abundance and prosperity.

## MALPRACTICE

If you are a doctor and you dream of malpractice, it means an increase in your patients and a boom in your practice. If you dream you are suing a doctor for malpractice, expect to sign legal papers.

## MALT

To dream of malt betokens a pleasant existence and riches that will advance your station. To dream of taking malted drinks denotes interest in something dangerous that will pay off well.

## MAMMOGRAM

To dream of having a mammogram with good results is a warning that you need to watch your health. If your mammogram comes out positive—indicating a problem—your health is fine.

## MAMMOTH

To dream of this extinct mammal implies that something from your past may come back to haunt you.

## MAN

To dream of a man, if he is handsome, well formed, and athletic, indicates that you will enjoy life vastly and come into rich possessions. If he is misshapen, you will meet disappointments, and many perplexities will involve you.

## MANACLES

If you dream of manacles or handcuffs, there will be a release of worries in your life. To dream of others in manacles speaks of the security and protection that surround you.

## MANHUNT

To dream you are the pursuer in a manhunt foretells a coming break in a friendship. To dream that you are being pursued means new friendships are in the offing.

## MANICURE

To dream of getting a manicure warns that you need to conserve your resources; something unexpected may come up that you will need to spend money on.

## MANNA

To dream of manna from heaven suggests unexpected blessings and monetary gain.

## MANNERS

To dream of seeing people practicing poor manners implies a failure to carry out undertakings because of a colleague's actions. If you meet people with affable manners, you will be pleasantly surprised by affairs of moment, with your luck taking a favorable turn.

## MAN-OF-WAR

To dream of a man-of-war indicates long journeys and separation from country and friends; dissension in political affairs is also portended.

## MANSION

To dream of being in a mansion indicates you will soon be wealthy. To see one from a distance foretells advancement.

## MANSLAUGHTER*

To dream that you are in any way connected with a manslaughter foretells a period of severe emotional stress when you may need to find help controlling your temper. To witness a manslaughter in a dream portends an unwelcome change.

*See *Killing, Murder.*

## MANTILLA

To dream of seeing a mantilla denotes an unwise enterprise that will bring you into unfavorable notice.

## MANURE

In dreams, manure is a favorable omen. The dream will be followed by much good, especially for farmers.

## MANUSCRIPT

To dream that you are writing a manuscript suggests financial gain and notoriety in the near future. To dream of reading another's manuscript implies a small financial loss, but nothing that can't be overcome.

To dream of a manuscript in an unfinished state forebodes disappointment. If you dream of its rejection by publishers, you will feel hopeless for a time, but eventually your desires will become a reality. If you lose it, you will be disappointed. If you see it burn, some work of your own will bring you profit and much acclaim.

## MAP

To dream of a map, or of studying one, suggests that you will contemplate a change in your business. Some disappointing things will occur, but much profit also will follow the change.

To dream of looking for a map means that a sudden discontent with your surroundings will inspire you with new energy, and thus your circumstances will improve.

## MAPLE

To dream of this tree or type of wood implies a happy family home life. To dream of maple syrup, maple sugar, or anything flavored with maple speaks of a happy love life and extraordinary sexual vigor.

## MARATHON

To dream that you are in a marathon means good health and well-being. To watch a marathon foretells the coming and going of a love affair.

## MARBLE

To dream of a marble quarry suggests that your life will be a financial success, but that your social surroundings will be devoid of affection.

If you dream of polishing marble, you will come into a pleasing inheritance. If you see marble broken, you will fall into disfavor among your associates.

## MARCH

To dream of the month of March portends disappointing returns in business.

## MARCHING

To dream of marching to the sound of music indicates that you are ambitious to become a soldier or a public official; consider matters well before making a final decision.

## MARDI GRAS

To dream of this holiday suggests happy times with family and friends—but with a cost attached, mental, physical, or financial.

## MARE*

To dream of seeing mares in pastures denotes success in business and congenial companions. If the pasture is barren, it foretells a period of poverty, but warm friendships.

*See *Horse*.

### MARGARINE

To dream of margarine cautions that you may have to rethink a plan or a home project.

### MARGARITA

To dream of this drink warns you to watch your desire to overindulge.

### MARIGOLD

To dream of seeing marigolds denotes contentment.

### MARIJUANA*

If you actually smoke this drug in your waking life, then the dream has no special significance. Otherwise, if you dream of using this drug, it suggests that something you are doing will discredit you.

*See *Reefer*.

### MARINER

To dream that you are a mariner implies a long journey to distant countries. Much pleasure will be connected with the trip.

### MARK

If you dream of a mark—a birthmark, a trademark, or a similar distinguishing feature—interesting new friends are coming your way.

### MARKET

To dream that you are in a market denotes thrift and busy activity in all occupations. An empty market indicates depression and gloom. Decayed vegetables or meat suggest losses in business.

### MARMALADE

To dream of eating marmalade denotes sickness and much dissatisfaction.

### MARQUEE

To see your name on a marquee means that honor and notoriety are in your future.

### MARRIAGE* (WEDDING)

To dream of seeing a marriage denotes enjoyment if the wedding guests attend in pleasing colors and are happy; if they are dressed in black or other somber hues, there will be mourning and sorrow for the dreamer.

If you dream of planning to marry, you may receive unpleasant news. If you are an attendant at a wedding, you will experience much pleasure from the thoughtfulness of loved ones, and business affairs will be unusually promising. To dream of any unfortunate occurrence in connection with a marriage foretells distress, sickness, or death in your family. For a young woman to dream that she is a bride, and be unhappy or indifferent, foretells disappointments.

*See *Bride, Nuptials.*

## MARS

To dream of this planet warns you to be careful of being argumentative and hot-tempered.

## MARSH*

To dream of walking through marshy places suggests illness resulting from overwork and worry. You will suffer much from the unwise conduct of a close relative.

*See *Swamp.*

## MARSHMALLOW

To dream of this spongy confection means happy times are in the offing.

## MARTINI

To dream of this alcoholic cocktail cautions you about your desire to indulge.

## MARTYR

To dream of martyrs suggests false friends, domestic unhappiness, and losses in areas that concern you most.

To dream that you are a martyr signifies separation from friends; enemies will attempt to slander you.

## MASCOT

To dream of a mascot means that sudden changes will soon be beneficial to your prospects.

## MASK

To dream that you are wearing a mask denotes temporary trouble, as your conduct toward a loved one will be misinterpreted and your efforts to aid that person will be misunderstood. Still, you will profit by the temporary misunderstanding.

To see others wearing masks suggests that you will combat falsehood and envy.

To simply see a mask in your dreams warns that someone may be unfaithful to you.

## MASON

To dream that you see a mason plying his trade denotes a rise in your circumstances; a more congenial social atmosphere will surround you. If you dream of seeing a meeting of the Order of Masons in full regalia, there are others besides yourself whom you must protect and keep from life's difficulties.

## MASQUERADE (DISGUISE)

To dream of being in masquerade hints that you will indulge in foolish and harmful pleasures to the neglect of business and domestic duties.

## MASQUERADE BALL

In dreams, a masquerade ball symbolizes unexpected surprises.

## MASS

To dream that you are attending a Catholic Mass predicts good fortune and blessings in the near future.

## MASSACRE

To dream of a massacre presages trouble on the global front.

## MASSAGE

To dream of getting a massage suggests that you are suspicious of a friend's motives. To give a massage means good news is approaching.

## MAST

To dream of seeing the masts of ships denotes long and pleasant voyages, the making of many new friends, and the gaining of new possessions.

To see the masts of wrecked ships implies sudden changes in your circumstances that will necessitate giving up on anticipated pleasures. If a sailor dreams of a mast, he will soon sail on an eventful trip.

## MASTECTOMY

To dream of getting a mastectomy heralds new love or pregnancy.

## MASTER

To dream that you have a master is a sign of your own inability to command others; you will do better work under the leadership of a strong-willed person. If you are a master and command many people, you will excel in judgment in the fine points of life and will hold high positions and possess much wealth.

## MASTER OF CEREMONIES

To dream that you are the emcee at an event means you will soon be recognized by your business associates or friends for a project you are currently working on.

## MASTERPIECE

To dream of observing a masterpiece foretells a surprise or unexpected gift. To dream of creating a masterpiece augurs a change in your personal life of your own doing.

## MASTURBATION

To dream of masturbating indicates a level of frustration in your waking life. This frustration is most likely linked to a relationship but not necessarily with sex.

## MAT

Keep away from mats in your dreams, as they will usher you into sorrow and confusion.

## MATCHES

To dream of matches denotes prosperity and change when least expected. If you strike a match in the dark, unexpected news and fortune are on the way.

## MATCHMAKER

If you are married and dream of going to a matchmaker, trouble lies ahead in your romantic partnership. If you are not married, this dream foretells a new love that will not last. To dream that you are a matchmaker predicts the coming of the love of your life.

## MATH

To dream of working on math problems means you will soon be taking account of your life. You may make some changes or decide that you are very content.

## MATINEE

To dream of going to a matinee suggests that a project you are working on will be completed earlier than expected.

## MATTING

To dream of matting foretells pleasant prospects and cheerful news from absent loved ones. If it is old or torn, vexing problems may arise.

## MATTRESS

To dream of a mattress suggests that you may assume new duties and responsibilities. To sleep on a new mattress in your dream signifies contentment with present surroundings.

To dream of a mattress factory indicates that you will be connected in business with thrifty partners and will soon amass wealth.

## MATZOH

To dream of this unleavened bread implies that something nice you have done for someone will be returned to you.

## MAUSOLEUM

To dream of a mausoleum indicates that a prominent friend will have trouble, become sick, or die. Finding yourself inside a mausoleum foretells your own illness.

## MAY

To dream of the month of May denotes prosperous times, and also pleasure for the young.

To dream of freakish May weather suggests that sudden sorrow and disappointment may cloud pleasure.

## MAYONNAISE

To dream of this condiment means that prosperity is on the horizon.

## MAYOR

To dream that you are the mayor tells you that a demotion is on the way at work.

## MAZE

To dream that you can find your way out of a maze suggests that your worries will be few. However, if you are lost and frightened while in a maze, you may have to change the way you do things to solve a problem that's vexing you.

## MEADOW

To dream of meadows predicts happy reunions and bright promises of future prosperity.

## MEAL*

To dream of enjoying your meal is a good omen. To dream of not enjoying it suggests that you will let trifling matters interfere with momentous affairs and business engagements.

*See *Eating.*

## MEASLES

To dream that you have the measles indicates that worry might interfere with your business affairs. To dream that someone else has this disease means that you will be troubled over the condition of others.

## MEASURING

To measure anything in a dream means that you will soon be reevaluating the direction your life is going in.

## MEAT*

If you dream of meat, it's a fortunate omen. To buy meat in a dream means you will be careful about risk-taking. Cutting meat means an increase in material wealth. Cooking meat suggests a change in your circumstances. Eating meat heralds good fortune.

*See *Beef.*

## MECHANIC

To dream of a mechanic denotes change in your dwelling place and a more active business. Advancement in wages usually follows this dream.

## MEDAL

To dream of medals denotes honors gained by application and industry. To lose one suggests misfortune through the unfaithfulness of others.

## MEDIAN DIVIDER

To dream of being frustrated because you can't cross a median divider tells you that events in your business life will be easy and satisfying.

## MEDICINE

To dream of medicine, if pleasant to the taste, means that trouble will come to you, but in a short time it will work for your good. If you take distasteful medicine, however, you will suffer a protracted illness, or some deep sorrow or loss will overcome you.

To give medicine to someone else denotes that you will work to injure someone who trusted you.

## MEDIEVAL PERIOD

To dream you are in medieval times warns you of a tendency to be closed-minded; you need to expand your thinking.

## MEDIUM

To dream of a going to a psychic medium means that you will have the correct instincts in an upcoming personal or business matter, and this will help you achieve your goals. To dream that you are a medium and able to predict the future suggests that you seek advice from others in an upcoming business or personal matter.

## MEGAPHONE

To dream of using a megaphone to amplify your voice means that you will have to be clear and precise in giving directions in an upcoming business project or personal matter. To hear someone else using a megaphone in a dream is a warning to listen carefully to those around you.

## MELANCHOLY

To dream that you feel melancholy over any event implies disappointment in what you thought were favorable undertakings.

To dream that you see others being melancholy denotes unpleasant interruptions in affairs. To lovers, it indicates separation.

## MELODY

To dream of a melody that is pleasing means great fortune. But if it is unpleasant, expect discord in personal or business relationships.

## MELON

To dream of melons denotes hope and a surprising turn of events in connection with a cherished goal.

## MEMOIR

To write a memoir in your dreams means that an upcoming event will create pleasant memories.

## MEMORABILIA

To dream of memorabilia of any kind means you have an obsession with the past that you need to let go of.

## MEMORANDUM

To dream that you write memoranda indicates that you will engage in an unprofitable business, and much worry will result for you. To see others writing memoranda signifies that some person will worry you with appeals for aid.

To lose a memorandum suggests a slight loss in trade. If you find one, you will assume new duties that will cause much pleasure to others.

### MEMORIAL

To dream of a memorial signifies that you will find occasion to demonstrate patience and kindness when trouble or sickness threatens your relatives.

### MEMORIZATION

To memorize something in your dreams and be able to retain it upon waking means that you will be furthering your education or knowledge. If you're unable to memorize or retain it, you need to expand your mind to let different ideas in.

### MENAGERIE

To dream of a menagerie suggests various troubles.

### MENDICANT

To dream of mendicants means you will meet with disagreeable interferences in your plans.

### MENDING

To dream of mending soiled garments implies that you will undertake to right a wrong at an inopportune moment; but if the garments are clean, you will be successful in adding to your fortune.

### MENOPAUSE

If a woman dreams that she is going through menopause, but she isn't, she might be facing a health problem in need of a doctor's attention. For a man to dream he is in menopause suggests that upcoming health problems will be easily solved.

### MENORAH

To dream of this Jewish candle holder used on the holiday of Hanukkah implies upcoming blessings.

### MENU

To dream of a menu indicates that a long, comfortable, and luxurious life lies ahead.

## MERCURY

To dream of mercury is significant of unhappy changes through the constant oppression of enemies.

## MERMAID

If you dream of a mermaid and it is a pleasant dream, you can expect things to go well in the near future. But if it was unpleasant, look for disappointment.

## MERRIMENT

To dream of being merry, or in merry company, suggests that pleasant events will engage you for a time, and affairs will assume profitable shapes.

## MERRY-GO-ROUND

A dream about a merry-go-round suggests that you will find yourself mulling over a troubling problem again and again until you find a solution.

## MESH

To dream of being entangled in the mesh of a net, or something similar, denotes that enemies will oppress you in a time of seeming prosperity.

## MESS

To dream of seeing a mess means that the problems currently creating confusion and angst will soon be resolved.

## MESSAGE

To dream of receiving a message suggests that changes will take place in your affairs. If you dream of sending a message, you will be placed in unpleasant situations.

## MESSENGER

If you dream of delivering good news, you will soon have a pleasant surprise via written communication, either letter or e-mail. If the message you are bearing is sad or bad news, then you will experience disappointments in contracts or legal matters.

If you dream that you have a happy message delivered to you, expect happy relationships in the near future. If it is sad, you will be disappointed in a relationship that is dear to you.

## MESSIAH

To dream of a messiah or prophet foretells blessings and happiness.

## METAL*

To dream of molten metal means that obstacles will seem impossible to overcome—but they are indeed solvable. Buying metal in your dream is a lucky omen. Selling metal indicates progress ahead, but only with much hard work.

*See individual types of metal.

## METAMORPHOSIS

To dream of seeing anything metamorphose suggests that sudden changes will take place in your life, for good or bad, depending on whether the dream was pleasant or frightful.

## METEOR

To dream of a meteor streaking across the sky foretells a sudden windfall. To dream of a meteorite crashing to Earth is even better: the windfall will be more than you have ever imagined.

## METER (PARKING)

To dream that you are putting money in a parking meter means you will soon have extra cash to save. If you dream of receiving a ticket because a meter ran out of time, you may soon incur an unexpected expense, so make sure that you save money for it beginning right away.

## METRIC SYSTEM

If you dream that you are measuring or counting using the metric system, and you do not normally use it, you will have to find another way to solve a problem rather than what you are currently doing.

## MICROCHIP

To dream of this semiconductor of electrical circuits means you will soon experience a brilliant idea for an upcoming project that will bring you notoriety.

## MICROFILM

To see yourself or another looking at something on microfilm warns you to pay close attention to the smaller details in an upcoming home or business project.

## MICROPHONE

To dream that you are using a microphone suggests that your advice and opinions will be heard loud and clear. To dream of someone else using one means you will have to be forceful with your advice and opinions if you hope to be heard.

## MICROSCOPE

To dream of a microscope implies that you will experience failure or small returns in your enterprises.

## MICROSURGERY

To dream of microsurgery warns that you may not be paying attention to details in a project or your life, and this may cost you financially. If you are performing the surgery in your dream, your attention to detail in a project will reap much more gain than you thought. To dream that you are having microsurgery performed on you suggests good health in the near future.

## MICROWAVE OVEN

To use a microwave oven in a dream denotes prosperity and financial gain, unless it wasn't food that you put into it; then this dream indicates financial loss.

## MIDWIFE

To see a midwife in your dreams signifies unfortunate sickness and a narrow escape from death.

## MIGRAINE

To dream of having this terrible headache foretells a problem that may cause you a lot of mental stress. You may need to seek help to alleviate this.

## MILDEW

To dream of mildew means that you will be disappointed in a romantic or platonic relationship.

## MILEPOST

To dream that you see or pass a milepost predicts that you will be assailed by fears in business or love.

If you see a fallen milepost, accidents are threatening to disorder your affairs.

## MILITARY

To dream of the military foretells peace of mind.

## MILK*

Cow's milk means good health; goat's milk, business advances.

For a farmer, to dream of drinking milk denotes abundant harvest and pleasure in the home; for a traveler, it foretells a fortunate voyage. This is a very propitious dream for women.

To see milk in large quantities signifies riches and health. To dream of dealing in milk commercially suggests great increase in fortune. To give milk away shows that you will be too benevolent for the good of your own fortune. Spilling milk means that you will experience slight losses and temporary unhappiness at the hands of friends.

To dream of spoiled milk implies that you will be tormented by petty troubles. If the milk is sour, you will be disturbed over the distress of friends. To dream of trying unsuccessfully to drink milk signifies that you will be in danger of losing something of value or the friendship of a highly esteemed person.

To dream of hot milk foretells a struggle, but the final result will be the winning of riches and desires. To dream of bathing in milk denotes the pleasure and companionship of friends.

*See *Buttermilk*.

## MILKING

If you dream of milking a cow and the liquid flows in great streams from the udder, you will see great opportunities withheld from you, but the end result will be favorable for you.

## MILKY WAY

To dream of the Milky Way galaxy means that your wishes will soon be granted.

## MILL

To dream of a mill indicates thrift and fortunate undertakings. A dilapidated mill, though, suggests sickness and misfortune.

## MILLDAM

To dream of seeing clear water pouring over a milldam foretells pleasant enterprises, of either a business or a social nature. If the water is muddy or impure, you will meet with losses, and troubles will arise where pleasure was anticipated. If the dam is dry, your business will assume shrunken proportions.

## MILLER

To see a miller in your dreams signifies that your surroundings will grow more hopeful.

## MILLIONAIRE

To dream of being a millionaire foretells profits in business. To dream of meeting a millionaire warns you to be careful of new friendships.

## MIMICRY

If you dream of mimicking someone, beware of that person. If you don't know the person, be careful of your friendships.

## MINE

To dream of being in a mine denotes failure. To own a mine, though, suggests future wealth.

## MINERAL

If you dream of minerals, your present unpromising outlook will grow brighter.

## MINERAL WATER

To dream of drinking mineral water foretells that fortune will favor your efforts. You will enjoy your opportunities to satisfy your cravings for certain pleasures.

## MINGLING

To find yourself mingling with strangers in a crowd foretells the loss of a friendship or business associate.

## MINIATURES

To dream of things in miniature means that a larger-than-life surprise or event is on the way.

## MINIMIZATION

To find yourself minimizing anything in a dream warns that you should pay special attention to business matters.

## MINING

To see mining in your dreams means that an enemy is seeking your ruin by bringing up past immoralities in your life. You are likely to make unpleasant journeys if you stand near the mine. If you dream of hunting for mines, you will engage in worthless pursuits.

### MINISTER*

To dream of a religious minister indicates an increase in status and improvement in your living conditions.

*See Preacher, Priest.

### MINIVAN

If you dream of this car and you don't own one in your waking life, you will soon have to help your business associates complete a project they are currently working on.

### MINK

To dream of this animal warns you to work harder at your career and that you have sly enemies to overcome.

If you kill one, you will win your desires.

### MINK COAT

To dream of a mink coat suggests that you should beware of greed and selfishness.

### MINORITY

To dream that you are in the minority means that you will soon be participating in a gathering of family and friends for a joyous occasion.

### MINT

To dream of the herb, the flavor, or the confection signifies improvement in your health. To dream of the place where money is minted means a rise in your social status.

### MINUET

To dream of seeing the minuet danced signifies a pleasant existence with congenial companions. If you dance it yourself, good fortune and domestic joys are foretold.

### MINUTE

To dream that you are watching the minutes on a clock means that you will have more time in your life for pleasure and happiness.

### MIRACLE

If you dream of a miracle, your future will be great.

## MIRE

To dream of going through mire indicates that your dearest wishes and plans will be put on hold temporarily because of unexpected changes in your surroundings.

## MIRROR*

To dream of seeing yourself in a mirror indicates that you will face many discouraging issues, and sickness will cause you distress and loss of fortune. It may also foretell unfaithfulness and neglect in marriage.

To see another face in the mirror alongside your own indicates that you are leading a double life. You will deceive your friends.

To see others in a mirror rather than yourself means they will act unfairly toward you to promote their own interests. To see animals suggests disappointment and loss in fortune.

To break a mirror in your dream portends an early and accidental death. Seeing an already broken one foretells the sudden or violent death of someone related to you.

*See *Glass, Looking glass.*

## MISBEHAVIOR

To dream that you are misbehaving foretells happy festivities in the near future. To dream of seeing others misbehave cautions you to be sure your behavior is serious enough.

## MISCARRIAGE

If you dream of a miscarriage and you are pregnant, this dream has no meaning. If you are single but not pregnant, the dream of a miscarriage foretells of news of a pregnancy or birth, but not necessarily yours. For a married woman, it predicts your own pregnancy. To watch a miscarriage or to know that someone has miscarried in a dream warns of trouble in your family.

## MISER

To dream of a miser suggests that you will struggle to find true happiness because of your own selfishness; love will disappoint you sorely.

To dream that you are miserly hints that others consider you obnoxious and conceited.

To dream that any of your friends are misers means that you may be distressed by the demands of others.

## MISERY

To dream that you are miserable foretells peace of mind and a happy environment. To dream of someone else's misery warns of a possible argument or quarrel with a friend.

## MISLEADING

If you dream you have been misled, help will be coming from a business associate. If you dream that you have been misleading someone, you will soon be called upon for help—but you won't be able to help, because of your own lack of experience or knowledge.

## MISMATCHED CLOTHING

To be aware that your clothing is mismatched in a dream suggests that a joyful event is coming.

## MISREPRESENTATION

To dream that you have been misrepresented means you have loyal and trusting friends. To dream that you are the one who is misrepresenting someone means you will soon be caught in a falsehood or doing something dishonest.

## MISSIONARY

To dream of being a missionary implies that a long-term plan will fail.

## MIST

To dream you are enveloped in a mist denotes uncertain fortunes and domestic unhappiness. If the mist clears, your troubles will be of short duration.

If you see others in a mist, you will profit by their misfortunes.

## MISTAKE

If you dream of taking responsibility for a mistake, financial gain is in the offing. To dream of blaming others for your mistake means financial loss.

## MISTLETOE

To dream of mistletoe foretells happiness and great rejoicing.

To the young, it predicts many pleasant pastimes. If seen with unpromising signs, however, disappointment will displace pleasure or fortune.

## MISTREATMENT

To dream of being mistreated means you are very loved and revered by your peer group. To mistreat someone else in a dream means you will lose a valuable friendship.

## MITTENS

To dream of mittens means you will soon have new love in your life. To dream of losing one suggests that you will soon experience a break in a relationship. But if you find the mitten in your dream, the relationship will be mended.

## MIXING

To dream of mixing anything in a dream means you will soon be incorporating different ideas in order to make a project move along faster.

## MOANING

To dream that you are moaning foretells a financial disruption that may be very difficult to rectify. To dream that you hear someone else moaning indicates the same thing—but the issue will be easily remedied.

## MOB

To dream of an angry mob foretells a group activity that could be dangerous to you.

## MOCCASINS

To dream of these shoes indicates that you will attain a level of spiritual enlightenment through the written word.

## MOCKERY

To mock someone in a dream means you need to beware of new people suddenly wanting to become your friend. To be mocked in a dream foretells new friendships.

## MOCKINGBIRD

To see or hear a mockingbird signifies that you will be invited to a pleasant gathering with friends, and your affairs will move along smoothly and prosperously.

## MODELS

To dream of a model suggests that your social affairs will deplete your purse; quarrels and regrets will follow.

## MODEM

To dream of buying or selling a modem means financial gain. To dream that you are attaching one to your computer suggests that you will be asked to learn something new to advance your career.

## MOLAR

To dream that you are having a molar pulled warns you to watch what you say because it will be misunderstood. To have a molar filled means you'll be asked to contribute your advice to solve a problem.

## MOLASSES

To dream of molasses is a sign that someone is going to extend you pleasant hospitality, and, through its acceptance, you will meet agreeable and fortunate surprises. To eat it suggests that you will be discouraged and disappointed in love. To find it smeared on your clothing means you will have disagreeable romances, and probably losses in business.

## MOLD (FUNGUS)

To dream of mold on anything indicates financial gain.

## MOLES

To dream of moles, the burrowing mammals, indicates secret enemies. If you dream of catching a mole, you will overcome any opposition and rise to prominence.

To see moles (spots) or blemishes on a person indicates illness and quarrels.

## MOLTEN

To see anything molten, whether metal, gold, or rock, means you will soon see a change for the better in a relationship.

## MONARCH

To dream you are visited by a monarch or attend an affair that puts you in contact portends great social success. To be a monarch in a dream indicates an unexpected job change.

## MONASTERY

To dream of visiting a monastery means the coming of blessings. To dream that you live in one means the blessings will be greater than you can imagine.

## MONEY*

To dream of finding money suggests small worries but large happiness. Changes will follow.

To pay out money denotes misfortune; to receive gold, great prosperity and unalloyed pleasures.

If you lose money, you will experience unhappy hours in the home and affairs will appear gloomy.

If you count your money and find a deficit, you will worry about making payments.

To dream of stealing money indicates that you are in danger and should guard yourself. To save money augurs wealth and comfort. To dream that you swallow money suggests that you may become mercenary. To look upon a quantity of money denotes that prosperity and happiness are within your reach.

To dream that you find a roll of currency, and someone claims it, foretells that you will lose in an enterprise by the interference of a friend. You will find that you are spending your money unwisely and living beyond your means. It is a dream of caution.

*See *Cash, Dimes.*

## MONEY MARKET

To dream that you open a money-market account foretells financial loss. Dreaming that you cash one in means financial gain.

## MONEY ORDER

To dream that you purchase a money order means that you will soon find yourself buying something you really don't need. To dream of receiving a money order indicates financial gain.

## MONK

To dream of seeing a monk, or of being a monk, means a change in your life that at first you might not see as a blessing—but it will turn into one.

## MONKEY

To dream of a monkey indicates that deceitful people will flatter you to advance their own interests.

To see a dead monkey signifies that your worst enemies will soon be removed.

## MONOGRAM

To dream of your initials on any item foretells business recognition. To dream of someone else's initials foretells a social embarrassment of some kind coming soon. Be careful what you are doing to draw attention to yourself.

## MONOPOLY (THE GAME)

To dream of playing Monopoly augurs a change of residence.

## MONORAIL

To dream of riding on a monorail means the coming of a trip, either for business or pleasure. To dream of watching a monorail train go by warns you to cancel a business or pleasure trip.

## MONSTER

To dream of being pursued by a monster indicates that sorrow and misfortune hold prominent places in your immediate future.

To slay a monster foretells that you will successfully cope with enemies and rise to prominent positions.

## MONUMENT

To dream of building a monument to someone or something suggests social embarrassment. To dream that you visit a national monument in any country indicates the coming of an invitation to attend a grand social affair.

## MOON*

To dream of seeing the moon prognosticates success in love and business affairs.

A weird-looking or otherwise altered moon denotes unpropitious romance, domestic infelicities, and disappointing enterprises of a business character. The moon in eclipse implies that contagion will ravage your community.

A new moon indicates an increase in wealth and congenial partners in marriage.

*See *Eclipse, Sun*.

## MOONSTONE

To dream of this semiprecious jewel suggests that you will soon be attracting love, or, alternatively, that you have the ability to remain calm during a troubled time in a relationship.

### MOOSE

To dream of this large animal means a good change is coming that will be beneficial for you. To dream of shooting a moose implies family troubles.

### MOPED

To dream of driving or riding on this mini-motorcycle is a dream of short-distance travel coming soon.

### MORGUE

To dream that you visit a morgue searching for someone foretells the shocking news of the death of a relative or friend.

If you see many corpses there, much sorrow and trouble will come to your attention.

### MORNING

To see the morning dawn clear in your dreams prognosticates the approach of fortune and pleasure.

A cloudy morning portends that weighty affairs will overwhelm you.

### MORNING SICKNESS

If you dream that you have morning sickness, and you are not pregnant, you will soon have a health problem that will not need medical attention but will heal itself. If you are pregnant, to dream that you have morning sickness signifies nothing.

### MOROCCO

To see Morocco in your dreams suggests that you will receive substantial aid from unexpected sources. Your love will be rewarded by faithfulness.

### MOROSENESS

If you find yourself morose in dreams, you will awaken to find the world, as far as you are concerned, going fearfully wrong.

To see others morose portends unpleasant occupations and unpleasant companions.

### MORPHINE

To dream that you or others are taking morphine suggests that you will need to make a decision quickly about a change in your relationships.

### MORTGAGE*

To dream that you put a mortgage on your property indicates that you are threatened with financial upheavals that will throw you into embarrassing positions.

To take or hold a mortgage against others implies adequate wealth to meet your obligations.

To find yourself reading or examining mortgages suggests great possibilities of love or gain.

To lose a mortgage contract implies loss and worry if it cannot be found again.

*See Deed.*

## MORTIFICATION

To dream that you feel mortified over any deed committed by yourself is a sign that you will be placed in an unenviable position before those to whom you most wish to appear honorable and just. Financial conditions will fall low.

To see mortified flesh denotes disastrous enterprises and disappointment in love.

## MOSAIC

To dream of this work of art means that you will soon be in contact with a long-lost friend. To dream of making mosaics suggests that you will soon be fitting pieces of your life together that will benefit you in the long run.

## MOSES

To dream that you see Moses means personal gain and marriage.

## MOSQUITO

To see mosquitoes in your dreams means you will strive in vain to remain impregnable to the sly attacks of secret enemies. Your patience and fortune will both suffer from designing people.

If you kill mosquitoes, you will eventually overcome obstacles and enjoy fortune and domestic bliss.

## MOSS

To dream of moss that is dry and discolored signifies disenchantment. If it is soft and green, it indicates romantic bliss.

## MOTH

To see a moth in a dream indicates that small worries will pressure you into hurried contracts, which will prove unsatisfactory. Quarrels of a domestic nature are in the forecast.

## MOTHER*

To see your mother in a dream as she appears in waking life signifies pleasing results from any enterprise.

If you engage her in conversation, you will soon have good news from issues you are anxious over.

For a woman to dream of her mother signifies pleasant duties and connubial bliss.

To see your mother emaciated or dead foretells sadness.

To hear your mother call you indicates that you are derelict in your duties, and that you are pursuing the wrong course in business.

To hear her cry as if in pain portends her illness or some affliction.

*See Parents.

## MOTHER-IN-LAW

To dream of your mother-in-law predicts that there will be pleasant reconciliations for you after a serious disagreement.

## MOTORCADE

To dream of watching a motorcade go by means troubles will soon disappear from your life. To dream of being in a motorcade predicts travel in the future.

## MOTORCYCLE

To dream of riding a motorcycle means travel, but not far away. To dream that you ride on one as a passenger suggests new friendships with the opposite sex.

## MOUND

Burial mounds in a dream foretell a pregnancy or birth announcement. But to make a mound of dirt, clay, or the like in your dream means you will be adding on to your home or residence.

## MOUNTAIN

If you ascend a mountain in your dream and the way is pleasant and verdant, you will rise swiftly to wealth and prominence. If the mountain is rugged and you fail to reach the top, you may expect reverses in your life and should strive to overcome all weakness in your nature. To awaken when you are at a dangerous point in your ascent suggests that you will find affairs taking a positive turn when they appear gloomy.

## MOURNING

To dream that you are in mourning is an omen of ill luck and unhappiness. If others mourn, disturbing influences among your friends may cause you unexpected dissatisfaction and loss; to lovers, this dream foretells misunderstanding and probable separation.

## MOUSE

To dream of mice foretells domestic troubles and the insincerity of friends. Business affairs will assume a discouraging tone. To kill mice suggests that you will conquer your enemies. To let them escape is significant of doubtful struggles.

If you dream of a single mouse, you need to be aware of someone whom you dislike who will stab you in the back or spread ugly rumors about you.

## MOUSETRAP*

To see a mousetrap in your dream signifies your need to be careful, because people have designs on you.

If you see the mousetrap full of mice, you will likely fall into the hands of enemies.

If you dream of setting a trap, you will artfully devise means to overcome your opponents.

*See Mice.

## MOUTH

A dream of an open mouth means you need to mind your own business when it comes to others. If you see teeth in the open mouth, untrue friendships are suggested. And if the mouth is small, financial gain is indicated. To dream of a large mouth foretells a valuable new friendship.

## MOVIE

To dream of enjoying a movie suggests pleasant times ahead socially. If you do not like the movie, you will be cheated on in a romantic relationship.

## MOVING

To dream of moving either your business or your home means that you will soon find peace and happiness right where you live or work without having to make any changes.

## MP3 PLAYER

To dream of using an MP3 player means you will be making pleasant memories that will last your lifetime.

## MUCUS

In dreams, mucus represents good health. If it is your own, it also indicates financial gain.

## MUD

To dream that you walk in mud denotes that you will have cause to lose confidence in friendships, and there will be losses and disturbances in family circles.

If you see others walking in mud, ugly rumors will reach you about a friend or employee. If you see mud on your clothing, your reputation is being assailed; to scrape it off signifies that you will escape the calumny of enemies.

## MUG

To dream of drinking from a mug means a warm and lasting relationship is on the horizon for you.

## MULBERRIES

To see mulberries in your dream suggests that sickness will prevent you from obtaining your desires; you will be called upon often to relieve suffering.

To eat mulberries signifies bitter disappointments.

## MULE*

If you dream of seeing or riding on a mule, you are engaging in pursuits that will cause you the greatest anxiety. If you reach your destination without interruption, however, you will be recompensed.

To be kicked by a mule foretells disappointment in love and marriage.

To see a dead mule portends broken engagements and social decline.

*See Donkey.

## MULTIPLICATION

To dream of performing this mathematical procedure warns you against spending money you don't have. To dream of teaching or being taught how to multiply means financial gain.

## MUMMY

To dream of a mummy means you will soon help someone find a solution to a problem. If you see yourself as a mummy, you are wrapped up in someone else's problem; you really should walk away from it.

## MUMS

In dreams, these flowers symbolize death.

## MURDER*

To see a murder committed in your dream foretells much sorrow arising from the misdeeds of others.

If you commit a murder, you are engaging in a dishonorable adventure that will leave a stigma upon your name. To dream that you are murdered suggests that enemies are secretly working to overthrow you.

*See *Killing, Manslaughter.*

## MUSCLES

If you dream of seeing your muscles well developed, you will have strange encounters with enemies, but you will succeed in surmounting their evil works and will gain fortune. If your muscles are shrunken instead, your inability to succeed in your affairs is portended.

## MUSEUM

To dream of a museum implies that you will pass through many and varied adventures in striving for what appears to be your rightful position. The knowledge you acquire will stand you in better light than if you had pursued the usual course to learning. If the museum is distasteful, you will have many causes for vexation.

## MUSHROOM

To see mushrooms in your dreams denotes unhealthy desires and unwise haste in amassing wealth, which may vanish in lawsuits and vain pleasures.

To eat them signifies humiliation and disgraceful love.

## MUSIC

To dream of hearing harmonious music heralds pleasure and prosperity. Discordant music foretells trouble with unruly children and unhappiness in the household.

## MUSICAL INSTRUMENT

To see musical instruments denotes anticipated pleasures. If they are broken, the pleasure will be marred by uncongenial companionship.

## MUSK

To dream of musk foretells unexpected occasions of joy. Lovers will agree and cease to be unfaithful.

## MUSSELS

To dream of water mussels denotes little money, but contentment and domestic enjoyment.

## MUSTACHE

To dream that you have a mustache warns you not to let irritations grow into major heartaches. To shave off a mustache in a dream indicates an unhappy experience with a current relationship, but a new love is on the horizon.

## MUSTARD

To see mustard growing and green foretells success and joy and some measure of wealth. To eat mustard seeds and feel the burning in your mouth indicates that you will repent bitterly some hasty action.

## MUTENESS

If you converse with a mute person in your dreams, unusual challenges in your life will prepare you for higher positions. To dream that you are a mute portends calamities and unjust persecution.

## MYRRH

To see myrrh in a dream signifies that your investments will give satisfaction.

## MYRTLE

To see myrtle in foliage and bloom in a dream says that your desires will be gratified, and pleasures will possess you.

## MYSTERY

If you find yourself bewildered by a mysterious event in your dream, strangers will harass you with their troubles and claim your aid. Such a dream also warns you of neglected duties, for which you feel much aversion. You will wind up in unpleasant complications at work.

## MYSTICISM

If your dream seems mystical and full of fantasy, it's a good omen of happiness and prosperity.

## MYTH

To dream of mythical characters or of reliving an ancient myth advises you that flattery will help you in a relationship or business dealing. Do not hesitate to spread it on thick when you can.

## NAGGING

To dream that you are nagging someone suggests that you have too much resentment; it needs to be released in a healthy way. If you dream of being nagged, be wary of who you tell your secrets to.

## NAILS (HARDWARE)

To see nails in your dreams indicates much toil and small recompense. To deal in nails shows that you will engage in honorable work, even if it be lowly. Rusty or broken nails indicate sickness and failure in business.

## NAKEDNESS*

To dream that you are naked betokens monetary luck and improvement in your personal circumstances. If you see others naked, you will uncover deception among friends. To dream that you suddenly discover your nudity and are trying to conceal it denotes you will be socially recognized for a good deed.

*See *Bare Naked*.

## NAME

To dream that you can't remember your name or that of someone else suggests a questionable business deal that you should investigate before signing any papers. To dream that someone calls you by the wrong name implies personal difficulties that will soon be rectified.

## NANNY

To dream of being a nanny foretells the need to be nurtured emotionally in the very near future. To dream of having a nanny means you will be the one to nurture a friend.

## NAP

To dream of taking a nap is a sign of emotional well-being and financial security.

## NAPKIN

To dream of a napkin foretells convivial entertainment in which you will figure prominently.

## NARROWNESS

To dream that something is excessively narrow suggests that you must overcome obstacles before you complete a project or reach a goal.

## NASA

To dream of NASA suggests that your goals are too lofty; you need to be more grounded and realistic.

## NATIVITY

To dream of the Nativity means many blessings.

## NATURAL CHILDBIRTH

If you dream of having a baby this way and you are not pregnant in waking life, a death is forecast. If you are pregnant, this dream has no meaning at all.

## NATURAL GAS

To dream that you are smelling natural gas implies travel for pleasure.

## NAUSEA

To dream of being nauseated means that your integrity may be challenged by untrustworthy friends or associates.

## NAVEL

To dream of your own belly button predicts a new adventure with long-term benefits. To dream of someone else's navel signals a new love relationship.

## NAVIGATION

To dream of studying navigation means you will be traveling soon. If you are a navigator in the dream, problems in life will seem very hard to deal with.

## NAVY

To dream of the navy denotes victorious struggles against frightful obstacles, and the promise of voyages and pleasure tours. If you seem frightened or disconcerted in your dream, you will have strange obstacles to overcome before you reach your goals. A dilapidated navy is an indication of unfortunate friendships in business or love.

## NAZI PARTY

To dream of this racist political party foretells extreme change in the way you view your spiritual beliefs.

## NEARSIGHTEDNESS

To dream that you are nearsighted signifies embarrassing failure and unexpected visits from unwelcome people.

## NEATNESS

If you dream of being extremely neat and find this disturbing, you need to get your business affairs in order before you lose money.

## NECK

To dream of seeing your own neck foretells approaching money. If you have a broken neck, you need to pay attention to loss and financial issues.

## NECKLACE

To dream of a necklace is a fortune dream about love. If the necklace is broken or falls off, however, it portends relationship disappointments.

## NECKTIE

To dream of having difficulty tying a necktie means you have an emotional problem that you would be wise to investigate and rid yourself of.

## NECROMANCER

To dream of a necromancer and his arts suggests that you are threatened by strange acquaintances who will influence you for evil.

## NECTAR

To dream of a bee or hummingbird feeding on nectar is a sign of prosperity and financial well-being.

## NECTARINE

To dream of this fruit means good luck.

## NEEDINESS

To dream that you are in need suggests that you will speculate unwisely, and distressing news of absent friends will depress you. To see others in need foretells that unfortunate affairs will affect both you and others.

## NEEDLE

To use a needle in your dream warns of approaching troubles.

To dream of threading a needle suggests that you will be burdened with the care of people outside your household.

To look for a needle foretells unnecessary worries. Finding a needle speaks of friends who appreciate you. To break one signifies loneliness and poverty.

## NEEDLEPOINT

To dream of doing needlepoint suggests happiness and contentment. If you dream of others doing it, look for opposition in business and deceit from close associates.

## NEGLIGEE

If you dream of wearing a negligee and you are a woman, you need to pay more attention to how you are taking care of yourself physically. If you are a man and you dream of wearing a negligee, you will soon meet a woman whom you will be very attracted to.

## NEIGHBOR

To see your neighbors in your dreams indicates that many profitable hours will be lost in useless strife and gossip. If the neighbors appear sad or angry, expect dissension and quarrels.

## NEON

To dream of anything illuminated in neon suggests clear and precise solutions to your problems.

## NEPHEW

To dream of your nephew implies that you are soon to come into good news.

## NERD

To dream of yourself as a nerd predicts new knowledge or advancement at work. If another person in your dream is a nerd, you should watch your arrogant attitude.

## NERVE GAS

To dream of poisonous gas foretells a health problem that should not be ignored.

## NEST EGG

If you talk about your nest egg in a dream, or hear someone else discuss it, you may see unexpected financial gain. To dream of talking about someone else's nest egg warns you to watch your spending.

## NET

To dream of ensnaring anything with a net foretells that you will be unscrupulous in your dealings and conduct with others.

To dream of an old or torn net suggests that your property has mortgages or attachments that will cause you trouble.

## NETTLES

If in your dreams you walk among nettles without being stung, you will be prosperous. If you are stung by them, you will be discontented with yourself and make others unhappy.

## NEUROSURGERY

To dream of having this type of surgery performed on yourself tells you to beware of possible depression. To dream of it performed on someone else is a sign of happiness.

## NEW AGE BELIEFS

To dream that you are interested in or practicing New Age concepts suggests embracing new spiritual beliefs.

## NEWS

To hear good news in a dream indicates that you will be fortunate in affairs and will have agreeable companions; but if the news is bad, contrary conditions will exist.

## NEWSCAST

To dream that you are broadcasting the news suggests that you will soon be telling secrets you should have kept to yourself. To watch a newscast indicates that you may learn a secret from a friend that you wish you'd remained ignorant of.

## NEWSLETTER

To dream of writing or editing a newsletter predicts good news in your family.

## NEWSPAPER

To dream of a newspaper suggests that fraud will be detected in your dealings and your reputation will be affected. If you print a newspaper, you will have opportunities to make foreign journeys and friends.

If you try to read a newspaper but fail, you will fail in an uncertain enterprise.

## NEWSPAPER REPORTER

If in your dreams you unwillingly see print journalists, you will be annoyed with small talk and quarrels. If you are a newspaper reporter in your dreams and you are not one in your waking life, there will be a varied course of travel offered you. Although you may experience unpleasant situations, there will be some honor and gain attached.

## NEW TESTAMENT

To dream of this holy book means many blessings.

## NEW YEAR

To dream of the new year signifies prosperity.

## NIBBLING

To dream of nibbling on anything implies a loss of money or personal property.

## NICKEL

To dream of this coin foretells unexpected gain—unless it is counterfeit, in which case it signifies minor illness.

## NICKNAME

To call someone by a nickname or to be called by a nickname in your dream warns you not to take chances in your personal or business life at this time.

## NIECE

To dream of a niece foretells freedom from worry.

## NIGHT*

If you are surrounded by dark night in your dreams, you may expect unusual hardships in your job. If the night seems to be vanishing, unfavorable life situations will get better.

*See *Darkness.*

## NIGHTCLUB

To dream of being in a nightclub foretells sad news.

## NIGHTGOWN*

If you dream that you are in your nightgown, you will be afflicted with a slight illness. To see others thus clad suggests unpleasant news of absent friends. Business will receive a setback.

*See *Clothes.*

## NIGHTINGALE

To dream that you are listening to the harmonious notes of a nightingale speaks of a pleasing existence, and prosperous and healthy surroundings. To see nightingales silent foretells slight misunderstandings among friends.

## NIGHTMARE

To dream of suffering from nightmares denotes wrangling and failure in business.

## NIPPLE

To dream of sucking on a nipple for nourishment suggests you should exercise care around your personal finances. Dreaming of a baby or child sucking on a nipple means release from worries. If you dream of looking at someone's nipples or someone looking at yours, expect happiness in your personal life.

## NOBEL PRIZE

To dream of receiving this award warns you against arrogance and pride. But if you dream that you are happy that someone else has won it, your personal relationships are heading toward happy times.

## NOBILITY

To dream of associating with nobility suggests that your aspirations are not of the right nature; you prefer show and pleasure to the development of the mind.

## NOISE

If you hear a strange noise in a dream, unfavorable news is presaged. If the noise awakens you, there will be a sudden change in your affairs.

## NOMINEE

To dream that you are a nominee suggests a demotion or layoff at work. If someone else is a nominee, that means a promotion or career change for the better.

## NONPROFIT ORGANIZATION

To dream of owning a nonprofit organization augurs financial gain. To dream of working at one indicates upcoming financial loss.

## NOODLES

To dream of noodles denotes progress in a cherished plan.

## NOOSE

To dream of a noose around your neck means good luck and fortune. If the noose is around someone else's neck, you must address a problem with self-esteem.

## NORTH

To dream of this direction or of traveling northward means you are going in the right direction in your life.

## NORTH POLE

To dream of being at the North Pole cautions that you have reached the highest level at your job; think about moving on to some other organization for advancement.

## NORTH STAR

In dreams, this star represents good luck and good fortune.

## NOSE

To see your own nose in a dream indicates force of character and consciousness of your ability to accomplish whatever enterprise you may choose to undertake. If your nose looks smaller than natural, there might be problems in your affairs. Hair growing on your nose indicates extraordinary undertakings that will be carried out by sheer force of character or will. A bleeding nose is prophetic of bad luck.

## NOTARY

To dream of a notary is a prediction of unsatisfied desires and probable lawsuits.

## NOTEBOOK

To dream of writing in a notebook advises you to take better care of your finances. To read something out of a notebook in your dream indicates financial gain.

## NOVEL

To dream of writing a novel suggests trouble in your career or personal life. Reading one implies happy social activities ahead.

## NOVEMBER

To dream of November augurs a season of indifferent success in all affairs.

## NOVENA

To dream of saying novenas predicts many blessings coming in the form that you have been asking for.

## NOVOCAINE

To dream of this painkiller predicts a sudden solution to a problem you thought was unsolvable.

## NOWHERE

To dream that you are going nowhere suggests that you will soon go very far in your personal and professional life.

## NOXIOUSNESS

To dream that something is noxious or that you smell noxious fumes portends physical well-being.

## NUCLEAR BOMB

To dream of witnessing a nuclear explosion predicts that the world as you know it will be spiritually, mentally, or emotionally destroyed and rebuilt for you in a positive way.

## NUGGET

To dream of nuggets of precious metal hints that an opportunity coming your way will affect your circumstances or surroundings positively.

## NUMBERS (FIGURES)

To dream of numbers indicates that unsettled conditions in business will cause you uneasiness and dissatisfaction.

## NUMBNESS

To dream that you feel a numbness creeping over you is a sign of illness.

## NUN

For a religiously inclined man to dream of nuns foretells that material pleasures will interfere with his spirituality. He would be wise to exercise self-control. For a woman to dream of nuns portends her widowhood or a separation from her lover. If she dreams that she is a nun, she is discontented with her present environment. If she discards the robes of her order in the dream, the longing for worldly pleasures may unfit her for her chosen duties.

Seeing a dead nun signifies despair over the faithlessness of loved ones; it also signifies impoverished fortune.

## NUPTIALS*

If a woman dreams of her nuptials, she will soon enter upon new engagements that will afford her distinction, pleasure, and harmony.

*See *Marriage, Wedding.*

## NURSE

To dream that a nurse is retained in your home foretells distressing illness or unlucky visiting among friends. To see a nurse leaving your house heralds good health in the family.

## NURSERY SCHOOL

To dream that you are a teacher in a nursery school cautions you to take better care of your spiritual and mental health. To dream of yourself as a student in a nursery school is a prediction of furthering your education.

## NURSING

For a woman to dream of nursing her baby denotes pleasant employment. If she is young, she will occupy positions of honor and trust. If a man dreams of seeing his wife nurse their baby, he will enjoy harmony in his pursuits.

## NUT

To dream of gathering nuts augurs successful enterprises and much success in love. If you dream of eating them, prosperity will aid you in satisfying your desires.

## NUTCRACKER

To dream of a nutcracker means troubles will soon be overcome.

## NUTMEG

In dreams, nutmegs symbolize prosperity and pleasant journeys.

## NYLON

To dream of nylon means that things in your life are not always as they appear; they call for a closer look.

## NYMPH

To see nymphs bathing in clear water implies that passionate desires will find an ecstatic realization. Convivial entertainments will enchant you. To see them out of their sphere denotes disappointment with the world. If you see them bathing, you will find favor and pleasure with others.

## OAK

To dream of a forest of oak trees signifies great prosperity in all areas of life. To see an oak covered with acorns denotes increase and promotion.

## OAR⋆

To dream of handling oars portends disappointment for you; you will sacrifice your own pleasure for the comfort of others.

To lose an oar denotes vain efforts to carry out plans satisfactorily. A broken oar represents interruption of an anticipated pleasure.

⋆See *Paddle*.

## OASIS

To dream of an oasis means that a new and exciting adventure is about to start in your life.

## OATH

When you take an oath in your dreams, prepare for dissension and altercations on awakening.

## OATMEAL

To dream of eating oatmeal signifies the enjoyment of worthily earned fortune.

## OATS

To dream of oats portends a variety of good things. To see rotting oats, however, foretells that sorrow will displace bright hopes.

## OBEDIENCE

To dream that you are obedient to another suggests a pleasant, uneventful period in life. If others obey you, you will command fortune and and be held in high esteem.

## OBELISK

An obelisk looming up stately and cold in your dreams is the forerunner of melancholy tidings.

## OBITUARY

To dream of writing an obituary forecasts that unpleasant duties will be thrust upon you. If you read one, news of a distracting nature will soon reach you.

## OBJECTION

To object to something in your dreams means the opposite: you will soon be in agreement with others over an upcoming personal matter or business issue.

## OBLIGATION

To dream of obligating yourself indicates that you will be stressed and worried by the thoughtless complaints of others. If others obligate themselves to you, you will win the regard of acquaintances and friends.

## OBNOXIOUSNESS

To dream of being obnoxious counsels that you must speak up in your waking life or be taken advantage of. If you dream of someone else being obnoxious, you need to watch your back with your friends.

## OBSCENITY

To dream that something is obscene foretells great beauty and comfort in your life.

## OBSERVATORY

To dream of viewing the heavens and beautiful landscapes from an observatory suggests your swift elevation to prominent positions and places of trust. For a young woman, this dream signals the realization of the highest earthly joys. If the heavens are clouded, however, your highest aims will not materialize.

## OCCULTIST

If you dream of listening to the teachings of an occultist, you will strive to elevate others to a higher plane of justice and forbearance. If you accept the occultist's views, you will find honest delight by keeping your mind and person above material frivolities and pleasures.

## OCCULT, MYSTICISM

To dream of the occult or mysticism means you will be told a secret of great advantage to you.

## OCEAN*

To dream of a calm ocean, whether sailing on it or not, is always propitious.

Dreams of being far out in the ocean and hearing the waves forebodes problems in business life and quarrels and stormy periods in the household. If you dream of yourself on shore and see the ocean waves foaming against one another, you may narrowly escape injury. To dream of seeing the ocean so shallow as to allow wading or a view of the bottom signifies prosperity and pleasure.

*See *Sea, Wave.*

## OCHER

In dreams, this mineral or color symbolizes spiritual blessings and enlightenment.

## OCTAGON

To dream of anything with eight sides means you will have many choices in career and personal life, all of them good.

## OCTOBER

To imagine that it is October predicts gratifying success in your undertakings. You will also make new acquaintances who will become lasting friends.

## OCTOPUS

To dream of this sea animal suggests that movement is afoot in your personal life or career. To dream that you are caught up in its tentacles warns you against using others to further your career.

## ODOR

In dreams, pleasant odors are good omens. Unpleasant ones predict anxieties that could be major or minor, depending on your attitude.

## OFFENSIVENESS

To dream of being offended denotes that errors will be detected in your conduct and will cause you inner rage while you attempt to justify yourself.

To give offense predicts many struggles before reaching your aims.

## OFFERING

To bring or make an offering in dreams indicates that you will be obsequious and hypocritical unless you cultivate higher views of duty.

## OFFICES (ELECTED)

To dream of holding an elected office signifies that your aspirations may lead you onto dangerous paths, but boldness will be rewarded with success. If you fail to secure a desired office, you will suffer keen disappointment.

To dream that you are removed from office signifies the loss of valuables.

## OFFSPRING

To dream of your own offspring denotes cheerfulness and the merry voices of neighbors and children.

To see the offspring of domestic animals portends an increase in prosperity.

## OGRE

If you dream of an ogre, be careful of hedonistic pleasures.

## OIL

To dream of anointing with oil foretells events in which you will be the particular moving power.

Quantities of oil prognosticate excesses in pleasure. For a man to dream that he deals in oil denotes unsuccessful romance, as he will expect unusual concessions. A woman who dreams that she is anointed with oil will be open to indiscreet advances.

## OILCLOTH

To dream of oilcloth warns that you will meet coldness and treachery.

## OIL PAINTING

If you are painting with oils in a dream, you will create something in your life that gives you pleasure. If you dream that you are admiring an oil painting, your friends will turn their backs on you in a time of need.

## OINTMENT

To dream of ointment indicates that your friendships will prove beneficial and pleasing.

## OLD MAN OR WOMAN*

To dream of seeing an old man or woman denotes great good luck.

*See *Faces, Man, Woman.*

## OLD TESTAMENT

To dream of the Old Testament means that many blessings are coming into your life.

## OLD-FASHIONED ITEM

To dream of anything being old-fashioned means new and exciting things are coming into your life.

## OLIVES

Gathering olives foretells favorable results in business and delightful surprises. If you take the olives from jars, it foretells conviviality. To break a jar of olives indicates disappointments on the eve of pleasure. Eating them signifies contentment and faithful friends.

## OMELET

In dreams, omelets represent good luck and financial gain.

## OMNIBUS*

To dream you are being drawn through the streets in an omnibus foretells misunderstandings with friends; you may make unwise promises.
*See *Bus*.

## ONION

Seeing quantities of onions in a dream represents the amount of spite and envy that you will meet by being successful. If you eat the onions, you will overcome all opposition. If you see them growing, there will be just enough rivalry in your affairs to make things interesting. Cooked onions denote placidity and small gains in business.

   To dream that you are cutting onions and feel the escaping juice in your eyes suggests that you will be defeated by your rivals.

## ONYX

To dream of wearing this semi-precious stone suggests that you will soon be able to get rid of a negative situation in your life. To dream of giving onyx augurs good luck.

## OPAL

To dream of opals means that you will come into a time of extreme good luck.

## OPEN-MINDEDNESS

To dream of being open-minded about a subject predicts that you will be forced to confront your normally narrow thinking.

## OPERA

To dream of attending an opera indicates that you will be entertained by congenial friends and will find your current affairs favorable.

## OPERATION

To dream of having an operation suggests a change in your lifestyle. To dream of observing an operation means unexpected news. If you are a doctor or are planning to have an operation in the near future, such dreams are insignificant.

## OPIUM

To dream of opium signifies that strangers will obstruct your chances of improving your fortune by sly and seductive means.

## OPOSSUM

To dream of this animal means you are ignoring a problem that needs to be addressed.

## OPPOSITE

To dream that you are the opposite of what you normally are implies that you are searching for spiritual, mental, or emotional balance.

## OPTICIAN, OPTOMETRIST

To dream of seeing an eye doctor means you are being too lazy and will be taken to task for it.

## ORACLE

To dream of this conduit of wisdom indicates that you will be given knowledge or will be told something in secret that is of great benefit.

## ORANGE (COLOR)

To see the color orange indicates expansion of spiritual pursuits, personal nourishment, and happy times.

## ORANGE (FRUIT)

Seeing orange trees or eating oranges in a dream signifies health and prosperous surroundings.

## ORANGUTAN

To dream of an orangutan warns that someone is using your influence to further selfish schemes.

## ORATION

To dream of delivering an oration predicts social embarrassment due to laziness. If you dream of listening to an oration, you need to rid yourself of a disturbing relationship.

## ORATOR

Being under the spell of an orator's eloquence in a dream denotes that you will heed the voice of flattery to your own detriment, as you will be persuaded to offer aid to unworthy people.

## ORBIT

To dream of planets or satellites in orbit suggests that you will go around and around a problem before you find a solution.

## ORCHARD

Dreaming of passing through blossoming orchards with your sweetheart heralds the delightful consummation of a long courtship. If the orchard is filled with ripening fruit, it denotes recompense for faithful service to those who serve under masters, and full fruition of designs for the leaders of enterprises.

To gather ripe fruit is a happy omen of plenty. Orchards infested with blight denote sad times, despite good conditions and wealth. If you dream of seeing a barren orchard, opportunities to rise in life will be ignored. If you see one robbed of its verdure by winter, you have been careless of the future by your enjoyment of the present.

Seeing a storm-ravaged orchard brings an unwelcome guest or duties.

## ORCHESTRA

To dream of belonging to or playing in an orchestra foretells pleasant entertainment. If you hear the music of an orchestra, you are well liked and favor will smile upon you.

## ORCHID

To dream of orchids advises you to curb your extravagant and exotic habits.

## ORDERS

To dream of obeying orders tells you that better times are ahead. To dream of giving orders indicates trouble in your relationships.

## ORGAN

To hear the pealing of a pipe organ signifies lasting friendships and well-established fortune. If you dream of rendering harmonious music on an organ, you will be fortunate along your path to worldly comfort, and much social distinction will be given you.

To hear doleful singing with organ accompaniment forecasts that you are nearing a wearisome task, and probable loss of friends or position.

## ORGANIST

To dream of an organist suggests that a friend will cause you much inconvenience from hasty action.

## ORGASM

To have an orgasm in a dream hints at financial security and positive personal relationships.

## ORGY

To dream of this decadent ritual means you need to start to do things in moderation.

## ORIFICE

In dreams, any opening in the body signifies good health and prosperity.

## ORIGAMI

To dream of the art of folding paper means good luck and fortune in your life.

## ORIOLE

To dream of this bird predicts profit from the sale of property or another asset.

## ORNAMENT

If you wear ornaments in dreams, you will have a flattering honor conferred upon you. If you receive them, you will be fortunate in undertakings. Giving them away denotes recklessness and lavish extravagance. Losing an ornament brings the loss of either a lover or a good job.

## ORPHAN

Dreaming of orphans means that the unhappy cares of others will touch your sympathies; sacrificing your own enjoyment will bring you joy. If the orphans are related to you, new duties will come into your life, causing estrangement from friends.

## OSTRICH

To dream of an ostrich suggests that you will amass wealth. If you catch one, your resources will enable you to enjoy travel and extensive knowledge.

## OTTER

To see otters is certain to bring waking happiness and good fortune.

## OTTOMAN*

Dreams in which you find yourself luxuriously reclining upon an ottoman foretell a time when you will need to sit back and rethink your situation, allowing the quietude to give you repose.

*See *Couch*.

## OUIJA BOARD

To dream of working on a Ouija board foretells the miscarriage of plans and unlucky partnerships. Seeing one fail to work suggests complications caused by substituting pleasure for business. If it writes fluently, you may expect fortunate results from a well-planned enterprise.

## OUTCAST

To be an outcast in your dream means you are well loved and cared for by friends and associates.

## OUTHOUSE

A dream featuring an outhouse portends financial gain through good luck.

## OUTLAW

To dream of being an outlaw means you are well respected by your colleagues. To dream of catching one warns you that someone you suppose to be a friend may betray one of your secrets.

## OUTLINE

To make an outline in your dream means that you will soon need to account for your spending; it may be wise to curtail unnecessary expenditures for a while.

## OUTPATIENT

To be an outpatient getting medical help in a dream foretells the happy outcome of a medical issue.

## OVATION

To receive a standing ovation in your dream cautions you not to fall behind in an important business project. To dream of giving an ovation portends business recognition.

## OVEN

To dream that your oven is red-hot denotes you will be loved by family and friends. If you are baking, temporary disappointments await. If the oven is broken, you will find frustration with events around you that are not working out as planned.

## OVERALLS

To dream of wearing overalls warns you that those you trust are engaging in a level of deception; you must uncover the truth.

## OVERCOAT

To dream of an overcoat suggests that other people's orneriness will bring you pain. To borrow one implies that you will suffer through mistakes made by strangers. If you see or are wearing a handsome new overcoat, you will be exceedingly fortunate in realizing your wishes.

## OVERLOOKING

To find yourself overlooking something you should have seen in your dream suggests that you need to keep an eye on your belongings. To be overlooked in a dream foretells social recognition.

## OVERPASS

To dream of driving under an overpass portends an argument with a family member.

## OVERREACTING

To dream that you are overreacting, or someone else is, warns you to pay closer attention to your relationships.

## OVERSEEING

If you dream you are overseeing a project or people, you will soon have to ask for help to solve a business problem. If you dream of being supervised, you can solve this problem without outside help.

## OVERSLEEPING

To dream that you are upset because you have overslept and missed something important suggests that you will have more than enough time for business and pleasure.

## OVERTURE

If you dream of listening to a musical overture, you will soon visit with someone you have not seen in a long time.

## OVERWEIGHT

To dream that you are overweight when, in waking life, you are not presages a health problem.

## OVULATION

To talk about or know you are ovulating in a dream indicates a serious illness that can be addressed with medical help.

## OWL

To dream of an owl connotes wisdom, underscoring that your judgment about a person or situation was accurate. Hearing the solemn, unearthly voice of an owl warns of bad luck and frustration.

## OX*

To see a well-fed ox signifies that you will become an influential person in your field. To see fat oxen in green pastures represents fortune and your rise to positions beyond your expectations. If they are lean, your fortune will dwindle. If you see oxen well matched and yoked, it betokens a happy and wealthy marriage, or that you are already joined to your true mate.

To see a dead ox is a sign of bereavement. If oxen are drinking from a clear pond or stream, you will end up with something or someone long desired.

*See *Cattle.*

## OYSTER

Opening oysters in a dream suggests that you have misplaced your confidence and are in danger of being cheated by someone you trust. Eating oysters portends good luck in love affairs. But if your main concern is business, this dream suggests that you will have to be more aggressive in asserting yourself if you want to succeed.

## OYSTER SHELL

To see oyster shells in your dreams signifies that you will be frustrated in your attempt to secure the fortune of another.

## PACEMAKER

In dreams, a pacemaker represents the renewal of an old love relationship.

## PACIFYING

To endeavor to pacify suffering implies that you will be loved for your sweetness of disposition. Pacifying the anger of others implies that you will labor for the advancement of others.

## PACING

To pace back and forth in a dream suggests that you are having too much fun and overdoing things. Be careful not to get physically run down.

## PACKAGE

If you dream that you are carrying a package, you are taking responsibility for a problem that is not yours; you need to step away.

## PACKING

If you see yourself packing in your dream, you are stuck in a rut and not going anywhere in the near future.

## PAD

A clean or new pad of paper in your dream suggests new opportunities.

## PADDING

To dream that you have something padded means you will soon have to deal with a dishonest friend.

## PADDLE*

To dream of breaking or losing a paddle portends moderately bad news. To dream of using one means you will overcome a health problem easily.
*See Oar.

## PAGE

To see a page in dreams denotes that you will contract a hasty union with someone unsuited to you. You will fail to control your romantic impulses.

If a young woman dreams that she is acting as a page, she is likely to participate in a foolish escapade.

## PAGEANT

To dream of a pageant of any kind suggests the return of a lost friend or relative.

## PAGE-TURNING

Turning pages in a book or magazine in your dream foretells a small financial gain.

## PAGODA

To see a pagoda in your dreams means you will soon go on a long-desired journey.

## PAIL

To dream of full pails is a sign of fair prospects and pleasant associations. An empty pail represents hard times.

## PAIN

To dream that you are in pain foretells useless regrets over a trivial transaction. To see others in pain warns you that you are making mistakes in your life.

## PAINKILLER

To dream of taking painkillers means you will be told you are in good health. But if you dream of taking them just to get high, you will suffer a health problem soon.

## PAINT AND PAINTING

To see newly painted houses in dreams foretells that you will succeed at a plan. If you accidentally get paint on your clothing, you will be made unhappy by the thoughtless criticism of others. To dream that you are using the brush yourself denotes that you will be well pleased with your present occupation.

If you dream of seeing beautiful paintings, you will find pleasure.

## PAINTBALL

To dream of this sport means you have a chance to accomplish something great. However, it also warns that you should proceed carefully so as not to be blindsided by co-workers. If you are stalking someone in your dream, you long for a challenge. Being stalked indicates hidden fears.

## PAJAMAS

To dream that someone is in pajamas (you or another person) foretells peace of mind with family members.

## PALACE

To dream of wandering through a palace and noting its grandeur signifies that your prospects are growing brighter. You will assume new dignity.

## PALISADE

To dream of palisades indicates that you will alter well-formed plans to please strangers, and by so doing will impair your own interests.

## PALL

To dream of seeing see a pall suggests sorrow and misfortune. If you raise the pall from a corpse, you will doubtless soon mourn the death of one you love.

## PALLBEARER

To dream of a pallbearer indicates that an enemy will provoke your ill feeling by attacking your integrity. A pallbearer carrying a coffin augurs a sudden change in your life.

## PALLET

To dream of a pallet foretells temporary uneasiness over your love affairs.

## PALM

To dream of looking at your palm indicates that you need look no farther to find what you require for success: you hold it all in the palm of your hand.

## PALMISTRY

To dream of palm-reading means you are contemplating your life's goals and direction.

## PALM SUNDAY

To dream of this holy day suggests the coming of many blessings in your life.

## PALM TREE

Palm trees seen in dreams symbolize hopeful situations and happiness of a high order.

## PALSY

To dream that you are afflicted with palsy indicates that you are making poor decisions in business. To see a friend so afflicted indicates uncertainty as to his or her faithfulness; sickness, too, may enter your home.

## PAMPHLET

If you dream that you are reading a pamphlet, you are about to embark on new education for your career. Handing out pamphlets suggests a job loss.

## PAN

To dream of a cooking pan heralds financial gain and prosperity in the very near future.

## PANCAKES

To dream of eating pancakes means that you will have excellent success in all enterprises undertaken at this time. Your affections are well placed; a home may be bequeathed to you.

To cook pancakes in a dream suggests that you are economical and thrifty in your home.

## PANDA

To dream of one of these adorable bears tells you that if you let go of worry, your troubles will go away—but you might need to compromise.

## PANE OF GLASS*

To dream of handling a pane of glass denotes that you are dealing in uncertainties. If you break it, your failure will be accentuated.

To talk to a person through a pane of glass suggests that obstacles in your immediate future will cause you no slight inconvenience.

*See Glass, Mirror.

## PANHANDLING

To dream that you are panhandling implies good luck in gambling. To dream that you give money to a panhandler warns of a financial loss.

## PANIC

If you dream that you panic, you will find much peace of mind and calmness surrounding you and your family now. To dream of others panicking while you stay calm means that you will have to deal with a family problem that you wanted to stay out of.

## PANORAMA

To dream of a panorama predicts that you will change your occupation or residence. You should curb your desire for a change of scene and friends.

## PANSIES

A dream of these flowers predicts an argument or misunderstanding with a friend.

## PANTHER

To see a panther and experience fright denotes that contracts in love or business may be canceled unexpectedly due to adverse influences working against you. But if you kill or overpower the animal, you will experience joy and be successful in your undertakings. If one menaces you by its presence, you will have disappointments in business. Other people will likely renege on their promises to you.

If you hear the growl of a panther and experience terror or fright, expect unfavorable news of reduced profit or gain, as well as social discord; if you're not frigthened in the dream, the news won't be as bad. As with all cats, seeing a panther in a dream is a warning, unless you kill it.

## PANTOMIME

To dream of seeing pantomimes indicates that your friends will deceive you. If you participate in pantomimes, you will have cause for offense.

## PANTRY

In dreams, a full pantry represents prosperity; an empty one, financial loss.

## PAPER, PARCHMENT

If you have occasion in your dreams to refer to or handle any paper or parchment, you will be threatened with losses. They are likely to be in the nature of a lawsuit.

## PAPRIKA

To dream of this spice warns you not to overspend in the very near future.

## PARABLE

To dream of parables denotes that you will be undecided as to the best course to pursue in addressing a business complication.

## PARACHUTE

To dream of an easily opened parachute means a happy love life. To dream that you have trouble opening one suggests that you will be let down by a love interest or close friend.

## PARADE

To dream that you lead a parade means you will be socially recognized. If you march in one, people may visit unexpectedly and become annoying. To dream of watching a parade augurs financial gain.

## PARADISE

To dream that you are in paradise implies that loyal friends are willing to aid you.

To dream that you set out to find paradise but find yourself bewildered and lost suggests that you will undertake enterprises that look feasible and full of promise, but they will prove disappointing and vexatious.

## PARALYSIS

Paralysis in a dream can be indicative of your emotional state. Perhaps you are feeling paralyzed about what to do in a situation. It can also be an indication of the sleep state. REM sleep often renders the person unable to move, as if paralyzed.

## PARASOL*

To dream of a parasol means emotional security. If it is ripped, your security is not assured.

*See Umbrella.

## PARCEL

If you dream that a parcel is being delivered to you, you will be pleasantly surprised by the return of an absent loved one or will be cared for in a world-class way.

If you carry a parcel, you will have an unpleasant task to perform. To drop one as you deliver it predicts the failure of a deal.

## PARDONING

To dream that you are endeavoring to gain a pardon for an offense you never committed implies that you will be troubled, seemingly with cause, over your affairs, but it will finally develop that events worked for your advancement. If you are guilty of the offense, on the other hand, you will realize embarrassment in affairs.

If you dream of receiving a pardon, you will prosper after a series of misfortunes.

## PARENTS*

To see your parents looking cheerful in your dream suggests harmony and pleasant associates. If your parents appear to you after they are dead, it is a message of love and warmth, and sometimes a warning. You should be careful in your dealings.

If you see your parents while they are living, and they are in your home and happy, the dream foretells pleasant changes for you.

To dream of seeing your parents looking robust and contented implies that you are in good shape; your business and love interests will flourish. *See Father, Mother.*

# PARK

To dream of walking through a well-kept park denotes enjoyable leisure. If you walk with your lover, you will be comfortably and happily married. Ill-kept parks devoid of green grass and foliage warn of unexpected reverses.

# PARKING

To dream that you are parking a vehicle means the ending of a friendship that does not work anymore.

# PARROT

To hear parrots chattering in your dreams signifies frivolity and idle gossip among your friends. Seeing parrots in repose denotes a peaceful interruption in family quarrels. If you see yourself trying to teach a parrot, you will have trouble in your private affairs. A dead parrot foretells the loss of friends.

# PARSLEY

To dream of parsley denotes hard-earned success; usually your surroundings are healthful and lively. To eat parsley is a sign of good health.

# PARSNIPS

To see or eat parsnips is a favorable omen of successful business or trade, but love will take on unfavorable and gloomy aspects.

# PARTING

To dream of parting from friends and companions suggests that many little vexations will come into your daily life. Parting from enemies betokens success in love and business.

# PARTNER

To dream of seeing your business partner indicates that you may need help from others in completing a project or task.

## PARTNERSHIP

To dream of forming a partnership denotes financial uncertainty.

To dissolve an unpleasant partnership in a dream suggests that things will arrange themselves according to your desires; if the partnership was pleasant, however, the dream implies disquieting news and disagreeable turns.

## PARTRIDGE

To see partridges in your dream predicts favorable conditions for the acquisition of property. To ensnare them signifies that you will be fortunate in meeting your expectations. Killing them foretells success; eating them, the enjoyment of deserved honors. If you see partridges flying, a promising future lies before you.

## PARTY

If you dream of attending a party of any kind for pleasure, you will find that life holds much good—unless the party is an inharmonious one. In this case, you need to work on your social skills.

## PASSENGER

To dream of seeing passengers arriving with their luggage denotes improvement in your surroundings. If they are leaving, you will lose an opportunity of gaining some desired property. If you are one of the passengers leaving home, you will be dissatisfied with your present situation and will seek to change it.

## PASSPORT

To dream of getting or using a passport signifies upcoming travel. If you dream of taking someone else's passport, travel plans will be delayed or canceled.

## PASSWORD

To dream of a password suggests that you will be able to address a slight trouble that will soon visit you.

## PASTEBOARD

To dream of pasteboard implies that unfaithful friends will deceive you concerning important matters. If you cut pasteboard, you will throw aside difficulties in your struggle to reach the top.

## PASTRY*

To dream of pastry suggests that you are enjoying sensual times and fulfilling moments.

*See Pie.

## PASTURE

In dreams, green pastures symbolize happiness and prosperity; withered and dry pastures, bad news. To dream of just-plowed pastures suggests that you will soon reach a goal you set for yourself. If your dream includes animals in the pasture, see the individual animals as well.

## PATCH

To dream that you have patches on your clothing suggests that you have no false pride. To see others wearing patches foretells a period of want.

To wear or see an eye patch implies surprising changes in your sex life.

## PATENT

To dream of securing a patent warns you to be careful and painstaking with any task you take on. If you fail to secure your patent, you will suffer failure due to your lack of ability.

## PATH

To dream that you are walking on a narrow and rough path, stumbling over rocks and other obstructions, predicts a rough encounter with adversity that will weigh heavily on you.

To dream that you are trying to find your path implies that you will fail to accomplish some work.

Walking along a pathway bordered with green grass and flowers speaks of your freedom from oppressive love.

## PAUNCH

To dream of someone with a large paunch denotes wealth and the total absence of refinement. A shriveled paunch foretells illness and reverses.

## PAUPER*

To dream that you are a pauper implies unpleasant events. Seeing paupers predicts a call upon your generosity.

*See Beggar.

## PAVEMENT

To dream of new or smooth pavement means easy times ahead. Bumpy or broken pavement speaks of jealousy between you and a friend.

## PAW

To dream of an animal paw warns that some of your friends are dishonest and disloyal.

## PAWNSHOP

If in your dreams you enter a pawnshop, you will find disappointments and losses in your waking life. To dream of seeing one hints that you haven't been trustworthy and are in danger of sacrificing your honorable name as a result of a salacious affair.

If you dream of pawning articles, you will have unpleasant scenes with your spouse or sweetheart and perhaps disappointments in business. Redeeming an article at a pawnshop suggests that you will regain things you lost.

## PAYING

To dream that you are paying a bill foretells financial security in the near future. To dream of being paid or having to pay someone else predicts an unexpected monetary gain.

## PEACE

If you dream of world peace, you will find happiness and contentment through spiritual learning.

## PEACH*

To dream of seeing or eating peaches indicates pleasurable times ahead.

To see them on trees with foliage suggests that you will secure some desired position or thing after much striving and risking of health and money.

Dried peaches warn you that foes may steal from you.

*See *Orchard*.

## PEACOCK

Peacocks are a good omen, signaling prestige, success, and contentment in your relationship and career. However, they can also indicate a problem with vanity and false pride.

To hear their harsh voices while looking upon their proudly spread plumage indicates that someone may cause you discomfort and uneasiness.

## PEANUT

In dreams, peanuts—whether in or out of the shell—represent social popularity.

## PEANUT BUTTER

To dream of peanut butter suggests that you feel sorry about something you have done and long to confess it.

## PEARLS

In dreams, pearls symbolize good business and trade and affairs of a social nature.

## PEARS

To dream of eating pears denotes fertility and prosperity. To admire the golden fruit suggests that fortune will wear a more promising aspect than formerly. Gathering them in your dream implies that pleasant surprises will follow quickly upon disappointment.

If you dream of preserving pears, you accept reverses philosophically. Baking them denotes uninspired love and friendships.

## PEAS

Dreaming of eating peas augurs robust health and the accumulation of wealth. Much activity is indicated for farmers.

To see peas growing denotes successful enterprises. Planting peas indicates that your hopes are well grounded; they will be realized. To gather them signifies that your plans will culminate in good and you will enjoy the fruit of your labors.

If you dream of canned peas, your brightest hopes will be filled with uncertainties for a short season, to be followed with success. Dried peas suggest that you are overtaxing your health. Eating dried peas in a dream reveals that you will, after much success, suffer a slight decrease in pleasure or wealth.

## PEASANT

To dream that you are a peasant suggests unexpected financial gain through inheritance or winnings. To dream of peasants foretells a small gain in finances through hard work.

## PEBBLES

In dreams, pebbles and small stones represent minor troubles and vexations in your life. To be throwing them, or to have them thrown at you, indicates that you are being oversensitive; minor criticisms tend to wound you.

## PECAN

If you dream of eating this appetizing nut, you will see one of your dearest plans come to full fruition; a seeming failure will prove a propitious source of gain.

To see pecans growing among leaves signifies a long, peaceful existence. Failure in love or business will follow if the pecan is bad. If the pecans you dream of are difficult to crack and the fruit is small, you will succeed after much trouble and expense, but returns will be meager.

## PEDALING

To dream of pedaling anything, such as a bicycle, means you will enjoy great reward from hard work.

## PEDDLING

In dreams, peddling your wares represents financial gain through dishonesty; be careful!

## PEDESTAL

To dream of placing something on a pedestal suggests that higher spiritual knowledge is coming to you through inspiration. If you dream of taking something off a pedestal, you will find occasion to look at your spiritual self and make changes for peace of mind.

## PEDICURE

To dream of receiving a pedicure means you will soon find rest from hard work. To give a pedicure in a dream means you will have to help someone you love reach a goal.

## PEEPING

To dream of hearing the peeping of chickens or birds betokens a pregnancy or birth announcement.

## PEG

To dream about hanging something on a peg suggests that you will be cleaning up some mental stress that has been a bother to you. To dream of hammering a peg into something advises you to try out various new ideas to clear up mental anguish.

## PELICAN

To dream of a pelican denotes a mingling of disappointments with successes. If you dream of catching a pelican, you will be able to overcome disappointing influences. Killing one denotes that you will cruelly set aside the rights of others. If you see them flying, you are threatened with changes that leave you uncertain.

## PEN

To dream of this writing implement warns that you are being led into serious complications by your love of adventure. If the pen doesn't write, you will be faced with a problem.

## PENALTY

To dream of penalties being imposed on you foretells duties that will rile you and leave you rebellious.

To pay a penalty denotes sickness and financial loss. If you escape the payment, you will be a victor in some contest.

## PENCIL

In dreams, pencils symbolize favorable occupations.

## PENDULUM

To dream of pendulums assures you that a sudden change in plans or routine will turn out for the better.

## PENGUIN

To dream of these birds reminds you that with patience, your troubles will soon be gone.

## PENIS*

No matter whose penis you dream about, it portends a pregnancy or birth announcement.

*See *Phallic symbol*.

## PENITENTIARY

To dream of a penitentiary suggests that coming engagements will result in your loss. To be an inmate of one foretells discontent in the home and failure in business. If you escape from one, you will overcome obstacles.

## PENNY*

To dream of pennies denotes unsatisfactory pursuits. Business will suffer; lovers and friends will complain of the lack of affection.

To dream of losing pennies signifies small deferences and failures. If you find pennies, prospects will advance to your advantage. Counting pennies suggests that you are businesslike and economical.

*See *Cent*.

## PENSION

To dream of drawing a pension foretells that you will be aided in your labor by friends. To fail in your application for a pension denotes that you will lose in an undertaking and will suffer the loss of friendships.

## PENTHOUSE

To dream of a penthouse warns that you are overspending and must watch your money. If you already live in one in your waking life, this dream means nothing.

## PEONY

In dreams, these flowers represent worry and anxiety.

## PEPPER

If you dream of pepper burning your tongue, you will suffer because of your love of gossip.

Seeing red pepper growing foretells a thrifty and an independent partner in marriage. To see piles of red pepper pods signifies that you will aggressively maintain your rights.

To grind black pepper denotes that you will be victimized by the wiles of ingenious men or women. To see ground black pepper in a peppermill on a table portends sharp reproaches or quarrels.

## PEPPERMINT

To dream of peppermint denotes pleasant entertainment and interesting affairs.

If you see it growing, you will participate in some pleasure that includes a dash of romance.

To enjoy drinks infused with peppermint hints that you will enjoy assignations with an attractive and fascinating person.

## PERCH

If you climb on a perch in your dream, you will soon experience a raise or promotion. To dream of a bird on a perch foretells good news about a change in your life.

## PERFORMING

If you dream of performing in a play or movie, you will soon be faced with a personality issue that you have kept hidden. It now needs to be brought out into the open.

## PERFUME

To dream of inhaling perfume is an augury of happy events. For you to perfume your garments and person implies that you will seek and obtain adulation. Being intoxicated by perfume indicates that excesses in joy will impair your thinking.

To spill perfume in dreams denotes that you will lose something that affords you pleasure. To break a bottle of perfume foretells that your most cherished wishes and desires will end disastrously, even while they promise a happy culmination.

To dream that you are distilling perfume means that your employments and associations will be of the pleasantest character.

## PERJURY

If you dream of committing perjury, you are being warned that some business deal will not be honest; be careful. To dream that others perjure themselves suggests that an injustice done to you in the past will soon be redressed.

## PERSPIRATION

To dream of perspiration foretells that you will come out of a difficulty that has stirred up much gossip with renewed honor.

## PEST

If you dream of being worried over a pest of any nature, disturbing elements will prevail in your immediate future. To see others thus worried predicts that you will be annoyed by a displeasing development.

## PETAL

To dream of petals falling is a sign that a friendship or relationship will soon end.

## PETTICOAT

To dream of seeing new petticoats denotes that pride in your belongings will make you an object of raillery among your acquaintances. If they are soiled or torn, your reputation may be in great danger.

## PETUNIA

In dreams, these flowers represent social pleasures, new hobbies, or vacation plans.

## PEWTER*

To dream of pewter foretells straitened circumstances.
*See *Dish.*

## PHALLIC SYMBOL*

To dream of any phallic symbol foretells the announcement of a pregnancy or birth.
*See *Penis.*

### PHANTOM*

To dream that a phantom pursues you foretells strange and disquieting experiences. If you see a phantom fleeing from you, trouble will diminish.
*See *Ghost*.

### PHARMACY

To dream of anything having to do with a pharmacy suggests a successful business deal.

### PHD

To dream of receiving this degree means advancement in your career. Giving one to someone else suggests a possible job loss.

### PHEASANT

Dreaming of pheasants heralds good fellowship among your friends.

### PHLEGM

To dream of clearing your throat of phlegm augurs happy news about a health problem. To dream of someone else spitting out phlegm warns you of a health problem that should not be ignored.

### PHOBIA

To dream of any kind of phobia means you will soon find that you are fearless in trying to achieve your goals or better your life.

### PHOSPHORUS

To dream of seeing phosphorus is indicative of evanescent joys.

### PHOTOCOPYING

To dream of making photocopies suggests that you are trying to be someone you aren't. Just be yourself and everything will work to your advantage.

### PHOTOGRAPH

If you see photographs in your dreams, you need to fully examine certain relationships in your life; you may be looking at them superficially. Ripping up a photo in your dream implies letting go. Having your photo taken indicates that you need to examine how others view you.

### PHYSICAL THERAPY

To dream that you are undergoing physical therapy implies that you are in great shape and should try some new physical challenge. If you dream that you are giving someone physical therapy, it is time for a checkup.

## PHYSICIAN

To dream of a doctor indicates a need for healing, whether spiritual, physical, emotional, or mental. To dream that you are a doctor indicates that you have the power to do the healing. To dream that you marry a doctor means you are being deceived.

## PIANO

In dreams, a piano represents a joyful occasion.

## PICKAX

To dream of a pickax suggests that a relentless enemy is working to overthrow you socially. A broken pickax portends disaster to all your interests.

## PICKLE

To dream of pickles denotes that you will follow worthless pursuits if you fail to call energy and judgment to your aid.

## PICKPOCKET

If you dream of a pickpocket, an enemy will succeed in harassing you and causing you loss.

## PICNIC

To dream of attending a picnic betokens success and real enjoyment. Dreams of picnics mean undiluted happiness to the young. To dream of storms or other interfering elements at a picnic implies the temporary displacement of profit and pleasure in love or business.

## PICTURE (LIKENESS)*

Pictures appearing before you in dreams prognosticate deception and the ill will of contemporaries.

To make a picture suggests that you will engage in an unremunerative enterprise. To destroy one means that you will be pardoned for using strenuous means to establish your rights. Dreams of buying pictures foretell worthless speculation.

If you dream of seeing your likeness in a living tree, you will be prosperous and seemingly contented, yet you will know disappointment when you reach out for companionship and the understanding of ideas and plans.

To dream of being surrounded by the best efforts of the Old Masters and modern painters denotes that you have an insatiable longing for ever-greater accomplishment. Compared with what you have presently achieved, your current success will seem poverty-stricken and miserable.

*See Paint and painting, Photograph.*

## PIE*

In dreams, eating pie indicates rewards for your hard work.

*See Pastry.*

## PIER

To stand on a pier in your dream denotes that you will be brave in your battle for recognition and you will be admitted to the highest places of honor. If you strive to reach a pier and fail, you will lose the distinction you most covet.

## PIERCING

To pierce anything in a dream foretells permanent changes in residence or career. To dream that you see someone else piercing something tells you that change is not good at this time.

## PIG*

To dream of a fat, healthy pig implies reasonable success in affairs. If you see pigs wallowing in mire, you will have hurtful associates, and your engagements will be subject to reproach.

*See Hog.*

## PIGEON

To dream of seeing pigeons and hearing them cooing above their cotes speaks of how proud you are of your children. To see them flying denotes freedom from misunderstanding, and perhaps news from those far away.

## PIGGYBACK RIDE

If you dream of giving a piggyback ride, you will have help from a friend or associate in an upcoming business or personal matter. To dream of getting a piggyback ride means you will have to solve a problem on your own.

## PIGTAILS

To dream of wearing this hairstyle means you will soon find yourself carefree after a difficult time. If you dream of assisting someone else tie pigtails, you will soon help someone find a solution to a personal problem.

## PILE, STACK

To put things in piles in a dream means you need to be more organized about the help you are willing to give; if you spread yourself too thin, you may not be able to fulfill a promise.

## PILGRIM

To dream of pilgrims predicts that you will go on an extended journey, leaving home and its dearest objects on the mistaken belief that it must be done for your loved ones' sakes.

To dream that you are a pilgrim portends struggles with poverty and unsympathetic companions.

## PILL*

To dream that you take pills indicates that you will have responsibilities to look after, but they will bring you much comfort and enjoyment.

To give pills to others signifies that you will be criticized for being disagreeable.

*See *Capsule.*

## PILLOW

To dream of a pillow denotes luxury and comfort.

## PILOT

To dream that you are a pilot suggests a new direction in your business or personal life.

## PIMP

To dream that you are associated with a pimp warns you to look closely at new financial and business opportunities. If you are the pimp, you can expect failure in a business dealing.

## PIMPLE

To dream of your flesh being full of pimples denotes worry over trifles. To see others pimpled signifies that you will be troubled by illness and complaints from others.

## PINBALL

If you dream of playing pinball, you must take more than one detour and avenue to solve a problem or conclude a project you are working on.

## PINCERS

To dream of feeling pincers on your flesh implies that you will be burdened by exasperating cares. Any dream of pincers speaks of misfortune.

## PINCHING

To dream of being pinched means you will become suddenly aware of a problem that needs an immediate solution. If you dream that you are pinching someone, a solution to a current problem is extremely hard to find.

## PINE

To dream of the smell of pine foretells mental stability and peace of mind.

## PINEAPPLE

To dream of pineapples is exceedingly propitious. Success will follow in the near future if you gather pineapples or eat them. If you dream that you prick your fingers while preparing a pineapple for the table, you will experience considerable vexation over matters that will finally bring pleasure and success.

## PINECONE

Pinecones in a dream represent unexpected news of a birth.

## PINE TREE

To see a pine tree in a dream foretells success in any undertaking.

## PING-PONG

If you dream that you cannot win a frustrating game of table tennis, you will have competition in a business matter; stay on your toes.

## PINK

To dream of the color pink suggests a happy time.

## PINKING SHEARS

A dream of these special sewing scissors implies that you can finish a chore rapidly without much stress.

## PINS

In dreams, pins represent personal differences and family quarrels. To dream of swallowing a pin predicts that accidents will put you in danger. To lose one implies a petty loss or disagreement. If you see a bent or rusty pin, you may lose esteem because of your careless ways. To stick one into your flesh suggests that someone will irritate you.

## PINSTRIPES

To dream of wearing a piece of clothing with pinstripes means you will become meticulous in a personal or business project and will reap great rewards.

## PINWHEEL

To dream of a pinwheel means your life will soon become more interesting and colorful.

## PIPE

Pipes seen in dreams are representatives of peace and comfort after many struggles.

Sewer, gas, and similar pipes denote unusual thought and prosperity in your community. Old and broken pipe signifies ill health and stagnation of business.

To dream that you smoke a pipe implies that you will enjoy the visit of an old friend; peaceful settlement of differences will also take place.

## PIRATE

To dream of pirates suggests that you will be exposed to the evil designs of false friends. If you dream that you are a pirate, your social standing will fall.

## PISTACHIO

In dreams, pistachios symbolize financial gain.

## PISTOL

Seeing a pistol in a dream generally denotes bad fortune. If you own one, you will cultivate a low, designing personality. If you hear the report of one being fired, you will be made aware of some scheme to ruin your interests.

To dream of shooting your own pistol signifies that you will become envious of some innocent person and will go far to avenge an imagined wrong.

## PIT

If you are looking into a deep pit in your dream, you will run silly risks in business ventures and will make people uncomfortable with your entreaties.

To fall into a pit denotes calamity and deep sorrow. To wake as you begin to feel yourself falling into a pit brings you out of distress in fairly good shape, however.

To dream that you are descending into a pit signifies that you knowingly risk health and fortune for greater success.

## PITA BREAD

To dream of making or eating pita bread suggests good cash flow.

### PITCHER (JUG)

To dream of a pitcher denotes that you are of a generous and congenial disposition. Success will attend your efforts. A broken pitcher implies loss of friends.

### PITCHFORK

Pitchforks in dreams represent struggles for betterment of fortune and some sort of great mental or physical labor.

To dream that you are attacked by someone wielding a pitchfork implies that you have personal enemies who would not hesitate to harm you.

### PITCHING

To dream of pitching a ball means the coming of happy news.

### PITY

To dream that you pity someone foretells arguments and frustration with friends and family. To dream that someone is pitying you means good luck, as does any dream in which you feel sorry for yourself.

### PIXELS

To dream of pixels on a television or computer screen suggests that elements of your life are coming together for happiness and well-being. If any of the pixels are missing, however, you must discover what is missing from your waking life and try to fix it.

### PIZZA

To dream of pizza means good fortune and gain in your life, especially financially.

### PLACEBO

If you dream of taking medicine while knowing it's a placebo and you are convinced that it's helping you, an unexpected find will help you solve a problem in your personal or business life.

### PLACE CARD

To dream of place cards suggests unexpected news and surprises, all good.

### PLACENTA

To dream of afterbirth means an upcoming pregnancy or birth announcement—unless you are pregnant, in which case the dream doesn't mean anything.

## PLAGUE

To dream of a plague denotes disappointing returns in business. If you are afflicted with the plague, you will keep your business in the black with the greatest maneuvering. If you are trying to escape a plague, some trouble that looks overwhelming is pursuing you.

## PLAID

To dream of this material or pattern tells you that new ideas from your friends will help you better your life.

## PLAIN*

To dream of crossing a plain implies that you will be fortunately situated, if the grasses are green and luxuriant; if the plain is arid, or the grass is dead, you will experience much discomfort and loneliness.

*See *Prairie*.

## PLAN

If you dream of looking at plans for a house or building, new friends and business associates will be very important to you. To dream of seeing yourself drawing plans suggests that you may be tricked into doing something that you don't want to, which could lead to financial loss.

To dream of making future plans suggests the need for delay, but everything will turn out fine in the end.

## PLANE (CARPENTRY TOOL)

If you dream of seeing carpenters using planes, things will progress smoothly in your undertakings.

## PLANET

To dream of a planet foretells an uncomfortable journey and depressing work.

## PLANK

Walking the plank is a good omen, if the board is sturdy, but you are warned to be unusually careful in your conduct after such a dream.

## PLANT

To dream of healthy plants portends good luck. Wilted plants suggest disappointment and difficulty coming into your life. To dream of repotting, watering, or feeding plants speaks of a comfortable home life.

## PLANTATION

In dreams, plantations symbolize financial gain and material success.

## PLASMA TELEVISION

To dream of this type of TV tells you that illusion and fantasy cloud your life. You need to get real and based in your truth.

## PLASTER

If you dream of seeing walls plainly plastered, it indicates that success will come, but it will not be stable.

To have plaster fall on you denotes unmitigated disasters and public exposure.

To see plasterers at work suggests that you will have sufficient competence to live above penury.

## PLASTIC

Dreaming of plastic speaks of friendships that add to your life.

## PLASTIC SURGERY

Unless you are undergoing reconstructive surgery, this dream warns that vanity and arrogance will be your downfall socially.

## PLATE*

To see a plate in your dream indicates social advantages. If it is empty, you suffer an emotional void.

*See *Dish*.

## PLATFORM

To dream of being on a platform suggests a rise in your social or career status.

## PLATINUM

If you dream of this precious metal, you will soon attain something you thought was out of reach.

## PLATYPUS

In dreams, this aquatic animal represents frivolity and enjoyment in your social life.

## PLAY (THEATER)*

To dream of watching a play and enjoying it foretells happy times. To dream of watching a play and not enjoying it warns of upcoming financial problems.

*See *Drama, Theater*.

## PLAYING

To dream of playing in general suggests good fortune, success, and love.

## PLEADING

To dream of pleading on behalf of yourself means life will be simple and you will have peace of mind. If it is on behalf of someone else, you will be asked to step in and help someone with a problem. You should not hesitate; your input may mean the difference in the outcome.

## PLEASURE*

To dream of pleasure suggests gain and personal enjoyment.

*See Joy.

## PLEDGE

To dream of taking a pledge implies a rise in your social or business status.

## PLEXIGLAS

To dream that you replace real glass with Plexiglas is a warning that things in your business or personal life may not be as clear or as easy as you first thought.

## PLIERS

To dream of this tool suggests that you will find a way around your current problem.

## PLOTTING

To dream of plotting against someone else reminds you that you must address the ups and downs in your business life in order to move forward. To dream of being plotted against foretells financial improvement.

## PLOWING

To dream of a plow signifies unusual success, and affairs will reach a pleasing culmination. To see people plowing denotes activity and advancement in knowledge and fortune.

## PLUCKING

In dreams, plucking something represents ridding yourself of unwanted associates.

## PLUGGING

To dream of a plug or of plugging something suggests financial gain through hard work.

## PLUMAGE

If you dream of feathered plumage and find it pleasing, good love relationships are in the offing. If the plumage displeases you, expect a broken relationship or marriage.

## PLUMBING

To dream of shiny and bright plumbing suggests that an unexpected opportunity will bring financial gain. Old, dull, or leaky plumbing predicts frustration and annoyance with a friend or colleague.

## PLUMPNESS

To dream of being plump or thinking someone else is pleasingly plump suggests financial stability in your life. To dream that you are unhappy with your plumpness or that you find someone else's chubbiness displeasing warns about upcoming spending issues and possible financial problems.

## PLUMS

In dreams, green plums signify discomfort, unless seen on trees. Ripe plums denote joyous occasions; they will be of short duration. To eat plums denotes that you will engage in flirtatious behavior.

If you dream of gathering plums, you will obtain your desires, but they will not prove as satisfying as you had imagined. If you see yourself collecting them from the ground and finding rotten ones among the good, you will be forced to admit that your expectations about life have not been realized, and that there is no life filled with pleasure alone.

## PMS

To dream of suffering from PMS foretells fertility problems and health issues.

## PNEUMONIA

To dream of this illness predicts health issues. You need to get a checkup.

## POCKET

To dream of your pocket is a sign of bad luck.

## POCKETBOOK*

If you find a pocketbook filled with money in your dreams, you will be quite lucky, gaining what you desire in nearly every instance. If the pocketbook is empty, you will be disappointed in some big hope. If you lose your own pocketbook, you will unfortunately disagree with a best friend.

*See *Purse*.

## POCKMARKS

To dream of seeing your face pockmarked suggests that you are being seen by others for your inner beauty. To dream of someone else's face being pockmarked reminds you to examine how you deal with others.

## PODCAST

To dream of a podcast means you will find the ability to learn something new that you never thought you could.

## POET

To dream of a poet means you will soon be asked for a monetary loan.

## POETRY

To dream of poetry betokens an interesting and unusual new friend.

## POINSETTIA

To dream of this Christmas plant suggests family harmony and stable relationships. If the poinsettia is dead or unhealthy, however, it foretells family arguments and discord.

## POISON*

To dream that you are poisoned suggests that a painful influence will immediately reach you. If you seek to use poison on others, you are guilty of base thoughts, or life will dissapoint you.

Throwing poison away in your dream denotes that by sheer force you will overcome unsatisfactory conditions. To handle poison, or see others with it, signifies that unpleasantness will surround you.

If an enemy or rival is poisoned, you will overcome obstacles. To recover from the effects of poison suggests that you will succeed after worry. To dream of taking strychnine or other poisonous medicine under the guidance of a physician cautions that you are undertaking an affair fraught with danger.

*See Cyanide.

## POISON IVY

To dream of this plant suggests that a painful misunderstanding will soon occur with a special friend.

## POKER (CARD GAME)

To play poker warns you against evil company.

## POKER (TOOL)

To dream of seeing a red-hot poker, or fighting using one, signifies that you meet trouble with combative energy.

## POLAR BEAR*

Polar bears in dreams suggest improvement in your social and financial circumstances. To see the skin of one denotes that you will successfully overcome any opposition.

*See *Bear*.

## POLECAT (SKUNK)

To dream of a polecat signifies salacious scandals. If you notice the odor of a polecat on your clothes, or otherwise smell it, you will find that your conduct is considered rude, and your affairs will prove unsatisfactory. To kill one reveals that you will overcome formidable obstacles.

## POLE-DANCING

To dream you are an exotic dancer, using a pole as a prop, foretells exciting and exotic adventures coming into your life.

## POLE-VAULTING

To dream of pole-vaulting suggests unexpected financial gain if you clear the pole; if you don't, financial loss is warned of.

## POLICE*

If you dream of the police trying to arrest you for a crime of which you are innocent, it foretells that you will successfully outstrip rivals. If the arrest is just, you will have a season of misfortune. To see police while you're out on parole indicates alarming developments in your affairs.

*See *Sheriff*.

## POLIO

To dream of having this disease indicates sound mental health.

## POLISHING

If you dream of polishing any article, high attainments will place you in enviable positions.

## POLITICIAN

To dream of a politician suggests displeasing companions and loss of time and means.

If you engage in political wrangling, misunderstandings and ill feeling will be shown you by friends.

## POLKA*

In dreams, dancing the polka symbolizes pleasant occupations.

*See Dancing.

## POLKA DOTS

To dream of this pattern suggests that confusion in an upcoming business project will cause you great frustration until the problem is solved.

## POLLEN

To dream of pollen suggests financial gain. To suffer an allergy from pollen in your dream warns you against unnecessary spending that could lead to a financial loss.

## POLLUTION

To dream that you are polluting implies that surrounding yourself with a beautiful environment will give you peace of mind and serenity.

## POLO

Dreaming of polo foretells an increase in material wealth.

## POLTERGEIST

To dream of these supernatural, playful creatures is a warning that being socially irresponsible could bring you embarrassment.

## POLYGAMY

To dream about polygamists, or that you are a polygamist, cautions you of mistrust and suspicion in a current love affair.

## POMEGRANATE

Dreaming of pomegranates shows that you will wisely use your talents for the enrichment of the mind rather than seeking pleasures that destroy morality and health. To eat one signifies that you will become captive to the personal charms of another.

## PONCHO

To dream of wearing a poncho means that help will come in times of trouble.

## POND*

To see a still, clear pond in your dream indicates that your life is fine and there is no immediate cause for concern. If the pond is muddy or choppy, you will have domestic quarrels.

*See Puddle, Water.

## PONY

To dream of ponies indicates that moderate speculation will be rewarded with success.

## POOL*

To dream of a swimming pool foretells social enjoyment, as long as the water is clear. If the pool is empty or the water is dirty, gambling will lead to financial loss.

*For playing pool, see *Billiards*.

## POOP

To dream of excrement denotes extreme financial gain and good fortune.

## POOR*

To dream that you or your friends are poor signifies worry and loss.

*See *Pauper*.

## POORHOUSE

To see a poorhouse in your dream warns you of unfaithful friends who care for you only so they can use your money and belongings.

## POPCORN

To dream of this snack food suggests abundance in friendship, fun, and love.

## POPE

Any dream in which you see the Pope represents your spiritual guidance, beliefs, and self. This is a good omen.

## POPLAR

To dream of seeing poplars is an omen of good, if they are in leaf or bloom.

## POPPIES

Poppies seen in dreams represent a season of seductive pleasures and flattering business, but they have unstable foundations. If you inhale the odor of one, you will be the victim of artful persuasions and flattery.

## PORCELAIN

To dream of porcelain signifies that you will have favorable opportunities of progressing in your affairs. To see porcelain broken or soiled denotes mistakes that will cause grave offense.

## PORCH

To dream of a porch implies that you will engage in new undertakings, and the future will be full of uncertainties. If you dream of building a porch, you will assume new duties.

## PORCUPINE

To see a porcupine in your dreams indicates that you will disapprove any new enterprise and repel new friendships with coldness. To see a dead porcupine signifies your abolishment of ill feelings and possessions.

## PORK*

If you eat pork in your dreams, you will encounter trouble; but if you merely see pork, you will come out of a conflict victoriously.

*See *Bacon*.

## PORPOISE

To see a porpoise in your dreams indicates a connection between your subconscious and conscious. Porpoises are spiritual mammals and portend a time of growth in your spiritual life.

## PORTER

Seeing a porter in a dream augurs decidedly bad luck. To imagine yourself a porter suggests humble circumstances. If you hire one, you will be able to enjoy whatever success comes to you.

## PORTFOLIO

To dream of a portfolio indicates that your employment will not be to your liking; you will seek a change in your location.

## PORTHOLE

To dream of looking through a porthole is not necessarily a bad omen, unless the water you are looking at is murky and rough; then you will have tough times ahead.

## PORTRAIT*

To dream of gazing on the portrait of a beautiful person indicates that, while you enjoy pleasure, you can feel the disquiet and treachery of such joys. You will suffer loss after dreaming of portraits.

*See *Likeness, Paint and painting, Photograph, Picture*.

## POST OFFICE

In dreams, a post office symbolizes generally unpleasant tidings and ill luck.

## POSTAGE

To dream of postage stamps suggests organization and remuneration in business. If you try to use canceled stamps, you will fall into disrepute.

To receive stamps signifies a rapid rise to distinction. Seeing torn stamps implies that there are obstacles in your way.

## POSTCARD

To dream of sending, writing, or buying a postcard means you will be embarrassed by something you have done in your past. To dream of receiving one denotes a financial embarrassment or loss.

## POSTPONEMENT

To dream of the postponement of a social or business affair portends an argument with someone close to you. If the postponement is of a trip, financial worries are coming.

## POT*

If you dream of a pot, unimportant events will cause you vexation. To see a broken or rusty one foretells keen disappointment.

*For the drug, see *Marijuana*.

## POTATOES

Dreaming of potatoes often brings good. To dream of digging them denotes success; eating them, substantial gain; cooking them, congenial employment. Planting them brings the realization of desires. To see potatoes rotting reveals vanished pleasure and a darkening future.

## POTBELLY

To see anything potbellied in a dream augurs luck and financial gain.

## POTLUCK

To dream of potluck meals indicates good fortune and physical well-being.

## POTPOURRI

If you dream of smelling potpourri and finding it pleasing, you'll experience relief from mental stress. If the smell is overpowering or annoying, something in your life is giving you much stress.

## POTTER

To dream of a potter denotes constant employment and satisfactory results.

## POTTER'S FIELD

To see a potter's field in your dreams warns of poverty and misery.

## POTTERY

If you dream of intact pottery, you will soon have a pleasant surprise. Broken pottery foretells broken engagements, promises, and business deals.

## POULTRY

To see dressed poultry in a dream reveals that extravagant habits will reduce your security in monetary matters.

## POUNDING

To dream that you are pounding something suggests frustration with business or in your personal life.

## POUND (WEIGHT)

To dream of weighing something in pounds foretells financial gain.

## POURING

To dream of pouring something or having something poured on you suggests an upcoming problem. The exact liquid being poured will indicate whether the problem will be easily remedied.

## POWDER

To see powder in your dreams reveals that you are dealing with unscrupulous people. You may detect them through watchfulness.

## POWER

To dream of power in any form is a dream of success.

## POWER OF ATTORNEY

To dream that you have obtained power of attorney over another means you will soon seek help in a legal matter. To dream that someone has power of attorney over you augurs good health and mental stability.

## POWER PLANT

To dream of a power plant means you will find the energy to complete a project that you never thought you could.

## POWWOW

To dream of this Native American ritual foretells upcoming blessings and spiritual enlightenment.

## PRACTICAL JOKE

To dream of playing a practical joke on someone suggests success in a business deal. If you dream of having such a joke played on you and find it funny, a problem with a friend or business associate is indicated. If the joke is not funny to you, expect disappointment in your personal life.

## PRACTICING

To dream of practicing something over and over again means advancement in your career.

## PRAIRIE

To dream of a prairie denotes that you will enjoy ease, even luxury and unobstructed progress.

An undulating prairie covered with growing grasses and flowers signifies joyous happenings. A barren prairie represents loss and sadness through the absence of friends. To be lost on one is a sign of sadness and ill luck.

## PRAISE

To dream of receiving praise foretells an unexpected gift of money. To dream of giving praise forewarns of an unanticipated expense.

## PRAYER

To dream of saying prayers foretells peace of mind and happiness in life. To hear others pray suggests loyal and lasting friendships.

## PREACHER*

To dream of a preacher denotes that your ways are not above reproach, and your affairs will not move smoothly. To dream that you are a preacher foretells losses in business; unsavory amusements will shake you up.

To hear preaching in a dream implies that you will experience misfortune. If you argue with a preacher, you will lose in a contest.

To see one walk away from you denotes that your affairs will proceed with renewed energy. If he or she looks sorrowful, reproaches will fall heavily upon you. To see a long-haired preacher warns of disputes with overbearing and egotistical people.

*See Minister, Priest.

## PRECIPICE*

To dream of standing over a yawning precipice portends misfortune and calamity. If you fall over the precipice, you will be engulfed in disaster.

*See Abyss, Pit.

## PREDICTION

To hear someone make a prediction in a dream foretells bad news. To dream that you are making a prediction warns you against putting yourself at risk.

## PREGNANCY

To dream that you are pregnant suggests that a new aspect of yourself is growing and developing. If the baby is sick or dying inside you in the dream, a project you put a lot of effort into may be falling apart. If you are pregnant and have this dream, it has no meaning.

## PREJUDICE

To dream of being prejudiced warns you that you may not be living your life in accordance with what you believe to be true.

## PREMATURITY

To dream of anything being premature suggests happiness and contentment in the near future. If you are pregnant and dream of a premature baby, the dream means nothing.

## PREMIERE

To dream that you are attending a premiere foretells a pleasant surprise and happy news in your family.

## PRESCRIPTION

To dream of filling a prescription for yourself suggests good health; for someone else, disappointment.

## PRESENT*

To receive presents in your dreams denotes that you will be unusually fortunate.

*See Gift.

## PRIDE

If you dream of being prideful, your integrity will soon be challenged. To dream of others being prideful suggests an advancement in your career.

## PRIEST*

A dream of a priest is an augury of ill, indicating the need for spiritual advice or guidance in your life.

*See Minister, Preacher.

## PRIME MINISTER

To dream of a prime minister means you will soon win a legal battle. To dream that you are the prime minister of a country means great social success.

## PRIMROSE

To dream of this little flower in the grass at your feet heralds joys laden with comfort and peace.

## PRINCE, PRINCESS

To dream of being this member of the royal family suggests an advancement in your social status; but this could be surrounded by jealousy, so you need to watch your back.

## PRINCIPAL

To dream of a school principal warns you to be careful about your driving; you might get a traffic ticket. To dream that you are the principal suggests that you will escape legal trouble.

## PRINTER

To see a printing-press operator in your dreams is a warning of poverty if you neglect to practice economy.

To dream of an office or computer printer implies that you will reach your goals, but only through your hard work.

## PRINTING PRESS

To be in a printing office in dreams denotes that slander will threaten you. To run a printing office is indicative of hard luck.

## PRISON*

To dream of a prison is the forerunner to misfortune if the prison encircles your friends or yourself.

To see anyone dismissed from prison denotes that you will finally overcome misfortune.

*See Jail.

## PRIVACY

To dream that your privacy suffers intrusion suggests that overbearing people worry you.

## PRIZE

To dream that you have won a prize signifies success and material gain.

## PRIZEFIGHT

To see a prizefight in your dreams suggests that controlling your affairs will give you trouble.

## PROCESSION

To dream of a procession indicates that you will have trouble fulfilling your obligations because of fear. If it is a funeral procession, sorrow is fast approaching and will throw a pall over your happiness.

## PROFANITY

To dream of profanity reveals that you cultivate traits that render you coarse and unfeeling toward your fellow man.

To dream that others use profanity is a sign that you will be injured in some way and probably insulted also.

## PROFESSOR

To dream of being a college professor means advancement in your career, unless you are a professor in waking life, in which case, it has no meaning. To dream of being instructed by a professor foretells a new hobby.

## PROFILE

To dream that you are writing a profile of yourself suggests that you will soon be examining your conscience and experiencing guilt for something you have done in the past. If you dream that you are reading another person's profile, your friends are honest and loyal.

To dream of viewing a person in profile foretells a problem with a friend or family member.

## PROFIT*

To dream of profits augurs success in your immediate future.
*See Gain.

## PROM

To dream of a prom foretells an unexpected and enjoyable social invitation.

## PROMENADING

To dream of promenading suggests that you will engage in energetic and profitable pursuits. To see others promenading signifies that you will have rivals in your pursuits.

## PROMISE

If you make a promise in a dream, you will forgive an enemy and gain a friend. To dream that you have received a promise betokens an unexpected event that will bring you great joy.

## PROMISSORY NOTE

If you dream of giving a promissory note to someone, an unexpected sum of money may enter your life. To dream of having to repay a promissory note suggests that you may suffer a financial loss because you didn't make sure the item was of value.

## PROOFREADING

To dream of proofreading warns you to be diligent in making sure that upcoming business projects are financially solvent.

## PROPAGANDA

To dream of influencing others using propaganda means you will have to hold your own against an underhanded attack on your reputation.

## PROPANE

To dream of this fuel means you will soon be setting the world on fire. All your previous ideas will come together and create a synergy that will benefit you.

## PROPELLER

To dream of a working propeller means a swift conclusion to an upcoming business deal. To dream of a stalled or broken propeller warns you that your carelessness or apathy will work against you and be someone else's gain.

## PROPERTY*

To dream that you own vast property predicts that you will be successful in your business affairs, gaining friends along the way.
*See *Wealth*.

## PROPHET

To dream of a prophet means you will have great blessings in your future and will enjoy an expanded spiritual base.

## PROPOSAL

To dream of making or receiving a proposal, if you are a woman, predicts great popularity among your friends and colleagues. If you are a man, it warns you not to trip yourself up by being too arrogant.

## PROSTITUTE

To dream that you are in the company of a prostitute indicates that you will incur the righteous scorn of friends for ill-mannered conduct.

To dream you are a prostitute indicates either that you secretly feel you are prostituting yourself for an unworthy cause, or perhaps that you need to deal with sexual repression.

## PROTOTYPE

To dream of a prototype means that you will have to acknowledge the efforts of others for the success of an upcoming project.

## PRUDERY

If you dream that you are a prude or someone else is, you are outspoken and may lose friends or colleagues in the near future.

## PRUNE

To dream of this dried fruit suggests that you will soon be undergoing a change of residence. If they are stewed in your dream, it foretells improving health.

## PSALM

To dream of reading, singing, or hearing psalms means blessings and abundance.

## PSYCHIC

To dream of a psychic means good luck and happy times. To dream you are a psychic suggests that you may need financial help for a monetary problem.

## PTOMAINE

To dream of having this food poisoning warns you to watch your diet.

## PUBIC HAIR

To dream of seeing this type of body hair predicts an announcement of pregnancy or birth.

## PUBLICITY

To dream of publicity for yourself or someone else warns that you are not handling your friends and family members kindly.

## PUBLISHING

To dream of a publisher foretells long journeys and aspirations to the literary craft.

For a publisher to reject your manuscript indicates that you will suffer disappointment at the miscarriage of cherished designs. If the publisher instead accepts your manuscript, you will rejoice in the full fruition of your hopes. If the manuscript is lost, you will suffer evil at the hands of strangers.

To dream of being involved with a publisher suggests financial loss.

Dreaming of having something published implies an improvement in your personal and financial life.

## PUDDING

To dream of seeing pudding denotes small returns from large investments. To eat pudding is proof that your affairs will be disappointing.

## PUDDLE

To find yourself stepping into puddles of clear water in a dream denotes vexation but some redeeming good in the future. If the water is muddy, unpleasantness will go a few rounds with you.

To wet your feet by stepping into puddles foretells that your pleasure will cause you harm afterward.

## PULPIT

To dream of a pulpit denotes sorrow and vexation. If you are in a pulpit, expect sickness and unsatisfactory results in business.

## PULSE

To dream of your pulse warns you to look after your affairs and health with care, as both are susceptible to debilitating conditions.

To dream of feeling the pulse of another signifies that you are committing depredations in pleasure's domain.

## PUMP

To see a pump in a dream suggests that energy and faithfulness to business will produce desired riches. Good health also is usually betokened by this dream.

A broken pump signifies that your means of advancing in life will be absorbed by family cares. To the married and the unmarried, it intimates wasted energies. If you work a pump, your life will be filled with pleasure and profitable undertakings.

## PUMPKIN

Any form of pumpkin in your dream represents a happy, comfortable home life.

## PUNCH (BEVERAGE)

To dream of drinking punch denotes that you prefer selfish pleasures to honorable distinction and morality.

## PUNCHING

To dream that you are punching anyone with a club or fist implies quarrels and recriminations.

## PUNCTURING

To dream that you are puncturing something means a change in residence.

## PUNISHMENT

If you dream you are being punished, you're about to become very popular. To dream that you are punishing someone else means you will be doing something that you will be very proud of.

## PUPPET

To dream of a puppet warns you to examine your career and personal life to see if you are being controlled.

## PUPPY*

To dream of puppies indicates that you will entertain the innocent and hapless and thereby enjoy pleasure. The dream also shows that friendships will grow stronger and fortune will increase if the pups are healthy and well formed; vice versa if they are lean and dirty.

*See Dog, Hound.

## PURCHASES

To dream of purchases usually augurs profit and advancement with pleasure.

## PURGATORY

To dream of purgatory means you will soon have to make a decision. You might not initially believe it is the right thing for you, but it will turn out to be a blessing.

## PURPLE

The color purple always is tied to psychic development, spiritual intuition, and development of spirit.

## PURRING

To dream of hearing purring augurs contentment and happiness.

## PURSE*

To dream of your purse being filled denotes associations where "good cheer" is the motto, and harmony and tender love make Earth a beautiful place.

To dream of your purse being empty suggests financial issues.

*See *Pocketbook*.

## PUSHING

To dream of pushing or being pushed foretells troubles that you will rise above.

## PUSSY WILLOW

In dreams, pussy willows symbolize comfort and security.

## PUTTY

To dream of working with putty suggests that you are taking hazardous chances with fortune. If you put a windowpane in with putty, you will seek fortune, with poor results.

## PUZZLE

To dream of solving a puzzle reveals that a current problem will be easily solved. If you cannot solve a puzzle in your dream, expect hard work ahead in solving a real-life problem.

## PYRAMID

To dream of pyramids tells you that many changes are coming. If you climb them, you will journey a long while before you find the gratification of desires.

To dream that you are studying the mystery of the ancient pyramids indicates that you will develop a love for the mysteries of nature and will become learned and cultured.

## PYTHON

To dream of this type of large snake warns you against your friends and colleagues being dishonest and backbiting.

## QUACK (CHARLATAN)

To see a quack in your dreams implies that you are alarmed over an illness and its improper treatment.

## QUADRILLE*

To dream of dancing a quadrille foretells a pleasant engagement that will occupy your time.

*See *Dancing*.

## QUADRIPLEGIC

To dream that you are a quadriplegic suggests that you are entering into a period of great stamina and good health. To dream of seeing someone else who is a quadriplegic indicates a health issue that needs to be addressed.

## QUADRUPLETS

To dream of four of a kind means that you will have double trouble, but it will be temporary and minor.

## QUAGMIRE

To dream of being in a quagmire implies an inability to meet obligations. To see others thus situated indicates that you will feel their failures. Illness is sometimes indicated by this dream.

## QUAIL

To see quail in your dream is a very favorable omen if they are alive; if they're dead, you will undergo serious ill luck.

To shoot quail foretells ill feelings toward you from your best friends. To eat quail signifies extravagance in your personal living.

## QUAKE

To dream of a quake suggests social stability and career recognition.

## QUAKER

To dream of a Quaker indicates that you will have faithful friends and an honest business. If you are a Quaker, you will behave honorably with your enemies.

## QUARANTINE

To dream of being quarantined means that you will be placed in a disagreeable position by the malicious intriguing of enemies.

## QUARREL

Quarrels in dreams portend unhappiness and fierce altercations. To a young woman, quarrels are the signal of unpleasantness fatal to a relationship, and to a married woman they bring separation or ongoing disagreement. To hear others quarreling denotes unsatisfactory business and disappointing trade.

## QUARRY

To dream of being in a quarry and seeing the workmen busy suggests that you will advance by hard labor.

An idle quarry signifies failure, disappointment, and, often, death.

## QUARTER

To dream of this coin means that an unexpected gift will surprise you.

## QUARTET

To dream of playing or singing in a quartet represents favorable affairs, jolly companions, and good times.

To see or hear a quartet foretells that you will aspire to something beyond you.

## QUARTZ

To dream of quartz speaks of being cheated financially; but if you trust your instincts, you will suspect this before it actually happens.

## QUAY

To dream of a quay denotes that you will contemplate making a long tour in the near future. To see vessels while standing on a quay suggests the fruition of wishes and designs.

## QUEEN*

To dream of a queen foretells successful ventures. If she looks old or haggard, however, disappointments will be connected with your pleasures.

*See Empress.

## QUESTIONING

To question the merits of a thing in your dreams warns that you will suspect someone whom you love of unfaithfulness, and you will fear for your investments.

To ask a question foretells that you will earnestly strive for truth and will be successful. If you are questioned, you will be unfairly dealt with.

## QUEUE

To dream that you are standing in or watching a queue means good family advice and generosity.

## QUICHE

To dream of eating quiche means financial well-being.

## QUICKSAND

If you find yourself in quicksand while dreaming, you will meet with loss and deceit. If you are unable to get out of the quicksand, you will be involved in overwhelming misfortune.

## QUIETUDE

To dream of quietude or absolute silence means you will have a mental shock that may require you to get help.

## QUILL

To dream of quills denotes to the literarily inclined a season of success. To dream of them as ornaments signifies a brisk trade and some remuneration.

## QUILT

To dream of quilts foretells pleasant and comfortable circumstances.

## QUINCE

Dreaming of cooked or jellied quince suggests that you are annoyed with a friend and the secrets he or she keeps. To dream of eating fresh quince cautions you to be more responsible in your finances.

## QUININE

To dream of quinine indicates that you will soon be possessed of great happiness, though your prospects for much wealth may be meager.

To take quinine foretells improvement in health and energy. You will also make new friends who will assist you in business.

## QUINTET

Dreaming of a quintet foretells new friends. To dream of listening to a quintet suggests that your friends are loyal and trustworthy.

## QUINTUPLETS

If you dream of anything in fives, obstacles in your path will be easily overcome and removed.

## QUIZ

To dream of taking a quiz foretells good luck. If you fail the quiz, however, you will have to deal with an uncomfortable situation in your life. If you pass, an upcoming problem will have an easy solution.

## QUOTA

To dream of meeting a quota in your dreams augurs new friends and business associates who will do well for you. To dream that you can't meet a quota implies a loss of a friend or business associate.

## QUOTE

To dream of quoting someone or something suggests social success. If you dream that you are being quoted, watch your back with a business associate or friend.

## RABBI

To dream of this Jewish scholar, regardless of your personal faith, suggests that things are going your way. But if you are Jewish and dream of a rabbi, it signifies prosperity through hard work.

## RABBIT*

To see a rabbit in your dream signifies luck, magical power, and success. Alternatively, rabbits symbolize abundance. In general, rabbits foretell a favorable turn of events, and you will be pleased with your progress.

To see white rabbits denotes faithfulness in love, to the married and the single. To see rabbits frolicking about implies that children will contribute to your joy.

*See *Hare*.

## RABIES

If you dream that an animal with rabies bites you, you will be betrayed by your dearest friend and much scandal will be brought to light.

## RACCOON

To dream of a raccoon indicates that you are being deceived by the friendly appearance of enemies.

## RACEHORSE

To dream of a racehorse in good health means unexpected luck. If the horse is in poor health, expect financial loss.

## RACETRACK

In dreams, a racetrack represents financial gain.

## RACING

To dream that you are in a race suggests that others aspire to the things you are working to possess. If you win, you will overcome your competitors.

## RACK

To dream of a rack suggests that you are giving much anxious thought to the uncertain outcome of some engagement.

## RACKET

To dream of a racket denotes that you will be foiled in some anticipated pleasure.

## RACQUETBALL*

To dream that you are participating in this sport means good health. To dream of watching someone play racquetball foretells a social event.
*See *Handball*.

## RADIATOR

To dream of a radiator that is cold suggests a loss of friendship. If you dream of a hissing radiator, beware of a shady business deal. To dream of an overheated car radiator warns of trouble in your love life.

## RADIO

If you dream of a radio and find the broadcasts pleasant, you will enjoy a happy home life. But if what you are hearing is displeasing, this indicates arguments and discord among family members.

## RADIOACTIVITY

To dream of anything radioactive means that your social and love life will soon be taking off.

## RADISH

To dream of seeing a bed of radishes growing is an omen of good luck. Your friends will be unusually kind, your business will prosper, and your anticipations will be happily realized. If you eat radishes, you may suffer slightly through the thoughtlessness of someone near to you.

## RAFFLE

To dream of raffling any article foretells that you will fall victim to speculation. If you are at a church raffle, you will soon find that disappointment is clouding your future.

## RAFT

To dream of a raft denotes that you will go into new locations to engage in enterprises that prove successful.

To dream of floating on a raft suggests uncertain journeys. If you reach your destination, you will surely come into good fortune. If a raft breaks, or any such mishap befalls it, you or a friend will suffer from an accident, or sickness will have unfortunate results.

## RAG

To dream of a clean rag foretells prosperity. A dirty rag portends financial loss.

## RAGE

To be in a rage and scolding people and tearing up things in a dream generally signifies quarrels and injury to your friends.

To see others in a rage is a sign of unfavorable conditions for business, and unhappiness in social life.

## RAGWEED

To dream of ragweed warns that if you don't address a problem, it will become a big annoyance.

## RAID

To dream of being raided warns against personal property loss. But if you participate in the raid, you will make a small financial gain in a very unusual way.

## RAILING

To dream of seeing railings indicates that some person is trying to obstruct your pathway in love or business.

To dream of holding on to a railing indicates that you will take a desperate chance to obtain something that you have set your heart on. It may be love or it may have a more material form.

## RAILROAD

If you dream of a railroad, you will find that your business needs close attention; enemies are trying to undermine you.

To see an obstruction on a railroad indicates foul play in your affairs.

To walk the cross-ties of a railroad signifies a time of worry and hard work. If you dream of walking the rails, expect much happiness from your skillful manipulation of affairs.

To see a railroad inundated with clear water foretells that pleasure will, for a short time, wipe out misfortune.

## RAIN

To dream of being out in a clear shower of rain suggests that you enjoy pleasure with the zest of youth, and prosperity will come to you. If the rain descends from dark clouds, you will feel alarmed over the gravity of your undertakings.

If you see and hear rain approaching, and manage to escape becoming wet, you will succeed in your plans and your ideas will advance rapidly.

To be sitting in the house and through a window see a downpour of rain means you will possess fortune, and passionate love will be requited.

To hear the patter of rain on the roof predicts a realization of domestic bliss and joy. Fortune will come in a small way.

If you dream that your house is leaking during a rain and the water is clear, it foretells that illicit pleasure will come to you rather unexpectedly; but if the water is filthy or muddy, you may expect that your affair will be exposed.

To find yourself regretting taking care of a chore badly while listening to the rain denotes that the way you seek pleasure will offend someone else's sense of propriety.

To see it rain on others foretells excluding friends from your confidence.

To see it raining on livestock foretells disappointment in business and unpleasantness in social circles. Stormy weather in dreams is always unfortunate.

## RAINBOW

To see a rainbow in a dream prognosticates unusual events. Affairs will assume a more promising aspect.

To see the rainbow hanging low over green trees signifies unconditional success in any undertaking.

## RAISINS

To dream of eating raisins implies that discouragement will darken your hopes when they seem about to be realized.

## RAKE

To dream of using a rake portends that work you have left to others will never be accomplished unless you superintend it yourself. A broken rake suggests that sickness or accident will bring failure to your plans. To see others raking foretells that you will rejoice in the good fortune of others.

## RALLY

To dream that you are rallying for a cause foretells an unexpected social affair that will bring you much joy. It is the same meaning if you are attending a rally.

### RAM*

To dream that a ram pursues you implies that misfortune threatens you. To see one quietly grazing means that you have powerful friends who will use their best efforts for your good.

*See *Lamb, Sheep*.

### RAMBLING

To dream that you are rambling through the country denotes that you will be oppressed by sadness and the separation from friends, but your worldly surroundings will be all that you could desire.

For a young woman, this dream promises a comfortable home but early bereavement.

### RAMROD

To dream of a ramrod denotes unfortunate adventures. You will have cause for grief. For a young woman to see one bent or broken suggests that a dear friend or lover will fail her.

### RANCIDITY

To dream of something becoming rancid or rotten warns against self-created health problems. Watch what you are eating and drinking.

### RANGER

To dream of a uniformed ranger implies travel.

### RANSOM

If you dream that a ransom is paid for you, you will find that you are deceived and tricked out of your money.

### RAPE

To dream that one of your acquaintances has been raped indicates that you will be shocked at the distress of some of your friends.

### RAPIDS

To imagine that you are being carried over rapids in a dream suggests that you will suffer appalling loss from the neglect of duty and the courting of seductive pleasures.

### RARE (COOKING)

To dream that meat is cooked rare portends trouble and a possible death.

### RARITY

To dream of a rare item of particular value foretells an unexpected gift.

## RASHES

To dream of a rash foretells an unpleasant argument or the ending of a friendship or relationship.

## RASPBERRY

To see raspberries in a dream suggests that you are in danger of entanglements that will be interesting but that you must escape from.

To eat raspberries means distress over circumstantial evidence in an event that is causing gossip.

## RAT*

To dream of rats suggests that you will be deceived and injured by your neighbors. Quarrels with companions are likely.

To catch rats means you will scorn the baseness of others and worthily outstrip your enemies. To kill a rat heralds your victory in any contest.

*See Mouse.

## RATIONING

Dreaming of rationing is a dream of abundance. But if you are the one doing the rationing, the dream suggests financial loss.

## RATTAN

To dream of rattan suggests that you depend largely on the judgment of others; you would be well served to cultivate independence in planning and executing your affairs.

## RATTLE

To dream of seeing a baby play with its rattle augurs peace and contentment in the home; enterprises will be honorable and full of gain.

## RATTLESNAKE

To dream of a rattlesnake foreshadows unexpected treachery from someone you trust. If you dream of only hearing the rattlesnake, you will be able to see it coming. If the snake bites you in a dream, it foretells an argument.

## RAT TRAP*

To dream of falling into a rat trap predicts that you will be victimized and will be robbed of a valuable object.

To see an empty trap signifies an absence of slander or competition. A broken one means that you will be rid of unpleasant associations.

If you dream of setting a trap, you will be made aware of the designs of enemies, and the warning will enable you to outwit them.

*See Mousetrap.

### RAVEN*

To dream of a raven denotes reverses in fortune and inhospitable surroundings.

*See Crow.

### RAVENOUSNESS

To dream that you are ravenously hungry suggests personal and family well-being.

### RAY (LIGHT)

To see a ray of sunshine through the clouds means the coming of blessings.

### RAZOR

To dream of a razor portends disagreements and contentiousness.

To cut yourself with one denotes that you will be unlucky in a deal you are about to make. Fighting with a razor foretells disappointing business; someone will keep you harassed almost beyond endurance.

A broken or rusty razor brings unavoidable distress.

### REACHING

To dream of reaching for something means your goal is farther away than anticipated. To dream that someone is reaching for you or for something that you have suggests that a goal is easily obtained.

### READING

To be engaged in reading in your dreams foretells that you will excel in work that appears difficult.

To see others reading reveals that your friends will be kind and are well disposed toward you.

If you give a reading or discuss reading, you will cultivate your literary ability. Indistinct or incoherent reading implies worry and disappointment.

### REAL ESTATE

To dream of a real-estate transaction indicates financial gain.

### REAPER

To dream of seeing harvesters busy at work denotes prosperity and contentment. If they appear to be going through dried stubble, crops will be poor and business will fall off.

To see idle reapers implies that something discouraging will occur in the midst of prosperity.

To see a broken harvesting machine signifies loss of employment or career disappointment.

## REBELLION

To dream of a rebellion of any kind foretells a happy social event with family or business associates.

## RECALLING

To dream that something is being recalled means you need to beware of repeating the same mistake over and over again.

## RECEIPT

To dream of a receipt is a promise of better times ahead.

## RECEPTION*

To dream of attending a reception predicts pleasant engagements. Confusion at a reception will cause you uneasiness.

*See *Entertainment*.

## RECIPE

To dream of a recipe means you need more social outlets. You are most likely working too much and need to add play in your life.

## RECITAL

Dreaming of giving a recital suggests that you are entering a period when you need to be alone to overcome a problem. To watch a recital in a dream means happy social events are in the offing.

## RECITATION

To dream of reciting something means you will be called upon to help with a problem because your opinion is valued. If you listen to someone reciting something in a dream, you must heed another person's words to solve a problem.

## RECLUSE

To dream of yourself as a recluse indicates the coming of happy social events and many invitations. To dream of observing a recluse means you need to get out and have more fun.

## RECONCILIATION

To reconcile in a dream suggests an upcoming argument or fight that could sever a relationship.

## RECORDING

To dream of a record player or tape recorder implies deterioration in your love life.

## RECOUNT

Dreaming of a recount denotes finishing a project very simply and easily.

## RECYCLING

To find yourself recycling anything in your dreams suggests the continuing of good times and pleasantness in your life.

## RED

To dream of this color or of any article that stands out because it is red indicates great passion and sensitivity in your emotional relationships.

## REDUCTION

To dream of successfully reducing anything predicts exciting new loves coming into your life.

## REDWOOD

To dream of these domestic conifers in their natural state suggests monumental gain in your personal life or career. To dream of working with this wood, as in lumber, augurs good changes in your personal or business life.

## REEF

To dream of a coral reef, or a reef of any type, foretells abundance, happiness, and well-being.

## REEFER*

To dream of smoking cannabis means you are taking way too many risks in your social life and will be embarrassed if you don't stop.

*See *Marijuana*.

## REFRIGERATOR

To see a refrigerator in your dreams portends that your selfishness will offend and injure someone trying to earn an honest livelihood.

## REFUGEE

To dream of a refugee warns you to take care of yourself before you take care of others. To dream of being a refugee means you will receive an unexpected favor done out of love.

## REGGAE

To dream of reggae music, style, or customs heralds pleasant surprises in your personal life and wonderful peace of mind.

## REGISTERING

To dream that someone registers your name at a hotel for you indicates that you will undertake some work that will be finished by others. If you register under an assumed name, you will engage in guilty questionable enterprise that will give you much uneasiness of mind.

## REGRET

To dream of regrets means you will soon be rejoicing about something wonderful.

## REINDEER

To dream of a reindeer signifies faithful discharge of duties, and remaining loyal to friends during times of adversity.

To drive reindeer implies that you will have hours of bitter anguish, but friends will attend you.

## REJECTION

To dream of yourself, or something you have done, being rejected foretells great social acceptance and recognition for your hard work. To reject someone else means the loss of a friend or business colleague.

## RELATIVE

To dream of any relative in your family forecasts freedom from worry. To dream of someone else's relative means you will soon be seeking help with a problem.

## RELIEF

To be relieved in a dream, or to wake up feeling relieved after a dream, foretells anxieties and worries ahead.

## RELIGION*

If you dream of discussing religion and you feel religiously inclined, you will find much to mar the calmness of your life, and business will turn disagreeable for you. If you judge yourself in the midst of religious rapture, you may almost be induced to give up your own personality to please someone whom you hold in reverent esteem.

To see religion declining in power denotes that your life will be more in harmony with creation than formerly. Your prejudices will not be so aggressive.

To dream that a minister tells you in a calm and friendly manner that he has given up his work foretells that you will be the recipient of unexpected tidings of a favorable nature; but if the minister speaks in a professional and warning way, it suggests that you will be overtaken in your deceitful intriguing, or that other disappointments will follow.

*See Revival.*

## REMEMBRANCE

To dream of a keepsake or souvenir suggests that pleasant memories will come back that relieve your anxieties and fears about an upcoming situation.

## RENDEZVOUS

To dream of having a rendezvous with someone you know means that soon you will get an invitation to a social event. To dream of having a rendezvous with a stranger or someone you don't know suggests that you will soon be making a good friend.

## RENT

To dream that you rent a house is a sign that you will enter into new contracts that will prove profitable.

To fail to rent out property signifies that there will be much inactivity in business.

To pay rent signifies that your finances will be satisfactory. If you can't pay your rent, it is unlucky for you; you will see a falling-off in business, and social pleasures will be of little benefit.

## REPAIRING

To dream of repairing something suggests a change that will be beneficial in your life.

## REPETITION

To dream of repeating something over and over augurs good fortune. To hear someone else repeating it means there may be a conflict in a personal relationship.

## REPLICA

Dreaming of a replica of anything implies an unexpected gift of jewelry or money.

## REPRIEVE

To be under sentence in a dream and receive a reprieve foretells that you will overcome a difficulty that is causing you anxiety.

## REPRIMAND

Dreaming of being reprimanded means the coming of a social or career-related honor. To be the one who is reprimanding, however, suggests a social or career-related embarrassment.

## REPRESENTATION

To dream that you are being represented means you will have help in a business project that will be beneficial to you. To dream that you are the one who is doing the representing indicates that you will have to rely on yourself in order to solve a problem.

## REPTILE*

If a reptile attacks you in a dream, there is trouble of a serious nature ahead for you. If you succeed in killing it, you will finally overcome obstacles.

To see a dead reptile come to life denotes that disputes and disagreements that you thought were settled will be renewed and pushed forward with bitter animosity.

To handle reptiles without harm to yourself suggests that you will be oppressed by the ill humor and bitterness of friends, but will succeed in restoring pleasant relations.

To see various kinds of reptiles augurs many conflicting troubles.

*See *Serpent, Snake.*

## REPUBLICAN

To dream of being a Republican when you are not means you will be seeking advice from someone you never thought you would.

## RESCUING

To dream of being rescued from any danger indicates that you will be threatened with misfortune and will escape with a slight loss. To rescue others foretells that you will be esteemed for your good deeds.

## RESERVOIR

If the water in the reservoir is full and clear in your dream, great prosperity is coming. If there is no water in it, this means difficulties—but not through your own actions. If the water in the reservoir is muddy or polluted, expect bad luck or heartache.

## RESIGNING

To dream that you resign from any position signifies that you will embark on new enterprises with unfortunate results. To hear of others resigning portends unpleasant tidings.

## RESISTANCE

Dreaming of resisting something foretells change. The change is for your benefit, so don't resist it.

## RESORT

To dream of a resort suggests a new romance, but it may not lead to anything permanent.

## RESTAURANT

To dream of an expensive restaurant or one that you've never visited or even seen points to a sudden expense. To dream of a restaurant that you patronize regularly suggests pleasant social activities in business. To dream of a "greasy spoon" predicts an increase in your income.

## RESTING

To dream of taking a rest means you will need to work extra-hard in your waking life.

## RESTROOM

In a dream, a restroom, whether dirty or clean, represents financial gain.

## RÉSUMÉ

To dream of your résumé means your career is safe. To dream of receiving a résumé from someone else suggests that you may have to worry about your job.

## RESURRECTION

If you dream that you are resurrected from the dead, you will have some great vexation but will eventually gain your desires.

To see others resurrected denotes unfortunate troubles that will be lightened by the thoughtfulness of friends.

## RESUSCITATION

To dream that you are being resuscitated indicates that you will have heavy losses, but will eventually regain more than you lose, and happiness will attend you.

If you resuscitate another, you will form new friendships that will give you prominence and pleasure.

## RETIREMENT

If you dream that you are retiring, you will soon have a career change.

## RETURNING

To return something in a dream warns you to watch your spending.

To dream that you are returning to a place you have been before is a warning not to travel in the near future.

## REUNION

If you dream of any kind of reunion, you will have help in furthering your career.

## REVELATION

To dream of a revelation, if it is of a pleasant nature, means that you may expect a bright outlook either in business or love; but if the revelation is gloomy, you will have many discouraging experiences to overcome.

## REVENGE

To dream of taking revenge is a sign of a weak and uncharitable nature, which, if not properly governed, will bring you troubles and loss of friends. If others avenge themselves on you, you will have much to fear from enemies.

## REVIVAL*

To dream that you attend a religious revival foretells family disturbances and unprofitable engagements.

If you take a part in the revival, you will incur the displeasure of friends by your contrary ways.

*See *Religion*.

## REVOLVER*

Any dream featuring a revolver suggests an injustice to you or someone else; you will have to fight hard to overcome it.

*See *Gun*.

## REVOLVING DOOR

To dream of a revolving door means situations in your life will go around and around until you change your approach. This dream indicates that you need to change your pattern.

## REWARD

To receive a reward in a dream portends unexpected good luck. To offer a reward means you need to stop being complacent.

## RHEUMATISM

To feel rheumatism attacking you in a dream foretells unexpected delay in the accomplishment of plans. To see others so afflicted brings disappointments.

## RHINESTONES

In dreams, rhinestones symbolize pleasures and favors of short duration.

## RHINOCEROS

To dream that you see a rhinoceros suggests that you will be threatened by a great loss and will have secret troubles. To kill a rhinoceros shows that you will bravely overcome obstacles.

## RHUBARB

To dream of rhubarb growing implies that pleasant entertainment will occupy your time for a while. To cook rhubarb foretells arguments in which you will lose a friend. To eat rhubarb denotes dissatisfaction with your current employment.

## RIB

To dream of seeing a person's ribs denotes poverty and misery.

## RIBBON

Seeing ribbons in your dreams suggests that you will have pleasant companions, and practical cares will not trouble you greatly.

## RICE

Rice is good to see in dreams, as it foretells success and warm friendships. Prosperity in all businesses is promised, and the farmer will be blessed with a bounteous harvest.

To eat rice signifies happiness and domestic comfort. To see it mixed with dirt or other impurities augurs sickness and separation from friends.

## RICHES*

To dream that you are possessed of riches indicates that you will rise to high places by your constant exertions and attention to your affairs.
*See Wealth.

## RIDDLES

To dream that you are trying to solve riddles means you will engage in something that will try your patience and involve a great deal of your money.

## RIDING

To dream of riding is unlucky. Sickness often follows this dream. If you ride slowly, you will have unsatisfactory results in your undertakings. Swift riding sometimes means prosperity under hazardous conditions.

## RIDING SCHOOL

To attend a riding school in your dream suggests that a friend will act falsely toward you, but you will throw off the vexing influence.

## RIGHT (DIRECTION)

To dream of the right side of anything, or of turning right, means you will soon be caught in a conflict between what you believe in and what your desires are. To dream of being right-handed when you are not suggests success in legal matters or a pleasant rise in social stature.

## RING

To dream of wearing rings signifies new enterprises in which you will be successful. To married people, a broken ring foretells quarrels and unhappiness; to lovers, separation. To see others with rings denotes increasing prosperity and many new friends.

## RINGWORM

If you dream of having ringworm appear on your skin, you will have a slight illness and some exasperating difficulty in the near future. If you see ringworm on other people, appeals for charity will beset you.

## RINK

To dream of an ice-skating rink denotes pleasant social events to come. A roller rink indicates an upcoming problem with a dishonest friend.

## RIOT

To dream of riots foretells disappointing affairs. If you see a friend killed in a riot, you will have bad luck in all endeavors; and the death, or serious illness, of someone will cause you distress.

## RIPENESS

To dream of ripe fruit or vegetables is a sign of prosperity. To dream that the produce is overripe, however, means financial trouble.

## RISING

To dream of rising to high positions indicates that study and advancement will bring you desired wealth.

If you find yourself rising high into the air, you will come into unexpected riches and pleasures, but you are warned to be careful of your engagements or you risk unpleasant prominence.

## RIVAL

To dream that you have a rival is a sign that you will be slow in asserting your rights and may lose favor with people of prominence.

If you find that a rival has outwitted you, it signifies that you will be negligent in your business and that your love of personal ease and comfort works to your detriment. If you imagine that you are the successful rival, this is good for your advancement, and you will find congeniality in your choice of a companion.

## RIVERS

If you see a clear, smooth, flowing river in your dream, you will soon enjoy delightful pleasures, and prosperity will be yours. If the waters are muddy or tumultuous, disagreeable and jealous contentions will feature in your life.

If you are waterbound by the overflowing of a river, temporary embarrassments may occur in your business, or you will suffer uneasiness lest some private escapade reach public notice and subject your reputation to harsh criticism.

If while sailing on a clear river you see corpses at the bottom, you will find that trouble and gloom follow swiftly upon present pleasures and fortune.

To see empty rivers denotes sickness and unusual ill luck.

## ROAD

Traveling over a rough, unknown road in a dream signifies new undertakings that will bring little but grief and loss of time.

If the road is bordered with trees and flowers, there will be some pleasant and unexpected fortune for you.

If friends accompany you, you will be successful in building an ideal home with happy children and a faithful spouse.

To lose the road foretells that you will make a mistake in deciding a question of business and will suffer loss, in consequence.

## ROADBLOCK

To encounter a roadblock in your dream is a sign that a problem you thought would be easily solved will be much harder. If you can get by the roadblock in your dream, then the problem will be easily fixed after all.

## ROAST

To see or eat a roast in a dream augurs domestic infelicity and secret treachery.

## ROBBER

To be a robber or encounter one in your dream means that you will fall romantically for someone who does not deserve your affection.

## ROBBERY

To dream that you lose your valuables in a robbery suggests unexpected gain. However, to dream that you lose money warns you to be careful how you handle your finances.

## ROBIN

To dream of this bird, the harbinger of spring, heralds great happiness.

## ROCKET*

To see a rocket ascending in your dream foretells sudden and unexpected elevation, successful wooing, and faithful keeping of the marriage vows. If you see rockets falling, unhappy unions may be expected.

*See Roman candle.

## ROCKING CHAIR

Rocking chairs seen in dreams bring friendly talk and contentment in any environment. To see a mother, wife, or sweetheart in a rocking chair betokens the sweetest joys that earth affords. To see vacant rocking chairs forebodes bereavement or estrangement; you will surely suffer misfortune in some form.

## ROCKING HORSE

To dream of riding a rocking horse foretells good luck in a personal matter.

## ROCKS*

To dream of rocks implies that you will meet reverses and suffer discord and general unhappiness. To climb a steep rock foretells struggle and disappointing surroundings.

*See Stones.

## ROGUE

To see or think yourself a rogue in a dream means that you are about to commit an indiscretion that will give your friends uneasiness of mind. You are likely to suffer from a passing malady.

## ROGUES' GALLERY

To dream that you are in a rogues' gallery foretells that you will be associated with people who fail to appreciate you. If you see your own picture, you will be overmatched by a tormenting enemy.

## ROLLER SKATES

To see young people on roller skates foretells that you will enjoy good health and feel enthusiastic over the pleasure you are able to contribute to others.

## ROLLING PIN

To dream that you use rolling pins as they are intended means happy family affairs. To use them otherwise is a warning against doing anything hasty in either personal or business matters.

## ROMAN CANDLE*

To see Roman candles while dreaming is a sign of speedy attainment of coveted pleasures and positions. To imagine that you have a loaded Roman candle and find it empty denotes that you will be disappointed with the possession of something you have long striven to obtain.

*See Rocket.

## ROMAN NUMERALS

In dreams, a Roman numeral represents financial gain.

## ROOF

To find yourself on a roof in a dream denotes unbounded success. To become frightened and think you are falling signifies that, while you may advance, you will have no firm hold on your position.

If you see a roof falling in, you will be threatened with a sudden calamity. If you repair or build a roof, you will rapidly increase your fortune.

To sleep on one proclaims your security against enemies and false companions. Your health will be robust.

## ROOK

To dream of rooks denotes that while your friends are true, they will not afford you the pleasure and contentment for which you long, as your thoughts and tastes will outstrip their humble ideas about how life should be lived.

A dead rook predicts sickness or death in your immediate future.

## ROOM

To dream that you enter a strange room cautions you to be true to your friendships. To dream that you find yourself in a strange room means success if it is furnished, but trouble if it's empty.

## ROOM SERVICE

To dream of room service predicts a comfortable time in your life.

## ROOSTER*

To dream of a rooster foretells that you will be very successful and rise to prominence, but you will allow yourself to become conceited over your rise. To see roosters fighting indicates altercations and rivals.

*See Chicken.

## ROOT CANAL

If you dream of this dental procedure, expect health concerns to arise soon.

## ROOTS

To dream of seeing the roots of plants or trees denotes misfortune, as both business and health will go into decline.

To use them as medicine warns you of approaching illness or sorrow.

## ROPES

Ropes in dreams signify perplexities and complications and uncertainty in romance.

If you climb a rope, you will overcome enemies who are working to injure you. To descend a rope brings disappointment to your most cheerful moments.

If you are tied with rope, you are likely to yield to love, against your better judgment.

To break rope signifies your ability to overcome enmity and competition. To tie ropes suggests that you will have power to control others as you may wish. To walk a rope shows that you will engage in some hazardous speculation, but will surprisingly succeed. If you see others walking a rope, you will benefit by the successful ventures of others.

To jump rope foretells that you will startle your associates with a thrilling escapade bordering upon the sensational. To jump rope with children shows that you are selfish and overbearing. To catch a rope with your foot denotes that you will be benevolent and tender in your ministrations.

To dream that you let a rope down from an upper window of a hotel to let in people below, thinking the proprietors would be adverse to receiving them, signifies that you will engage in an affair that will not look proper to your friends, but will afford you pleasure and interest.

## ROSARY

To say or hear this Catholic prayer predicts blessings and contentment.

## ROSE

To dream of seeing roses blooming and fragrant suggests that a joyful occasion is nearing, and you will possess the faithful love of your sweetheart.

Withered roses signify the absence of loved ones. White roses, if seen without sunshine or dew, denote serious if not fatal illness.

To inhale the fragrance of roses brings unalloyed pleasure.

## ROSEBUSH

To see a rosebush in foliage but without blossoms indicates that prosperity surrounds you. A dead rosebush foretells misfortune and sickness for you or relatives.

## ROSEMARY

Rosemary, if seen in dreams, denotes that sadness and indifference will cause unhappiness in homes where there is every appearance of prosperity.

## ROSETTE

To wear rosettes in dreams or see them on others is significant of a frivolous waste of time; though you will experience the thrills of pleasure, it will bring disappointments.

## ROTTING

To dream of seeing or smelling anything rotting is a sign of trouble. You might also hear of a death.

## ROUGE (BLUSH)

To dream of using rouge implies that you will practice deceit to obtain your wishes.

To see others with rouge on their faces warns that you are being artfully used to further the designs of some deceitful people. If you see it on your hands or clothing, you will be found out in a scheme. If it comes off your face, you will be humiliated before a rival and lose your lover by your deceit.

## ROULETTE

To play or watch this game of chance warns that you will soon experience a financial loss if you are not careful.

## ROUNDABOUT

To dream of seeing a traffic circle implies that you will struggle unsuccessfully to advance in fortune or love.

## ROWBOAT

To dream that you are in a rowboat with others reveals that you derive much pleasure from the companionship of happy, worldly people. If the boat capsizes, you will suffer financial losses by engaging in seductive enterprises.

If you find yourself defeated in a rowing race, you will lose favor with your sweetheart to your rivals. If you are the victor, though, you will easily obtain your romance. Your affairs will move agreeably.

## ROWING

To dream of rowing foretells steady progress in your field of choice.

## RSVP

If you dream of receiving or giving an RSVP, a spell of disappointment and disillusionment lies ahead in your romance.

## RUBBER

To dream of being clothed in rubber garments is a sign that you will have honors conferred upon you because of your steady and unchanging purity and morality. If the garments are ragged or torn, be cautious in your conduct; scandal is about to attack your reputation. If you find that your limbs stretch like rubber, it is a sign that illness is threatening you, and you are likely to use deceit in your wooing and business.

To dream of rubber goods denotes that your affairs will be conducted on a secret basis, and your friends will fail to understand your conduct in many instances.

## RUBBING

To dream of rubbing something suggests gain in your life, either materially or in a business matter.

## RUBBISH

To dream of rubbish suggests that you will manage your affairs badly.

## RUBY

To dream of a ruby means that you will be lucky in business or love. For a woman to lose one augurs the approaching indifference of her lover.

## RUDDER

If you dream of a rudder, you will soon make a pleasant journey to foreign lands, and new friendships will be formed. A broken rudder augurs disappointment and sickness.

## RUDENESS

If you are being rude to someone in your dream, it means that those around you think highly of you. If someone is rude to you, someone close to you will soon have a problem with you.

## RUG

A new, clean rug in a dream means good luck. An old, worn-out rug signifies financial trouble on the horizon.

## RUINS

To dream of ruins indicates broken engagements in romance, distressing conditions in business, destruction to crops, and failing health. To dream of ancient ruins foretells that you will travel extensively, but there will be a note of sadness mixed with the pleasure and the realization of a long-cherished hope. You will feel the absence of a friend.

## RULER

To measure anything in your dream with a ruler means that you will achieve your goal with careful planning and action.

## RUM

To dream of drinking rum foretells that you will have wealth but will lack moral refinement.

## RUNNING

To dream of running in the company of others is a sign that you will participate in some festivity and will find that your affairs are growing toward fortune. If you stumble or fall, you will lose property and reputation.

Running alone indicates that you will outstrip your friends in the race for wealth, and you will occupy a higher place socially. If you run from danger, you will be threatened with losses and will despair of adjusting matters.

If you dream of others running, you will be oppressed by the threatened downfall of friends.

## RUNWAY

Dreaming of walking down a runway portends social recognition of a positive nature. To watch others walk down a runway in your dream means upcoming travel.

## RUPTURE

To dream that you are ruptured indicates that you will have physical disorders or disagreeable problems. If you see others ruptured, you will be in danger of irreconcilable quarrels.

## RUSHING

If you dream you are rushing, pleasant and leisurely times lie ahead.

## RUST

To dream of rust on articles such as old pieces of metal signifies the decline of your surroundings. Sickness, loss of fortune, and false friends are filling your sphere.

## RUT

To dream that you are physically stuck in a rut means that you will soon be moving forward with a current problem that has vexed you, thanks to help from an unexpected source.

## RV (RECREATIONAL VEHICLE)

Dreaming of towing or driving a recreational vehicle suggests that you will be traveling soon for pleasure. If you dream that you are living in one, expect great financial gain in the future.

## RYE

To see rye is a good sign. Prosperity will envelop your future in brightness.

To see coffee made of rye means that your pleasure will be tempered with sound judgment and affairs will proceed without friction.

To see livestock entering rye fields forecasts prosperity.

## RYE BREAD

To see or eat rye bread in your dream suggests a cheerful and well-appointed home.

## SABBATH

If you dream of this holy day and you are not Jewish, blessings and good fortune are coming your way.

## SABOTAGE

To dream of any type of sabotage predicts arguments and disagreements with family or business associates that could be serious. Please watch your aggression.

## SACK

To dream of a full sack means good luck. An empty sack in your dream warns of obstacles you must overcome.*

## SACRIFICE

To dream of making a sacrifice heralds blessings and well-being. To dream of witnessing a sacrifice means spiritual inspiration will be coming your way.

## SADDLE

To dream of saddles foretells news of a pleasant nature; also unannounced visitors. You are also, probably, to take a trip that will prove advantageous.

## SADNESS

To dream of being sad means you will soon find that your troubles are over.

## SAFARI

To dream of a safari suggests financial gain in your future.

## SAFE*

To dream of seeing a safe denotes security from discouraging affairs of business and love. If you try to unlock a safe in your dream, you worry over the failure of your plans to reach maturity. To find a safe empty denotes trouble.

*See *Cupboard*.

## SAFE-DEPOSIT BOX

To dream of a safe-deposit box means you will soon be receiving a gift. Taking something out of a safe-deposit box portends an unexpected invitation.

## SAFETY PIN

To dream of a safety pin assures success in everything in the weeks to come.

## SAFFRON

Saffron seen in a dream warns you that you are entertaining false hopes; bitter enemies are interfering secretly with your plans for the future.

To drink a tea made from saffron foretells that you will have quarrels and alienation in your family.

## SAGE

To dream of sage suggests that thrift and economy will be practiced by your staff or family.

## SAILING*

To dream of sailing on calm waters foretells easy access to blissful joys and immunity from poverty and whatever brings misery. Sailing on a small vessel reveals that your desires will not exceed your power to possess them.

*See *Ocean, Sea.*

## SAILOR

To dream of sailors portends long and exciting journeys.

## SAINT

To dream of a saint suggests unusual blessings and difficulties being overcome.

## SAKE

To dream of this Japanese rice wine augurs good luck.

## SALAD

To dream of eating or making a salad suggests the approach of good luck in money matters and an increase in social status.

## SALARY

If you dream you are not being given a salary increase, you are likely to see financial gain through an unexpected source. If you request a raise and it is granted in your dream, this portends a monetary loss. Paying a salary to someone foretells unexpected good luck with money.

### SALE

To dream of a sale suggests an increase in material possessions through a valuable gift or legacy. If you sell something at a sale, expect an increase in your overall wealth.

### SALMON

Dreaming of salmon indicates that good luck and pleasant duties will employ your time.

### SALMONELLA

To dream of this food poisoning portends good health.

### SALON

To dream of being in a salon is a warning of disloyal and dishonest friends.

### SALT

Salt is an omen of discordant surroundings when seen in dreams. You will usually find after dreaming of salt that everything goes awry, and quarrels and dissatisfaction show themselves in the family circle.

To salt meat portends that debts and mortgages will harass you.

### SALTPETER

To dream of saltpeter indicates that changes in your lifestyle will lead to some unconquerable grief.

### SALUTE

To salute or be saluted in your dream suggests that social recognition and respect among your colleagues are on the way.

### SALVATION ARMY

To dream of this charitable organization foretells contentment in your personal life.

### SALVE

To dream of a salve implies that you will prosper under adverse circumstances and convert enemies into friends.

### SAMPLES

To dream of receiving merchandise samples signifies improvement in your business.

### SAND

To dream of sand is indicative of losses.

## SANDAL

To dream of a sandal or a pair of comfortable sandals suggests a new romance. If the sandals hurt your feet or are on someone else in the dream, you need to take care of monetary concerns.

## SANDBOX

To dream of a playing in sandbox foretells a happy time.

## SANDPAPER

To dream of sandpaper means irritation involving relatives and close friends.

## SANDWICH

To dream of a sandwich implies an improvement in your personal and business life.

## SANGRIA

If you dream of this alcoholic concoction, a festive and joyous time is awaiting you.

## SANITARY NAPKIN

If you dream of this personal hygiene product and it is clean and new, expect the announcement of a pregnancy or birth. If the pad is not clean, it indicates possible illness or death.

## SANSKRIT

To dream of Sanskrit means that you will separate yourself from friends in order to investigate occult subjects.

## SAPPHIRE

To dream of sapphires betokens fortune and gain.

## SARDINES

To eat sardines in a dream foretells that distressing events will come your way unexpectedly.

## SARI

If you dream of a sari and you are not from a culture that dresses in them, your beauty will be noticed and commented on.

## SARONG

To dream of this article of clothing suggests that you are noted for your beauty and grace.

## SASH

To dream of wearing a sash foretells that you will seek to retain the affections of a flirtatious person.

## SATAN*

To dream of Satan predicts dangerous adventures; you will be forced to use strategy to keep up honorable appearances.

To dream that you kill him suggests that you desert wicked or immoral companions to live upon a higher plane. If he comes to you under the guise of literature, you are warned against promiscuous friendships, and especially flatterers. If he comes in the shape of wealth or power, you will fail to use your influence for harmony or for the elevation of others. If he takes the form of music, you are likely to succumb to his wiles.

To feel that you are trying to shield yourself from Satan implies that you will endeavor to throw off the bondage of selfish pleasure and will seek to give others their just deserts.

*See *Devil, Dragon.*

## SATELLITE

To dream of satellites orbiting the earth augurs good news arriving via mail, phone, or Internet.

## SATELLITE DISH

To dream of a satellite dish means you will soon be corresponding with an old friend whom you haven't heard from in a while.

## SAUERKRAUT

In dreams, this dish symbolizes good health and happy social occasions.

## SAUNA

If you dream you are in a sauna and find it a pleasant experience, spiritual enlightenment will be coming your way. To find the experience unpleasant and stifling is a warning that you need to explore your spirituality.

## SAUSAGE

To dream of making sausage denotes that you will be successful in many undertakings. To eat it suggests that you will have a humble but pleasant home.

## SAVIOR

To dream of being a savior means you will soon be asked to help someone solve a problem. To dream of the Christian Savior foretells blessings and good fortune.

## SAW

To dream of using a handsaw indicates an energetic and busy time and a cheerful home life.

To see big saws in machinery predicts that you will oversee a major enterprise that will yield a fair return. For a woman, this dream suggests that she will be esteemed and her counsel will be heeded.

To dream of rusty or broken saws denotes failure and accidents. If you lose a saw, you will engage in affairs that culminate in disaster. To hear the buzz of a saw indicates thrift and prosperity. To find a rusty saw indicates that you will probably restore your fortune. To carry a saw on your back suggests that you will carry large, but profitable, responsibilities.

## SAWDUST

To dream of sawdust signifies that grievous mistakes will cause distress and quarreling in your home.

## SAXOPHONE

To dream of hearing this musical instrument forecasts a happy and pleasurable time ahead. If you dream of playing the saxophone and you don't know how to in waking life, expect a rise in your social or business status.

## SCAB

To dream of a scab suggests an increase in material wealth.

## SCABBARD

To dream of a scabbard suggests that a misunderstanding will be amicably settled. If you wonder where your scabbard can be, you will face overwhelming difficulties.

## SCAFFOLD

To dream of a scaffold suggests keen disappointment in failing to secure the object of your affection.

If you ascend a scaffold, you will be misunderstood and censured by your friends for an action that you never committed. To descend one predicts that you will be guilty of wrongdoing and will suffer the penalty.

If you fall from one, you will be unexpectedly surprised while engaged in deceiving others and causing injury to them.

## SCALDING

To dream of being scalded indicates that distressing incidents will blot out pleasurable hopes.

## SCALES

To dream of weighing on scales implies that justice will temper your conduct, and you will see your prosperity increasing.

## SCALLOPS

To dream of this seafood in a raw form suggests an upcoming trip for pleasure. Eating or cooking scallops in your dream predicts an improvement in your living conditions.

## SCANDAL

To dream that you are an object of scandal implies that you are not careful to select good and true companions, but rather enjoy having reckless men and women contribute to your pleasure. Trade and business of any kind will decrease after this dream.

## SCANNER

To dream of a scanner suggests that you will have to redo a project you thought was finished.

## SCAR

If you dream of scars on someone else, you will endure a short period in which things in life fluctuate before they settle down. To dream of scars on yourself warns you to stop doing things that make you ashamed.

## SCARCITY

To dream of scarcity foretells sorrow in the household and failure.

## SCARECROW

To dream of a scarecrow means that what used to frighten you no longer will. You now have enough courage to face it.

## SCARF

To dream of a scarf suggests a happy love affair.

## SCARLET FEVER

To dream of scarlet fever suggests that you are in danger of sickness or you are in the power of an enemy. To dream that a relative dies suddenly of scarlet fever foretells that you will be overcome by villainous treachery.

## SCEPTER

To imagine in your dreams that you wield a scepter suggests that you will be chosen by friends for positions of trust; you will not disappoint their estimate of your ability.

To dream that others wield the scepter over you indicates that you will seek employment under the supervision of others rather than by exerting your energy and acting for yourself.

## SCHEDULE

To dream of making a schedule means you need to beware of wasting your time. To dream of following a schedule augurs a business trip that will prove beneficial to your career.

## SCHIZOPHRENIA

To dream that you are schizophrenic indicates a period of mental well-being in your life. To dream that someone else is schizophrenic means you might suffer from depression.

## SCHOLARSHIP

To dream of receiving a scholarship predicts financial gain. To dream of giving one means you will soon offer help to a friend.

## SCHOOL

To dream of attending school indicates distinction in literary work. If you are young and at school in the dream, you will find that sorrow and reverses will make you sincerely long for the simple trust and pleasures of days of yore.

To dream of teaching school foretells that you will strive for literary attainments, but the bare necessities of life must first be met. To visit the schoolhouse of your childhood days suggests that discontent and discouraging incidents overshadow the present.

## SCHOOLTEACHER

To dream of a schoolteacher implies that you are likely to enjoy learning and amusements in a quiet way. If you are a teacher, you are likely to be successful with literary and other works.

## SCIENTIST

To dream of a scientist suggests improvement in your social or business status.

## SCISSORS

To dream of scissors is an unlucky omen; wives will be jealous and mistrustful of their husbands, and sweethearts will quarrel and nag each other mercilessly and with recrimination. Dullness will overcast business horizons.

To dream that you have your scissors sharpened suggests that you will have hateful work to do. If you break the scissors, expect quarrels and separations. If you lose them, you will seek to escape from unpleasant tasks.

## SCOLDING

If you dream of being scolded, it's a warning that you are being overconfident. To scold someone in a dream predicts a family argument.

## SCOOTER

To ride a scooter in your dream or see someone else riding one suggests that joy and happiness are on the horizon.

## SCORE

To dream of a score warns you against jealousy around you.

## SCORPION

To dream of a scorpion reveals that false friends will take advantage of opportunities to undermine your prosperity. If you fail to kill the scorpion, you will suffer loss from an enemy attack.

## SCRABBLE™

To dream of playing SCRABBLE is a dream of good luck. But if you are having trouble making a word while you play, you need to watch your negative thoughts.

## SCRAPBOOK

To dream of a scrapbook suggests that you will soon have disagreeable acquaintances.

## SCRAPING

To dream of scraping any hard surface foretells the end of a friendship and that this loss will prove beneficial to you.

## SCRATCHING

To scratch others in your dream indicates that you will be ill-tempered and fault-finding in your dealings with others.

If you are scratched, you will be injured by the enmity of someone deceitful.

To dream that you scratch your head suggests that strangers will annoy you by their flattering attentions, which you will feel are designed to win favors from you.

## SCREAMING

To dream of other people screaming suggests distressing news. To dream you are screaming is a good omen for all that concerns you.

## SCREECH OWL

To dream that you hear the shrill, startling notes of the screech owl indicates that you will be shocked at news of the illness or death of a dear friend.

## SCREEN

To dream of a screen implies that you will soon be trying to cover up or hide a mistake that you have made.

## SCREW

To dream of seeing screws denotes tedious tasks to perform and peevishness in companions. It also warns you to be economical and painstaking.

## SCREWDRIVER

To dream of screwdrivers means your goal will be accomplished—but only through diligence and hard work on your part.

## SCRIBBLING

To find yourself scribbling in a dream implies frustration with a love affair or serious relationship. To dream of someone else scribbling speaks of peace of mind.

## SCRIPTURE

In dreams, holy writing represents blessings, good fortune, and spiritual advancement.

## SCRUBBING

To find yourself scrubbing something in a dream is a sign of happier times ahead. But if the scrubbing produces no good result, this means your troubled times will continue for a while.

## SCULPTOR

To dream of a sculptor foretells that you will change from your present position to one less lucrative but more distinguished.

## SCUM

To dream of scum (as is seen on stagnant water) suggests disappointment over a lack of social success.

## SCYTHE

To dream of a scythe reveals that accidents or sickness will prevent you from attending to your affairs or making journeys. An old or broken scythe implies separation from friends, or failure in some business enterprise.

## SEA*

To dream of hearing the lonely sighing of the sea suggests that you are entering a sad time. Dreams of the sea prognosticate unfulfilled longings; although you may enjoy physical pleasure, inwardly you crave something that the flesh cannot fulfill.

*See *Ocean, Wave.*

## SEAGULL

To dream of a seagull flying overhead means having freedom from financial problems. To dream of a seagull sitting on the beach implies a financial problem that you will need help to solve. To see these birds anywhere other than on the shore is a warning of financial loss.

## SEAHORSE

To dream of this sea creature predicts a pleasant trip for you.

## SEAL (ANIMAL)

To dream that you see seals denotes that you are striving for a place above your power and ability. Dreams of seals usually reveal that you have high aspirations; discontent may goad you into struggles to advance your position.

## SEAM

To dream of the seams on anything warns you to watch your spending.

## SEAMSTRESS

To see a seamstress in a dream portends that unexpected bad luck will keep you from pleasant visits.

### SÉANCE

To attend or host a séance in your dream means you will need to ask for help with an upcoming problem in your personal or business affairs.

### SEAPORT

To dream of visiting a seaport indicates that you will have opportunities to travel and acquire knowledge, but there will be some who will object to your planned tours.

### SEARCHING

To search for something but not know what you are searching for implies that you could be wasting your time in a meaningless activity or relationship. If you know what you are searching for but you are not able to find it, a relationship that seems good at the moment will soon end. To find what you are searching for predicts a happy and pleasant new relationship.

### SEARCHLIGHT

To dream that you see, or are in the beam of, a searchlight is a sign that your hard work will soon pay off. To see searchlights in the sky portends world problems such as war and conflict.

### SEASHELLS

To see seashells on the shore but not pick them up in your dream suggests that you will find it hard to decide among your many choices. To gather seashells means you have made good choices in life and will soon gather your rewards.

### SEASICKNESS

To dream that you are seasick predicts a time of illness that will pass quickly. To dream that someone else is seasick means you are in good health.

### SEAT

To think, in a dream, that someone has taken your seat implies that you will be bothered by people calling on you for aid.

To dream that someone is offering you a seat suggests that you need to be open to receiving advice.

### SEAT BELT

To wear or fasten a seat belt in your dream means you feel confined to a relationship or job that may need to change. To dream of fastening or removing someone else's seat belt suggests that you have made a good decision in your relationships and should stay where you are.

## SEAWEED

If you dream of seaweed, you will soon be asked to do something that goes against your principles.

## SECOND HAND (CLOCK)

To watch the second hand on a clock implies that a problem you have been mulling over will not be solved solely by you. You should seek another opinion.

## SECRET

To dream you are keeping secrets indicates that you have not fully tapped into your hidden power.

## SECRETARY

To dream that you are a secretary implies that you are stuck in a poor career choice and should consider a change. To hire a secretary in a dream means social and professional recognition.

## SECRET ORDER

There is a vision of selfish and designing friendships for one who joins a secret order in dreams.

## SEDUCTION

To dream of being seduced, sexually or otherwise, indicates that you feel you have no power to choose in a certain area in your life.

## SEED

To dream of seeds foretells increasing prosperity, though present indications appear unfavorable.

## SEESAW

To dream of this playground toy suggests that a new love affair will be short-lived.

## SELF-DEFENSE

To find yourself practicing self-defense in a dream portends well-being and happiness.

## SELF-SERVICE

To dream of anything that is self-service indicates that you have loyal and trusted friends.

## SELLING

To dream of selling property or possessions is a portent of unexpected financial gain. To dream that you have to sell yourself suggests a coming health issue that you should not ignore.

To dream that you have sold anything denotes that unfavorable business will worry you.

## SEMEN

To dream of this male bodily fluid foretells a pregnancy or birth.

## SENATOR

If you dream of a senator and you are male, you will be asked to do a favor for a friend. If you are a woman, this dream indicates an improvement in your social status.

## SENTRY

To dream of a sentry indicates that you will have kind protectors and that your life will go on smoothly.

## SEPARATION

To dream of a separation of any kind means you will soon reach a better understanding in your love life.

## SEPTIC TANK

To dream of a septic tank foretells good fortune and financial gain.

## SEQUINS

To dream of sequins foretells a pleasant surprise in a social affair.

## SERENADE

If you hear a serenade in your dream, you will receive pleasant news from absent friends, and your hopes will not fail you. If you are one of the serenaders, many delightful things lie in your future.

## SERMON

To dream of hearing a sermon suggests a delay in future plans. If you dream of delivering a sermon, doubts about a friend are groundless.

## SERPENT*

To dream of serpents is indicative of an upcoming disappointment.

*See *Reptile, Snake.*

## SERVANT

To dream of a servant is a sign that you will have good fortune, despite gloomy appearances. Anger is likely to push you into unnecessary worry and quarrels.

To discharge a servant foretells regret and loss. To quarrel with one in your dream indicates that you will, upon waking, have real cause for censuring someone derelict in duty. To be robbed by one shows that you have someone near you who does not respect the laws of ownership.

## SEWAGE

To dream of sewage suggests very good luck and good fortune.

## SEWING

To dream of sewing new garments foretells that domestic peace will crown your wishes.

## SEX*

To dream of changing your sex implies honor and success in family matters. To dream of sexually teasing someone, or of being teased, means that a goal you are working toward will prove unworthy.

*See *Intercourse*.

## SHABBINESS

If you dream of something shabby, things will go very well in your financial life.

## SHACKLE

To dream of shackles suggests freedom and peace of mind in your personal and business life.

## SHADOW

To dream of shadows means not everything you are seeing is real.

## SHAKER (RELIGIOUS SECT)

To dream of seeing members of the sect called Shakers in a dream denotes a change in your business.

If you imagine you belong to the Shakers, you will unexpectedly renounce all former ties and seek new pleasures in distant locales.

## SHAKING, SHAKING HANDS

To dream of shaking indicates health issues you need to address in the near future.

To shake someone's hand in a dream speaks of renewed or reconciled friendships and also suggests that a new business venture is on the horizon.

## SHAME

To feel shamed in a dream implies positive social recognition and career advancement. But if you shame someone else in a dream, you will suffer embarrassment for saying the wrong thing.

## SHAMPOO

To dream of shampoo indicates that you will engage in undignified affairs to please others.

If you have your own head shampooed, you will soon make a secret trip that will bring much enjoyment.

## SHAMROCK

To dream of a shamrock means good luck, of course. Good luck and fortune are on the horizon.

## SHANTY

To dream of a shanty indicates that you will leave home in the quest of health. This also warns of decreasing prosperity.

## SHARK

To dream of sharks suggests formidable enemies. To see a shark pursuing and attacking you denotes that unavoidable reverses will sink you into despondency and foreboding. If you see sharks sporting in clear water, jealousy is secretly but surely bringing you disquiet and misfortune while you bask in the sunshine. Dreaming of a dead shark implies reconciliation and renewed prosperity.

## SHARPSHOOTER

To dream of being a sharpshooter cautions you to be very diligent in an upcoming project if you hope to gain anything financially from it. To dream of being shot at by a sharpshooter signifies a rise in social status.

## SHAVING

To merely contemplate getting a shave in a dream suggests that you will plan for the successful development of enterprises, but will fail to generate energy sufficient to succeed.

To dream of shaving yourself foretells that you will govern your own business and dictate to your household. If your face appears smooth, you will enjoy quiet, and your conduct will not be questioned by your companions. If your face is old and rough, there will be many squalls.

If your razor is dull and pulls your face, you will give your friends cause to criticize your private life.

If your beard is gray, you will be absolutely devoid of any sense of justice for those having claims against you.

To dream of shaving your head or any part of your body until it is bare indicates your desire to reveal your true self to others.

## SHAWL

To dream of a shawl indicates that someone will flatter and favor you. To lose your shawl foretells sorrow and discomfort.

## SHEARS

To see shears in your dream denotes that you will become miserly and disagreeable in your dealings. If you see them broken, you will lose friends.

## SHEAVES

To dream of sheaves heralds joyful occasions. Prosperity holds before you a panorama of delightful events, fields of enterprise, and fortunate gain.

## SHEEP*

To dream of shearing sheep predicts that a season of profitable enterprises will shower down upon you.

If you dream of flocks of sheep, there will be much rejoicing as you prosper.

To see them looking scraggy and sick means that you will be thrown into despair by the miscarriage of some plan that promised rich returns.

*See Lamb, Ram.

## SHEERNESS

To dream of something that is sheer is a dream of good luck.

## SHEET

To dream of sheets that are clean and neatly folded augurs financial gain. If the sheets are soiled or messy, this instead suggests a financial loss.

## SHEET METAL

To see sheet metal in your dream denotes that you are listening to the admonitions of others, with unfortunate results. To walk on sheet metal signifies distasteful engagements.

## SHELF*

To dream of a shelf, or something on a shelf, implies an unexpected delay in your plans.

To see empty shelves in dreams indicates losses and consequent gloom. Full shelves augur happiness and contentment through the fulfillment of hope and effort.

*See *Store*.

## SHELLS*

To walk among and gather shells in your dream denotes extravagance or the desire to be protected or sheltered from something in your waking life.

*See *Mussels, Oyster*.

## SHELTER

To dream that you are building a shelter signifies that you will escape the designs of enemies. If you are seeking shelter, you will be guilty of cheating and will try to justify yourself.

## SHEPHERD

To dream of shepherds watching their flocks portends bounteous crops and pleasant relations for the farmer, and also much enjoyment and profit for others.

To see shepherds idle foretells sickness and bereavement.

## SHERIFF*

To dream of seeing a sheriff indicates that you will suffer great uneasiness over the uncertainties that loom before you.

To imagine that you are elected sheriff or feel interested in the office implies that you will participate in an affair that will afford you neither profit nor honor.

If you escape arrest by the sheriff, you will be able to further engage in illicit affairs.

*See *Police*.

## SHERRY

To dream of drinking sherry means you will soon enjoy good health, prosperity, and wealth.

## SHIN

To dream of banging, bruising, or injuring your shin foretells financial difficulties in the near future.

## SHINGLE (ROOFING MATERIAL)

To dream of a shingle suggests success through hard work and strong effort.

## SHIP*

To dream of ships foretells honor and unexpected elevation to ranks above your mode of life.

To hear of a shipwreck portends a disastrous turn of affairs. To lose your life in one suggests that you will have an exceedingly close call on either your life or honor.

If you see a ship on her way through a tempestuous storm, you will be unfortunate in business transactions and will be challenged to find a way to cover up something from the public, as your partner in the affair will threaten you with betrayal.

If you see others shipwrecked, you will seek in vain to rescue a friend from disgrace and insolvency.

*See *Boat, Deck.*

## SHIRT

To dream of putting on your shirt foreshadows preparing yourself for some new venture.

To lose your shirt augurs disgrace in business or love. A torn shirt represents misfortune and miserable surroundings. A soiled shirt denotes that contagious diseases will become an issue for you.

## SHOCK

To dream of being shocked or in shock implies the overcoming of present difficulties in your life.

## SHOEMAKER

To see a shoemaker in your dream warns that indications are unfavorable for your advancement.

## SHOES

To dream of seeing your shoes ragged and soiled suggests that you will make enemies by your insensitive criticism.

To have them polished in your dream foretells improvement in your affairs, and an important event will give you satisfaction. New shoes augur changes that will prove beneficial. If they pinch your feet, you will be uncomfortably exposed to the practical joking of the fun-loving companions of your sex.

To find them untied suggests losses, quarrels, and ill health. To lose them is a sign of desertion and divorce.

To dream that your shoes have been stolen during the night, but you have two pairs of stockings or socks, implies that you will have a loss in one area but will gain in another.

### SHOOTING*

To dream that you see or hear shooting signifies unhappiness between married couples and sweethearts because of selfishness; it also bodes dissatisfaction in business and other projects due to negligence.

To dream that you are shot and are feeling the sensations of dying denotes that you may meet unexpected abuse from the ill feelings of friends; if you escape death by waking up, you will be fully reconciled with them later on.

*See *Pistol.*

### SHOOTING STAR

To dream of a shooting star portends an unexpected gift or a wish coming true.

### SHOP*

To dream of a shop forecasts that you will be opposed by scheming and jealous friends in every attempt you make for advancement.

*See *Store.*

### SHOPLIFTER

To dream you are a shoplifter implies the coming of a gift. To see a shoplifter in your dream indicates an upcoming loss from theft.

### SHORT CIRCUIT

To dream of something short-circuiting implies that something you are about to purchase will last well.

### SHOTGUN

To dream of a shotgun foretells domestic trouble and worry.

### SHOULDER

To see your own shoulders signifies your ability to take care of your responsibilities. To dream of seeing naked shoulders foretells happy changes that will make you look at the world in a different light than formerly.

## SHOUTING

If you are shouting in a dream, or if you hear shouting, you will soon need to speak up in a business dealing.

## SHOVEL

To see a shovel in a dream signifies laborious but pleasant tasks. A broken or old one implies frustrated hopes.

## SHOWER*

To dream of taking a shower means the cleansing of your personal life and spiritual renewal.

*See Rain.

## SHREW

If you dream of a shrew, you will have a big job keeping a friend in a cheerful frame of mind, and you may be unfit yourself for the experiences of everyday existence.

## SHRINE

To dream of any kind of shrine denotes many blessings coming your way.

## SHRIVELING

To see something shriveled means bad news is on the horizon.

## SHROUD

To dream of a shroud augurs sickness and its attendant distress and anxiety, coupled with the machinations of false friends. Business will threaten a decline after this dream.

To see shrouded corpses denotes a multitude of misfortunes. To see a shroud removed from a corpse suggests that quarrels will result in alienation.

## SHRUBS

To dream of shrubs foretells peace of mind and prosperity if the shrubs are healthy. If they are dying or sickly in your dream, this suggests difficulties in business relations.

## SHUFFLING

To dream that you are shuffling your feet, or someone else is, predicts possible crises in a love affair or marriage.

## SHUFFLEBOARD

To dream of playing this game or watching it played predicts indecision in many aspects of your life; they will need to be addressed.

## SHUTTLE

To dream that you are on a shuttle implies short trips for pleasure.

## SHY

To be shy in a dream portends success in your current affairs. To dream of others being shy suggests a setback in a personal or business matter.

## SIBLING

To dream of a sibling implies good family harmony. But if you dream that you have siblings and you don't in your waking life, this means the coming of new friendships.

## SICKNESS

To dream of sickness is a sign of trouble and real sickness in your family. Discord is sure to find entrance also.

To dream of your own sickness is a warning to be unusually cautious of your person.

To see any of your family pale and sick foretells that some event will break unexpectedly upon your harmonious hearthstone.

## SIDE

To dream of seeing only the side of an object suggests that some person is going to treat your honest proposals with indifference.

If you dream that your side pains you, vexations in your affairs will test your patience.

## SIDEWALK

To dream of a clean, well-kept sidewalk foretells travel. If you dream that the sidewalk is broken, cluttered, or hard to pass along, you need to examine your motor vehicle for repair.

## SIEVE

To dream of a sieve suggests that you will soon make an annoying transaction, probably to your loss. If the mesh of the sieve is too small, you will have the chance to reverse a decision unfavorable to yourself. If too large, you will eventually lose what you have recently acquired.

## SIGHING

To dream that you are sighing over any trouble or sad event denotes that you will have unexpected sadness, as well as some redeeming brightness in your season of trouble.

To hear the sighing of others foretells that the misconduct of dear friends will oppress you with the weight of gloom.

## SIGN

To dream of a sign, specifically a road sign, augurs an opportunity to make an important change.

## SIGNAL

To dream of a signal means you are finally getting your long-desired wishes, and your ambitions are coming to fruition.

## SIGNATURE

To dream of placing your signature on something suggests a small financial gain. To dream of seeing others' signatures means your friends and associates will prove loyal.

## SIGN LANGUAGE

If you don't know sign language in your waking life, but you are doing it or understanding it in your dream, this is a sign of spiritual enlightenment and mental clarity.

## SILENCE

To dream of silence and find it frustrating warns that you may need to watch what you say to those around you; you might misspeak and be taken the wrong way. To dream of enjoyable silence implies that your words will be cherished and honored.

## SILHOUETTE

To dream of a silhouette bodes contentment and happiness in your life.

## SILK CLOTHING

To dream of wearing silk clothes is a sign of high ambitions being gratified; friendly relations will be established between those who were estranged.

## SILKWORM

If you dream of silkworms, you will engage in very profitable work, which will also place you in a prominent position. To see them dead or cutting through their cocoons signifies reverses and trying times.

## SILO

To dream of a silo means abundance and easy living.

## SILVER

To dream of silver is a warning against depending too much on money for real happiness and contentment.

To find silver money is indicative of shortcomings in others. You draw hasty conclusions too frequently for your own peace of mind.

To dream of silverware denotes worry and unsatisfied desires.

## SIM CARD

To dream of a Subscriber Identity Module card, which activates your cell phone, indicates that you will soon connect with someone from your past whom you have pleasant memories about.

## SIMMERING

To dream you are watching something simmer means you need to say what is on your mind right now to guard against losing your temper—you are close to the boiling point.

## SINGING*

To hear singing in your dreams betokens a cheerful spirit and happy companions. You are soon to hear promising news from the absent. If you are singing while everything around you gives promise of happiness, jealousy will insinuate a sense of insincerity into your joy. If there are notes of sadness in the song, you will be unpleasantly surprised by the turn your affairs will take. Ribald songs signify gruesome and extravagant waste.

*See *Hymn.*

## SINGLE

For married people to dream that they are single foretells that their union may not be harmonious. It could also indicate that they need to find a spirit of independence in their union.

## SINISTER

Anything that appears sinister in nature in your dream is actually a blessing.

## SINK

To dream of a sink, kitchen or otherwise, augurs unhappy news about a friend.

## SISTER

For a man to dream of his sister means emotional security. For a woman, it speaks of domestic disagreements.

## SITTING

To dream of sitting means that things in your life may be going up and down in the near future, but they will indeed improve over time.

## SKELETON

To dream of seeing a skeleton is prognostic of illness, misunderstanding, and injury at the hands of others, especially enemies.

To dream that you are a skeleton is a sign that you are worrying unnecessarily and should cultivate a milder disposition. If you imagine that a skeleton is haunting you, this foretells an accident or death; or the trouble may take the form of financial disaster.

## SKIDDING

To dream of uncontrollable skidding means a problem that is weighing heavily on your mind is being made worse by your indecision. This dream is a warning that you need to reach a conclusion.

## SKIING

To dream of this sport whether in snow or on water means you are balancing the physical, emotional, mental and spiritual aspects of your life.

## SKIN

To dream of clear skin implies happiness in family and home life. To dream of damaged or pimply skin suggests problems in your love life. A dream of peeling skin means a time of unhappiness and an ending in a relationship that will open the door for a new love.

## SKINNY-DIPPING

To find yourself or others skinny-dipping implies a release from your worries and problems.

## SKIPPING

To dream of skipping or to see someone skipping suggests unexpected help in a relationship or business problem. To dream of skipping rope means you are well liked and cared about.

## SKIRT

To dream of short or tight skirts is a warning of financial problems. Long or full skirts augur financial gain.

## SKULL

To dream of skulls grinning at you is a sign of domestic quarrels. Business will be reduced if you handle the skulls.

To see a friend's skull denotes that you will receive injury from a friend because you are preferred to him or her.

To see your own skull suggests that you will be the servant of remorse.

## SKUNK

To see or smell a skunk in a dream foretells a social disappointment. But do not worry: new opportunities are coming that will be very pleasing.

## SKY*

To dream of the sky signifies distinguished honors and interesting travel with cultured companions, if the sky is clear. Otherwise, it portends disappointed expectations.

To see the sky turn red portends public disquiet.

*See *Firmament, Heaven.*

## SLANDERING

To dream that you are slandered is a sign of your untruthful dealings and ignorance. If you slander anyone, you will feel the loss of friends through selfishness.

## SLAPPING

To dream that you get slapped suggests a gain in your social status. However, to dream of seeing someone else getting slapped or of slapping someone portends that you will be embarrassed socially.

## SLEEPING

To dream of sleeping on clean, fresh beds denotes peace and favor from those whom you love. To sleep in unnatural resting places foretells sickness and broken engagements.

To sleep beside a little child betokens domestic joy and reciprocated love. If you see others sleeping, you will overcome all opposition in your pursuits. To dream of sleeping with a repulsive person or object warns you that your love and interest in something may wane.

GUSTAVUS HINDMAN MILLER *

## SLEEVE

Dreaming of wearing short sleeves suggests a small disappointment in your personal life. Long sleeves predict social recognition.

## SLEIGH

To see a sleigh in your dreams suggests that you will fail in a romantic adventure and incur the displeasure of a friend. To ride in a sleigh foretells injudicious engagements on your part.

## SLIDING

To dream of sliding portends disappointment. To slide down a hillside implies that you will be deceived into ruin by flattering promises.

## SLIPPERS

To dream of slippers warns that you might be sluggish when it comes to your current dreams; you need to get a better foothold before you proceed. It could also suggest that you need to rest.

## SLOT MACHINE

To dream of anything to do with slot machines warns you to save money for an unexpected expense.

## SMALLPOX

To see people with smallpox in a dream denotes unexpected and shocking sickness.

## SMILING

Dreaming of yourself or someone else smiling suggests happy times ahead.

## SMOKE

To dream of smoke foretells that you will be perplexed by doubt and fear. To be overcome by smoke denotes that dangerous people are victimizing you with flattery.

## SNAIL

To see snails crawling in your dream signifies that unhealthful conditions surround you. To step on them denotes that you will come in contact with disagreeable people.

## SNAKE*

To dream of snakes warns of trouble in various forms.

To see them wriggling and falling over others foretells struggles with fortune and remorse. If you kill them, you will feel that you have used every opportunity for advancing your own interests or respecting those of others. You will enjoy victory over enemies.

If you walk over snakes, you live in fear of sickness. If they bite you, you may succumb to evil influences and enemies. To dream that a snake coils itself around you and darts its tongue out at you is a sign that you will be placed in a position where you are powerless.

If you dream of handling snakes, you will use strategy to aid in overthrowing opposition. If snakes turn into unnatural shapes, your troubles will be dispelled if treated with indifference, calmness, and willpower.

To see or step on snakes while wading or bathing denotes that there will be trouble where unalloyed pleasure was anticipated. To see them bite others foretells that some friend will be injured and criticized by you.

*See Reptile, Serpent.

## SNEEZING

To dream that you sneeze denotes that hasty tidings will cause you to change your plans. If you see or hear others sneeze, some people will bore you with visits.

## SNOUT

To dream of snouts foretells dangerous seasons for you. Enemies are surrounding you, and difficulties will be numerous.

## SNOW

Snow in a dream signifies your inhibitions and repressed emotions, which need to be expressed. You also may be feeling neglected.

To find yourself in a snowstorm denotes sorrow and disappointment at failing to enjoy some long-expected pleasure. If you eat snow, you will fail to realize your ideals.

To see dirty snow foretells that your pride will be humbled. If you see it melt, your fears will turn into joy. To see large white snowflakes falling indicates a fresh start.

To see snowcapped mountains in the distance warns you that your longings and ambitions will bring no worthy advancement. To see the sun shining through landscapes of snow foretells that you will conquer adverse fortune and be possessed of power.

To dream of snowballing implies that you will have to struggle with dishonorable issues; if your judgment is not well grounded, you will suffer defeat. If you dream of being snowbound or lost, there will be a wave of ill luck breaking upon you.

### SNUFF

If you dream of snuff, your enemies are seducing the confidence of your friends.

### SOAP

To dream of soap foretells that friends will lead to interesting entertainment. It is best to interpret this symbol against the backdrop of the rest of the dream. It could also mean that there is a situation, relationship, or part of your environment that you need to clean up.

### SOBBING

Dreaming of sobbing, regardless of the source, suggests the coming of good news.

### SODA FOUNTAIN

To dream of being at a soda fountain denotes pleasure and profit after many exasperating experiences.

If you treat others to soda-fountain and other delectable iced drinks, you will be rewarded for your efforts, though the outlook appears full of contradictions.

### SOLDIER

To see soldiers marching in your dream foretells for you a period of flagrant excess, but at the same time you will be promoted to positions above rivals. To see wounded soldiers is a sign that the misfortunes of others are causing serious complications in your affairs. Your sympathy will outstrip your judgment.

If you dream that you are a worthy soldier, you will enjoy the fulfillment of your ideals.

### SOMNAMBULIST

To imagine while dreaming that you are a somnambulist portends that you will unwittingly consent to some agreement or plan that will bring you anxiety or misfortune.

### SON

To dream of your son, if you have one, as handsome and dutiful, foretells that he will afford you proud satisfaction and will aspire to high honors. If he is not handsome and dutiful, there is trouble ahead.

## SOOT

If you see soot in your dreams, you will meet with ill success in your affairs.

## SORCERER

To dream of a sorcerer foretells that your ambitions will undergo unexpected disappointments and change.

## SORES

To dream of seeing sores suggests that illness will cause you loss and mental distress. Dressing a sore foretells that your personal wishes and desires will give way to the pleasure of others. To dream of sores on yourself portends decay of health and impaired mental prowess.

## SORROW

To dream of sorrow reveals that you are entering a period of great comfort and peace.

## SOUL

To dream of seeing your soul leaving your body signifies that you are in danger of sacrificing yourself to useless designs, which will dwarf your sense of honor and cause you pain.

To dream that you are discussing the immortality of your soul suggests that you will have opportunities to gain the knowledge you desire and the pleasure of inspired conversation with intellectuals.

## SOUP

To dream of soup is a forerunner of good tidings and comfort. If you see others taking soup, you have many good opportunities ahead of you.

## SOURNESS

To dream of eating something sour suggests that you are looking too often to material things to make you happy. You need to look closer at your values.

## SOVEREIGN

To dream of a sovereign denotes increasing prosperity and new friends.

## SOWING

To dream that you are sowing seed foretells fruitful promises. To see others sowing portends much business activity, which will bring gain to all.

## SPADE

To dream of this kind of shovel indicates that you have work to complete that gives you much annoyance.

If you dream of the suit of cards, you will be enticed into folly that brings you grief and misfortune.

## SPAGHETTI

Dreaming of this pasta heralds a time of celebration.

## SPARROW

To dream of sparrows means that you will be surrounded by love and comfort, and this will gain you popularity. To see them distressed or wounded foretells sadness.

## SPEAR

Dreaming of using a spear or seeing one used foretells the clearing of obstacles from your personal and business paths and new happiness.

## SPECTACLES

To dream of spectacles foretells that strangers will cause changes in your affairs. To dream that you see broken spectacles suggests estrangement.

## SPEECH

To dream of giving a speech means improved social status. And to dream that you hear one implies loyalty among your friends and business associates.

## SPELLING

To dream that you spell something correctly denotes success in business. Misspelling it warns you against backstabbing friends and business associates.

## SPENDING

To dream of spending is actually a warning to be tight with your money at present and save rather than spend.

## SPHINX

To dream of this ancient wonder means that you will soon find the answer to a question that has been vexing you.

## SPICE

To dream of spice indicates that you will probably damage your own reputation in search of pleasure.

## SPIDER

To dream of a spider suggests that you will be careful and energetic in your labors, and your fortune will be amassed to pleasing proportions. To see one building its web foretells that you will be happy and secure in your own home. To kill one signifies quarrels. If one bites you, you will be the victim of unfaithfulness and will suffer from enemies in your business. If you dream that you see many spiders hanging in their webs around you, expect fortune, good health, and friends.

To dream of a large spider confronting you signifies that your elevation to fortune will be swift, unless you are in dangerous contact with the spider.

To imagine that you are running from a large spider suggests that you will lose fortune. If you kill the spider, you will eventually come into a fair estate.

## SPIDERWEB

To dream of spiderwebs denotes pleasant associations and fortunate ventures.

## SPINNING

To dream that you are spinning suggests that you will engage in an enterprise that will be all you could wish.

## SPIRITS

To see spirits in a dream denotes that some unexpected trouble will confront you—unless you know the spirits, in which case there is a message you will need to decipher.

## SPITTING

To dream of spitting denotes unhappy terminations of seemingly auspicious undertakings. For someone to spit on you foretells disagreements and alienation of affections.

Spit from a dog represents loyalties from your friends and colleagues. Saliva from a horse suggests an increase in prosperity; from other animals, the overcoming of obstacles and opposition.

## SPLEEN

To dream of a spleen portends a misunderstanding with some party who will injure you.

## SPLENDOR

To dream that you live in splendor indicates that you will have much material success.

To see others thus living signifies pleasure derived from the interest that friends take in your welfare.

## SPLINTER

To dream of splinters sticking into your flesh suggests that you will have many vexations from members of your family or jealous rivals. If while you are dreaming, you get a splinter in your foot, you will soon make or receive a visit that will prove extremely unpleasant. Your affairs will go slightly wrong through your continued neglect.

## SPONGE

Sponges seen in a dream indicate that deception is being practiced on you. If you use a sponge for an eraser, you will be the victim of folly.

## SPOOL

To dream of spools of thread foretells some long and arduous tasks that, when completed, will meet your expectations. If the spools are empty, disappointments are in store for you.

## SPOON

To see or use spoons in a dream denotes advancement. Domestic affairs will afford contentment.

To think a spoon is lost suggests that you will be suspicious of wrong-doing. To steal one is a sign that you deserve censure for contemptible meanness in your home. To dream of broken or soiled spoons indicates loss and trouble.

## SPOTS

Viewing spots on anything in your dream foretells new opportunities coming your way in business or personal affairs.

## SPRING (SEASON)

To dream that spring is advancing is a sign of fortunate undertakings and cheerful companions. To see spring appearing unnaturally warns of disquiet and loss.

## SPURS

To dream of wearing spurs indicates that you will engage in some unpleasant controversy. To see others with them on means that a feeling of enmity is about to get you into trouble.

## SPYGLASS

To dream that you are looking through a spyglass suggests that changes will soon occur to your disadvantage. To see a broken or imperfect spyglass foretells dissension and loss of friends.

## SPYING

To dream that spies are harassing you denotes dangerous quarrels and uneasiness. If you dream that you are a spy, you will make unfortunate ventures.

## SQUALL

To dream of squalls foretells disappointing business and unhappiness.

## SQUASH

To dream of squash means you will make the most of upcoming opportunities.

## SQUIRREL

If you dream of seeing squirrels, pleasant friends will soon visit you. You will also see advancement in your business.

Killing a squirrel denotes that you will be unfriendly and disliked. To pet one signifies family joy. To see a dog chasing one foretells disagreement and unpleasantness among friends.

## STABLE

In dreams, a stable signifies fortune and advantageous surroundings. To see a stable burning denotes successful changes, or that one may be seen on fire in waking life.

## STAG

If you see stags in your dream, you will have honest and true friends and will enjoy delightful entertainment.

## STAGE (THEATER)

To dream that you are on stage and comfortable means your career choice is a good one; you should try for advancement when you can. To be uncomfortable on stage suggests a possible loss of your job, which will put you on the path of a new and exciting career.

## STAGECOACH DRIVER

To dream of a stagecoach driver signifies that you will go on a strange journey in quest of fortune and happiness.

## STAIN

To see a stain on your hands or clothing while dreaming foretells that trouble over small matters will assail you.

To see a stain on the garments of others, or on their flesh, foretells that someone will betray you.

## STAIRS

To dream of walking up a stairway foretells good fortune and much happiness. If you fall down the stairs, you will be the object of hatred and envy. If you walk down, you will be unlucky in your affairs, and romance will be unfavorable.

To see broad, handsome stairs speaks of approaching riches and honors.

To see others going down a stairway indicates that unpleasant conditions will take the place of pleasure. Sitting on stair steps denotes a gradual rise in fortune and delight.

## STALLING

To dream of stalling suggests that you expect impossible results from some enterprise.

## STALLION

To dream of a stallion foretells prosperous conditions, in which you will hold a position that confers honor upon you.

If you dream of riding a fine stallion, you will rise in position and affluence in a phenomenal way; however, your success will warp your morality and sense of justice.

## STAMMERING

To dream that you stammer in your conversation suggests that worry and illness will threaten your enjoyment. To hear others stammer signifies that unfriendly people will delight in annoying you and giving you needless worry.

## STAMP

To dream of stamps of any kind augurs a good financial forecast.

## STANDARD-BEARER

To dream that you are a standard-bearer denotes that your occupations will be pleasant, but varied. If you see others acting as standard-bearers, you will be jealous of a friend.

## STARFISH

To dream that you see, find, or pick up a starfish predicts new friendships.

## STARING

To dream of being stared at predicts a social embarrassment. If you are doing the staring, you need to focus more on yourself and your problems, not on those of the people around you. In other words, mind your own business.

## STARS

To dream of looking at clear, shining stars foretells good health and prosperity. If they are dull, trouble and misfortune lie ahead.

To see a shooting or falling star denotes sadness and grief. If you see stars appearing and vanishing mysteriously, strange changes and events may occur in the near future.

If you dream that a star falls on you, there will be a bereavement in your family. To see stars rolling around on the earth is a sign of formidable danger and trying times.

## STARVING

To dream of starving portends unfruitful labor and a dearth of friends. To see others in this condition presages misery and dissatisfaction with present companions and employment.

## STATIC

To dream of static on a radio or television warns of erratic and unusual behavior in relationships of those around you.

## STATION

To dream that you are waiting at any kind of station (gas, train, and so forth) betokens unexpected happy news. To dream you are leaving a station forecasts financial gain.

## STATIONERY

To dream of personal writing paper augurs an increase in prosperity.

## STATUES

To see statues in dreams signifies estrangement from a loved one. Lack of energy will cause you disappointment in realizing your wishes.

## STEAK

To dream of rare or uncooked steak portends bad news. Cooking steak predicts an increase in social activity; eating it, an increase in income.

## STEALING

To dream of stealing, or of seeing others commit this act, foretells bad luck and loss of character. To be accused of stealing denotes that you will be misunderstood and will suffer as a result, but you will eventually find that this brings you favor. To accuse others denotes that you will treat someone rudely.

## STEAM

To dream that you are burned by steam suggests dishonesty among friends. Hearing the sound of steam means quarrels and disagreement. To dream that you turn off something steaming means you should make a wish.

## STEAM BATH

To dream of a steam bath means you need to take time to reevaluate your relationships. If you dream of emerging from one, your cares will be temporary.

## STEAMROLLER

To operate a steamroller in a dream indicates success in your personal life. But if you dream you are hit or run over by one, expect hostility and dissention among friends and family.

## STEEL

To dream of steel suggests enduring love and friendship. To dream of handling it portends good success—unless it is featured in weapons or blades, which indicates a warning against jealousy.

## STEEPLE

To see a steeple rising from a church is a harbinger of sickness and reverses. A broken one points to death in your circle of friends. To climb a steeple foretells that you will have serious difficulties, but will surmount them. To fall from one portends losses in trade and ill health.

## STENCILING

To dream of stenciling something means you may have to repeat a problem in order to learn from it.

## STEPS*

To dream that you ascend steps suggests that fair prospects will relieve anxiety. If you descend them, you may find misfortune. If you fall down them, you are threatened with unexpected failure.

*See Stairs.

## STEPSISTER

To dream of a stepsister denotes that you will have unavoidable care and annoyance thrust upon you.

## STEREO

A dream featuring a stereo implies travel abroad.

## STERLING (MONEY)

To dream of this type of money—British Sterling—portends unexpected money gifts. If this silver is shiny in your dream, look for a new and inviting friendship. If the silver is dull, you need to evaluate your friendships to see who doesn't fit anymore.

## STEROIDS

To dream that you are injecting steroids means that you are lying to yourself about a personal relationship. If you see someone else injecting steroids, you will make a new and loyal friend.

## STETHOSCOPE

To dream of a stethoscope foretells unusual accomplishments on your own or with associates. There will be trouble and recriminations in love.

## STEW

To dream of serving or cooking stew foretells news of a birth. To dream of eating it indicates a surprise reunion with an old friend.

## STICK

In dreams, sticks are an unlucky omen. A stick may be an instrument of punishment or power. If you are punishing an animal with a stick, you may have negative feelings about yourself and your nature. The people you hit with a stick may represent a part of yourself that you are in conflict with.

## STICKINESS

To dream of something being sticky tells you that a problem will be around for quite a while before it is solved.

## STICKSHIFT

To dream of smoothly driving with a stickshift suggests that the road ahead will be smooth and easy. To dream that you are having difficulty driving a stick forecasts a dilemma in your business.

## STILLBIRTH

To dream of a stillborn baby denotes that a distressing incident will come to your notice.

## STILTS

To dream of walking on stilts indicates that your fortune is not secure. If you fall from stilts, or feel them break beneath you, you will be precipitated into embarrassment by trusting your affairs to the care of others.

## STINGING

To feel that any insect stings you in a dream is a foreboding of bad news and unhappiness.

## STINKING

To dream of something that smells awful suggests that your friends are honest and straightforward.

## STITCHING

To dream of stitching means that you will be clearing up a personal matter, which will then bring you happiness.

## STOCK EXCHANGE

To dream of being at a stock exchange portends a change in your financial well-being, either good or bad.

## STOCKINGS*

To dream of stockings denotes that you will derive pleasure from dissolute companionship.

*See Knitting.

## STOCK MARKET

To dream of a stock-market gain means you need to watch your money. But if you lose in the stock market in your dream, expect good luck with your finances.

## STOMACH

To dream of having pain in your stomach signifies good health. If you dream that you have a fat stomach and you do not, you need to see a doctor.

## STONEMASON

To see stonemasons at work while dreaming foretells disappointment. To dream that you are a stonemason portends that your labors will not be fruitful and your companions will be dull and uncongenial.

## STONES*

To see stones in your dreams foretells numberless perplexities and failures. To walk among rocks or stones predicts that an uneven and rough pathway will be yours for at least a while. If you throw a stone, you will have cause to admonish a person. If you deign to throw a pebble or stone at a belligerent person, an evil you fear will not come to pass because of your untiring attention to right principles.

*See Rocks.

## STOOP

To dream of the stoop of a front porch suggests an unexpected invitation to a social event that will bring you much happiness.

## STOOPING

If you stoop to pick something up in your dream, discovery of a new talent or hobby can bring you financial gain.

## STOPWATCH

To dream of a stopwatch suggests that you will soon need to take stock of your finances and make changes to avoid loss.

## STORAGE BATTERY

If you dream of a storage battery, opportune speculations will return handsome gains to you.

## STORE*

To dream of a store filled with merchandise foretells prosperity and advancement. An empty one denotes failure and quarrels. If you find yourself in a department store, you will derive much pleasure from various sources of profit.

If you sell goods in a store, your advancement will be accelerated by your energy and the efforts of friends.

*See Shop.

## STORK

To dream of storks implies that troubles are on the horizon, but they will be small and easy to overcome.

## STORM*

To see and hear a storm approaching foretells continued sickness, unfavorable business, and separation from friends, which will cause distress. If the storm passes, your afflictions will not be so heavy.

*See *Hurricane, Rain.*

## STORY

If you dream of writing a story, a time of sadness is about to come. To dream of reading or listening to a story predicts happy times.

## STOVE

To see a stove in your dream means that much unpleasantness will be minimized by your timely intervention.

## STRAITJACKET

To dream of a straitjacket suggests that an upcoming project will enjoy smooth sailing.

## STRANGERS

To dream of strangers predicts happy times with valued friends. If they please you, expect good health and pleasant surroundings; if they displease you, look for disappointments. To dream you are a stranger denotes abiding friendships.

## STRANGLING

To dream of being strangled means you need to overcome your fears to reach a goal. To dream of strangling someone warns you to listen to your intuition regarding someone you like but should not trust.

## STRAW

If you dream of straw, your life is threatened with emptiness. Seeing straw piles burning portends prosperous times. To feed straw to stock foretells that you will make poor provisions for those depending upon you.

## STRAWBERRY

To dream of strawberries is favorable to advancement and pleasure. You will obtain some long-wished-for object. To eat strawberries denotes requited love. To deal in them implies abundant harvest and happiness.

## STRAYING

To find yourself dreaming of straying means you may have to take a different approach in a personal or business affair or problem.

To find a stray in your dream foretells a new friendship that will prove loyal and loving.

## STREAM

If you dream of a stream that is clear and flows smoothly, your life will as well. But if the stream is rough, obstacles and troubles and trials are coming into your life. The rougher the water, the harder the journey.

## STREET

To dream that you are walking on a street foretells ill luck and worries. You will almost despair of reaching the goal you aspire to. If you dream that you're on a familiar street in a distant city and it appears dark, you will make a journey soon, but it will not afford the profit or pleasure contemplated. If the street is brilliantly lighted, you will engage in pleasure that passes quickly, leaving no comfort.

To pass down a street and feel alarmed lest a thug attack you warns that you are venturing upon dangerous ground in advancing your pleasure or business.

## STREETCAR

To dream of hopping onto a streetcar implies travel. To dream of jumping off a streetcar predicts a new home or residence.

## STRENGTH

To dream of being very strong means you are aiming too high in an ambition or goal. If you watch someone showing off strength in a dream, a passionate love affair will turn ugly.

## STRESS

To dream of being stressed heralds the coming of happiness.

## STRIKE (BOWLING)

To dream that you bowl a strike predicts financial gain.

## STRIKING (HITTING)

To dream of striking someone or being struck implies progression toward a much-desired goal in your profession or personal life.

## STRIKING (ORGANIZED LABOR)

To witness workers on strike augurs a promotion or advancement in your career.

## STRING

To dream of small bits of string warns you that you need to deal with repressed fear. To dream of using string implies happiness and well-being—the longer the string, the more happiness will be yours.

## STRING BEAN

To dream of string beans is a good dream. Eating them suggests happy social times ahead. Cooking or serving them indicates a change in residence.

## STRIPPING

To dream of doing a striptease warns you against being too promiscuous. To strip furniture suggests the renewal of a contract for your career.

## STROKE

To dream of having a stroke means you need a medical checkup. If you dream of someone else having a stroke, expect news of an illness.

## STROLLER

To dream of pushing a baby stroller suggests news of a pregnancy or birth—unless you are pregnant, in which case the dream has no significance.

## STRONGBOX

To dream of putting items into an empty strongbox lets you know that you will soon unexpectedly have to spend money on a broken item. To dream that you are taking something out of a full strongbox indicates financial gain.

## STRUGGLING

To dream of struggling foretells serious difficulties; but if you gain victory in your struggle, you will also surmount these obstacles.

## STUB

To dream of a stub from anything predicts an unexpected windfall.

## STUDIO

If your dream features a studio of any kind, pleasant social affairs are in the offing.

## STUDYING

To dream of studying something and understanding it foretells new knowledge and financial gain. To study something you don't understand augurs problems with money.

## STUMBLING

If you stumble in a dream while walking or running, you will meet with disfavor, and obstructions will bar your path to success; but you will eventually surmount them, if you do not fall.

## STUMPS

To dream of a stump implies that you are to have reverses and will depart from your usual mode of living. If you see fields of stumps, you will be unable to defend yourself against the encroachments of adversity.

To dig or pull up stumps signifies that you will extricate yourself from the environment of poverty by throwing off sentiment and pride and meeting the realities of life with a determination to overcome whatever opposition you may encounter.

## STUTTERING

If you dream of stuttering, and you don't stutter when awake, you will be able to find the words you need to get your point across when the time comes.

## STYLIST

If you dream of visiting a stylist for your hair, makeup, or fashion, you will change your outlook about certain friendships and colleagues.

## STYROFOAM™

To dream of this synthetic material suggests that some things you once thought to be true are not: they are false or illusionary.

## SUBMARINE

To dream of a submarine means you are currently hiding an issue that cannot be solved until it surfaces.

## SUBPOENA

To dream of serving or being served a subpoena foretells legal problems.

## SUBWAY

To dream of a subway suggests small disappointments or setbacks; but do not be discouraged, for these will clear up.

## SUCCESS

To dream of being a success means you will indeed succeed in your personal or business life, whichever is of most concern to you.

## SUCKLING*

To see the young suckling denotes contentment and favorable conditions for success.

*See *Nursing.*

## SUDS

In dreams, suds represent happy and joyous times.

## SUFFOCATING*

To dream that you are suffocating suggests that you will experience deep sorrow and mortification as a result of the conduct of someone you love. Be careful of your health after this dream.

*See *Smoke.*

## SUGAR

To dream of sugar denotes that you will be hard to please in your domestic life and will entertain jealousy while seeing no cause for anything but satisfaction and secure joy. There may be worries, and you might see your strength and temper taxed after this dream.

If you eat sugar in your dreams, you will have unpleasant matters to contend with for a while, but they will turn out better than expected.

## SUGAR TONGS

To dream of sugar tongs portends disagreeable tidings of wrongdoings.

## SUICIDE

To commit suicide in a dream indicates that misfortune will hang heavily over you.

To see or hear of others committing this deed warns that their failure will affect your interests. If you dream that a friend commits suicide, you may have trouble finding the answer to a very important question.

## SUITCASE

A dream of a suitcase indicates upcoming travel.

## SULFUR

To dream of sulfur warns you to use discretion in your dealings, for you are threatened with foul play. To eat sulfur indicates good health and pleasure.

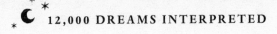 

## SUN*

To dream of seeing a clear, shining sunrise foretells joyous events and prosperity, which give delightful promise. To see the sun at midday denotes the maturity of ambition and indicates unbounded satisfaction. A dream of a sunset is prognostic of joys and wealth passing their zenith, and warns you to care for your interests with renewed vigilance.

Seeing the sun shining through clouds denotes that troubles and difficulties are losing hold on you and prosperity is nearing. If the sun seems weird or is in an eclipse, there will be stormy and dangerous times, but these will eventually pass, leaving your business and domestic affairs in better shape than before.

*See *Eclipse*.

## SUNBURN

To dream of being sunburned means you need to watch your health.

## SUNFLOWER

To dream of a sunflower betokens emotional and mental happiness and contentment.

## SUNGLASSES

If the sunglasses are prominent in a dream, you are hiding behind something that will no longer serve you emotionally.

## SUPERMARKET

If a supermarket is featured in your dream, it suggests abundance and happiness.

## SURGEON

To dream of a surgeon indicates that you are threatened by enemies close to you in business.

## SURGICAL INSTRUMENT

To see surgical instruments in a dream foretells your dissatisfaction at the indiscreet behavior a friend displays toward you.

## SURVEY

To dream of a survey warns you that you may lose something if you are not careful.

## SWALLOW

To dream of swallows is a sign of peace and domestic harmony.

To see a wounded or dead swallow signifies unavoidable sadness.

## SWAMP*

To walk through swampy places in dreams foretells that you will be the object of adverse circumstances. Your inheritance will be uncertain, and you will undergo keen disappointments in love matters.

*See *Marsh*.

## SWAN

To dream of seeing white swans floating upon placid waters foretells prosperous outlooks and delightful experiences.

To see a black swan denotes illicit pleasure, if it is near clear water. A dead swan speaks of satiety and discontent.

If you see swans flying, pleasant anticipations will be realized soon.

## SWASTIKA

To dream of this symbol warns you that you are being too forceful or too easily influenced by others. You need to change your behavior.

## SWEARING

To dream of swearing denotes some unpleasant obstructions in business.

If you are swearing before your family, disagreements will soon arise due to your disloyal conduct.

## SWEEPING

To dream of sweeping suggests that you will gain favor in the eyes of your spouse, and children will find pleasure in the home. If you think the floors need sweeping, and you neglect them for any reason, distresses and bitter disappointments await you in the approaching days.

## SWEET OIL

Sweet oil in dreams implies that considerate treatment will be withheld from you in some unfortunate occurrence.

## SWEET TASTE

To dream of any kind of a sweet taste in your mouth indicates that you will be praised for your pleasing conversation and calm demeanor at a time of commotion and distress.

To dream that you are trying to get rid of a sweet taste foretells that you will oppress and deride your friends, incurring their displeasure.

## SWELLING

To dream that you see yourself swollen indicates that you will amass fortune, but your egotism will interfere with your enjoyment of it.

To see others swollen foretells that advancement will meet with envious obstructions.

## SWIMMING*

To dream of swimming is an augury of success if you find no discomfort in the act. If you feel yourself going down, much dissatisfaction will present itself to you.

To swim underwater forecasts struggles and anxiety.

*See *Diving.*

## SWINGING

To dream of a swing or of swinging suggests that your patience and perseverance will indeed pay off.

## SWING SET

To dream of a swing set that is empty means your life is very balanced and easy. If anyone is swinging on it, your indecision will cause you problems.

## SWISS CHEESE

To dream of Swiss cheese implies that you will come into possession of substantial property, and healthful amusements will be enjoyed.

## SWITCH

To dream of a switch foretells changes and misfortune; you may meet discouragements in momentous affairs. A broken switch foretells disgrace and trouble.

If you dream of a railroad switch, travel will cause you much loss and inconvenience.

## SWITCHBOARD

To dream of a switchboard implies an expansion in your circle of friends. There are new friendships on the horizon.

## SWORD

To dream that you wear a sword indicates that you will fill some public position with honor.

To have your sword taken from you denotes your vanquishment in rivalry.

If you see others bearing swords, altercations will be attended with danger. A broken sword foretells despair.

## SYMPHONY*

To dream of symphonies heralds delightful occupations.

*See *Music*.

## SYNAGOGUE*

To dream of a synagogue is an indication of your longing for spiritual comfort and aspiration to higher levels of enlightenment.

*See *Church*.

## SYRINGE

To dream of a syringe indicates that a false alarm about the gravity of a relative's condition will reach you. To see a broken syringe suggests that you are approaching a period of ill health or worry over slight mistakes in business.

## SYRUP

To dream of this sweetener means joy and happiness are on the way.

## TABASCO™

To dream of this hot sauce predicts an exciting new romance. If you are married or in a relationship right now, the dream suggests that an interesting new friend will bring joy to your life.

## TABLE

To dream of setting a table preparatory to a meal foretells happy unions and prosperous circumstances.

To see empty tables signifies poverty or disagreements. Clearing away a table indicates that pleasure will soon assume the form of trouble and indifference.

To eat from a table without a tablecloth foretells that you will be independent, and the prosperity or conduct of others will no longer influence you. A soiled tablecloth means that quarreling will follow pleasure.

A broken table implies declining fortune. To see someone standing or sitting on a table foretells that to obtain your desires, you will be guilty of indiscretions.

## TABLOID

To dream that you are published in a tabloid foretells social embarrassment for you.

## TACK

If you dream of tacks, many inconveniences will plague you.

## TACO

To dream of this Mexican food predicts financial gain.

## TADPOLE

To dream of tadpoles indicates that uncertain speculation will bring cause for uneasiness in business.

## TAIL

To dream of seeing only a tail suggests an unusual annoyance where pleasure seemed assured. To cut off the tail of an animal foretells that you will suffer misfortune by your own carelessness. To dream that a tail is growing on you predicts that your evil ways will cause you untold distress, and strange events will cause you confusion.

## TAILOR

To dream of a tailor portends that worries will arise on account of a journey. If you have a misunderstanding with a tailor, you will be disappointed in the outcome of some scheme. For a tailor to measure you indicates that you will have quarrels and disagreements.

## TALCUM POWDER

Anything having to do with talcum powder in a dream suggests that you will soon discover the softer side of someone you know.

## TALISMAN

To dream that you wear a talisman implies that you will have pleasant companions and enjoy favors from the rich.

## TALKING

To dream of talking denotes that you will soon hear of the sickness of relatives, and there will be worries in your affairs.

If you hear others talking loudly, you may be accused of interfering in the affairs of others. If you think others are talking about you, you are menaced with illness and disfavor.

## TALLOW

To dream of tallow warns that love and wealth will quickly vanish.

## TAMALE

To dream of tamales means a new friendship that will prove useful to you.

## TAMBOURINE

To dream of a tambourine predicts that you will find enjoyment in an unusual event.

## TAM-O'-SHANTER

To dream of a tam-o'-shanter predicts happy and joyous events.

## TAMPON

To dream of a new tampon foretells a pregnancy and birth. A used tampon is a warning of health issues.

## TANGERINE

To dream of this fruit suggests good times and good fortune.

## TANGLE

To dream of something being tangled tells you that now is the time to sort out confusion in your affairs and avoid embarrassment.

## TANGO

To dream of this dance suggests that quick decisions will be profitable.

## TANK

To dream of a storage tank implies that you will be prosperous and satisfied beyond your expectations. A leaking tank denotes loss.

If you dream of an army tank, you will find peace of mind around a problem that has been bothering you for some time.

## TANNERY

To dream of a tannery denotes contagion and illness. Loss in trade is portended.

To dream that you are a tanner suggests that you will have to engage in work that is not to your taste, but there will be others dependent upon you.

If you buy leather from a tannery, you will be successful in your undertakings, but will not make many friends.

## TAP-DANCING

To dream of tap-dancing foretells gaiety and celebration in your life. To watch others tap-dancing in your dream predicts a pleasant surprise.

## TAPE

To dream of tape denotes that your work will be both wearisome and unprofitable.

## TAPE MEASURE

To use a tape measure in a dream means that you will soon be held accountable for something you thought you could get away with.

## TAPE RECORDER

Any reference to a tape recorder in a dream suggests that you will soon find yourself repeating a request before it will actually be fulfilled.

## TAPESTRY

To dream of seeing rich tapestry foretells that luxurious living will be to your liking; if the tapestries are not worn or ragged, you will be able to gratify your inclinations.

## TAPEWORM

To dream of seeing or having a tapeworm portends disagreeable prospects for health or pleasure.

## TAPIOCA

To dream of this pudding betokens financial gain.

## TAPPING

Dreaming that you hear the tapping of something and find it annoying suggests that you will soon have a disagreement with a family member or friend.

## TAR

If you see tar in dreams, it warns you against the pitfalls and designs of treacherous enemies. To have tar on your hands or clothing denotes sickness and grief.

## TARANTULA

To see a tarantula in your dream signifies that enemies are about to overwhelm you with loss. If you kill a tarantula, you will be successful after much ill luck.

## TARGET

To dream of a target suggests that an unpleasant affair will pull your attention away from other more pleasant ones.

## TASSEL

To see tassels in a dream implies that you will reach the height of your desires and ambitions.

## TASTING

To dream of tasting something means you will experience delays in your projects or personal affairs.

## TATTOO

To see your body appearing tattooed foretells that some difficulty will cause you a long and tedious absence from your home.

To see tattoos on others suggests that strange relationships will make you an object of jealousy.

If you dream that you are a tattoo artist, you will estrange yourself from friends because of your fancy for some type of strange experience.

## TAVERN

To dream of a tavern predicts that too much entertaining will be your downfall.

## TAXES

To dream of paying your taxes indicates that you will succeed in destroying evil influences rising around you.

If others pay your taxes, you will be forced to ask aid of friends. If you are unable to pay them, you will be unfortunate in experiments you are making.

## TAXI

To dream of riding alone in a taxi suggests that you will have a comfortable life. To dream of being in a taxi with someone else warns you against scandal.

## TAXIDERMY

To dream of taxidermy means you need to keep your eyes open because things are not what they appear to be.

## TB (TUBERCULOSIS)

To dream of tuberculosis is a dream of good health and well-being.

## TEA

To dream that you are brewing tea indicates that you will be guilty of indiscreet actions and will feel deeply remorseful.

To dream of drinking tea with friends suggests that social pleasures will lose their appeal for you; you will seek to change these feelings by serving others in their sorrow.

To see dregs in your tea warns you of trouble in love and in your social life. Spilling tea in a dream is a sign of domestic confusion and grief. To find your tea chest empty portends much disagreeable gossip and news. If you dream that you are thirsty for tea, you will be surprised by uninvited guests.

## TEACHER

To dream of being a teacher warns that if you want to avoid unpleasant repercussions from being at cross purposes with yourself, you must be decisive and firm in your decisions.

## TEACUP

To dream of teacups suggests that you'll attend and enjoy social events.

## TEAKETTLE

To dream of seeing a teakettle foretells sudden news that will likely distress you.

## TEARS

To dream that you are in tears indicates that an affliction will soon envelop you. If you see others shedding tears, your sorrows will affect the happiness of others.

## TEASING

To find yourself teasing anyone in a dream means that you will be loved and sought after because of your cheerful and amiable manner. Your business will be successful eventually.

To dream of being teased implies that you will win the love of happy, well-to-do people.

## TEDDY BEAR

To dream of a teddy bear means that you will soon experience security and safety in your life.

## TEETH

An ordinary dream of teeth augurs an unpleasant contact with sickness or disquieting people.

If you dream that your teeth are loose, expect failures and gloomy tidings. If the doctor pulls your tooth, you will endure a desperate illness; if not fatal, it will be lingering. If you have cavities in your teeth filled, expect to recover lost valuables after much uneasiness. To clean or brush your teeth foretells that some great struggle will be demanded of you if you hope to preserve your fortune.

To dream that you are having a set of false teeth made predicts that severe burdens will fall upon you, and you will strive to throw them aside.

If you lose your teeth, you will have burdens that crush your pride and demolish your affairs.

To dream that you have your teeth knocked out denotes sudden misfortune. Either your business will suffer, or deaths or accidents will come close to you.

To examine your teeth warns you to be careful of your affairs, as enemies are lurking near you. If they appear decayed, your business or health will suffer from intense strain. To dream of spitting out teeth portends sickness, your own or in your immediate family. For one tooth to fall out foretells disagreeable news; two, unhappy states that you will be plunged into through no carelessness on your part.

To admire your teeth for their whiteness and beauty suggests that you'll get your wishes and live happily ever after.

## TELEGRAM

To dream that you receive a telegram foretells unpleasant tidings. A friend is likely to misrepresent matters that are of much concern to you.

To send a telegram is a sign that you will be estranged from someone near you, or that business will disappoint you. To see or be in a telegraph office implies unfortunate engagements.

## TELEMARKETING

To dream that you are being haunted by telemarketers is a dream of upcoming good news.

## TELEPATHY

To dream that you have telepathy betokens exciting news arriving in the mail.

## TELEPHONE

If you dream of a telephone, you will have rivalry where you least expect it. If the phone is out of order, look to receive sad news.

## TELESCOPE

To dream of a telescope suggests unfavorable seasons for love and domestic affairs, and business will be changeable and uncertain. To look at planets and stars through one portends journeys that will afford you much pleasure but later cause you much financial loss. To see a broken telescope, or one not in use, signifies that matters will head out of the ordinary with you, and trouble may be expected.

## TELEVANGELIST

To dream of televangelists predicts an unexpected spiritual awakening. To dream that you are a televangelist warns you to examine your spiritual balance.

## TELEVISION

To dream of watching a show on television and enjoying it suggests that your life is going in the right direction. If you don't like what you are watching, you are currently being influenced by other people who bear you ill will.

## TELLER

To dream that you give money to a bank teller heralds financial gain. To dream that you receive money from a bank teller suggests a financial loss.

## TEMPER

To dream of losing your temper means that you could lose the support of a friend or colleague. A dream of others losing their temper means that you may need a change of location or personal environment for things to work out.

## TEMPERATURE

To be aware of the temperature, whether hot or cold, in your dream suggests good luck and a possible gambling win, if you play the number of the temperature.

## TEMPEST★

To dream of tempests augurs a siege of calamitous trouble; friends will treat you with indifference.

*See *Cyclone, Storm.*

## TEMPTATION

To dream that you are surrounded by temptations implies that you will be involved in some trouble with an envious person who is trying to undermine the confidence your friends have in you. If you resist the temptations, you will be successful in some affair.

## TEMPURA

To dream of this Japanese form of batter-fried food indicates good fortune and financial gain.

### TENANT

For a landlord to see his tenant in a dream means that he will have business trouble and vexation. To dream that you are a tenant implies that you will suffer a business failure. If a tenant pays you money, you will be successful in something.

### TENNIS

If you dream that you are watching others play tennis, you might experience health issues. To dream that you are playing tennis means you will have good health.

### TENT

To dream of being in a tent foretells a change in your affairs. To see a number of tents suggests journeys with unpleasant companions. If the tents are torn or otherwise dilapidated, there will be trouble for you.

### TENTACLES

To see the tentacles of a fish or an animal in your dream means that you will have many options to choose from in a problem that you have been working on. To dream that you are tangled in tentacles cautions that you will need help for that problem from an outside source.

### TEPEE

To dream of a tepee means many blessings coming your way.

### TEQUILA

To dream of tequila portends a celebration or upcoming surprise. To dream of being drunk on this alcohol warns of mental depression and emotional ill health.

### TERMINAL

To dream of being in a terminal predicts unexpected business and personal travel.

To dream of the terminals of an electric circuit implies that an idea or possible solution to a problem will have to go around and around to come to fruition.

### TERMINAL ILLNESSES

To dream of a terminal illness suggests very good health.

### TERMITE

To dream of these insects foretells an emotional issue that will wear away at your nerves.

## TERROR

To dream that you feel terror about any object or event indicates that disappointment and loss will envelop you.

To see others in terror means that the unhappiness of friends will seriously affect you.

## TEST

To dream of failing a test suggests that your ambitions or goals are set too high and you will be disappointed. If you pass the test, you will have no major problems in achieving your goals. To dream of simply taking a test reminds you that slow and steady will win the race; in other words, you just need to stay the course and things will turn out all right.

## TESTICLES

A dream of healthy testicles suggests social popularity and a rise in your career status. The larger the genitals, the bigger the gain. However, to dream of diseased testicles means you are spending too much time having fun at social affairs.

## TESTIFYING

To dream that you have to testify implies that someone will soon be asking you for your help. To have someone testify against you in your dream portends a new friendship that will be very beneficial in your business or personal life.

## TEXT

To dream of being in a dispute over a text foretells unfortunate adventures for you. If you try to recall a text, you will meet with unexpected difficulties. If you are repeating one and pondering over it, you will have great obstacles to overcome to gain your desires.

## TEXT MESSAGE

To dream of sending or receiving text messages on your cell phone means you will soon be hearing from an old friend or acquaintance.

## THANKSGIVING

To dream of this festive fall holiday betokens good news and happy times.

## THATCHING

To dream that you thatch a roof indicates that sorrow and discomfort will surround you. If you find that a roof you have thatched with straw is leaking, danger may threaten, but by your rightly directed energy the danger can be averted.

## THAWING

To dream of seeing ice thawing foretells that some affair that has caused you much worry will soon give you profit and pleasure. To see the ground thawing after a long freeze augurs prosperous circumstances.

## THEATER

To dream of being at a theater suggests that you will have much pleasure in the company of new friends. If you are one of the players, your pleasures will be of short duration.

If you dream of trying to escape from a theater during a fire or other incident, you will engage in some hazardous enterprise.

## THERAPY

To dream that you are in therapy, either mental or physical, is a sign of good health if it follows an illness in your waking life. To dream you are the one giving the therapy suggests that you will soon hear news of someone's health problem.

## THERMOMETER

To dream of looking at a thermometer denotes unsatisfactory business and disagreements in the home. To see a broken one foreshadows illness. If the mercury seems to be falling, your affairs will assume a distressing shape. If it is rising, you will be able to throw off bad conditions in your business.

## THERMOSTAT

To dream of a thermostat means you will soon have to make a snap decision in a personal matter.

## THIEF*

To dream that you are a thief and are pursued by officers is a sign that you will meet reverses in business and your social relations will be unpleasant. If you pursue or capture a thief, you will overcome your enemies.

*See Stealing.

## THIGHS

To dream of seeing thighs denotes unusual good luck and pleasure. To see wounded thighs foretells illness and treachery.

# THIMBLE

If you use a thimble in your dreams, you will have many others to please besides yourself. To lose a thimble implies poverty and trouble. An old or broken thimble suggests that you are about to act unwisely in some momentous affair.

To receive or buy a new thimble portends new associations in which you will find contentment. To dream that you use an open-ended thimble, but find that it is closed, indicates that you will have trouble, but friends will aid you in escaping its disastrous consequences.

# THINNESS

To dream you are painfully thin (if you are not in real life) portends an emotional health problem that will need your attention. To dream of seeing painfully thin people suggests that a health issue that has been worrying you will go away.

# THIRST

To dream of being thirsty shows that you are aspiring to things beyond your present reach; but if your thirst is quenched with pleasing drinks, you will obtain your wishes. If you see others thirsty and drinking to slake their thirst, you will enjoy many favors at the hands of wealthy people.

# THISTLE

Even though this is a prickly plant, the purple flower you see in your dream indicates that a current health matter will be rectified and you will experience a time of healing and well-being.

# THORN

To dream of thorns is an omen of dissatisfaction, and evil will surround every effort toward advancement. If the thorns are hidden beneath green foliage, secret enemies will interfere with your prosperity.

# THOROUGHBRED

To dream of any animal being a thoroughbred implies that you will be rewarded through your pure thoughts and deeds.

# THREAD*

To dream of thread indicates that your fortune lies at the end of an intricate path. If you see broken threads, you will suffer loss through the faithlessness of friends.

*See Spool, Twine.

## THREAT

Any form of threat warns you to watch a propensity to gamble or take chances.

## THRESHING

To dream of threshing grain denotes great advancement in business and happiness among families. But if there is an abundance of straw and little grain, you will undertake unsuccessful enterprises.

To dream of breaking down or having an accident while threshing portends some great sorrow in the midst of prosperity.

## THRESHOLD

To dream of carrying something over a threshold foretells a new relationship. To dream that you are being carried over a threshold predicts a pregnancy or birth announcement.

## THRIFT SHOP

To dream of a thrift shop suggests the coming of money, luck, and prosperity.

## THROAT

To dream of seeing a well-developed and graceful throat portends a rise in position. If you dream that your throat is sore, you will be deceived in your estimation of a friend and will have anxiety over the discovery.

## THRONE

If you dream of sitting on a throne, you will rapidly rise to favor and fortune. To descend from one portends much disappointment for you. If you see others on a throne, you will succeed to wealth through the favor of others.

## THRUSH

To dream of this small bird betokens peace and contentment in your life.

## THUMB

To dream of seeing a thumb suggests that you are a favorite. If you are suffering from a sore thumb, you will lose in business and your companions will prove disagreeable.

To dream that you have no thumb implies loneliness. If your thumbs seem unnaturally small, you will enjoy pleasure for a time; if abnormally large, your success will be rapid and brilliant. A soiled thumb indicates gratification of promiscuous desires. If your thumb has a very long nail, you are liable to fall into evil by seeking strange pleasures.

## THUNDER

To dream of hearing thunder indicates that you may be threatened with reverses in your business. If you are in a thundershower, trouble and grief are close to you. To hear terrific peals of thunder that make the earth quake portends great loss and disappointment.

## THYME

In dreams, this herb represents monetary gain.

## TIARA

To dream of wearing this head ornament means that you will soon be invited to lively social events. To dream of someone else wearing one suggests that you are being too serious.

## TICK

To dream that you see ticks crawling on your flesh is a sign of impoverished circumstances and ill health. You may have to get to the hospital in a hurry. To mash a tick denotes that you will be annoyed by treacherous enemies. If you see large ticks on livestock, enemies are endeavoring to get possession of your property by foul means.

## TICKET

To dream of a ticket augurs news of delay. You will have to wait for something that you have wanted.

## TICKLING

To dream of being tickled denotes insistent worries and illness. If you tickle others, you will throw away much enjoyment through weakness and folly.

## TIC-TAC-TOE

To dream of this game foretells the arrival of unexpected news.

## TIDAL WAVE

To dream of a tidal wave that is free of debris portends an amazing career and personal change that will be very beneficial to you. If the water is dirty and carrying debris, it warns of hard times ahead.

## TIDE

To dream of a high tide means new opportunities. An incoming tide suggests an increase in financial resources. A low tide advises that you must make a change somewhere in your life. An outgoing or ebbing tide means the ending of a problem.

## TIGER

If you dream of a tiger advancing toward you, you will be tormented and persecuted by enemies. If it attacks you, failure will bury you in gloom. If you succeed in warding it off or killing it, you will be extremely successful in all your undertakings.

To see a tiger running away from you is a sign that you will overcome opposition and rise to high positions. To see tigers in cages foretells that you will foil your adversaries. Tigerskin rugs suggest that you are going to enjoy luxurious ease and pleasure.

## TIGHTROPE

To dream of a tightrope warns that you need to take special care of a personal or business matter in order for it to benefit you.

## TILE

To dream of broken tiles warns against unnecessary risks in business. Dreams of whole tiles foretell good business speculation that will turn in your favor.

## TILL

To dream of seeing money and valuables in a till predicts success: your love affairs will be exceedingly favorable. An empty one denotes disappointed expectations.

## TIMBER★

To see timber in your dreams is an augury of prosperous times and peaceful surroundings. If the timber appears dead, there will be great disappointments for you.

★See *Forest.*

## TIME BOMB

To dream of undetonated time bombs foretells an invitation to a party or social event. If the bomb goes off, unexpected change in your personal life may not be good for you.

## TIME CAPSULE

To dream of a time capsule speaks of pleasant memories and reconnection with an old friend.

## TIME ZONE

To be aware of change in time zones in your dream means you will unexpectedly be asked to do something that may have a profound impact on your life.

## TIN

To dream of this material in its molten state suggests obstacles in your path that you will need to overcome. Buying or selling tin implies progress after troubled times.

## TINSEL

To dream of this Christmas ornamentation warns that even though something may be pleasing to your eye or ear, it is not necessarily true.

## TIPSINESS

To dream that you are tipsy indicates that you will cultivate a jovial disposition, and that the cares of life will make no serious inroads into your conscience. Seeing others tipsy reveals that you are unconcerned as to the demeanor of your associates.

## TIPTOEING

To dream of tiptoeing suggests that biting your tongue may not be advisable. Perhaps you need to speak up in a particular situation.

## TIRE

To dream of changing a tire means you need more rest. Buying a tire predicts a solution to a problem. A blowout means problems with a jealous friend. If you lose your tire, you need more self-control.

## TIREDNESS

To dream of being excessively tired warns you against overdoing things; you should slow down in your daily life, or see a doctor.

## TISSUE

To dream of tissues means help is on the way for a business matter.

## TNT

To dream of dynamite that is not detonated implies solutions to a problem. To watch it explode denotes unexpected change.

## TOAD

To dream of toads signifies unfortunate adventures. To kill a toad foretells that your judgment will be harshly criticized. If you put your hands on a toad, you will be instrumental in causing the downfall of a friend.

## TOADSTOOL

To dream of a toadstool means that you might have to fight to reach your goal. Prepare yourself for hard work.

## TOASTING

To dream of toasted bread foretells financial gain.

To make a toast or have one made in your honor implies honor and respectability in the workplace.

## TOBACCO

To dream of tobacco denotes success in business affairs but poor returns in love. To use it warns you against enemies and extravagance. To see tobacco growing foretells successful enterprises. To see it dry in the leaf ensures good crops for farmers and subsequent gain for tradespeople.

To dream of smoking speaks of amiable friendships.

## TOBOGGAN

To dream of riding this winter sled implies a swift end to a current problem. If you watch others on a toboggan, you will have to ask for help.

## TODDY

To dream of drinking a toddy signifies that interesting events will soon change your plan of living.

## TOILET

To dream of a toilet is a sign of unexpected gain in money or property and overall good fortune and abundance.

## TOKEN

To dream of tokens means that a financial problem may be larger than you think. Be diligent and realize that it isn't as small as it appears.

## TOLLBOOTH

To dream of paying money at a tollbooth means that you will realize financial gain. But if you do not pay the toll, you need to be aware of thievery and dishonesty when it comes to your money and investments.

## TOMATO

To dream of eating tomatoes signals the approach of good health. To see them growing denotes domestic enjoyment and happiness.

## TOMB

To dream of seeing tombs suggests sadness and disappointment in business. Dilapidated tombs portend death or desperate illness. To dream of seeing your own tomb predicts your sickness or disappointment. To read the inscription on tombs foretells unpleasant duties.

## TONGUE

To dream of seeing your own tongue suggests that you will be looked upon with disfavor by your acquaintances. If you see the tongue of another, scandal may vilify you. To dream that your tongue is affected in any way means that your carelessness in talking will get you into trouble.

## TOOTHACHE

To dream of a toothache means that what you have to say will be taken seriously. Choose your words wisely.

## TOOTHBRUSH

To dream of using a toothbrush augurs happy times. To dream of losing it predicts your inability to speak your mind when you must.

## TOOTHLESSNESS

To dream that you are toothless suggests your inability to advance your interests; and ill health will cast gloom over your prospects. To see others toothless means that enemies are trying in vain to injure your reputation with false charges.

## TOOTHPICK

To dream of toothpicks indicates that small anxieties will harass you unnecessarily if you give them your attention. If you use a toothpick, you will be a party to a friend's injury.

## TOPAZ

To see topaz in a dream tells you that fortune will be liberal in her favors and you will have very pleasing companions.

## TOP HATS

To dream of wearing this type of formal hat foretells a possible death. To see another person wearing a top hat foretells travel.

## TOP (TOY)

To dream of a top means that you may be involved in frivolous difficulties, especially due to indiscriminate friendships. To see one spinning speaks of wasting your means in childish pleasures.

## TORAH

If you dream of reading this holy scroll and you are not Jewish, blessings are foretold.

## TORCH*

To dream of seeing torches foretells amusement and favorable business. To carry one denotes success in love. For it to go out denotes failure and distress.
*See *Lamp, Lantern.*

## TORNADO

If you dream that you are witnessing a tornado, expect profound change that will be beneficial to you. To be in a tornado is double good luck.

## TORRENT

To dream that you are looking upon a rushing torrent suggests that you will have unusual trouble and anxiety.

## TORTILLA

To dream of this Mexican flat bread signifies prosperity.

## TORTOISE

To dream of this slow-moving reptile implies security in your home and steady progress in your business affairs.

## TORTURING

To dream of being tortured suggests that you will undergo disappointment and grief through the machination of false friends. If you are torturing others, you will fail to carry out well-laid plans for increasing your fortune. If you are trying to alleviate the torture of others, you will succeed after a struggle in business and love.

## TOTEM

To dream of a totem betokens new friends who will broaden your mind.

## TOUCAN

To dream of this tropical bird tells you that happiness and peace of mind will finally be yours.

## TOURIST

To dream that you are a tourist predicts that you will engage in some pleasurable affair that will take you away from your usual residence. To see tourists indicates brisk but unsettled business and anxiety in love.

## TOWEL

To dream of clean towels implies good health and material comfort; dirty towels, frustration coming in your personal life; and paper towels, a period of financial setbacks.

## TOWER

To dream of seeing a tower suggests that you will aspire to high positions. If you climb one, you will succeed in your wishes; but if the tower crumbles while you descend, you will be disappointed.

## TOWNHOUSE

To dream of a townhouse warns you to set your goals higher in your life for greater achievement.

## TOY

To see new toys in dreams foretells family joys; but if they're broken, death or sickness will rend your heart with sorrow. If you see children at play with toys, a happy marriage is indicated. To give away toys in your dreams suggests that you will be ignored socially by your acquaintances.

## TRADING

To dream of trading denotes fair success in your enterprise. If you fail, trouble and annoyances will overtake you.

## TRAFFIC

To dream of watching traffic means you may need help in solving a problem. To drive in traffic reveals a problem within your family that will soon be solved. To be in a traffic jam reminds you that patience will be needed to overcome obstacles. If you dream of a traffic accident, health problems are indicated.

## TRAGEDY

To dream of a tragedy foretells misunderstandings and grievous disappointments. If you are implicated in it, a calamity will plunge you into sorrow and peril.

## TRAIL

To dream of following a trail means that you will achieve your goal if you persevere. To dream of being lost on a trail suggests that you are wasting time in relationships.

## TRAILER

To dream of a trailer foretells a complete change in your personal and business life.

## TRAIN

If you see a train of cars moving in your dreams, you will soon have cause to make a journey. If you are on a train and it appears to be moving smoothly along though there is no track, you will be much worried over some affair that will eventually prove to be a source of profit to you. To see freight trains in your dreams portends changes that will tend to elevate your position.

## TRAITOR

To see a traitor in your dream predicts that you will have enemies working to despoil you. If someone calls you a traitor, or if you so imagine yourself, unfavorable prospects are suggested.

## TRAMP

To dream of being a tramp foretells peace of mind and improving circumstances in your life. If you dream of helping a tramp, expect a rise in your social status. But to refuse to give help to a tramp predicts harder work and smaller rewards in your career.

## TRAMPOLINE

To dream of a trampoline means you are wasting time in your career. You need to change jobs.

## TRANSFIGURATION

To dream of the Transfiguration of Jesus foretells that your faith in humankind's own nearness to God will raise you above trifling matters and elevate you to an important position, in which capacity you will be able to promote the well-being of the downtrodden and persecuted.

If you see yourself transfigured, you will stand high in the esteem of honest and prominent men.

# TRANSPLANT

Any kind of organ transplant in a dream suggests the renewal of a cherished goal that you will indeed achieve.

# TRAP

To dream of setting a trap implies that you will use intrigue to carry out your designs. If you are caught in a trap, you will be outwitted by your opponents. If you catch game in a trap, you will flourish in whatever vocation you may choose.

If you see an empty trap, expect misfortune in the immediate future. An old or broken trap denotes failure in business; sickness in your family may follow.

# TRAPDOOR

To dream of a trapdoor portends an astonishing revelation that will improve your life.

# TRAPEZE

To dream of a trapeze tells you that problems will be solved with ease.

# TRAVELING*

To dream of traveling signifies profit and pleasure combined. Traveling through rough unknown places portends dangerous enemies, and perhaps sickness; over bare or rocky steeps, it signifies apparent gain, but loss and disappointment will swiftly follow. If the hills or mountains are fertile and green, you will be eminently prosperous and happy.

To dream that you travel alone in a car suggests that you may make an eventful journey, and affairs will be worrying.

To travel in a crowded car foretells fortunate adventures and new and entertaining companions.

*See Journey.

# TRAY

To see trays in your dream indicates that your wealth will be foolishly wasted, and surprises of an unpleasant nature will shock you. If the trays seem to be filled with valuables, though, surprises will come in the form of good fortune.

# TREASURE

If you dream of finding treasures, you will be greatly aided in your pursuit of fortune by some unexpected generosity. If you lose treasures, bad luck in business and the inconstancy of friends are foretold.

### TREE*

To dream of trees in new foliage foretells a happy consummation of hopes and desires. Dead trees signal sorrow and loss. To climb a tree is a sign of swift advancement and favor. To cut one down or pull it up by the roots denotes that you will waste your energy and wealth foolishly. To see green trees newly felled portends unhappiness coming unexpectedly to scenes of enjoyment or prosperity.

*See Forest.

### TREMBLING

To dream of trembling augurs good health and happiness.

### TRENCH*

To see trenches in dreams warns you of distant treachery. You will sustain loss if you're not careful in undertaking new enterprises or in associating with strangers.

To see filled trenches denotes the buildup of anxiety in your life.

*See Ditch.

### TRIAL

To dream of being on trial warns you to be cautious in anything new in business.

### TRIANGLE

To dream of a triangle foretells separation from friends; love affairs will terminate in disagreements.

### TRIPE

To see tripe in a dream means sickness and danger. To eat tripe denotes that you will be disappointed in some serious matter.

### TRIPLETS

To dream of seeing triplets foretells success in affairs where failure was feared. For a man to dream that his wife has triplets signifies a pleasant termination to some affair that has long been in dispute.

To hear newborn triplets crying signifies disagreements that will be speedily reconciled to your satisfaction. If a young woman dreams that she has triplets, she will suffer loss and disappointment in love, but will succeed to wealth.

### TROPHY

To see trophies in a dream signifies that some pleasure or fortune will come to you through the endeavors of mere acquaintances. For a woman to give away a trophy implies doubtful pleasures and fortune.

### TROUSERS

To dream of trousers foretells that you will be tempted to perform dishonorable deeds. If you put them on wrong-side out, you will become obsessed with something.

### TROUT

To dream of seeing trout signifies growing prosperity. Eating trout suggests that you will be in good health. To catch a trout with a hook foretells pleasure. If it falls back into the water, you will have a short season of happiness. To catch trout with a net is a sign of unparalleled prosperity. To see them in muddy water shows that your success in love will bring you to grief and disappointment.

### TROWEL

To dream of a trowel means that you will meet with unfavorable reactions in business. If you see a trowel rusty or broken, unavoidable ill luck is fast approaching you.

### TRUCK

To dream of a truck suggests comfort in your life and good social standing.

### TRUMPET

To dream of a trumpet denotes that something of unusual interest is about to befall you. To blow a trumpet signifies that you will gain your wishes.

### TRUNK

To dream of trunks foretells journeys and ill luck. Packing your trunk suggests that you will soon go on a pleasant trip. To see the contents of a trunk thrown about in disorder predicts quarrels and a hasty journey from which only dissatisfaction will accrue. Empty trunks foretell disappointment in love and marriage.

### TRUSS

If you see a truss in your dream, ill health and unfortunate business engagements are predicted.

## TRUST

To dream of trusts foretells indifferent success in trade or law. If you imagine you are a member of a trust, you will be successful in designs of a speculative nature.

## TUB

To dream of seeing a tub full of water denotes domestic contentment. An empty tub proclaims unhappiness and the waning of fortune. A broken tub suggests family disagreements and quarrels.

## TULIP

To dream of planting tulips means a small disappointment, but to see them in bloom or to gather them speaks of happiness.

## TUMBLING

To dream that you tumble off of anything denotes that you are given to carelessness; you should strive to be prompt in your affairs. To see others tumbling is a sign that you will profit from the negligence of others.

## TUMOR

To dream of a tumor foretells good health and new and interesting responsibilities that you will embrace.

## TUNNEL

To dream of going through a tunnel is bad for those in business and in love. To see a train coming toward you while you're in a tunnel foretells ill health and change in occupation. To pass through a tunnel in a car denotes unsatisfactory business and much unpleasant and expensive travel.

To see a tunnel caving in portends failure and enemies. To look into a tunnel indicates that you will soon be compelled to face a desperate issue.

## TURBAN

To dream of a turban means something is being hidden from you that you will need to investigate. It has to do with your social status.

## TURF

To dream of a racing turf reveals that you have pleasure and wealth at your command, but your morals may be questioned by your most intimate friends. A green turf indicates that interesting affairs will hold your attention.

### TURKEY

To dream of seeing turkeys signifies abundant gain in business. To see them dressed for the market denotes improvement in your affairs. To see them sick or dead predicts that stringent circumstances will cause your pride to suffer.

To dream of eating turkey foretells a joyful occasion approaching.

If you dream of turkeys flying, expect a rapid transition from obscurity to prominence. To shoot them as game is a sign that you will amass wealth unscrupulously.

### TURKISH BATH

To dream of being in a Turkish bath foretells that you will seek health far from your home and friends, but you will have much pleasurable enjoyment. To see others at a Turkish bath signifies that pleasant companions will occupy your attention.

### TURNIP

To see turnips growing indicates that your prospects will brighten, and that you will be much elated over your success. To eat them is a sign of ill health. To pull them up from the ground predicts that you will improve your opportunities and your fortune thereby.

Eating turnip greens is a sign of bitter disappointment. Turnip seed predicts future advancement.

### TURPENTINE

To dream of turpentine foretells unprofitable and discouraging engagements in the near future.

### TURQUOISE

To dream of turquoise suggests that you will realize a desire that will greatly please you.

### TURTLE

To dream of seeing turtles signifies that an unusual incident will cause you enjoyment and will improve your business. To eat turtle soup says that you will find pleasure in situations of intrigue.

### TUTOR

To dream that you are a tutor means you will soon learn something new. If you dream that you are taught by a tutor, you will be teaching someone something new.

### TWEEZERS

To see tweezers in a dream augurs uncomfortable situations that fill you with discontent. Your companions may abuse you.

### TWILIGHT

To dream of the twilight suggests that some romantic difficulties are on the horizon—but they will only be annoying, not devastating.

### TWINE*

To see twine in your dream warns you that your business is assuming complications that will be hard to overcome.

*See Thread.

### TWINS

To dream of seeing twins foretells security in business and faithful and loving contentment in the home. If the twins are sickly, you will have disappointment and grief.

### TYPE

To see type in a dream portends unpleasant transactions with friends.

### TYPEWRITER

To dream of a typewriter means a step forward in your career. But if you have problems with the device, you may need to overcome certain obstacles to advance your career.

### TYPHOID FEVER

To dream that you are affected with this disease warns you to beware of enemies and look well to your health. An epidemic of typhoid fever augurs depressions in business; good health will undergo disagreeable changes.

## UDDER

To dream of an udder foretells pleasant news.

## UFO

Dreaming of a UFO suggests that profound spiritual change is coming.

## UGLINESS

To dream that you are ugly denotes that you will have a difficulty with your sweetheart, and your prospects will suffer.

## UKULELE

To dream of a ukulele predicts happy news.

## ULCER

To see an ulcer in a dream signifies loss of friends and distance from loved ones. Affairs will remain unsatisfactory.

To dream that you have ulcers denotes that you will become unpopular with your friends by giving yourself up to foolish pleasures.

## ULTRASOUND

This foretells a health problem that will be easily solved.

## ULTRAVIOLET

To dream of ultraviolet light suggests that you will see things with much more clarity than you have before in your business and personal life.

## UMBILICAL CORD

Unless you are pregnant already, this dream foretells a pregnancy or birth announcement.

## UMBRELLA*

To dream of carrying an umbrella indicates that trouble and annoyances will beset you.

If you see others carrying them, you may receive an appeal for charity.

If you borrow one, you will have a misunderstanding, perhaps with a close friend. To lend one portends injury from false friends. To lose one denotes trouble with someone who holds your confidence.

If you see one torn to pieces or broken, you will be misrepresented and maligned. Carrying a leaky one denotes that you will be in pain and feel displeasure toward your sweetheart or companions.

To carry a new umbrella over you in a clear shower, or in sunshine, heralds exquisite pleasure and prosperity.

*See *Parasol*.

### UMPIRE

If you dream of disagreeing with an umpire, you may soon need to rethink an idea for a project in order for it to reach completion.

### UNCLE

To see your uncle in a dream portends sad news.

### UNCONSCIOUSNESS

To dream you are unconscious warns you to get a health checkup, just in case you might have some health issues that have gone undetected. To dream of someone else being unconscious suggests bad health.

### UNDERGROUND

If you dream of being in an underground habitation, you are in danger of losing reputation and fortune.

To dream of riding on an underground railway foretells that you will engage in a peculiar speculation that will contribute to your distress and anxiety.

### UNDERLINING

Dreaming of anything underlined cautions you to pay special attention to your finances right now.

### UNDERPASS

If you dream of an underpass, you may encounter an obstacle in your personal life that causes you pain, but you will be able to overcome it.

### UNDERSTUDY

To dream you are an understudy for someone else implies honor and recognition. If you dream that someone is your understudy, you are being easily led and need to be careful.

## UNDERTAKER

Dreaming of an undertaker foretells news of a wedding or birth.

## UNDERTOW

To dream of being caught in an undertow means you will soon be a comfort to someone who is grieving.

## UNDERWEAR

To dream of clean underwear predicts good news. If the underwear is dirty, financial gain is indicated.

## UNDRESSING

To dream that you are undressing suggests that scandalous gossip will overshadow you.

To see others undressed is an omen of stolen pleasures, which will rebound with grief.

## UNFAITHFULNESS

To dream of being unfaithful suggests that you will be tempted to do something that goes against your character; be prudent. If someone is being unfaithful to you, your friends and family will rally behind you.

## UNFORTUNATE CIRCUMSTANCE

To dream that you are unfortunate is significant of loss to yourself and trouble for others.

## UNHAPPINESS

The greater the unhappiness in your dream, the greater the joy that will be coming.

## UNICORN

A dream of this mythical creature betokens a period of beneficial change.

## UNIFORM

To see a uniform in your dream denotes that you will have influential friends to aid you in obtaining your desires.

To see people arrayed in strange uniforms foretells the disruption of friendly relations with another power by your own government. To see a friend or relative looking sad while dressed in uniform, or as a soldier, predicts ill fortune or continued absence.

## UNION

To dream of a labor union means you soon will have business associates who will prove beneficial to you.

## UNIVERSITY

To dream of this place of higher learning is a good omen of success and financial well-being.

## UNKNOWN*

To dream of meeting unknown people foretells change for good, or for bad, depending on whether or not the person is good looking.

To feel that you are unknown denotes that strange things will cast a shadow of ill luck over you.

*See Mystery.

## UNTYING

To dream of untying something predicts success in a venture that you have undertaken.

## UPSIDE-DOWN

To dream you are upside-down tells you that life is actually going smoothly; there will be no ups and downs unless you bring them on yourself.

## URGENCY

To dream that you are being insistent about the urgency of something signifies that you will soon have the ability to slow your life down and make good progress.

## URINAL

To dream of a urinal suggests that disorder will predominate in your home.

## URINE

To dream of seeing urine denotes the release of tension and worries in your life.

## URN

To dream of an urn foretells that you will prosper in some respects, and in others disfavor will be apparent. If you see broken urns, unhappiness will confront you.

## USHER

To dream of an usher implies that good social contacts will prove beneficial to you financially.

## USURPER

To dream that you are a usurper foretells that you will have trouble in establishing a good title to property.

If others are trying to usurp your rights, there will be a struggle between you and your competitors, but you will eventually win. If a young woman has this dream, she will be a party to a spicy rivalry in which she will win.

## UTERUS

To dream of a uterus portends an engagement or pregnancy.

## VACANCY

To dream that you are in a building or apartment that is vacant suggests a new beginning in your life.

## VACATION

To dream of being on vacation predicts unexpected gain or a gift.

## VACCINATION

To dream of being vaccinated speaks of your susceptibility to those around you.

To see others vaccinated shows that you will fail to find contentment where it is sought, and that your affairs will suffer decline in consequence.

## VACUUM CLEANER

To dream of this cleaning appliance augurs success in a love affair. But if the vacuum cleaner is broken, there will be trouble.

## VAGINA

To dream of a healthy vagina means pregnancy and good health. But if it is diseased, it is a warning that your love relationships may be unhealthy or dysfunctional, and possibly abusive.

## VAGRANCY

To dream that you are a vagrant portends poverty and misery. To see vagrants is a sign of contagion invading your community. To give to a vagrant denotes that your generosity will be applauded.

## VALEDICTORIAN

To dream of being a valedictorian means you will be overlooked for a promotion or career advancement.

## VALENTINE

To dream that you are sending valentines foretells that you will lose opportunities to enrich yourself.

## VALET

To dream of having a valet suggests social or community recognition. To dream of being one implies a possible job loss.

## VALLEY

To dream of walking through green and pleasant valleys foretells great improvements in business; lovers will be happy and congenial. If the valley is barren, the reverse is predicted. If marshy, illness or vexations may follow.

## VAMPIRE

To dream of vampires warns that you need to be more serious and responsible.

## VAN

To dream of a van foretells good news.

## VANILLA

To dream of this flavoring means that a social invitation will be arriving shortly.

## VARNISHING

To dream of varnishing anything denotes that you will seek to win distinction by fraudulent means. To see others varnishing foretells that you are threatened with danger from the effort of friends to add to their own possessions.

## VASE

To dream of a vase suggests that you will enjoy the sweetest pleasure and contentment in your home life. If you drink from a vase, you will soon thrill with the delights of stolen love. To see a broken vase foretells sorrow. For a young woman to receive a vase signifies that she will soon obtain her dearest wish.

## VASECTOMY

Unless you have already had a vasectomy, this dream foretells a pregnancy or birth.

## VAT

To see a vat in your dreams foretells anguish and suffering at the hands of cruel people whose clutches you have unwittingly fallen into.

## VATICAN

To dream of the Vatican signifies that unexpected honor will fall within your grasp. You will make the acquaintance of distinguished people if you see royal personages speaking to the pope.

## VAULT

To dream of a vault denotes bereavement and other sorrow.. To see a vault for valuables signifies that your fortune will surprise many, as your circumstances will appear to be meager. To see the doors of a vault open implies loss and treachery of people whom you trust.

## VCR

To dream of a VCR foretells a pleasant reunion with an old friend.

## VEAL

To dream of eating veal betokens good luck.

## VEGETABLE

To dream of eating vegetables is an omen of strange luck. You will think for a time that you are tremendously successful, but will find to your sorrow that you have been grossly imposed upon. Withered or decayed vegetables bring unmitigated woe and sadness.

## VEGETARIANISM

If you dream that you are a vegetarian, and you aren't in your waking life, you will experience a health issue.

## VEHICLE

To ride in a vehicle while dreaming threatens loss or illness. To be thrown from one foretells hasty and unpleasant news. To see a broken-down vehicle signals failure in important affairs. If you buy a vehicle, you will reinstate yourself in your former position. Selling a vehicle in your dream denotes an unfavorable change in affairs.

## VEIL

To dream that you wear a veil suggests that you will not be perfectly sincere with your lover and you will be forced to use stratagems to retain him or her. If you see others wearing veils, you will be maligned and defamed by people you thought were your friends. An old or torn veil warns you that a web of deceit is being thrown around you with sinister design.

To dream of seeing a bridal veil foretells that you will make a successful change in the immediate future, with much happiness accruing to your position. For a young woman to dream that she wears a bridal veil indicates that she will engage in an affair that will afford her lasting profit and enjoyment. If it gets loose, or any accident befalls it, she will be burdened with sadness and pain.

To throw a veil aside indicates separation or disgrace.

To see mourning veils in your dreams signifies distress and trouble, and embarrassment in business.

### VEIN

To see your veins in a dream ensures you against slander, if they are normal. To see them bleeding denotes that you will have a great sorrow from which there will be no escape. If you see them swollen, you will rise hastily to distinction and places of trust.

### VELCRO™

To dream of Velcro suggests that your relationships are steadfast and loyal.

### VELVET

To dream of velvet portends very successful enterprises. If you wear velvet, some distinction will be conferred upon you.

To see old velvet means your prosperity will suffer from your extreme pride. If a young woman dreams that she is clothed in velvet garments, she will have honors bestowed upon her, and the choice among several wealthy lovers.

### VENEER

To dream that you are veneering indicates that you will systematically deceive your friends; your actions will be of a misleading nature.

### VENEREAL DISEASE

To dream that you have a venereal disease cautions you to watch your health.

### VENISON

To dream of venison suggests social embarrassment.

### VENTRILOQUIST

If you dream of a ventriloquist, an affair is going to prove detrimental. If you think yourself one, you will not conduct yourself honorably toward people who trust you.

## VERANDA

To dream of being on a veranda predicts your success in an affair that is giving you anxiety.

An old veranda denotes the decline of hopes, and disappointment in business and love.

## VERMIN

Vermin crawling in your dreams signify sickness and much trouble. If you succeed in ridding yourself of them, you will be fairly successful, but if not, death may come to you or your relatives.

## VERTIGO

To dream that you have vertigo foretells the loss of domestic happiness; your affairs will suffer a gloomy outlook.

## VESSEL (SHIP)*

To dream of vessels denotes labor and activity.

*See Ship.

## VEXATION

If you are vexed in your dreams, you will find many worries asssail you when you first arise. If you think some person is vexed with you, it is a sign that you will not soon reconcile a slight misunderstanding.

## VIAGRA™

A dream featuring this drug cautions you against having too much pride.

## VICE

To dream that you are favoring any vice signifies that you are about to endanger your reputation by letting evil entice you. If you see others indulging in vice, ill fortune will engulf the interest of a relative or associate.

## VICTIMIZATION

To dream that you are the victim of any scheme foretells that you will be oppressed and overpowered by your enemies. Your family relations will also be strained.

To victimize others denotes that you will amass wealth dishonorably and will prefer illicit relations, to the sorrow of your companions.

## VICTORY

To dream that you win a victory indicates that you will successfully resist the attacks of enemies.

## VIDEO

To dream of a video warns you that there may be too much illusion in your love life; you need to see things more clearly.

## VILLAGE

To dream that you are in a village indicates that you will enjoy good health and find yourself comfortably provided for. To revisit the village home of your youth augurs pleasant surprises and favorable news from absent friends. If the village looks dilapidated, though, or the dream itself is indistinct, trouble and sadness will soon come to you.

## VINE

To dream of vines is propitious of success and happiness. Good health is in store for those who see flowering vines.

If the vines are dead, you will fail in a momentous enterprise. To see poisonous vines foretells that you will be the victim of a scheme that will impair your health.

## VINEGAR

Any dream of vinegar involves inharmonious and unfavorable aspects. To dream of drinking vinegar indicates that you will be exasperated and worried into assenting to something that fills you with evil foreboding. To use vinegar on vegetables foretells a deepening of already distressing affairs.

## VINEYARD

To dream of a vineyard suggests favorable speculations. To visit a poorly kept vineyard filled with bad odors tells you that disappointment will overshadow the events you most look forward to.

## VIOLENCE

To dream that any person does you violence implies that you will be overcome by enemies. If you do other people violence, you will lose fortune and favor by a reprehensible way of conducting your affairs.

## VIOLET

To see or gather violets in your dream heralds joyous occasions in which you will find favor with some superior. To see violets dry or withered denotes that love will be spurned and thrown aside.

## VIOLIN

To see or hear a violin in your dreams foretells harmony and peace in the family; financial affairs will cause no apprehension. If you attempt to play a violin and are unsuccessful, you will lose favor and aspire to things you can never possess. A broken violin indicates sad bereavement and separation.

## VIPER

To dream of a viper warns that calamities are threatening you. If you dream that a many-hued viper—one capable of throwing itself into many pieces, or disjointing itself—attacks you, your enemies are bent on your ruin and will work together, discreetly, to displace you.

## VIRGIN

To dream of a virgin foretells comparative luck in your speculations.

## VISITING

If you visit in your dreams, you will soon enjoy a pleasant occasion. If your visit is unpleasant, your happiness will be marred by the actions of malicious people.

For a friend to visit you predicts news of a favorable nature. If the friend appears sad and travel-weary, there will be a note of displeasure growing out of the visit, or other slight disappointments may follow. If he or she is dressed in black or white and looks pale or ghastly, serious illness or accidents are predicted.

## VODKA

To dream of being drunk on vodka is a warning against thievery.

## VOICES

To dream of hearing calm and pleasing voices denotes pleasant reconciliations; high-pitched and angry voices signify disappointments and unfavorable situations.

To hear weeping voices shows that sudden anger will cause you to inflict injury on a friend.

If you hear the voice of God, you will make a noble effort to rise higher in unselfish and honorable principles, and will justly hold the admiration of high-minded people.

Hearing the voice of distress, or a warning voice calling to you, implies your own serious misfortune or that of someone close to you. If you recognize the voice, it often portends accident, illness, death, or loss.

If you hear your name called in a dream by strange voices, your business may fall into a precarious state. Strangers may lend you assistance, or you might fail to meet your obligations.

To hear the voice of a friend or relative suggests the desperate illness of one of them and may involve death; in the latter case you may be called upon to stand as guardian over someone.

Lovers hearing the voice of their beloved should heed the warning. If they have been negligent, they should make amends. Otherwise, they may suffer separation from misunderstanding.

To hear the voice of the dead may be a warning of your own serious illness or of business worries due to bad judgment.

### VOLCANO

To see a volcano in your dreams predicts violent disputes that threaten your reputation as a fair-dealing and honest citizen.

### VOLLEYBALL

To dream of playing this game or watching it played represents good health and emotional well-being.

### VOLUNTEERING

To dream of volunteering to do anything augurs a promotion at work.

### VOMITING

To dream of vomiting is a sign that you will be afflicted with a malady that threatens invalidism, or that you will be connected with a racy scandal.

If you see others vomiting, you will be made aware of the false pretenses of people trying to engage your aid. For a woman to dream that she vomits a chicken, and it hops off, predicts that she will be disappointed in a pleasure by the illness of a relative. Unfavorable business and discontent are also predicted.

If it is blood you vomit, you will find illness a sudden and unexpected visitor in your life. You will be cast down with gloomy forebodings, and children and domesticity in general will cause you discomfort.

### VOODOO

To dream of voodoo is a warning against letting undesirable associates lead you astray.

### VOTING

If you dream of casting a vote on any measure, you will be engulfed in a commotion affecting your community.

To vote fraudulently foretells that your dishonesty will overcome your better inclinations.

## VOUCHER

To dream of vouchers foretells that diligent effort will overcome the attempt to wrest fortune from you. If you sign a voucher, you have the aid and confidence of those around you, despite the evil workings of enemies. To lose a voucher implies that you must struggle with relatives in order to maintain your rights.

## VOW

To dream that you are making or listening to vows predicts that complaints may be made against you of unfaithfulness, in business or in some love contract. To take the vows of a church indicates you will bear yourself with unswerving integrity through a difficulty. To break or ignore a vow portends that disastrous consequences will attend your dealings.

## VOYAGE

To make a voyage in your dreams foretells that you will receive money besides that which your labors win for you. A disastrous voyage implies incompetence and false loves.

## VULTURE

To dream of vultures signifies that some scheming person is bent on injuring you, and you will not prevail unless you see the vulture wounded or dead.

## WADDING

To wad something in a dream brings consolation to the sorrowing, and indifference to unfriendly criticism.

## WADING

If you wade in clear water while dreaming, you will partake of evanescent but exquisite joys. If the water is muddy, you are in danger of illness or some sorrowful experiences.

## WAFER

Wafers, if seen in a dream, predict an encounter with enemies. To eat one suggests impoverishment.

## WAFFLE

To dream of this breakfast food suggests an increase in financial and social activity.

## WAGER

To dream of making a wager signifies that you will resort to dishonest means to forward your schemes.

If you lose a wager, you will be hurt by someone you know. To win one reinstates you in favor with fortune. If you are not able to put up a wager, you will be discouraged and humiliated by adversity.

## WAGES

Wages, if received in dreams, bring unlooked-for good to those engaging in new enterprises.

To pay out wages indicates that you will be confounded by dissatisfaction.

To have your wages reduced warns you that unfriendly interest is being taken in you. An increase of wages suggests unusual profit in any undertaking.

## WAGGING

To dream of something wagging implies laughter and good times.

## WAGON

To dream of a wagon denotes that you will be unhappily mated, and many troubles will prematurely age you.

To dream of driving one down a hill is ominous of proceedings that will fill you with disquiet and will cause you loss. To drive one uphill improves your worldly affairs.

To drive a heavily loaded wagon denotes that duty will hold you in a moral position, despite your efforts to throw it off. To drive into muddy water is a gruesome prognostication, bringing you into a vortex of unhappiness and fearful foreboding.

To see a covered wagon foretells that you will be surrounded by mysterious treachery, which will retard your advancement. A broken wagon represents distress and failure.

## WAIF

To dream of a waif denotes personal difficulties and special ill luck in business.

## WAILING*

A wail falling upon your ear while in the midst of a dream brings fearful news of disaster and woe.

*See *Weeping*.

## WAIST

To dream of a round, full waist denotes that you will be favored by an agreeable dispensation of fortune. A small, unnatural waist foretells failure and recriminations.

## WAITER

To dream of a waiter signifies you will be pleasantly entertained by a friend. To see one cross or disorderly portends that offensive people will thrust themselves upon your hospitality.

## WAITING LIST

To dream of a waiting list means an upcoming project will run more smoothly and quickly than you anticipated.

## WAKE

To dream that you attend a wake suggests that you will sacrifice an important engagement to enjoy an ill-favored assignation.

## WALKING*

To dream of walking through rough briar-entangled paths indicates that you will be much distressed over your business complications, and disagreeable misunderstandings will produce coldness and indifference.

If you walk in pleasant places, you will be the possessor of fortune and favor.

To walk in the night brings misadventure and unavailing struggle for contentment.

*See *Wading.*

## WALKING STICK, CANE

To see a walking stick in a dream foretells that you will enter into contracts without proper deliberation and will consequently suffer reverses. If you use a stick in walking, you will be dependent on the advice of others.

If you admire handsome canes, you will entrust your interests to others, and they will be faithful.

## WALLET

To see wallets in a dream signifies that pleasant burdens will await your decision to assume them.

An old or soiled wallet implies unfavorable results from your labor.

## WALLPAPER

To dream of wallpaper warns that someone is covering a truth up and lying to you.

## WALLS

To dream that a wall is obstructing your progress suggests important victories in your affairs. If you jump over it, you will overcome obstacles and win your desires.

If you force a breach in a wall, you will succeed in the attainment of your wishes through sheer tenacity of purpose. If you demolish it, you will overthrow your enemies.

To build a wall foretells that you will carefully lay plans and solidify your fortune to prevent failure and to keep away designing enemies.

## WALNUT

To dream of walnuts is an omen of prolific joy and favor. To dream that you crack a decayed walnut indicates that your expectations will end in bitterness and heartbreaking failure.

## WALTZING

To see the waltz danced in your dream foretells pleasant relations with a cheerful and adventurous person.

## WAND

To dream of a wand suggests that you will be learning to appreciate the important things in life.

## WANTING

To dream that you are in want suggests that you have unfortunately ignored the realities of life and chased folly to her stronghold of sorrow and adversity. If you find yourself contented in a state of want, you will heroically bear the misfortune that threatens and will see the clouds of misery disperse.

To relieve want signifies that you will be esteemed for your disinterested kindness but will feel no pleasure in doing good.

## WAR

To dream of war foretells unfortunate conditions in business, and much disorder and strife in domestic affairs.

For a young woman to dream that her lover goes to war indicates that she will hear of something detrimental to her lover's character. To dream that your country is defeated in war is a sign that it will suffer revolution of a business and political nature. Personal interest will sustain a blow either way.

If you dream of victory in war, there will be brisk activity along business lines, and domesticity will be harmonious.

## WARDROBE

To dream of your wardrobe indicates that your fortune will be endangered by your attempts to appear richer than you are. If you imagine that you have a scant wardrobe, you will seek association with strangers.

## WAREHOUSE

To dream of a warehouse denotes a successful enterprise. If it is empty, you may be cheated and foiled in some plan to which you have devoted much thought and maneuvering.

## WARLOCK

To dream of this male witch warns that negativity is surrounding you from someone you thought you could trust.

## WARRANT

To dream that a warrant is being served to you indicates that you will engage in important work that will give great uneasiness regarding its outcome and profitability.

If you see a warrant served to someone else, your actions may bring you into fatal quarrels or misunderstandings. You are likely to be justly indignant at the wantonness of a friend.

## WARTS

If you are troubled with warts on your person in your dreams, you will be unable to successfully parry the thrusts made at your honor. To see warts leaving your hands foretells that you will overcome disagreeable obstructions to fortune. To see warts on others shows that you have bitter enemies near you. If you doctor your warts, you will struggle hard to ward off threatened danger to you and yours.

## WASHBOWL

To dream of a washbowl signifies that you will find new interests that afford much enjoyment to others.

To bathe your face and hands in a bowl of clear water predicts that you will soon consummate a romance that will bind you closely to someone who interested you before passion enveloped you.

If the bowl is soiled or broken, you will rue an illicit engagement that gives others pain and affords you small pleasure.

## WASHING*

To dream of washing something warns you to mind your own business. If you heed this warning, your relationships will be pleasant.

To dream that you are washing yourself signifies that you pride yourself on the numberless liaisons you maintain.

*See Bathing, Washbowl.

## WASP

Wasps, if seen in dreams, suggest that enemies will scourge and spitefully vilify you.

If a wasp stings you, you will feel the effect of envy and hatred. If you kill wasps, you will be able to throttle your enemies and fearlessly maintain your rights.

## WASTE, WASTING

To dream of wandering through waste foreshadows doubt and failure where the promise of success was once bright before you.

To dream of wasting your fortune indicates that you will be unpleasantly encumbered with domestic cares.

## WATCH

To dream of a watch suggests that you will be prosperous in well-directed speculations. If you look at the time on a watch, your efforts will be defeated by rivalry. If you break a watch, distress and loss will menace you.

To drop a watch crystal foretells carelessness or very unpleasant companionship.

If you dream of stealing a watch, a violent enemy may attack your reputation. To make a present of one speaks of the pursuit of undignified recreation.

## WATER*

To dream of clear water foretells that you will joyfully realize prosperity and pleasure. If the water is muddy, you will be in danger, and gloom will occupy pleasure's seat.

If you see water from a flood rise up in your house, you will struggle to resist evil; but unless you see it subside, you will succumb to dangerous influences.

If you find yourself bailing it out, but with feet growing wet, then trouble, sickness, and misery will cause you grief, but you will forestall them by your watchfulness. The same interpretation may be applied to muddy water rising in vessels.

To fall into muddy water is a sign that you will make many bitter mistakes and will suffer poignant grief therefrom. To drink muddy water portends sickness, but if what you drink is clear and refreshing, that brings the favorable consummation of fair hopes.

To sport with water predicts a sudden awakening to love and passion. To have it sprayed on your head suggests that your passionate awakening to love will be mutual.

*See *Flood, Pond, Puddle.*

## WATER CARRIER

If you see water carriers passing in your dreams, your prospects will be favorable in fortune, and love will prove no laggard in your chase for pleasure. If you dream that you are a water carrier, you will rise above your present position.

## WATERFALL

Dreaming of a waterfall predicts that you will secure your wildest desire, and fortune will be exceedingly favorable to your progress.

## WATER LILY

To dream of water lilies, or to see them growing, foretells prosperity after sorrow.

## WATERMELON

To dream of this fruit on the vine warns you against a casual love affair that may be harmful. In any other form, it denotes unexpected travel.

## WAVE*

To dream of waves means turmoil if they are muddy or rough. Clear waves indicate something coming to you that is good.

*See *Ocean, Sea.*

## WAX TAPER

To dream of lighting wax tapers denotes that some pleasing occurrence will bring you into contact with friends long absent. To blow out the candles signals disappointing times; sickness will forestall expected opportunities to meet distinguished friends.

## WEALTH

To dream that you are possessed of much wealth signifies that you will energetically charge yourself to meet the problems of life with the force that compels success. To see others wealthy speaks of friends who will come to your rescue in perilous times.

## WEAPON

To dream of using a weapon against another person means you will soon need to watch your back with your friends. To have someone use a weapon on you predicts a new friendship.

## WEASEL

To see a weasel in your dreams bent on a marauding expedition warns you to beware of the friendships of former enemies, as they will devour you once your guard is down. If you destroy a weasel in your dream, you will succeed in foiling deep schemes laid for your defeat.

## WEATHER

To dream of the weather foretells fluctuations in your fortune. Now you progress immensely, only to be suddenly confronted with doubts and rumblings of failure.

If you dream of reading the reports of a weather bureau, you will change your place of abode after much weary deliberation, but the change will benefit you.

## WEATHER VANE

In dreams, a weather vane symbolizes good luck and happiness.

## WEAVING

To dream that you are weaving signifies that you will baffle any attempt to defeat you in the struggle to build an honorable fortune.

If you see others weaving, you will be surrounded by good health and energy.

## WEB (SPIDER)

To dream of webs warns you that deceitful friends will cause you loss and displeasure. If the web is inelastic, you will remain firm in withstanding the attacks of those envious people who are seeking to obtain favors from you.

## WEDDING*

To attend a wedding in your dream foretells an occasion that will cause you bitterness and delayed success.

*See *Bride, Marriage.*

## WEDDING CLOTHES

To dream of wedding clothes signifies that you will participate in pleasing works and will meet new friends. To see them soiled or in disorder reveals that you will lose close relations with some much-admired person.

## WEDDING RING

To dream that a wedding ring is bright and shiny suggests that you will be shielded from cares and infidelity.

If it should be lost or broken, much sadness will come into your life through a death.

To see a wedding ring on the hand of a friend, or some other person, denotes loyalty among friends.

## WEDGE

To dream of a wedge indicates that you will have trouble in some business arrangements, which will be the cause of separation from relatives.

## WEDLOCK

To dream that you are in the bonds of an unwelcome wedlock predicts that you will be unfortunately implicated in a disagreeable affair.

## WEEDING

To dream that you are weeding suggests difficulty in proceeding with some work that will bring you distinction. If you see others weeding, you should be fearful that enemies will upset your plans.

## WEEDS

To dream of weeds warns against dishonest and dishonorable friendships.

## WEEPING*

Weeping in a dream foretells ill tidings and disturbances in your family. To see others weeping signals pleasant reunions after periods of sadness and estrangement.

*See Wailing.

## WEEVIL

To dream of weevils portends loss in trade and falseness in love.

## WEIGHING

To dream of weighing yourself indicates that you are approaching a prosperous period. If you set yourself determinedly toward success, you will victoriously reap the full fruition of your labors.

Should you dream of weighing others, you will be able to subordinate their wishes to your interest.

## WELCOMING

To dream that you receive a warm welcome in society suggests that you will become distinguished among your acquaintances and will have deference shown you by strangers. Your fortune will approximate what you had hoped it would become. To accord others welcome reveals that your congeniality and warm nature will be your passport into pleasure.

## WELL

To dream that you are stuck in a well suggests that you will succumb to adversity through your misapplied energies. You will let strange elements direct your course.

To fall into a well signifies that overwhelming despair will possess you. For a well to cave in promises that enemies' schemes will overthrow your own. If you see an empty well, you will be robbed of a fortune if you allow strangers to share your confidence. To see a well with a pump in it shows that you will have opportunities to advance your prospects.

If you dream of an artesian well, your splendid resources will gain you admittance into the realms of knowledge and pleasure. Drawing water from a well augurs the fulfillment of ardent desires; but if the water is impure, there will be unpleasantness.

## WELT

To see welts on your body or on someone else's predicts a pleasant love affair.

## WETNESS

To dream that you are wet indicates that a pleasure may involve you in loss and disease. You are warned to avoid the blandishments of seemingly well-meaning people.

## WET NURSE

To dream that you are a wet nurse portends that you will be widowed or have the care of the aged or of little children.

## WHALE

To dream of seeing a whale approaching a ship indicates that you will struggle between duties and will be threatened with loss of property. If the whale is killed, you will happily decide between right and inclination, and will encounter pleasing successes. If you see a whale overturn a ship, you will be thrown into a whirlpool of disaster.

## WHALEBONE

To see or work with whalebone in your dreams foretells an alliance that will afford you solid benefit.

## WHEAT

To see large fields of growing wheat in your dreams augurs encouraging prospects. If the wheat is ripe, your fortune will be assured and love will be your joyous companion.

To see large, clear grains of wheat running through a thresher signifies that prosperity has opened her portals to the fullest for you. If you see wheat in sacks or barrels, your determination to reach the apex of success is soon to be crowned with victory, and your love matters will be firmly grounded.

To dream of a granary that is not well covered, with its contents exposed to rain, suggests that while you have amassed a fortune, you have not secured your rights; you will see your interests diminishing at the hands of enemies. If you rub wheat into your hand and eat it, you will labor hard for success and will obtain what is yours and will protect your rights.

To dream that you climb a steep hill covered with wheat, pulling yourself up by the stalks, implies that you will enjoy great prosperity and thus be able to distinguish yourself in any chosen pursuit.

### WHEELBARROW

To dream of pushing a wheelbarrow predicts exciting new friendships. An empty wheelbarrow indicates sad news, however; one upside-down suggests added responsibilities that will prove gratifying.

### WHEELCHAIR

If you dream of being in a wheelchair—and you are not confined to one in waking life—an accident may loom. To see someone else in a wheelchair indicates unexpected news, but it might not be good.

### WHEELS

To see swiftly rotating wheels in your dreams indicates that you will be thrifty and enterprising in your business, and will be successful in pursuits of domestic bliss.

To see idle or broken wheels proclaims the death or absence of someone in your household.

### WHETSTONE

To dream of a whetstone foretells sharp worries; pay close attention to your affairs if you hope to avoid difficulties. You are likely to be forced into an uncomfortable journey.

### WHIP

To dream of a whip signifies dissension and unfortunate friendships.

## WHIRLPOOL

To dream of a whirlpool portends imminent danger in your business. Unless you are extremely careful, your reputation will be seriously blackened by a disgraceful intrigue.

## WHIRLWIND

To dream that you are in the path of a whirlwind suggests that you are confronting a change that threatens to overwhelm you with loss and calamity.

## WHISKEY

Whiskey is not fraught with much good. Disappointment in some form is likely to appear following such dreams. To dream of seeing and drinking whiskey suggests reaching a desired object after many disappointments. If you only see it, however, you will never obtain the result you hoped and worked for. And to dream of drinking it alone foretells that you will sacrifice your friends for your selfishness.

If you dream of whiskey in bottles, you will likely be careful of your interests, protecting them with energy and watchfulness, thereby adding to their value.

If you dream of destroying whiskey, you may lose your friends through your ungenerous conduct.

## WHISPERING

To dream of whispering indicates that you will be disturbed by the gossiping of people near you.

If you hear a whisper coming to you as advice or a warning, you stand in need of aid and counsel.

## WHISTLING

To hear a whistle in your dream forecasts that you will be shocked by some sad news, which will change plans for innocent pleasure. To dream that you are whistling foretells a merry occasion in which you expect to figure prominently. This dream for a young woman indicates indiscreet conduct and failure to get what she wishes for.

## WHITE

In dreams, anything that is notably white represents good luck and purity.

## WHITE LEAD

To dream of white lead suggests that relatives or children are in danger because of your carelessness.

## WHITE MOTH

To dream of a white moth foretells unavoidable sickness, although you will be tempted to accuse yourself or another of some wrongdoing that you are sure has caused the complaint.

## WHITEWASHING

If you dream that you are whitewashing, you may seek to reinstate yourself with friends by ridding yourself of offensive habits and companions.

## WIDOW

To dream that you are a widow indicates that you will have many troubles through malicious people. If a man dreams that he marries a widow, he may see some cherished undertaking crumble in disappointment.

## WIFE

For a man to dream of his wife denotes unsettled affairs and discord in the home. If his wife is unusually affable, he may receive profit from some important venture in trade.

## WIG

To dream that you wear a wig indicates that you will soon make an unpropitious change. If you lose a wig, you will incur the derision and contempt of enemies. To see others wearing wigs is a sign of treachery entangling you.

## WILDLIFE

To dream of wildlife implies peace of mind and a comfortable life.

## WILD LIVING

To dream that you are running about wild foretells a serious fall or accident. To see others doing so suggests that unfavorable prospects will cause you worry and vexation.

## WILL

To dream that you are making your will foretells momentous trials and tribulations. If you dream that a will is against your interests, you may have disputes and disorderly proceedings to combat in some event soon to transpire. If you fail to prove a will's validity, you are in danger of libelous slander.

To lose one is unfortunate for your business. To destroy one warns you that you are about to be a party to treachery and deceit.

## WILLOW

To dream of willows suggests that you will soon make a sad journey, but you will be consoled in your grief by faithful friends.

## WIND

To dream of the wind blowing softly on you signifies that great fortune will come to you through the death of someone dear to you. If you hear the wind sighing, you will wander in estrangement from one whose life is empty without you.

To walk briskly against a strong wind signifies that you courageously resist temptation and pursue fortune with a determination not easily put aside. For the wind to blow you along against your wishes portends failure in business undertakings and disappointments in love. If the wind blows you in the direction you wish to go, you will find unexpected and helpful allies or you will realize that you hold natural advantages over a rival.

## WINDMILL

To see a windmill operating in your dreams foretells abundant fortune and great contentment. To see a broken or idle windmill signifies adversity coming upon you unaware.

## WINDOW

To see windows in your dreams is an augury of the unhappy culmination of what were bright hopes. You will see your fairest wish go down in despair. Fruitless endeavors will be your portion.

To see closed windows is a representation of desertion. If they are broken, you will be hounded by miserable suspicions of disloyalty from those you love.

To sit in a window indicates that you will be the victim of folly. To enter a house through a window warns that you will be found out while using dishonorable means for a seemingly honorable purpose. To escape by one indicates that you will fall into a trouble whose toils will hold you unmercifully close.

If you look through a window as you pass and strange objects appear, you will fail in your chosen avocation and lose the respect for which you risked health and contentment.

## WINDPIPE

To dream that something is stuck in your windpipe, or someone else's, cautions you to watch your finances.

## WINDSURFING

To dream of this sport portends social affairs that will prove good for finances.

## WINE

To dream of drinking wine betokens joy and friendship. To dream of breaking bottles of wine foretells that your love and passion will border on excess.

To see barrels of wine prognosticates great luxury. To pour wine from one vessel into another signifies that your enjoyments will be varied and that you will journey to many notable places. To dream of dealing in wine denotes that your occupation will be remunerative.

## WINE CELLAR

To dream of a wine cellar suggests that superior amusements or pleasure will come your way, to be enjoyed at your bidding.

## WINEGLASS

To dream of a wineglass indicates that a disappointment will affect you seriously, as you will fail to see any hint of trouble until you are shocked into it.

## WINGS

To dream that you have wings signifies that you will experience grave fears for the safety of someone on a long journey away from you.

To see the wings of birds denotes that you will finally overcome adversity and rise to positions of wealth and honor.

## WINKING

Dreaming of someone winking at you warns you to watch your reputation.

## WINTER

To dream of winter is a prognostication of ill health and dreary financial prospects. After this dream, your efforts will not yield satisfactory results.

## WIRE

To dream of wire indicates that you will make frequent but short journeys that will be to your detriment.

Old or rusty wire signifies that you will be possessed of a bad temper, which will give troubles to your kindred.

If you see a wire fence in your dreams, you may be cheated in some trade that you have in view.

## WISDOM

To dream that you are possessed of wisdom signifies that your spirit will be brave under trying circumstances, and you will be able to overcome these trials and rise to prosperous living. If you think you lack wisdom, it implies that you are wasting your native talents.

## WISHBONE

To dream of a wishbone augurs an unexpected gift and marks a great time for taking risks.

## WISHING WELL

Dreaming of a wishing well indicates that help from friends is forthcoming when needed.

## WISTERIA

In dreams, this flowering vine symbolizes happiness and love in your domestic life.

## WITCH

To dream of witches indicates that you, with others, will seek adventures that afford hilarious enjoyment, but that these will eventually rebound, to your mortification. Business will suffer if witches advance upon you; home life may be disappointing.

## WITNESSING

To dream that you bear witness against someone who is innocent in a court of law means that you will have misfortune of some sort coming your way. If others bear witness against you, you will be compelled to refuse favors to friends in order to protect your own interests. If you are a witness for a guilty person, your fortunes will turn for the better.

## WIZARD

To dream of a wizard suggests that you are going to have a big family, which will cause you much inconvenience as well as displeasure. For young people, this dream implies loss and broken engagements.

## WOLF

To dream of a wolf implies that you have a thieving person in your employ, who will also betray secrets. To kill a wolf indicates that you will defeat sly enemies who seek to overshadow you with disgrace. To hear the howl of a wolf reveals to you a secret alliance that aims to defeat you in honest competition.

## WOMAN

To dream of a woman foreshadows intrigue. To argue with one foretells that you will be outwitted.

## WOOD*

To dream of wood suggests that your business ventures will be solid in the upcoming future.

*See individual species of wood.

## WOODEN SHOE

To dream of a wooden shoe is significant of lonely wanderings and penniless circumstances.

## WOODPECKER

To dream of this noisy bird warns you to watch your tongue and behavior, because you may find yourself being argumentative.

## WOODPILE

To dream of a woodpile denotes unsatisfactory business and misunderstandings in love.

## WOODS

To dream of woods signifies a natural change in your affairs. If the woods appear green, the change will be lucky; if they are stripped of verdure, it will prove calamitous.

To see woods on fire implies that your plans will reach satisfactory maturity. Prosperity will beam with favor upon you.

To dream that you deal in firewood indicates that you will win fortune through determined struggle.

## WOOL

To dream of wool is a pleasing sign of prosperous opportunities to expand your interests. To see soiled or dirty wool foretells that you will seek employment with those who detest your principles.

## WORKHOUSE*

To dream that you are in a workhouse foretells an event that will cause you harm and loss.

*See Jail, Prison.

## WORKING

To dream that you are hard at work denotes that you will win merited success by concentrating your energy on achieving your goal.

To see others at work suggests that hopeful conditions will surround you. If you dream of looking for work, you will be benefited by some unaccountable occurrence.

## WORKSHOP

To see workshops in your dreams implies that you will use extraordinary schemes to undermine your enemies.

## WORMS

To dream of worms implies that you will be oppressed by the low intriguing of disreputable people. To use worms as fish bait in your dreams foretells that by your ingenuity, you will use your enemies to good advantage.

## WOUND

To dream that you are wounded signals distress and an unfavorable turn in business.

To see others wounded denotes that injustice will be accorded you by your friends.

To relieve or dress a wound signifies that you will have occasion to congratulate yourself on your good fortune.

## WRAPPING

To wrap something in your dream suggests a satisfactory end to a job or project.

## WREATH

To dream that you see a wreath of fresh flowers betokens great opportunities for enriching yourself. A withered wreath predicts sickness and wounded love.

To see a bridal wreath foretells a happy ending to uncertain engagements.

## WRECKS

If you see a wreck in your dream, you may be harassed by fears of destitution or sudden failure in business.

## WREN

In dreams, this little bird is a harbinger of pleasant news.

## WRESTLING

To dream of wrestling with someone or something warns that bad luck is on the horizon. Do not gamble. To see wrestlers in your dream means good luck.

## WRINKLES

To dream of having facial wrinkles predicts an increase in popularity.

## WRITING*

To dream that you are writing foretells a mistake that will almost prove to be your undoing.

To see writing denotes that you will be upbraided for your careless conduct. A lawsuit may cause you embarrassment.

To try to read strange writing signifies that you will escape your enemies only by being conservative in your business affairs.

*See *Letter.*

## X-RAY

In dreams, X-rays symbolize good health and peace of mind.

## YACHT

To see a yacht in a dream denotes happy recreation away from business and troubles. A stranded yacht represents an unsatisfying engagement or festivity.

## YAM

To dream of yams warns of a health issue.

## YARDSTICK

To dream of a yardstick predicts that even though you will succeed in business, much anxiety will possess you.

## YARN

To dream of yarn suggests success in your business and an industrious companion in your home.

## YAWNING

If you yawn in your dreams, you will search in vain for health and contentment.

To see others yawning suggests that you will see some of your friends in their misery. Sickness will keep them from their usual tasks.

## YEARBOOK

Dreaming of a yearbook augurs an unexpected message from a long-lost friend.

## YEARNING

To feel in a dream that you are yearning for the presence of anyone denotes that you will soon hear comforting tidings from absent friends.

## YEAST

To dream of yeast foretells unexpected wealth.

## YELLOW

If this color is prominent in your dreams, it signifies new beginnings, happiness, and confidence.

## YELLOW BIRD

To see a yellow bird flitting about in your dreams signifies that a great event is about to happen. To see a yellow bird sick or dead warns that you will suffer for another's wild folly.

## YEW TREE

To dream of a yew tree predicts illness and disappointment.

## YIELDING

To dream of yielding to another's wishes denotes that by weakness and indecision, you will throw away a great opportunity to elevate yourself. If others yield to you, exclusive privileges will be accorded you and you will be elevated above your associates. If you receive poor yield for your labors, you may expect cares and worries.

## YODELING

To dream of this Alpine type of singing suggests good luck in business and with friends.

## YOGA

Dreaming of yoga foretells spiritual advancement and peace of mind.

## YOGURT

In dreams, this food represents good health and prosperity.

## YOKE

To dream of seeing a yoke indicates that you will unwillingly conform to the customs and wishes of others.

To yoke oxen in your dreams signifies that your judgment and counsel will be accepted submissively by those dependent upon you. If you fail to yoke the oxen, you will be anxious over some old friend you haven't seen in a while.

## YOUTH

To dream of seeing young people foretells the reconciliation of family disagreements and favorable times for planning new enterprises. To dream that you are young again suggests that you will make mighty efforts to recall lost opportunities, but will nevertheless fail.

## YUCCA

To dream of yucca signifies spiritual and material comfort in life.

## YULE LOG

To dream of a Yule log indicates that your joyous anticipations will be realized by your attendance at great festivities.

## ZEBRA

If you dream of a zebra, you will be interested in varied and fleeting enterprises. To see one wild in its native country suggests that you will pursue a chimerical fancy that will return you little pleasure upon possession.

## ZENITH, THE

To dream of the zenith foretells great prosperity. You will win the suitor of your choice.

## ZEPHYR

To dream of soft zephyrs denotes that you will sacrifice fortune to obtain the object of your affection and will find reciprocal affection in your wooing.

## ZINC

To work with or to see zinc in your dreams indicates substantial and energetic progress. Business will be healthy. To dream of zinc ore promises the approach of success.

## ZIPPER

This portends social problems if a zipper is broken or stuck. But to dream of a zipper that fastens easily augurs satisfaction in your social life.

## ZODIAC, THE

To dream of the zodiac is a prognostication of unparalleled rise in material worth, but also indicates moderate peace and happiness. To see the zodiac appearing weird indicates that untoward grief is hovering over you; only strenuous efforts can dispel it.

To study the zodiac in your dreams suggests that you will gain distinction and favor by your involvement with strangers. If you approach the zodiac or it approaches you, you will succeed in your investments beyond your wildest imagination, to the wonderment of others. To draw a map of the zodiac signifies future gain.

## ZOO

If you dream of visiting zoological gardens, you will likely have a varied fortune. At times it seems that enemies overpower you; at times you stand in the front rank of success. You will also gain knowledge by travel and sojourn in foreign countries.